Susan Glaspell and the Anxiety of Expression

Language and Isolation in the Plays

KRISTINA HINZ-BODE

McFarland & Company, Inc., Publishers
Jefferson, North Carolina, and London

Frontispiece: portrait of Susan Glaspell by Jerry Farnsworth courtesy of the Highland House Museum, Truro Historical Society, Truro, Mass., USA.

LIBRARY OF CONGRESS CATALOGUING-IN-PUBLICATION DATA

Hinz-Bode, Kristina, 1971–
    Susan Glaspell and the anxiety of expression : language and isolation in the plays / Kristina Hinz-Bode.
        p.   cm.
    Includes bibliographical references and index.

    ISBN 0-7864-2505-9 (softcover : 50# alkaline paper) ∞

    1. Glaspell, Susan, 1876–1948 — Criticism and interpretation.   2. Individuality in literature.   3. Socialization in literature.   I. Title.
    PS3513. L35Z69   2006
    818'.5209 — dc22   2006001508

British Library cataloguing data are available

On the front cover: Susan Glaspell with two dogs (photographer: Underwood & Underwood). Henry W. and Albert A. Berg Collection of English and American Literature, The New York Public Library, Astor, Lenox and Tilden Foundations.

Manufactured in the United States of America

McFarland & Company, Inc., Publishers
    Box 611, Jefferson, North Carolina 28640
    www.mcfarlandpub.com

Susan Glaspell and the
Anxiety of Expression

To Bärbel and Gerhard Hinz,
who taught me to value
both thought and feeling.

Acknowledgments

This book has seen several stages before arriving at its present state, and many people have encouraged me on the way.

At the Friedrich-Schiller-University of Jena, my academic home in Germany for many years, I thank my mentor Kurt Müller for introducing me to American drama and to Susan Glaspell. Without his valuable advice my study would not be what it is. I also thank Wolfgang G. Müller for his encouragement during the earliest stages of this project, and Karl M. Meessen at the Jena Law Faculty, both for a job that granted me financial independence during an important phase of orientation and for his slight regret when I chose literature over law, after all.

At the University of Berne, Fritz Gysin's support made possible my stay in Switzerland. At the Ludwig-Maximilians-University of Munich, Ulla Haselstein welcomed me into the circle of her graduate students and offered me the opportunity to teach. To Daniel Göske at the University of Kassel I am infinitely grateful for his positive response to the first version of this book and for giving it the crucial impulses and solid support without which it would not have reached its final form.

In the world of Glaspell studies, I thank all those who have willingly exchanged ideas with me over the years: Gerhard Bach for his ready help with information and material from the start, and for introducing me to the rest of the crowd. Linda Ben-Zvi for organizing an inspiring conference at the University of Tel Aviv. Elaine Aston and Marcia Noe for their interest and help with material. More recently, Martha Carpentier, for taking me under her wings during the first Glaspell Play Reading Marathon at Provincetown and for discovering the sundial of *Tickless Time*, and J. Ellen Gainor, for her great last-minute generosity both with missing material and with advice. I also thank Susan Kurtzman, curator at the Highland House Museum in Truro, Mass., for granting me permission to use Jerry Farnsworth's portrait of Susan Glaspell, and Valentina Cook at the Glaspell Estate for her permission to quote from Glaspell's unpublished plays "Chains of Dew" and "Springs Eternal" and from other materials not yet out of U.S. copyright.

For the financial support without which many of these encounters would not have come to pass, I thank the Friedrich-Naumann Foundation of Germany, which financed the core three years of my research, and the University of Jena as well as the state of Thuringia, which granted additional means for the trip to Tel Aviv and during interim periods.

On a more personal note, I would like to mention those friends and colleagues whose ever-present eagerness for intellectual exchange has had its firm share in giving the book its present form. Thank you Stephanie Wolf, Eveliina Juntunen, Melanie Schmelcher, Christine Wögerbauer, Sibylle Drack, Gabriela Hilti-Saleem, Nicole Soost, Torsten Graff, Gundula Müller-Wallraff, Claudia Ernst, Gabriele Spengemann, Tom Clark, Daniel Bengsch!

Last but not least, I thank my family for bearing with me to the end, and my husband, Hans-Peter Bode, for deeming this project important every single step of the way.

Table of Contents

Introduction

Until quite recently, Susan Glaspell was usually mentioned in two contexts: as co-founder of the Provincetown Players, the group that staged Eugene O'Neill's first plays, and as author of the one-act *Trifles*, a work which has been celebrated as the prototype of feminist drama in America. I first encountered Glaspell's oeuvre in C.W.E. Bigsby's collection of four of her plays: *Trifles*, *The Outside*, *Inheritors*, and *The Verge*. I was fascinated by all four works. What struck me most was the intensity and philosophical depth with which this American writer treated language both as a theme in its own right and as a means for her aesthetics as a dramatist. With her persistent interest in the function of communication and the relation between art and life, Susan Glaspell joins in the pursuit of other American and European authors of her period to come to terms with the epistemological crisis of the modern age. And while I was intrigued by the gender differences portrayed in the plays of Bigsby's collection, I still saw their female characters' troubles as examples of a universally human dilemma: the experience of life as lived both essentially apart from and irreducibly connected to others.

When I began to research the literature available on Glaspell in the late 1990s, however, I realized that her reception had been overridingly feminist since her initial re-discovery three decades before. *Trifles* and its short-story version "A Jury of Her Peers" had become classics of "female ways of reading" through the groundbreaking work of scholars such as Judith Fetterley and Annette Kolodny. *The Outside* was perceived as an illustration of how women succeed in restoring life where men can only fail. And *The Verge* was read as a showcase for a Cixousian *écriture féminine* that prefigured the concept itself by half a century. I could not find much on *Inheritors*— possibly because, as Barbara Ozieblo still writes in 2000, "it is the least overtly feminist" of the four works that Bigsby decided to include in his edition.[1]

Such readings were thrilling in that they foregrounded the remarkable sensitivity with which Glaspell portrays issues of gender, politics, and power

1

in her works — and these interpretations had been vital in re-establishing her as an important American author in the first place. They did not, however, address my impression that there were more complex and more universal issues at stake in Glaspell's plays than the opposition of the sexes. After all, it was one of the play's male characters, the sociable Mr. Hale, who presented the possibility of human community to Minnie Wright when he tried to convince his reticent neighbor to "go in with [him] on a party telephone" in *Trifles* (36). In *The Outside* Allie Mayo would never have been shocked back into life had it not been for the appearance of the (male) life-savers and their stubborn attempts to rescue a drowned stranger against all odds. And Claire Archer's success in achieving "outness" and "otherness" in *The Verge* at the expense of Tom Edgeworthy's life and her own complete isolation, I felt, could hardly be called a triumphant solution for women battling against society's imprisoning gender expectations.

Luckily, by the late 1990s several scholars had begun to call for a new approach to Glaspell criticism, including a more sophisticated re-appraisal of her oeuvre as a whole. It is true that Susan Glaspell is still known first and foremost for her connection to the Provincetown Players, one of the nation's most influential "little theatres" in the 1910s and early 1920s. But Glaspell (1876–1948) was a successful author of fiction before she began writing for the theatre, and she continued her career in both genres long after her time with the Provincetown Players. Her oeuvre includes not only fourteen plays but more than fifty short stories and nine novels, many of which were highly acclaimed both by the critics and by the reading public of her own time. In the early 1990s occasional voices thus began to demand that the author's acknowledged status as "Glaspell, the dramatist" and "Glaspell, the woman writer" should be regarded only as the starting point for further investigations into her literary achievements. In her *Research and Production Sourcebook* (1993) — itself an invaluable reference work which minutely "illustrates the rise and fall and rise once more of [Glaspell's] critical reputation" (12) — Mary E. Papke pointed out that her bibliography of secondary sources was, "of course, only provisionally closed. [...] Hers is a fascinating story, the conclusion of which now depends upon a new generation of Glaspell scholarship" (14). And Linda Ben-Zvi, one of the most prominent scholars in the field, stated only two years later: "Glaspell criticism has moved to a second stage — assessing the work of this important writer, no longer arguing her case" ("O'Neill's Cape(d) Compatriot," 131).

Indeed, both Papke's *Sourcebook* and Ben-Zvi's collection *Susan Glaspell: Essays on Her Theatre and Fiction* (1995) are markers of such a new stage in Glaspell criticism. Recent editions of her works have documented a growing interest in the wider range of the author's writings. Bigsby's selection of plays was followed by her short story collection *Lifted Masks*, first published in 1912 and reedited by Eric S. Rabkin in 1993. Persephone Books in London has reissued two of Glaspell's novels (*Fidelity* in 1999 and *Brook Evans* in 2000). Linda Ben-Zvi only recently presented her new edition of *Road to the Temple*, Glaspell's 1927 biography of her husband George Cram Cook (2005), and an annotated collection of her complete plays, edited by Ben-Zvi and J. Ellen Gainor, is scheduled to appear in 2006. What is more, several book-length studies attest that with the beginning of the new millennium Glaspell scholarship has both accelerated in pace and widened in scope. Barbara Ozieblo's critical biography (2000), the first after Marcia Noe's ground-breaking study *Susan Glaspell: Voice from the Heartland* (1983), was followed by Martha C. Carpentier's study of *Susan Glaspell's Major Novels* (2001; the first monograph dealing exclusively with the writer's long fiction), and — a "first" once again — by J. Ellen Gainor's study of her complete plays, *Susan Glaspell in Context* (2002). In 2003 the Susan Glaspell Society was founded, and since then its web page has been able to celebrate several new publications, among these another Glaspell biography (Ben-Zvi, 2005) and a second collection of essays edited by founding members Carpentier and Ozieblo and expected to appear in 2006.[2] Last but not least, the expanding criticism on Glaspell has lately been flanked by a resurging interest in the group for which she first began to write her plays, as is attested by studies such as Cheryl Black's 2002 monograph on *The Women of Provincetown: 1915–1922* and the recent edition of Edna Kenton's early history of *The Provincetown Players and the Playwrights' Theatre, 1915–1922* (2004).

The new phase in Glaspell criticism is a welcome and exciting development for anyone who knows more of this author's compelling oeuvre than *Trifles* and "A Jury of Her Peers." At the same time, while recent publications have sometimes discussed Glaspell's hitherto undervalued fiction, most readings of her works are still somewhat narrowly focused on "women's issues." Veronica Makowsky's 1993 monograph *Susan Glaspell's Century of American Women* traces the "maternal metaphor" through Glaspell's writings (9). A preeminently feminist interest drives most of the essays collected by Ben-Zvi in 1995, and a concentration on the artist's personal and social position *as woman* also dominates Barbara Ozieblo's biography. As one of the two most recent studies on Glaspell's works Carpentier's discussion of her novels, too, presents a predominantly feminist approach in its concentration on Glaspell as the writer of a "female 'semiotic'" (1), and 15 of the 21 entries on Glaspell listed in the MLA Bibliography between 2000 and 2004 focus on issues of gender and refer to either *Trifles*, "Jury," or *The Verge*.

Hence, while J. Ellen Gainor was not the first to point out that Glaspell's canonization as a woman author presents a double-edged success, her comprehensive study of Glaspell's dramatic oeuvre is the first to resolutely move beyond her perception in the "academic mainstream" as nothing more than a "token [representative] of [her] group" — that is, of women's writing (2). Gainor's engaging readings refuse to employ any one specific theoretical framework, and they do not restrict themselves to a single thematic concern. Instead, Gainor "seeks to introduce and explore a number of the historical, social, political, literary, and theatrical contexts that informed Glaspell's dramaturgy," and she argues that "[it] is this close engagement with her culture that makes Glaspell's theatrical work important historically, creatively, and intellectually" (3).

My own study of Glaspell's plays shares a number of Gainor's premises, first and foremost her conviction that a synthetic reading of Glaspell's works will show that her "feminism" — however one wants to define this concept — is only one characteristic feature of her writings.[3] Moreover, I agree that the full range of Glaspell's interests and artistic achievements is best explored by an approach which remains open to diverse methods and theories. Whereas Gainor concentrates on the intricate web of historical and cultural contexts Glaspell engages with in her plays, however, I want to draw attention to a particular cluster of images and ideas about language and communication that inform her writings from her first turn-of-the-century stories to her final play and novels in the 1940s. My contention is that Glaspell develops a view on language and art in her works which links them to the innovative plays of European dramatists as diverse as August Strindberg, Henrik Ibsen, Anton Chekhov, George Bernard Shaw, and Georg Kaiser, as much as to the modernist visions of her American contemporaries T.S. Eliot and Ezra Pound and to the philosophical thought not only of Friedrich Nietzsche and Ludwig Wittgenstein but of many later 20th-century thinkers. What Glaspell sees and dramatizes as the most profound human experience, both for her female and male characters, is a paradoxical sense of being simultaneously isolated from and connected to others — and a corresponding feeling of being forever caught between one's individuality and one's social existence.

In this context, questions about the nature of language and the function of communication emerge as one of Susan Glaspell's central artistic concerns throughout all of her works. An approach which discusses the various angles from which she develops these themes throughout her career, therefore, is useful in two ways: first, in opening up the view on Glaspell's entire oeuvre as an aesthetic entity which is tuned to the most daring artistic and philosophical notions of her time, and second, in putting into perspective her current classification as a woman author interested primarily (or even exclusively) in "female" themes. Of course, the very observation that issues of language and communication feature so prominently in Glaspell's works has enhanced the gender-based readings of the past thirty years. After all, research in the field of gender studies has shown that men and women use language in fundamentally different ways, and feminist thought since the 1970s has demonstrated how patriarchal linguistic dominance has served to silence women throughout Western history. While such readings have brought into focus the fascinating ways in which Glaspell's works anticipate late 20th-century ideas of sexual difference, my study shows that her over-arching artistic concern with the nature of communication often *transcends* such aspects of difference. This is precisely why Glaspell's art can speak to many audiences and readers, regardless of gender, age, nationality, class, or historical context. And while this is true for all of her writings, my study focuses on her plays because the meta-level of the artist's own means of expression takes on an additional edge in the genre of drama. In the theatre, the creative act of making sense of the world is turned into a collective com-municative endeavor. This aspect, which acquires even more significance in Glaspell's case through the Provincetown Players' pronounced philosophy of a communal drama, informs her use of language both as theme and as a medium of artistic expression in all of her plays.

My first chapter offers a brief biographical overview which connects Glaspell's persistent literary theme of individuality versus communality to her conservative Midwestern roots and her life as an avant-garde artist. The following chapter sets up the theoretical and heuristic background for my reading of the plays. Throughout her oeuvre Susan Glaspell inhabits three different subject positions in her debates on the function of language: that of the self as unmarked by gender, that of a specifically female point of view ("woman"), and that of the artist and her — or his! — art as a special case of human expression. These points of view are often in conflict yet constantly interact with each other. I draw on various theories of communication — some transcending aspects of gender, others focusing on sexual difference, still others conceiving of art as analogous to language — in order to disen-tangle the many levels of meaning which Glaspell generates in this context. Among others, ideas discussed here include those of Ludwig Wittgenstein and Martin Heidegger, Luce Irigaray and Hélène Cixous, Julia Kristeva and Judith Butler. Is language capable of expressing our innermost thoughts? Do words shape reality in a way the individual cannot control? Can art take over where mere verbal communication is bound to fail? Such questions have troubled diverse thinkers and writers through centuries, and Susan Glaspell approaches them from ever varying perspectives in her plays.

If one focuses on Glaspell's underlying assumptions about communica-tive processes, one is struck by the fact that the frequently noted indetermi-nacy of her plays (often seen as an annoying "open-endedness") results from the way in which she constantly intertwines two contradictory conceptions of language and, by analogy, of art. On the one hand, she treats these media as vehicles to transmit thoughts and ideas from one isolated mind to the other. On the other hand, she just as often presents the creation of meaning as a more communal, intersubjective act in which reality is shaped in communication and "truth" is never absolute. Each of these two notions contains one positive and one negative conceptual consequence. The idea of language as a representative system of signs — based as it is on a semiotic concept of sender, message, transmitter, and receiver — may support the idealist stance that meaning, if private, can be transferred from one human mind to the other without serious distortion. Or it can foster the skeptic's fear that in our fundamental isolation it is ultimately impossible to understand each other. In contrast, the alternative notion insists that meaning does not exist prior to social contact in the first place. While this concept suggests that we depend on the cooperation of others to make sense of any given situation, at the same time it entails the possibility of achieving real change in the parameters of our social existence — if we embark on that project in a cooperative act of creating new meaning out of old notions. These are the paradigms which govern Glaspell's treatment of language and communication whenever she puts her pen to paper. It is against this background that she dramatizes a surprisingly broad range of forces which influence the way her characters — women and men, artist figures and ordinary people — perceive their lives and engage with the world. And this is what makes her plays so relevant to today's audiences.

When Glaspell was first rediscovered for a wider critical audience, two books reopened the debate on her contribution to American letters: Arthur E. Waterman's volume in the Twayne author's series (1966) and Gerhard Bach's German study *Susan Glaspell und die Provincetown Players* (1979). Both critics favored Glaspell's drama over her fictional writings, yet both identified an overarching agenda in her entire oeuvre when they located a persistent concern with "the meaning of life" in all of her works — dramatic and fictional. As Bach pointed out in a 1978 article: "*Life's meaning* is the central question underlying all of Glaspell's literary efforts, before, during, and after her affiliation with the Provincetown Players" ("Susan Glaspell — Provincetown Playwright," 37).

From today's perspective, both Waterman and Bach seem unaware of the gender bias inherent in such a totalizing concept of human experience as the condition of "*man*kind." In Arthur Waterman's study especially, this gender bias is certainly evident in his every remark on Glaspell's literary "greatness." What is more, many scholars have since pointed out that the same bias continues to influence the perception of Glaspell's work up to the present day — most notably in C.W.E. Bigsby's otherwise path-breaking criticism. Referring to Bigsby's claim that "Susan Glaspell's theme throughout her career" was "the *man* at odds with society," Elaine Aston has summed up feminist objections to such a frequently voiced "male perspective" by arguing that it "overlooks Glaspell's central concern which was to speak on behalf of the *woman* at odds with society" ("Meeting the Outside," 57, Aston's emphasis). Since I read Glaspell's works as sophisticated attempts to make sense of life both from a pointedly gendered position *and* from a wider interest in the human condition as such, my approach acknowledges the fundamental tensions which her art creates between a notion of universally valid concepts and an understanding of life as always dominated by concrete circumstance. It is this very ambivalence which Glaspell shares with many modern and postmodern writers of American and European literature.

In detailed analyses which form the core part of this study, I concentrate on eight of Glaspell's fourteen plays, beginning with her 1916 one-act *Trifles* (her first solo-piece for the stage and the play which has generated her fame as a feminist writer) and ending in 1943 with her final play *Springs Eternal*. While Glaspell's last drama was never produced on stage, my consideration of the unpublished typescript, held by the New York Public Library, provides valuable insights for a thorough understanding of her published oeuvre. The other plays analyzed in detail are *The People*, *The Outside*, *Bernice*, *Chains of Dew*, *The Verge*, and *Alison's House*. Glaspell's remaining six dramas are drawn on only selectively in these readings, either because the problem of language and communication is not one of their dominant thematic concerns, or because they are collaborations for which it would be difficult to determine Glaspell's individual contribution. Instead, my final chapter discusses the themes of language and communication in Glaspell's entire oeuvre by placing these remaining plays in the context of her fictional writings both before and after her engagement with the Provincetown. Thus, my brief discussions of the plays *Suppressed Desires*, *Close the Book*, *Woman's Honor*, *Tickless Time*, *Inheritors* and *The Comic Artist* are framed by a consideration of Glaspell's three early novels (*The Glory of the Conquered*, *The Visioning*, *Fidelity*) and a look at one of her last fictional works, *Norma Ashe* (1942). Surveying her creative career with the help of a number of less-known pieces in both genres, this final chapter thus opens up the view on Glaspell's oeuvre as a surprisingly consistent aesthetic entity — an entity which, for all its unquestionable originality, is situated within the broader context of various transnational movements in 20th-century philosophy and art.

Most Glaspell critics have seen her as firmly rooted in the American scene. Indeed, J. Ellen Gainor's "one overarching agenda" is to "convince [her] readers that the most compelling way to approach Glaspell is as an American writer" (9). My own focus on the function of language and communication in Glaspell's works serves to compliment this overly exclusive view. As a European student of American literature and culture, I cannot but see Susan Glaspell as a writer who operated in a literary environment which often transcended national boundaries. Hence she offers less a culturally specific than a uniquely personal as well as a more universal, transnational analysis of human experience. As Glaspell passionately argued not only in her Pulitzer Prize-winning play *Alison's House*: The power of art and its gift to the world lies in its ability to respect difference and still reach directly to the human heart.

1. Social Rebel or Conventional Woman?

Community as Threat and Blessing in Susan Glaspell's Life and Art

Ever since her first success as a writer Susan Glaspell has been hailed as well as scorned both for her popular fiction and for her avant-garde drama; she has been labelled a traditionalist as well as a social rebel, and her literary achievements have been called anything from brilliant to minor to second-class. To be sure, these contradictory reactions find their explanation partly in the diverse historical and professional backgrounds of the individuals who voice them. At the same time, they have their roots in a variety of contradictions pervading Glaspell's works themselves. Ardent calls for women's liberation can be found next to sympathetic versions of Victorian womanhood, a celebration of the author's Midwestern, pioneer roots is set against a harsh criticism of her native region's narrow-minded conservatism, and radical experiments in style are combined with more traditional forms of artistic expression.

Such inconsistencies have often puzzled Glaspell's critics, even more so since they seem to pervade not only the artist's literary works but many of her life decisions as well. Barbara Ozieblo includes both the circumstances of Glaspell's life and her artistic creations when she begins her critical biography with the remark: "I have read her plays, novels, and letters again and again, trying to understand why the rebel in her chose so often to acquiesce to convention" (*Susan Glaspell* 1). Almost twenty years earlier Marcia Noe also pointed to a direct connection between the "paradoxes in [Glaspell's] work and personality" (*Susan Glaspell* 10). As a result of this "close relationship between [Glaspell's] art and her life" — already posed by Arthur Waterman in 1966 (7) — critics have often approached her oeuvre through a "close linkage of biographical accounting and literary evaluation" (Bach, rev. of Noe, 97).

As is the case with any other single critical stance, of course the usefulness of "biographical accounting" has its limits if taken exclusively or even predominantly to an author's works. Glaspell herself discusses these limits in her 1930 play *Alison's House*, whose story is inspired by the life of Emily Dickinson — without, however, altogether denying the relevance of an artist's life experience for her art. Indeed, while time and again Glaspell's works celebrate the capacity of art to enhance many different points of view, she also argues repeatedly that the artist's own voice remains a crucial factor in this dialogue. It is for this ambivalence in her writings that I feel justified in beginning my own discussion of Glaspell's drama with a glance at the story of her life. From my specific vantage point, one answer to Ozieblo's question of "why the rebel in her chose so often to acquiesce to convention" can be found in the persistent way in which Glaspell displays her protagonists' uncompromising urge for self-expression in conflict with a similarly existential need to keep in contact with the community they find themselves a part of. Since this sense of self as both isolated from and irreducibly connected to others — a basic theme in all of Glaspell's writings — finds its obvious corollary in many of the author's life experiences, for my critical response to her plays, too (as for many other critics' readings), Glaspell's biography provides a relevant frame and backdrop.[1]

Susan Glaspell was born in Davenport, Iowa, on 1 July 1876, the second of three children to Alice and Elmer Glaspell.[2] Hers was a family with strong pioneer roots: When her great-grandparents came to make a new start for themselves along the Mississippi River in 1839, only four years after the town of Davenport was founded by Colonel George Davenport on the former site of an Indian village, they were among the first to settle this part of the Midwest. The Glaspells, if a middle-class and not very well-to-do family, were active and respected members of their community. Raised in the Davenport public school system, Susan Glaspell developed a strong sense of belonging to her native region, a sense of home that would accompany her through all the stages of her later life.

Accordingly, as Marcia Noe observes, "Susan Glaspell was [...] a girl who could take pride in her family's old-Davenport heritage and claim her rightful place in Davenport society" (14). At the same time, although the young Glaspell "aspired to membership in the [town's] elite clubs, literary, musical, and social," she did not "belong to the right set of people" — her family was not affluent enough (Ozieblo, *Susan Glaspell* 17, 18). It was perhaps adequately enough, therefore, that in pursuit of her early urge for writing Glaspell took on the position of *Society Editor* to Davenport's *Weekly Outlook* in 1896, two years after her high school graduation. In her reports on "the activities of Davenport's elite," thus Ozieblo recounts, the twenty-year-old "soon started writing sprightly commentaries on any aspect of Davenport morals and mores that caught her fancy" (*Susan Glaspell* 20). Gradually, Glaspell began to reflect not only on the positive values of her native community but also on the stifling influence which social norms such as "respectability" and "tradition" had come to exert on the ideals of personal freedom and creativity since the days of her pioneer ancestors — especially, one might add, if one was a woman. When she entered Drake University in Des Moines, Iowa, in 1897 "by Iowa standards" her "college enrolment was an audacious act for a young woman of the 1890s" (Noe, *Susan Glaspell* 15).

During her university years, Glaspell always managed to foster her social interests and to vigorously pursue her academic studies at the same time. Her activities included the position as Vice-President of the Debating Society as well as frequent contributions to the college's literary magazine, the *Delphic*. Having received her bachelor of philosophy degree in 1899, she first stayed on as statehouse and legislative reporter for the *Des Moines Daily News*, adding occasional editorial commentary to her work in a column called "The News Girl." As she had always wanted to pursue a professional career in writing, however, in 1901 (aged twenty-five) she decided to quit her job in order to concentrate all of her energies on this goal. Drawing from her observations as news reporter and social columnist, Glaspell was soon able to support herself financially with the regular publication of her short stories in popular magazines. After spending the summer of 1902 at the University of Chicago doing post-graduate work in literature, she returned to Davenport to "find that she had become somewhat of a local celebrity" (Noe, *Susan Glaspell* 22). Two years later, she was firmly set on her literary career.

While at this point in her life Glaspell's literary success finally began to yield her access to Davenport's elite social circles (including a ladies' literary group called the Tuesday Club to which she was elected in 1907), she was also drawn to the quite openly rebellious, "free-thinking" atmosphere among certain intellectuals who "found Davenport to be a city where tolerance prevailed over narrow-mindedness" (Noe, *Susan Glaspell* 23). Stimulated by the refreshingly liberating ideas she encountered among the members of the socialist Monist Society, Glaspell joined this group in their debates on political and philosophical issues. As Marcia Noe comments on the contradictions in Glaspell's social life at this time:

> Susan's simultaneous association with the Tuesday Club and the Monist Society reflected the conflicting aspects of her personality. On Tuesday afternoons, Susan the society girl sipped tea with Davenport matrons; on Sundays, Susan the social reformer plotted with free-thinkers and socialists to win influence in the Davenport political scene [*Susan Glaspell* 23].

It was at these meetings that Glaspell first met George Cram Cook, aristocratic classics scholar, artist, and social visionary from her hometown, who would develop into an important influence in her life and art during the following years.[3] In 1907 Cook — whose family occupied a prominent position in Davenport's public life — had just quit his teaching position at the University of Stanford and had returned to live at his family's estate near Buffalo to "raise vegetables and write" (Noe, *Susan Glaspell* 24). Like Glaspell's family, the Cooks could take pride in a distinguished pioneer background. Where the Glaspells had never been upper class, however, the Cooks belonged to Davenport's high society. As Susan Glaspell remembers in 1927: "George Cram Cook grew up in a town that had a Cook Memorial Library, the Cook Home, and a Cook Memorial Church. I am constrained to say again — there having been no Glaspell Home for the Friendless— these things are relevant" (*Road* 13).

Soon the inner circle of the Monist Society was gathering regularly at Cook's home, and Glaspell came to be among the most frequent visitors. By the end of that year, ardently debating each other's social ideals and literary inspirations (Glaspell was working on her first novel), she and Cook had become infatuated with each other. But Cook, divorced from his first wife, was engaged to the Chicago journalist Mollie Price, whom he married in 1908. Glaspell's visits to the Cook estate became less frequent as she spent a lot of time in New York and Chicago arranging the publication of her novel. When *The Glory of the Conquered* was published in 1909 to meet immediate success, the news reached her in Europe, where she had been touring the Netherlands and Belgium with her friend Lucy Huffaker before settling more permanently in Paris.

On her return to Davenport, Glaspell renewed her contacts to the old circle from the Monist Society. Rumors soon making the rounds about the nature of the relationship between her and "Jig" Cook seemed justified when Cook left his wife and two children early in 1911 and moved to Chicago, where he began to assist his socialist friend Floyd Dell with the *Chicago Evening Post*'s Friday Literary Review. Glaspell, in the meantime, concerned herself with the publication of her second novel, *The Visioning*, which came out later that year. Having faced the conservative mores of Davenport society as well as the more moderate reception of her second long work, she met up again with Cook in Chicago, and the two were married in Weehawken, New Jersey, on 14 April 1913. Drawn by the "lively tales of free expression" (Noe, *Susan Glaspell* 47) reaching them from New York, they decided to move to the East Coast, settling in Provincetown, Massachusetts, for the summers while spending the winter months among New York's bohemian intellectuals in the city's bustling Greenwich Village.

It was here in New York that in 1915 (the same year that saw the publication of Glaspell's third novel, *Fidelity*) the one-act which was to inspire the birth of the Provincetown Players was written in collaboration between Cook and Glaspell. *Suppressed Desires*, a satire on the fad for Freudianism which had recently taken hold of Greenwich Village, was both artists' first venture into the genre of drama. Bored with the plays produced on Broadway the couple had decided to amuse themselves with writing a play of their own. When the result of their joint effort was rejected by their friend Lawrence Langner of the Washington Square Players—one of New York's first little theatres, which they had helped found earlier that year in an effort to "counter Broadway with the works of Ibsen and Strindberg" (Noe, *Susan Glaspell* 38)—Cook and Glaspell moved on to produce their play themselves. As Mary E. Papke recounts, *Suppressed Desires* was first presented in a private performance on 15 July 1915 "at the home of Hutchins Hapgood and Neith Boyce in Cape Cod on a double bill with Neith Boyce's *Constancy*" (16).

This evening marked the informal beginnings of what one might call the "Provincetown idea." Since his college days at Harvard, George Cram Cook had marvelled at the Greek model of democratic artistic expression, admiring especially the communal Dionysian spirit which had brought about the birth of drama in ancient Greece. Having readily taken in the spirit of an intrinsically national expression of art as put on stage by the Irish Players during their visit to Chicago in 1911, by 1915 Cook had long picked up the enthusiasm of a developing new form of drama coming to life in the country's little theatre movement.[4] His dream was to create a true community theatre which would promote an indigenous American drama, "a place of unity and harmony where the playwright was also director, producer, and actor" (Noe, *Susan Glaspell* 48). Among the spirited and gifted Provincetown crowd of 1915, this vision was received with open minds and hearts: "Buoyed up by the possibility of creating in their own little theatre a new type of drama, the Provincetown artists took over Mary Heaton Vorse's studio property, transforming it by late summer into the Wharf Theatre" (Papke, *Susan Glaspell* 16). In September, they publicly restaged their first two plays along with two others, and a year later, after the Provincetown Players were formally incorporated, the group moved to New York, opening their Playwrights' Theatre on MacDougal Street.

Susan Glaspell, then, came to the stage through circumstance — and, as her autobiographical accounts have it, through the inducement of her husband. For the third bill of the Provincetown Players Cook announced a play by Glaspell which had yet to be written. In an often-quoted passage of *The Road to the Temple*, Glaspell's biography of her husband, she recounts how her first independent dramatic effort came to life as she sat in the auditorium of the Wharf Theatre across the street from her home in Provincetown, looking on at the stage and giving her ideas the freedom to take form in the actual space before her.[5] *Trifles*, which premiered at the Wharf Theatre on 8 August 1916, was to become one of the most successful American one-acts, frequently anthologized as the perfect example of a well-structured play and most consistently received throughout time by her critical audiences.

During the following six years, Susan Glaspell wrote ten more plays to be staged by the Players, in accordance with Provincetown policy playing an active part in most of their original productions (both as actress and as director). For the sake of the project she had given up her novel-writing, publishing only the odd short story now and then. The plays she wrote as she found herself immersed in the inspiring atmosphere created by the intimate Provincetown venture were received as highly innovative not only by her fellow explorers of a new dramatic art. Almost instantly, Glaspell was acknowledged as a crucial figure to the development of a new and distinctly national drama by those reviewers who saw beyond the superficial aesthetics of their contemporary Broadway theatre. When critics began to think of the young Eugene O'Neill — who had met up with the Players in 1916 with his legendary "trunk full" of plays (Glaspell, *Road* 253) — as the father of modern American drama, in those early years they rarely failed to see in Glaspell its mother at the same time.[6]

Yet this comparison between Glaspell and O'Neill also opens up the view on a significant difference in the two writers' involvement with the genre of drama. While Eugene O'Neill had been committed to writing plays before he joined the Provincetown Players and continued to pursue an ever accelerating career in the theatre after the group had long dissolved, Glaspell's career as a dramatist is inseparably connected to those early years in Greenwich Village and Cape Cod. It virtually ended when she followed her husband to Greece in 1922, into a future which would never again provide her with a community similar to the one constituted by the spirited Provincetown venture of the 1910s and early 1920s. That this community both provided her with an intellectually stimulating environment and offered her a deeply appreciated safety-net of human contact is evident in the way in which Glaspell described these years in retrospect:

> We were supposed to be a sort of "special" group — radical, wild. Bohemians, we have even been called. But it seems to me we were a particularly simple people, who sought to arrange life for the thing we wanted to do, needing each other as protection against complexities, yet living as we did because of an instinct for the old, old things, to have a garden, and neighbors, to keep up the fire and let the cat in at night [*Road* 235–36].[7]

When Glaspell wrote these lines in 1927, only five years had passed since the original Provincetown Players had dispersed. Yet as is apparent from this passage, at this point in her life she was already looking back at her time with the Players as an experience irretrievably lost in the past. Much has been written about the inevitable way in which, the very moment the experiments born in their midst came to meet commercial success, the Provincetown Players had also come face to face with their end as a freely experimental amateur theatre.[8] It was Cook himself who in unquestioning dictatorship had turned against all votes when he spent nearly all of the group's money on building a concrete dome for the production of Eugene O'Neill's *The Emperor Jones* in the fall of 1920. Yet when the play made such a stir among the theatre-going public that its production was offered the chance to be moved uptown, it was again Cook who saw that with professionalism and commercialism his dream of a communal drama had come to an end. Determined to give the child of his vision "good death" (see Glaspell, *Road* 309), he decided to close this chapter of his life and to pursue instead a dream even more deeply rooted in his heart. In March 1922, even before the Players ended their final season with Glaspell's *Chains of Dew*, the couple had sailed for Greece, Jig Cook's often longed-for "spiritual homeland" (Papke, *Susan Glaspell* 7).

That Glaspell followed her husband to Greece at a time when she had just begun to make herself a name as a guiding beacon for her country's national drama is one of her life decisions most frowned upon by her biographers. After all, it was Cook's dream, not Glaspell's, which the couple pursued with this remove from New York, and no-one could have foreseen that their stay in the country whose ancient traditions George Cook so greatly valued would be cut off prematurely by his sudden death. In 1924, after less than two years among the shepherds and peasants of Parnassos, Susan Glaspell was left to return to the United States alone — her husband gone, and their theatre no longer waiting for her at her arrival.[9]

For in Jig's and Susan's absence, the Provincetown Players had been turned into a decidedly different playhouse with openly commercial aims. Significantly, this had been the very thing which the group's two co-founders had sought to prevent before they had left the country. Acting upon "a strong sense that the original ideal needed guarding" — thus Provincetown chronicler Robert Károly Sarlós recounts — just a few days before their departure Glaspell and Cook had met with Eugene O'Neill, Cleon Throckmorton, Edna Kenton, and Eleanor Fitzgerald in a final session of the Players' executive committee. Eager to ensure that neither name nor theatre could be misused in the announced one-year interim they had initiated the decision to legally incorporate the group (Sarlós 144).[10] Unimpressed by their founders' legal actions, however, O'Neill (who had supported Cook's plans for incorporation while the latter was still in New York), Kenneth Macgowan, and Robert Edmund Jones — the "triumvirat," as they would be called from now on — had moved to form a new group from the remnants of the original community in Cook's and Glaspell's absence. As Barbara Ozieblo sums up the significant changes that had been made in the process:

> Macgowan had successfully transformed the Provincetown Players Inc. from a membership to a stock company; he had then "sold" the Players' assets to a newly formed group, which took the name of the Experimental Theater Inc. This group was to perform at the Provincetown Playhouse [*Susan Glaspell* 228].

To Glaspell, even worse than this de facto appropriation of the old name was the fact that the new group was not willing to pay tribute to the late George Cram Cook and his ideal of a communal theatre. For their embittered tone alone, the remarks with which Sarlós quotes Jig's widow from a May 1924 letter to Eleanor Fitzgerald and "all those new members of the Provincetown Players" is worth reprinting here at length:

> It savors a bit of wanting to profit by a thing and at the same time saying "We don't owe nothing to nobody."
> Since you are not Provincetown Players I do not think you should call yourself Provincetown something else and let people go on calling you Provincetown Players. And since you are not the Provincetown Players I do not see why you should add members to our organization.
> [...] Now one thing more. Hard to say, but while I am at it, I'm going to get it said. [...] There was a man named Jig Cook. He gave some eight years of his life to creating the P. Playhouse. If it had not been for him there would not be that place in which you now put on your plays. He worked until he had worked himself out, and then he went away, and he died. You are profiting by what he did and you have forgotten him.... There was no mention of Jig on the new Program, nor when the play for which he put in the dome was revived. It is not a spirit that will ever make the kind of place he made.[11]

Only a few days later, thus Sarlós tells the end of Glaspell's involvement with the group she had helped to create, she "resigned 'from the new organization into which membership in the Provincetown Players may have carried me.' [...] She concluded with a terse farewell: 'Fitzie, and all of you, for this letter is for all of you, from very deep down, I am through'" (Glaspell to Fitzgerald, 31 May 1924; as qtd. in Sarlós, *Jig Cook* 152, see also Sarlós' fn. 45).

Glaspell's painful fall-out with what had become of the old theatre and of the community which had once "protected" her against the "complexities of life" put an end to her activities as a playwright for some time to come. Determined to keep her husband's memory alive she began work on two new projects: a collection of Cook's poems entitled *Greek Coins*, and his biography, *The Road to the Temple*. Cook's poems were published in 1925, yet Glaspell's self-set task to create a believer's monument of her husband's life was complicated not only by the difficulty of keeping her own person out of the picture. Possibly even more disturbing was the unexpected interference of a new love. In the summer of 1924, when Glaspell was still struggling for her old disciplined working routine, she met the young writer Norman Matson. While some of her old Provincetown friends saw Matson as an upstart and intruder, others were able to see that he shared Glaspell's interests and that their relationship brought her back to life after she had so tragically lost Jig (see Noe, *Susan Glaspell* 54 f). Yet although her love for Matson may have given Glaspell consoling warmth, fresh excitement, and a new strength to face the future, presumably it also caused her serious pangs of guilt to intermingle with her thoughts of Jig — *The Road to the Temple* finally appeared in 1927 (see Ozieblo, *Susan Glaspell* 230).

Eventually, however, Glaspell did move ahead by picking up her original career as a novelist. Between 1928 and 1931 three new books appeared with her old publisher Frederick Stokes: *Brook Evans* (1928), *Fugitive's Return* (1929), and *Ambrose Holt and Family* (1931). Only three times did she go back to writing for the stage after 1922, and only two of the three pieces were produced. Interestingly enough, when Glaspell again set her mind on writing drama even before her first new novel reached the market, once again the effort was made for her partner — this time, Norman Matson. As it turned out, however, while Glaspell's first co-production for the stage had tipped off the founding of the Provincetown Players twelve years before, this time her partner's interest in the theatre was not enough to keep her in the dramatic mode. Glaspell's and Matson's 1927 piece *The Comic Artist* premiered in London with limited success and only came to New York in 1933, where it was likewise greeted with less than luke-warm tones. Moreover, three year's after the publication of this play Glaspell's new drama *Alison's House*, produced by Eva Le Gallienne's New York Repertory Company, won her the Pulitzer Prize, but it could win no public acclaim. To the contrary, when it was moved uptown in May 1931 after the award had been announced, a harsh debate broke loose over the merits of her latest play, and the Pulitzer committee's decision was heavily criticized by most reviewers as a mistake. This was a bitter experience for Glaspell, who, as much as she had been surprised by the news herself, had been "thrilled with the Pulitzer award, the highest honor she had ever received" (Noe, *Susan Glaspell* 59). Lacking Jig Cook's encouragement as much as the support of the original Village community, in the face of these disappointments she turned away from writing drama except for one last attempt towards the end of her life. *Springs Eternal*, her final play, was rejected by Lawrence Langner when Glaspell submitted it to the Theatre Guild in 1944 and was never produced on stage.[12]

Yet whatever had been the reasons for Glaspell's prolonged silence as a playwright after 1922 — a changed Provincetown Playhouse (which, along with everything else, welcomed women's participation much less than it had in the beginning years),[13] the loss of her husband and his enthusiasm for the stage, her preoccupation with Cook's poems and biography, her early-set personal preference for fiction — after the critical debate over *Alison's House* ten years later Glaspell did not only turn from writing for the stage. Following the release of her sixth novel, *Ambrose Holt and Family*, in 1931, the woman who had been consistently productive ever since she started writing as a teenager would publish nothing much at all for nearly an entire decade. In 1932 Norman Matson, her life companion for eight steady years, left her for the 19-year-old daughter of one of Glaspell's and Cook's Greenwich Village friends, getting married to the girl when she was already expecting his child. This came as such a shock to Glaspell that she, "middle-aged and in failing health, [...] was tempted to withdraw from life to ensure that she would not be hurt again" (Noe, *Susan Glaspell* 65). And although, as Noe goes on to say, she "did not do so, because she realized to do this would be to go against all she had believed and written about," she apparently struggled with this personal crisis to an extent that hampered her literary productivity for a long time to come.[14]

Instead, in 1936 Glaspell accepted a job as director of the Midwest Play Bureau for the Federal Theatre Project in Chicago. For two years she put all her weight and energy into this government project whose aim it was to find and produce the plays of American playwrights. Even though she had ceased to write plays herself, at sixty Glaspell was thus able to link up once more with the prominent interests of her Provincetown years. Nevertheless, in 1938 she decided to give up her job with the project[15] and moved back to Provincetown, where she found a lively society of artists "who drank and talked shop together, drifting in and out of each other's homes as the members of the Provincetown Players did twenty years earlier" (Noe, *Susan Glaspell* 70). Here in Provincetown, which had been her home away from home ever since she had left Davenport, Susan Glaspell spent the last ten years of her life as a welcome, active and much-respected member of her community. Here she died on 27 July 1948, at the age of seventy-two, having published three more novels and a children's tale to add to her rich literary legacy.[16]

As one of many critics to ponder over the striking inconsistencies in Susan Glaspell's life and art, Marcia Noe has put her finger on the fact that Glaspell was always the "society girl" as much as she was a rebel against social norms. Always actively involved with her immediate community, she greatly enjoyed and depended on the support of her friends and family — an emotional dependence which included a certain desire for acceptance by society in a broader sense. Yet while she grew up in a community whose Midwestern ties to the pioneer tradition she greatly valued, at the same time Glaspell also experienced a sense of alienation from the conservatism of her native region. Her personal convictions urged her to follow her own mind and heart even when her inner voice was in conflict with other people's beliefs, causing pain to herself and others. For Susan Glaspell, to live one's life to the fullest meant to live it according to one's own standards, unhampered by stiff social norms. Simultaneously, her view of life included that this could not be achieved without striving to come to lasting terms of understanding and acceptance with one's fellow human beings.

Glaspell's personal philosophy thus provided the roots for many contradictory elements in her life and oeuvre. Although she was convinced that conservative social norms stood in the way of individual truthfulness and freedom, when Cook left his wife and two children to marry her in 1913 no avant-garde desire to shock society had encouraged her in her feelings. Instead, she chose to embark on a marriage to Cook herself which in many ways turned out to be "quite a traditional one" (Noe, *Susan Glaspell* 36).[17] Likewise, it was not a modern decision against traditional family values and in favor of an uninterrupted professional career which left Glaspell without children. To the contrary, it caused her much pain that after a miscarriage during their first year of marriage and because of a heart lesion then discovered she could never have children of her own. "I do not know how to tell the story of Jig without telling this," she writes in *The Road to the Temple.* "Women say to one: 'You have your work. Your books are your children, aren't they?' And you look at the diapers airing by the fire, and wonder if they really think you are like that..." (239).

Indeed, that Glaspell radically broke with traditional social norms in her life decisions yet often enough adhered to them at the same time is especially apparent in her partnerships. Despite the fact that she was among the most liberated women of her time — a professional writer and always the bread-winner in her relationships— she habitually put her partner's achievements before her own. "'[Susan] subordinated herself completely, always to the man of the moment, was *anything* but a feminist, and always sad when work of her own succeeded more than my father's— or after, Norman Matson's,'" thus Marcia Noe quotes Nilla Cook, Glaspell's stepdaughter, from a 1976 letter (*Susan Glaspell* 10). J. Ellen Gainor has rightly pointed out that this much-quoted statement is certainly problematic in that Cook's daughter never seems to have specified her personal definition of "feminism" in this context (see *Susan Glaspell* 264 f.). Nevertheless, the impression remains among scholars that Glaspell never claimed for herself the position she deserved as a female artist. As Ozieblo, too, still states with some impatience: "[In] spite of living an extraordinary life for a woman of her time and her undoubted triumphs and popularity as a playwright and novelist, Glaspell constantly ceded center stage to the men she loved" (*Susan Glaspell* 3). Indeed, it seems that the almost self-effacing pose which the successful artist is said to have upheld in her love relationships extended to her public appearances as well. As late as 1940, one journalist reports that at a cocktail party hosted by Glaspell's publishers to celebrate her new novel the guest of honor persistently complimented every attending writer on *his* latest book before anyone could compliment her on her own work: "It was really difficult to make Miss Glaspell stay even on the edge of the limelight; she seemed naturally to begin talking about any subject rather than herself" ("Turns with a Bookworm").

It seems plausible enough to read Glaspell's habitual display of modesty both in her private and in her public life as the expression of her adherence to a Victorian ideal of True Womanhood constantly at odds with her unconventional New Woman's life. With an eye on yet another striking parallel between Glaspell's life and her dramatic works, however, one might also speculate that these gestures of self-effacement were an expression of the artist's very refusal to have her works pinned down to her personal life. Interestingly enough, the part seldom quoted of Nilla Cook's remark about Glaspell's tendency to "subordinate herself to the man of the moment" is the way in which it is introduced in Noe's biography: "'The reason no one has discovered anything about [Glaspell's] life is that she very much wanted it that way,' said her stepdaughter, Nilla Cook" (*Susan Glaspell* 10).

Just as Glaspell absented many of her characters from her stage only to demonstrate how easily their identities are co-opted by others in their absence (see, for instance, my chapters on *Trifles*, *Bernice*, and *Alison's House*), it appears that she made a point of absenting herself from the historical record in all but her artistic works. For not only did Glaspell change the date of her birth in biographical accounts and withdrew her own experience to the status of vague between-the-lines allusions in her literary representation of Cook's life. As Ozieblo explains, another interesting circumstance renders the biographer's task difficult in Glaspell's case:

> Joining the ranks of many famous writers, Glaspell destroyed her personal letters; her extant diaries [...] are mostly empty, a few pages half-filled with cryptic sentences to remind her of ideas for plays or stories. The biographer must rely on the traces of her life that she could not destroy, such as her plays and novels, and the letters and autobiographies of friends, in which she is but a minor character in the drama of their lives [*Susan Glaspell* 3].

It was "[w]ith no help from Glaspell," then, that Ozieblo "approached the more intimate aspects of her life" (*Susan Glaspell* 3). As this biographer readily acknowledges that her thoroughly researched study presents her "version of one of the 'six or seven thousand selves'—posited by Virginia Woolf in every human being—awaiting us in Susan Glaspell," she highlights the fact that this version is as much a *construct* as is any image which audiences might create of Glaspell's absent characters with the help of her on-stage ensembles. True enough, indeed: What remains for us to examine are the literary works themselves—with all their inconsistencies and paradoxes intact.

In her early critical biography, Marcia Noe has identified "the one consistent element in Susan Glaspell's life and writings, in light of which the paradoxes and irreconcilable elements seem less perplexing. First and foremost, Susan Glaspell was not a feminist, a bohemian, a socialist, an expatriate, an eulogist, or critic of the Midwest, but an idealist" (*Susan Glaspell* 10). To J. Ellen Gainor, this label of "Glaspell, the idealist" (chosen by Waterman, too, to pin down the overarching characteristic of this writer's oeuvre),[18] is too reductive a rubric to "support all the various positions Glaspell seems to project through her writing"—as is Gerhard Bach's term of "life's meaning" (*Susan Glaspell* 264, 266). Instead, Gainor calls Glaspell a "political writer" and suggests that this "construction [...] allows for greater flexibility in the critical and theatrical exploration of her work" (266). Yet Gainor's claim that Glaspell "chose her writing, particularly her drama, as her [...] form of activism" (264) highlights Glaspell's persistent belief in the possibility of social change through art, and with this emphasis points back directly to earlier identifications of the idealist's stance in her works. As Noe went on to explain in her book, Glaspell's idealism "is not a commitment to any one belief so much as it is a belief in belief, a faith in faith [...]" (*Susan Glaspell* 10). What my readings will show is that this "faith in faith"—often faltering but always renewed—is consistently aimed at the possibility of living one's life to its full potential against all social restrictions while at the same time finding reconciliation and strength in one's connection to others.

Glaspell's artistic vision, indeed, does not evolve around the struggle of the human soul with God or Fate, as has been said of her fellow-Provincetowner Eugene O'Neill.[19] Instead, it is concerned throughout with the relationship between the individual soul and her fellow human beings. That Glaspell grapples with the nature of this relationship time and again in terms of human expression, be it language or non-verbal communication, words or silence, social actions or art, is a special feature of her work which has its immediate biographical link in the fact that she wanted to be a writer from an early age and pursued this aim with vigor through her entire life. In search of a way to reconcile the two basic notions of individuality and communality in human existence, both in her life and in her art Susan Glaspell set her highest hopes on the possibility of successful self-expression and communication.

2. Language and Communication

Theoretical Points of Departure

In 1932, the theatre critic Ludwig Lewisohn wrote about Susan Glaspell and her plays:

> She is a Puritan struggling toward freedom, toward unaccustomed expression. [...] She is a dramatist a little afraid of speech. [...] She wants to speak out and to let her people speak out. [...] She brooded and tortured herself and weighed the issues of expression [*Expression* 393–94].

Fifty-five years later, redirecting critical attention to Glaspell's works with his annotated edition of four selected plays, C.W.E. Bigsby explains:

> Susan Glaspell does indeed weigh the issues of expression. They are the essence of her work. Neither was she unaware of the extent to which her own freedoms were circumscribed by a language which tied her to social and biologic function. Her plays both placed this concern at their centre and constituted a statement of her own independence [*Plays* 29].

No one encountering the plays of Susan Glaspell can fail to notice the central importance assigned to notions of language, self-expression, and communication in these works. As the two quotations above aptly illustrate, however, exactly what is the meaning attached to these notions and what are the effects called forth by the dramatist's specific ways of dealing with them cannot as easily be agreed upon. Glaspell poses no clear-cut problems in her art, as little as she offers any ready-made solutions. The very vagueness of the term chosen by her contemporary Lewisohn to define one of her most central concerns bears witness to the difficulties of pinning down any unambiguous messages connected with these "issues of expression" in her plays. What is more, where Lewisohn (otherwise an ardent admirer of Glaspell's works) "aches for a word to release the dumbness" (on *Trifles*, *Drama* 105), Bigsby finds her work "best when it is least articulate" (on *The Outside*,

"Susan Glaspell," 28). And while feminist criticism has read the unique way in which Glaspell puts to use her artistic medium both as a revalorization of female expression and as the dramatic presentation of woman's silencing in patriarchy, the question whether the dramatist's own communication has to be judged an aesthetic success or failure still causes heated debates among her critics today.

Susan Glaspell's plays present a steady process of contemplation, experimentation and debate, and her works constantly seem to shift grounds in emphasis and position. Not only does her engagement with the notions of language and communication take place on a number of different thematic levels. Throughout her oeuvre the playwright persistently takes up three distinct if interchangeable vantage points in relation to these issues: that of an otherwise unmarked position of the self as connected or opposed to human community, that of a specifically gendered experience, and that of artistic expression and the artist's role in society. In order to disentangle the complex ways in which Glaspell mixes all of these angles both in individual works and from play to play, it is useful to explore them against the backdrop of a number of related communicational theories. As will soon become apparent, in their programmatic attempt to explain how we succeed (or fail) to communicate with each other, all theories of language are inevitably linked to the question of what constitutes "meaning" in human interaction. In this way, any concept of communication includes a systematic understanding of how human beings make sense of their lives and of their relation to others—the very issues which lie at the heart of Susan Glaspell's writings.

Defining and Relating the Self: A Philosophy of Language

Approaching the concept of language from a perspective which remains inherently "gender-blind," two views have surfaced as opponents in a variety of disciplines (philosophy, linguistics, speech communication, semiology) throughout the 20th century. While these two notions are often posited as incompatible in their theoretical assumptions, they are relevant to a reading of Glaspell's oeuvre precisely because they can be found to exist side by side in her works—a circumstance that might be able to account for many of the contradictions pervading her art.

In my following presentation of the two concepts in question, I am guided by three parallel approaches which have challenged the "old" view with a "new" one. For one, I base my discussion on the still ongoing debates over the German philosopher Ludwig Wittgenstein and the change in his thinking from his 1922 *Tractatus Logico-Philosophicus* to his *Philosophical*

Investigations (1945–49, trans. 1953). Secondly, I find the two rival principles pointedly distinguished in the works of the British linguist Roy Harris, who has profoundly challenged traditional assumptions of his field since the early 1980s. And thirdly, I approach the issue with the help of John Stewart, American scholar of speech communication, who in his 1995 study *Language as Articulate Contact* (a phrase I will borrow for my own purposes) advances a post-semiotic philosophy of communication built on descriptions of language as developed by Martin Heidegger, Hans-Georg Gadamer, Martin Buber, and Mikhail Bakhtin. What my play-by-play analyses will show against this theoretical background is how thoroughly Susan Glaspell anticipated not only late 20th-century feminist thinkers, but many other notions developed in connection to the so-called "linguistic turn."

Perhaps the more familiar of the two concepts at issue here, the idea of language as a representational system of signs has been a pervasive one for as long as the Western world can remember.[1] Roy Harris calls it the telementational model for its basic conviction that language is the means with which thoughts or ideas are transferred from one human mind to another. John Stewart terms it the symbol model, since any version of it rests on the belief that words stand for something else. Both scholars point out that as a model explaining the nature of language, it is made up of a number of suppositions so closely interrelated that none could be abandoned without damaging the model as a coherent whole.[2]

It is arguably the most basic of these convictions that to see language as a transmitter of thoughts from one mind to another is to presuppose the existence of two different worlds, one linguistic and one non-linguistic (the "world of words" as opposed to the "world of facts" or "objective reality"). As a second assumption, the linguistic world is taken to consist of a number of identifiable units (phonemes, words, sentences, utterances, speech acts etc.) which are understood to stand in a representational relationship with the elements making up the other, non-linguistic world. Hence, language is seen as a system of signs and fixed meanings which can be observed, studied and described as such — a composite consisting of distinct elements and guided by distinct rules. Finally, this theory assumes that as a representative system language is used by human beings in order to achieve their communicative goals — to make themselves understood, that is, for the purpose of "getting something done" in the non-linguistic world. It is a significant consequence of such an understanding that the notions of "language" and "communication" are seen as distinctly separate from each other: the first is simply a tool employed in order to achieve the latter.

Inherent in this model of language is the idea that humans stand in a subject-object relationship to the world as well as to language itself. As Stewart explains:

> [T]he claim that language instrumentally represents, assumes the *prior* existence of humans who are already-constituted and capable of intending and representing. It also presupposes the existence of worlds which are objectively given and thus capable of being intended and represented [113–14; emphasis in the original].

In this way, the symbol model poses the individual as the Kantian-Cartesian metaphysical subject, a unified self living in an unmediated relationship to the world.[3] Importantly, such a view makes way for a skepticism capable of questioning the entire process of communication: If language is nothing but a tool we use to transmit thoughts and ideas from one mind to another, one can easily draw the conclusion that meaning itself is inherently private. And, consequently (as Charles Altieri sums up this idea), "once the words are taken as primarily signs of something else, once verification depends on people's intentions or on their particular intuitions of the reality referred to, there will always be a gap between direct experience and linguistic expression" (1400).

While this dilemma has occupied thinkers across the centuries (engendering differing modes of repair-work from various quarters),[4] the possibility of complete miscommunication remains a built-in feature of the symbol model of language, and the point of attack for fundamental skepticists has remained intact. If truth is to be found outside of language, successful communication and understanding between subjects is ultimately a matter of faith: "The hearer must presuppose that he is interpreting the speaker as the speaker intends: but the speaker's intention and the hearer's interpretation are, at best, constituted by inner states of each respectively, not accessible to themselves, let alone to the other" (Dummett 202). As a result, the moment that the metaphysical subject loses this faith in the process of communication and is forced to give up the idealist stance, s/he is left to a state of complete isolation without any dependable way of reaching another human being. Significantly, as I will show in my analyses of Susan Glaspell's plays, it is this devastating conclusion precisely which many of her characters are forced to face.

Even if the difficulties inherent in the symbol model of language have long been under discussion, the representational view proves to be a particularly stubborn habit of mind. As one scholar remarks in a discussion of Ludwig Wittgenstein's philosophy: "The conviction that the meaning of a word is the object for which it stands is a conviction that dies hard" (Quigley 214). On the other hand, throughout the 20th century a growing number of voices have been raised to criticize the telementational model in its entirety, rejecting the very ways in which the concepts of language, understanding, and meaning have traditionally been theorized. Among the earliest of these voices, in his *Philosophical Investigations* Wittgenstein turns upside down his own representational notion of language as put forth in his earlier *Tractatus Logico-Philosophicus* (1922). While Wittgenstein, notably, moves his emphasis to a notion which is founded in the very necessity of not developing yet another *theory*, later thinkers point out the need for a substitutive systematic view. As John Stewart notes, with Heidegger, Gadamer and Bakhtin, "at least three prominent contemporary philosophers working from at least two distinct traditions call for a post-semiotic account of the nature of language" (105).

The starting point common to all rejections of the representational model of language is the claim that it often fails to conform to our everyday experience.[5] As Quigley explains, moving along a series of concrete examples Wittgenstein illustrates that language — instead of serving as a transmitter for our thoughts — has "a multitude of [...] functions embedded in a multitude of language-games that we regularly play" (215). A key passage of his work, Wittgenstein goes on to explain this concept: "[T]he term 'language-*game*' is meant to bring into prominence the fact that the *speaking* of language is part of an activity, or of a form of life" (*Investigations* I, § 23; emphasis in the original). It is this understanding of language as a primal, contextualized activity which is shared by all accounts that challenge the representational model.

In effect, such a notion takes issue with all basic features of the representational model.[6] In its understanding of language as our very mode of living, it runs counter to the telementational conviction that the human subject is able to occupy a detached vantage point over against an independently given sphere of objective facts — be it "world" or "language." Instead of positing the world of facts and the world of words as two independent spheres which can be described and analyzed in scientific terms, the understanding of language as constitutive articulate contact claims that human experience is of only one world, and this world is linguistic. As Stewart, in a reference to Martin Heidegger, explains:

> [T]he subject-object analyses of humans begin one giant step too far into the problematic, because, prior to any operations as subjects over against a more-or-less "objective" world, humans engage in a variety of everyday practices into which we are socialized but that *we do not represent in our minds* [28; Stewart's emphasis].

This primary mode of human existence is what Heidegger has labeled "being-in-the-world," and as the notions of "socialization" and "engagement" in the quote above indicate, it is fundamentally and irreducibly a mode of involvement with other humans — a "being-*with*," according to Heidegger's terminology in his *History of the Concept of Time*. Hence what Stewart calls the process of our "everyday coping" characteristically takes place *through language* — in communicative acts of human contact. With this understanding, the notions of language and communication blend into one: Communication is pointedly *not* "a matter of transporting information and experiences from the interior of one subject to the interior of the other one." Rather "it is a matter of being-with-one-another becoming manifest in the world, [...] which itself becomes manifest in speaking with one another" (Stewart 110–11).

Importantly, then, since language is the very way in which we make sense of our existence, it is our linguistic grasping of it which constitutes reality for us in the first place. As Stewart explains: "human worlds are collaboratively constructed (modified, developed, razed, reconstructed) in speech communication" (111). It is at this point that an understanding of language as *constitutive* articulate contact comes into play. In order to describe the dynamic involved, Stewart coins the term "worlding," as a "process that *happens in address-and-response, in speaking-and-listening, that is, in verbal-nonverbal talk*" (ibid.; Stewart's emphasis). Such an understanding of the function of language insists that "features of human worlds do not first exist and then get spoken or written of, they come into being in talk" (113).

John Stewart's notion of "worlding" (or "languageing," as he also calls it) is in line with Gadamer's argument that we live in "a world not of things but of *meaning*," and it describes the same phenomenon Wittgenstein is concerned with in creating his concept of language-games.[7] Significantly, such an insistence on the all-embracing role of linguisticality in human experience does not deny the facticity of objects. Instead, it stresses that

> [w]hatever truth the affirmation of facticity enjoys is due to coherence and consensus not correspondence. No Archimedian observation post is available to render "relative" all worldviews that are allegedly dependent on other, less secure vantage points" [Stewart 117].[8]

In this way, what the concept of language as articulate contact suggests is that we "cannot explain our activities by recourse to extra-linguistic facts, but neither can we consider the possibility that all there is is language or mind *as opposed to* getting in touch with the facts" (Guignon 669; emphasis in the original).

One of the most important consequences of this idea is that it removes the very grounds for doubting whether people "really" understand each other. As described above, the existential problem which arises from the symbol model of language is the realization that if "consciousness is a process of representing some external reality, it follows that [it] is always interpretation, always the imposition of tenuous forms on an unknowable but felt flux" (Altieri 1405). Wittgenstein, however, insists that only if we look at a word "'from outside' [do we] become conscious that it could be interpreted thus or thus." In contrast, "if it is a step in the course of [our] thought, then it is a stopping place that is natural to [us], and its further interpretability does not occupy (or trouble) [us]" (*Investigations* I, § 235). For Wittgenstein, "[t]he real discovery is the one that makes me capable of stopping doing philosophy when I want to.— The one that gives philosophy peace, so that it is no longer tormented by questions which bring *itself* in question" (ibid. § 133). With this stance, he fights off the demons of both skepticism and solipsism, in effect rejecting the very starting point for all philosophical thinking — the idea that "secure understanding is only possible if we first doubt everything that *can* be doubted, and then remove all these doubts" (ibid, § 87). Instead, as Quigley explains the way in which the philosopher later elaborates on this idea, in our everyday language-games "[m]any things count as certain for us because of the forms of life we have experienced" (222). In other words, we know things to be true because of our own as well as other people's experience — because we are "familiar with [them] as a certainty" (Wittgenstein, *On Certainty* § 272). Truth, then, is not something outside of our everyday lives or human histories; it is found in the very way we constitute our world in habitual language-games (or, in John Stewart's phrase, in the act of "worlding").[9]

Consequently, for Wittgenstein the meaning of a word is not the "object" it "stands for," but "its use in the language" (*Investigations* I, § 23). Such an understanding takes into consideration that concepts "don't just have a use, they have a history of use, and though we are free to revise [the existing meaning of a concept], we are not free to ignore it" (Quigley 220). On the one hand, this idea allows the conclusion that the skeptic's doubt as to the possibility of communication is an attitude which simply does not make sense in the face of our every-day experiences of the world. After all, the concept of doubt, as part of our ongoing language-games, is habitually brought into play only in the context of a contrasting residue of concepts which indeed remain certain. As Quigley sums up this idea:

> Things stand fast for us not because of external grounds but because of conventional history of use, because of established forms of life, because of inherited characteristics of discourse, [...], because of all those things we have learned to exempt from doubt in order to investigate things it seems more fruitful to doubt. [In fact, there is a] necessity of leaving something exempt from doubt if the word *doubt* is to function at all [224–25].

On the other hand, experiences of a failure of language are as much a part of our daily lives as are our habitual ways of understanding one another. Indeed, it is precisely in these moments that a suspicion as to whether our dealings in the world might not be based on arbitrary interpretations imposes itself on us: "[I]nterpretations are problematic precisely because they are called for only when our normal procedures break down" (Altieri 1406–07).

Significantly, however, the notion of language as articulate contact changes such experiences of a breakdown in our procedures of understanding from an indication of our minds' ultimate *isolation* to a realization that we are fundamentally *connected* in our human existence: Experiences of miscommunication form an integral part of the ordinary communicative process of "worlding."

To understand our world as "languaged," then, pointedly includes those instances in which we experience meaning as lying outside the realm of words. For, as John Stewart explains:

> although one may not be able satisfactorily to label an emotion or to capture an aesthetic experience in a sentence or paragraph, linguisticality nonetheless pervades these experiences of meaning. The fact that one isolates a given state of being as "an emotion," an object as "a work of art," and a response to it as "overwhelming" or "ineffable" all reflect cultural categories [...] that one has learned communicatively [116].

Once more, the emphasis here is on the term "communication" as a profoundly intersubjective activity. Ultimately, what our experiences of failed expression illustrate is that although our human world comes into being in communication, we do not create it individually: we do not "world" alone. Language and meaning are fundamentally contextualized in human existence — this is the idea put forth in Wittgenstein's notion of meaning as use, and it is basic to all later critiques of the symbol model.[10] Within his own framework, Stewart emphasizes:

> Of course, no individual initiates this process [of *worlding*]; each of us is born into a family that, in the context of its culture and speech community, bequeaths us a world that, as we mature, we more- or less-substantively alter. Thus human worlds are not constituted *de novo*, but from what we inherit [113; Stewart's emphasis].

Consequently, this understanding entails the realization that although we are "participants in public language-games which are not grounded on anything outside our lives," nevertheless these language-games, "insofar as they constitute our lives, [...] are not something we create or can fully master" (Guignon 660). At the heart of this model of language is the recognition that there is no human nature or mode of being before or indeed independent of cultural experience and social construction. Putting forth an alternative understanding of human existence, it draws the conclusion that although we cannot impose our will on reality as we (?) choose — that is, although our habits of mind are not easily changeable — neither are the instances of our lives the result of unalterable "facts" imposed on us from some authoritative position outside of our existence as social beings. Strikingly, all throughout Susan Glaspell's dramatic oeuvre both these aspects of cultural determination and of creative freedom play a significant role — even as they exist side by side to her struggle with the questions of isolation and connection provoked by the opposing model of language as a representational system of signs.

Finally, one of the most crucial features characterizing the notion of language as constitutive articulate contact lies in the fact that in its particular view of human nature it preserves and idea of the "self" as a recognizable entity. Even as the model rejects the idea of the solitary Kantian-Cartesian subject situated at a distance from objective reality, it replaces this notion with the concept of a "speaking subject" whose existence is profoundly contextual, relational and communal.[11] Bent on its central requirement of making sense with regard to our every-day experiences of life, such an understanding acknowledges the commonplace perception of ourselves as coherent entities which are characterized by more-or-less stable identities. Allowing that these identities are never fixed but always in motion (engaged, as it were, in a constant process of worlding), this theory insists that part of our thus constituted understanding of human existence is the notion of a self which is "I."

Consequently, while the view of language as articulate contact posits the self as nothing other than that which is constituted through language in a continuous engagement with other human beings, it nevertheless runs counter to the idea of the "death of the self" as it has been announced by 20th-century deconstructionists.[12] Along with Ludwig Wittgenstein, many thinkers who call for a pragmatic understanding of language are guided by the conviction that our sense of self is vital to our emotional, physical and psychic well-being.[13] Arguing along the same lines in her own (artistic) instances of expression, Susan Glaspell frequently discusses the problem of identity in precisely this context. In many of her plays her protagonists are presented as individuals whose well-being is threatened as they struggle to both free themselves of and at the same time define themselves within a web of communicational contacts which create the notions of self and other in a constant reciprocal process.[14] (And in many instances Glaspell seems to advise her audience that if one must not reject the essential communality of existence, one should turn it into an instrument of power instead.)

The Gender Experience: Women's Voice and L'écriture féminine

Whereas up to this point the theories presented here have disregarded the possibility of gender-related differences in our understanding of language, for an examination of Glaspell's drama it is also necessary to clarify the theoretical basis which many critics have employed to highlight her "uniquely female" voice. In fact, while the import of gender in her works has been obvious to Glaspell's audiences from the start, interpretations still differ greatly when it comes to defining the female aspects of expression at stake. A frequent starting point for analysis is the observation that all of Glaspell's protagonists are women, and this fact is then employed in arguing the consistency with which she has handed over centre stage to the feminine point of view. However, during the further development of such argumentations the all-incorporating notion of the "female voice" allows for readings which pursue differing aims and at times even cross each other out in their theoretical presuppositions. More often than not, confusion rules as to what exactly constitutes the "feminine point of view" in Glaspell's plays, or the rendering of "woman's experience," or the mode of "feminine writing" indiscriminately referred to. What, indeed, are the defining pillars of a "female language?" Are the concepts evoked — such as the French coinage of an *écriture féminine* or the American socio-linguistic notion of genderlects— meant to be understood as empirical givens or theoretical postulates? In what ways is the idea of a feminine identity driven by underlying concepts of a human nature?

Prominent 20th-century debates related to these issues evolve around a core of ideological concerns: the discussion on "equality versus difference" in gender relations is linked to disagreements over the existence of a "female essence," while in an argument over variations such as biological versus cultural or strategical essentialism the very notion of essence itself is hotly debated when applied to questions of sex and gender. The stakes involved in these issues are high: they concern the possibilities of a liberation from biological as well as cultural or social determinism. Yet if one links these debates with the language philosophies I have discussed above, it becomes apparent that the very clash of theories regarding a female language has its origins in the same opposition outlined there — the opposition between the idea of a primal human nature existing prior to our socialization, and the notion of our human existence as an irreducibly communicative activity. Again, my interest in tracing this conflict lies in the conviction that both concepts work side by side in Glaspell's plays— even as she shifts her position from a gender-neutral to a pointedly female sense of self.

Based on an understanding which posits sexual difference as a primal fact in human existence, during the mid-1970s a number of theoretical concepts evolved which located women's "difference" to men in their essentially different relation to language.[15] Engaging with contemporary discourses such as Lacan's psychoanalytic interpretations of the "Imaginary" and the "Symbolic" or Derrida's philosophical concepts of deconstruction and *différance*, these ideas combine a description of the patriarchal status quo with feminist postulates of resistance and subversion. The debate includes differing views with regard to speech and writing, coining a specific terminology for both: *parler femme*, translated into "womanspeak" or "speaking (as) woman," and *écriture-au-féminine* ("writing-in-the-feminine"), or, in a more compact phrasing, *écriture féminine* ("female/feminine writing").

The notion of *parler femme* has been developed first and foremost in the writings of the psychoanalyst and philosopher Luce Irigaray. In Margaret Whitford words, Irigaray's concern with the spoken element of language results from her understanding that "identity [is] enacted at least partly in self-positioning in language vis-à-vis an interlocutor" (*The Irigaray Reader* 3). While this statement seems to resonate the idea of language as articulate contact, what is central to Irigaray's understanding of a specifically *feminine* identity in this context is the notion that our language is always already situated "within a particular symbolic system known as patriarchy" (ibid.).

The concept of the symbolic system brought into usage here is taken from a Lacanian reading of Freudian psychoanalytical theory. As Toril Moi explains, Lacan distinguishes a pre–Oedipal Imaginary in which the child (male or female) "believes itself to be a part of the mother, and perceives no separation between itself and the world" from the subsequent establishment of the Symbolic Order, when the intrusion of the father destroys this original unity (*Sexual/Textual Politics* 99). It is in the Oedipal crisis that the child acquires a sense of self as a separate entity, a sense brought about by the loss of unity with the maternal body and marked by the emergence of language. As the development of the self's inherently linguistic subject position is initiated through the appearance of the father (establishing the notions of difference and absence in the child's psyche), from this point onwards the feminine (the female body) is defined as "that which is absent" or, more pointedly, as "the other."

According to this theory, the only possible subject position within the Symbolic Order is a masculine subject position. The little girl inevitably sees herself as "a little man without a penis," she is defined only in terms of lack. Luce Irigaray, in her influential study *Speculum of the Other Woman*, shows how patriarchal discourse throughout history has defined woman solely in this enigmatic way, as man's other, the negative of the norm. Woman's own subject position, a feminine identity completely apart from the male subject, has remained unthinkable: Language by necessity traps woman in the position of the other. More precisely, according to Irigaray, since patriarchal logic defines woman only in relation to man, she is turned not into "an actual other," but always into "the other of the same," without ever achieving the status of an independent subject irreducible to the male subject.[16] Consequently, in the patriarchal Symbolic Order women are faced with two equally painful choices with regard to the possibilities of their self-expression: Either they adopt male language in a gesture of accepting its deceptive garment of universality, or they are left to speechlessness and silence, thus retreating to a state prior to the emergence of language, a position within the inarticulate and unified Imaginary (see Makward 95–105).

However, woman cannot simply choose to remain within the realm of the Imaginary, either, as this would equal a failure to establish a sense of identity within language and would therefore result in madness. (Hence the idea that the female hysteric attempts to speak her femininity in her disjointed, unintelligible utterances; see Irigaray, "Questions," 138.) Instead, Irigaray postulates that women need to work on the disruption of the Symbolic language from *within*, in an empowering attempt to confirm their female identity as different and completely apart from male identity. Significantly, here

> the issue is not one of elaborating a new theory of which woman would be the *subject* or the *object*, but of jamming the theoretical machinery itself [...]. [Women] should not put [the question] in the form 'What is woman?' but rather, repeating/interpreting the way in which, within discourse, the feminine finds itself defined as lack, deficiency, or as imitation and negative image of the subject, they should signify that with respect to this logic a *disruptive excess* is possible on the feminine side ["The Power of Discourse," 126; Irigaray's emphasis].

In this vein, Irigaray develops her concept of "*speaking (as) woman*" as "an attempt to provide a place for the 'other' as feminine"—whatever the (feminine) characteristics of this "actual other" may then turn out to be ("Questions," 137). Although she argues that female language cannot be defined (as it would immediately be captured within the language of the Symbolic, the "economy of the logos"), she nevertheless gives certain attributes to a "feminine *style*": "This 'style,' or 'writing,' of women tends to put the torch to fetish words, proper terms, well-constructed forms. [...] *Simultaneity* is its 'proper' aspect—a proper(ty) that is never fixed in the possible identity-to self of some form or other. It is always *fluid* [...]" ("The Power of Discourse," 126). In a move which considerably complicates the question of feminine expression, Irigaray then connects these attributes of simultaneity and fluidity to the very nature of the female body, to the multiplicity of woman's sexual organs and her *jouissance*.[17] Thus, a disruptive strategy which otherwise might have been employed by anyone striving to work against the patriarchal Symbolic Order, including men, is significantly turned into something naturally accessible only to women by virtue of their "other" *morphology*.[18]

Interestingly, at the same time that Irigaray formulates her idea of "speaking (as) woman" as a theoretical postulate she also detects it as an empirical fact taking place within women-only groups (see, for example, "Questions," 137). As she sums up her findings "obtained from research into the way in which little girls, adolescent girls, and women speak," Irigaray proposes "an interpretation of the characteristics of feminine language" ("The Question of the Other," 15). In her core argument she explains that the "language the most aware of the other is that of the little girl," that the little girl "always respects the existence of two subjects, each having the right to speak," and that girls and women — in contrast to boys and men — "almost always prefer a relationship with the other over a relationship with the object" (ibid. 16). Again, what is significant about Irigaray's observations on the differences in male and female speech is the way in which she interprets their origins: "Why does the little girl like dialogue so much? Doubtless because as a woman, born of woman, with the qualities and characteristics of a woman, including the ability to give birth, the little girl finds herself, as soon as she is born, in the position of having relationships with two subjects" (ibid. 17). And to state her point even more sharply, she continues:

> And it's not just a question of sociohistorical determination or a certain alienation of the feminine which could be done away with by making it equal to the masculine [...]. [Women's language] demonstrates an inherent richness which leaves nothing to be desired from men's language, in particular, a taste for intersubjectivity, which it would be a shame to abandon in favor of men's more inaccessible subject-object relations [ibid.].

Thus, whether as theoretical postulate or as empirical given Irigaray locates the origins of the differences between men and women in the specificity of the female body. Whether one calls this theoretical stance a kind of biological, cultural, or strategical essentialism or even renders the very term useless by denying essence to essentialism itself, the fact remains that at the core of her theories lies the understanding

> that *sex [sexe] is a primal and irreducible dimension of subjective structure.* We are sexuate and we produce sexuate forms. [...] No world can be produced or reproduced without sexual difference. Everything is sexuate: plants, animals, the gods, the elements of the universe. [...] [Thus], to date, no one has been able to assert that they belong to a monosexuate or asexuate universe [Irigaray, "The Three Genres," 146, 149; emphasis in the original].[19]

Significantly, in a development parallel to the discussions on the concept of *parler femme* it is this same question of a "female essence" which has fed a passionate debate over Hélène Cixous's concept of an *écriture féminine.* Here, the issue under fire is already problematized in the ambivalence of the French term *féminine.* Toril Moi has pointed out that it "has long been an established practice among most feminists to use 'feminine' (and 'masculine') to represent *social constructs* [...], and to reserve 'female' and 'male' for the purely biological aspects of sexual difference" (*Sexual/Textual Politics* 65; emphasis in the original). Again, what is at stake in this differentiation is the possibility of liberating women from pre-conceived notions of a universal female/feminine identity. Defining "feminism" as "a theoretical and political practice committed to the struggle against patriarchy and sexism" ("Men Against Patriarchy," 182), Moi claims that it is especially crucial for feminist critics to distinguish between social and biological definitions, since "patriarchal oppression consists of imposing certain social standards of femininity on all biological women, in order precisely to make us believe that the chosen standards for 'femininity' are *natural*" (*Sexual/Textual Politics* 65; Moi's emphasis).

Yet the issues involved in a definition of femininity and a female language are as paradoxically interwoven in Cixous as they are in Irigaray. More than once, Cixous has taken pains to stress that for her, "feminine" and "masculine" writing do not depend on the biological sex of the author.[20] In her understanding of the nature of writing she involves the ideas of *différance* and deconstruction developed by Jacques Derrida. With the French philosopher, she opposes the way meaning is produced in the opposition of hierarchical binary oppositions. Dual sets of terms, thus Toril Moi explains Cixous' stance, such as Culture/Nature, Activity/Passivity, Head/Emotions, Logos/Pathos etc., throughout "Western philosophy and literary thought" have "always in the end come back to the fundamental 'couple' of male/female [...] with its inevitable positive/negative evaluation" (*Sexual/ Textual Politics* 104–05). Against this imprisoning concept of meaning, Cixous sets the Derridean notion of *différance*: Meaning is produced through the "free play of the signifier," it is "never truly present, but is only constructed through the potentially endless process of referring to other, absent signifiers" (ibid.). *Différance*, then, includes both "difference" and "deferral" as the process in which each "'next' signifier [...] give[s] meaning to the 'previous' one [...] *ad infinitum*" (ibid.). Such an understanding, as Moi explains the concept, "implies a fundamental critique of the whole of Western philosophical tradition, based as it is on a 'metaphysics of presence,' which discerns meaning as fully present in the Word (or Logos)" (ibid.). According to Derrida, in Moi's words, there can be

> no 'transcendental signified' where the process of deferral somehow would come to an end. Such a transcendental signified would have to be meaningful *in itself*, fully present to itself, requiring no origin and no end other than itself. An obvious example of such a 'transcendental signified' would be the Christian concept of God as Alpha and Omega, the origin of meaning and final end of the world. Similarly, the traditional view of the author as the source and meaning of his or her own text casts the author in the role of transcendental signified [ibid].[21]

Hence what Cixous calls "feminine writing" is a language strategy based on the concept of *différance*. It is a writing bent on disrupting the patriarchal logic of binary closure, on disturbing and "deconstructing" the language of *phallogocentrism* and its view of the subject as static, unified, ever-present.[22] In this frame, feminine texts are "texts that 'work on the difference'" — regardless of whether they were written by a woman or a man (Cixous as qtd. by Moi, ibid. 108). They are texts which can admit that the "difference is in us," which work with an understanding that "the subject is a non-closed mix of self/s and others," suggesting that "I is the open set of the trances of an I by definition changing, mobile, because living-speaking-thinking-dreaming" (Cixous, "Preface," xviii, xvii, xviii). In line with such a view of the feminine, male writers are readily posited on the feminine side of writing (see Cixous, "First Names of No One," 28).

Seen in this way, feminine writing — similar to Irigaray's *parler femme* — marks a cultural position taken up within the patriarchal Symbolic Order, not a sexual essence with a fixed meaning, and the "terms 'masculine' and 'feminine' [...] can be viewed as markers which could be exchanged for any others" (Sellers, "Introduction," xxviii). On the other hand, the notion of sexual difference is as vital to Cixous as it is to Irigaray. It is worth noting that if a subversive position towards patriarchal logic were all that defined "feminine" writing, one might just as well call it "anti-patriarchal" instead and avoid the entire problematic question of sexual essence. But Cixous's understanding of an *écriture féminine*, like Irigaray's concept, goes further. It is closely bound up with a specific concept of sexuality, or more precisely of *bisexuality*. In her *La Jeune Née — The Newly Born Woman*, Cixous defines the traditional idea of bisexuality to be "the fantasy of a complete being, [...] Ovid's Hermaphrodite, less bisexual than asexual, not made up of two genres but of two halves. Hence, a fantasy of unity. Two within one, and not even two wholes" (41). To this, she opposes "the *other* bisexuality [...] — that is to say the location within oneself of the presence of both sexes, evident and insistent in different ways according to the individual, the non-exclusion of difference or of a sex [...]." This "other" bisexuality "does not annihilate differences but cheers them on, pursues them, adds more" (ibid.). Again, although Cixous grants that men, too, can live — and write — this kind of inclusive bisexuality, she links it to a kind of femininity determined specifically by *woman's* position in the patriarchal Symbolic Order. Consequently, while this femininity, marked by the inclusion of sexual difference within subjectivity, is cultural on the one hand, it is at the same time inherently connected to the female body. Quoting Cixous, Sellers explains:

> For Cixous, then, sexual difference is important in the role it plays in determining gender behaviour, with its capacity to uphold or challenge the existing order, rather than as anatomical difference per se. Cixous nevertheless contends that sexuality is vital, seeing in the differences between the sexes the potential for alternative insights and ways of understanding the world. She suggests that women's real or imagined experiences of preg-

nancy and childbirth, for example, entail the possibility of a radically different relation to the other: [...] "There is a bond between woman's libidinal economy — her *jouissance*, the feminine Imaginary — and her way of self-constituting a subjectivity that splits apart without regret" ["Introduction," xxviii].

Hence Cixous's idea of femininity — as does Irigaray's—continuously oscillates between the poles of (cultural) position and (biological) essence. What is more, the "other" which the feminine, according to Cixous, is able to admit to is not even Irigaray's "actual other." As the critic Lisa Gasborrone has accurately shown, Cixous's "other" is not located on the outside, enabling woman to engage in a Bakhtinian dialogic discourse as a "process of 'interanimation' in which self and other create one another continually" (Gasborrone 5, quoting Bakhtin). Instead, her "location of otherness totally within the parameters of the [female] self results in its negation. In short, she cancels otherness out" (ibid.). Cixous thus shares the specific theoretical presuppositions of all sexual difference-promoters: similar to Luce Irigaray, she works with the fundamental conception of a primal sexuate universe. In Lisa Gasborrone's words: "Cixous's feminine self is [...] a *pre-existing entity*. Silenced up until now, she has always been there, beneath the surface" (Gasborrone 16; my emphasis).

Consequently, although both Irigaray and Cixous at first sight seem to come down on an understanding of language as "constitutive articulate contact" — stressing the way identity is formed within communication, criticizing the notions of fixed meanings — they nevertheless adhere to the theoretical presuppositions connected to the representational model of language and meaning in that their theories imply the existence of a human nature prior to and independent of human socialization. As both insist on the necessity for the female self to express herself through language, the only difference is that in their view, this primal human nature is not gender-neutral but irreducibly sexuate. Significantly, with an eye on Susan Glaspell's most obviously feminist pieces such as *Trifles* and *The Verge*, and in reference to the host of unique "female stutterers" who figure so prominently all throughout her oeuvre, critics have read her works as creating early instances of both *parler femme* and *écriture féminine*. Yet Glaspell's writing does not only allow interpretations in the essentialist vein. It is similarly open to an understanding of sexual difference as a *cultural* phenomenon.

As I have shown, in an interesting turn of their theories both Irigaray and Cixous link their idea of "woman" to the concept of a "natural" female acceptance of human intersubjectivity. With this emphasis on the special importance of interpersonal relationships for women, both thinkers link up with a broad field of empirical research performed on the Anglo-American scene of gender studies. Especially Irigaray's findings on the specific way(s) in which women habitually use language in conversation stand in relation to a frame of research on gender differences in communication which has been conducted in a number of diverse disciplines in the Anglo-American context over the past twenty years. Analyzing the ways in which language is employed and interpreted in every-day conversations, studies in this area have acknowledged the existence of two different registers of speech, distributed in a striking pattern of opposition between women and men. Similar to Irigaray's research, these studies observe that boys and girls, women and men engage the world in fundamentally different ways, as they experience the relationship of self and other differently.

However, although Irigaray and the researchers involved in these studies presumably work with similar raw material (actual language use between people in Western cultures),[23] their interpretations take on a different focus as they are guided by differing theoretical systems. While Irigaray poses sexual difference in language use as something more basic than "just a question of sociohistorical determination" ("The Question of the Other," 17), most Anglo-American studies stress their conviction that the various modes of engaging with the world are universal to human nature and are distributed to create gender oppositions only in the context of our socialization within Western culture. The psychologist Carol Gilligan, for instance, who in her influential 1982 publication *In a Different Voice* has revealed "two [distinct] ways of speaking about moral problems" as being clearly distributed in a pattern of contrast between women and men ("two modes of describing the relationship between other and self"), insists that women's "different voice" is "characterized not by gender but theme. Its association with women is an empirical observation, [...] [it is] not absolute" (2).

Gilligan refers to earlier research when she traces the beginnings of "basic sex differences [...] in personality development" back to early childhood, to the period of the first three years of life, when "for both sexes the primary caretaker [...] is typically female" (50). Since "mothers tend to experience their daughters as more like, and continuous with, themselves" while they "experience their sons as a male opposite," a developing sense of female identity is connected to the experience of continuation and attachment while the emergence of male identity is linked to a sense of differentiation and individuation:

> Consequently, relationships [...] are experienced differently by women and men. [...] Since masculinity is defined through separation while femininity is defined through attachment, male gender identity is threatened by intimacy while female gender identity is threatened by separation. Thus males tend to have difficulty with relationships, while females tend to have problems with individuation [Gilligan 8].

According to Gilligan's work the different emphasis boys and girls as well as men and women place on the issues of individuation and interdependence can be observed at any age and stage in the human life cycle. By the time they reach adulthood, women and men have developed two different systems of understanding and engaging with the world, each system reflecting one side of "the paradoxical truths of human experience — that we know ourselves as separate only insofar as we live in connection with others, and that we experience relationship [sic] only insofar as we differentiate other from self" (63). Gilligan's research shows that while males of any age often define the nature of a moral dilemma as an abstract equation presenting itself as the formal problem of "how to exercise one's rights without interfering with the rights of others," women (and girls) habitually reveal a different point of view. For them, a "moral problem arises from conflicting responsibilities [to oneself and to others] rather than from competing rights and requires for its resolution a mode of thinking that is contextual and narrative rather than formal and abstract" (21, 19). Women, Gilligan concludes, live in a world which is determined by a "network of connection, a web of relationships that is sustained by a process of communication," while male reality is structured by a "hierarchical ordering" of values, rights, and power (32–33; see also 62–63).

Continuing along similar lines with her own research, the American sociolinguist Deborah Tannen approaches what she calls the existence of two different "genderlects" from the position of a "cultural difference framework": From her point of view, "systematic differences in women's and men's characteristic styles" develop "because boys and girls grow up in what are essentially different cultures" (*Gender and Discourse* 7, 11). Women and men move in "different worlds of words" since they engage the world in different ways: men as "individual[s] in a hierarchical social order in which [they are] either one-up or one-down," and women as "individual[s] in a network of connections" (*You Just Don't Understand* 24–25). In a world structured by hierarchies, she explains further, "conversations are negotiations in which people try to achieve and maintain the upper hand if they can, and protect themselves from others' attempts to put them down and push them around. Life, then, is a contest, a struggle to preserve independence and avoid failure" (ibid. 25). In a world characterized by connections, on the other hand, "conversations are negotiations for closeness in which people try to seek and give confirmation and support, and to reach consensus. They try to protect themselves from others' attempts to push them away. Life, then, is a community, a struggle to preserve intimacy and avoid isolation" (ibid.).

Interestingly, the same female emphasis on attachment and communication that is evident in Gilligan's and Tannen's research has also come to the surface in a 1987 study on women's conceptions of knowledge and truth. The findings of this study are significant in the context of trying to define a female language in that they show that women often use a metaphor of growth which describes an increasing knowledge of the world and personal understanding of truth as the process of "gaining a voice." This is remarkable insofar as conceptual notions of knowledge and truth have traditionally favored the image of gaining *insight*, instead. As Goldberger et al. point out:

> The tendency we observed for women to ground their epistemological premises in metaphors suggesting speaking and listening is at odds with the visual metaphors— such as equating knowledge with illumination, knowing with seeing, and truth with light — that scientists and philosophers most often use to express their sense of mind. [...] [S]uch analogies have led to a favored cultural model for truth and the quest for mind. Visual metaphors, such as "the mind's eye," suggest a camera passively recording a static reality and promote the illusion that disengagement and objectification are central to the construction of knowledge. Visual metaphors encourage standing at a distance to get a proper view, removing — it is believed — subject and object from a sphere of possible intercourse [207–08].

These findings suggest that while the "official" ("male") ways of knowing favor objectivity, detachment, and an abstract notion of truth, at the heart of female epistemology lie the concepts of engagement, subjective knowledge formed by experience, and the notion of private, relative truth. In the female mind, then, personal growth is understood as a process characterized by dialogue, not by observation and deduction.— This, of course, is precisely the gendered stance which has been identified to lie at the heart of Glaspell's most famous one-act, *Trifles*. In my own reading of this much-discussed play, however, I will argue that its supposedly gendered opposition in engaging with the world embodies nothing other than the very contrast of a representational versus an integrational understanding of language. In this way, my discussion will shift emphasis from a discussion of gender differences in *Trifles* to an analysis of what it portrays as *common to both* men and women in their experience of the world (see chapter 3).

Although coming from a completely different theoretical background, the above-quoted research in the Anglo-American context resonates Irigaray's findings of a systematic "alternation between a masculine choice of subject-object relations and a feminine choice of subject-subject relations" ("The Question of the Other," 16), sharing her observations with regard to women's taste for intersubjectivity (or interdependence, dialogue). Yet in their concluding terminology, the two approaches seem diametrically opposed to each other. Irigaray's central statement is that the patriarchal Symbolic Order — and therefore, men's thinking —functions through a fundamental Logic of the Same, whereas women are naturally capable of accepting "true difference" and the existence of "an other subject." Research working within the cultural difference framework, quite to the contrary, stresses men's inclination to preserve their own difference vis-à-vis an interlocutor, in comparison to women's habitual leaning towards aspects of sameness in interpersonal relations. Significantly, it is not in their observations as to what constitutes the female as opposed to the male voice that these approaches differ from each other, but in their underlying theoretical assumptions concerning the question of a human nature, and in their specific political goals in relation to the position of women within patriarchal society.

As Irigaray's thinking works from the fundamental understanding that sexual difference — may it be biologically or culturally defined — is an irreducible fact of human subjectivity, she argues against all feminist theories and strategies of "equality." In her eyes, such strategies accept the patriarchal Logic of the Same to the continuing detriment of women. Instead of adopting the patriarchal view of man as "universal," Irigaray is convinced, women need to accept their difference as "actual otherness" and create for themselves an independent female identity within the Symbolic Order. In her attempt to revalorize feminine subjectivity she thus camps on the same side with those feminists who accept the current content of a cultural man/woman dichotomy but strive to change the negative connotations of many "female traits" to expressively positive ones. Examining such approaches to the question of femininity, Christine Delphy explains that any insistence on sexual difference works with an epistemological model which she calls the "additive approach":

> Now such a view implies that the parts, which exist before the whole, have a meaning, and indeed a nature — an *essence*— of their own. It implies furthermore that the parts that make up any reality — the physical, social, or psychic world — are always the same, in number and in content, and are there to stay; therefore, that which we perceive is what *reality* is made up of: if we perceive two sexes for instance, it is because there *are* two sexes; that society or its instances— language for one instance — intervene only to rank these pre-existing realities [...]. The additive approach is thus necessarily essentialist [201–01; Delphy's emphasis].

In contrast to this view, many studies stressing the cultural/social aspects of existing gender differences have done so in order to defeat the very notion of a female essence. Fearing the forces of biological and cultural determinism, this kind of research has felt a conceptual need to deny essence to femininity in order to make social equality between the sexes feasible in the first place.[24] Against the view of pre-existing sexual differences (the existence of a "male human nature" and a "female human nature," see Delphy 203), there has been set the belief in a pre-existing "*human* nature" which is indeed universal and, therefore, non-gendered. Significantly, as Delphy puts it, studies working on the side of "equality" between women and men, insisting that observed gender differences are "only" cultural, have worked from "an implicit belief that somehow underlying social and cultural structures, there exists a 'human nature' that could surface if given the chance" (204). That throwing off one's socially formed gender identity is not as easily accomplished as this belief suggests, however, is an experience persistently thematized in many of Susan Glaspell's works—and a realization which inevitably leads to a concept of sex and gender as neither primal nor cultural, but as "constituted in articulate contact."

While Toril Moi—as one critic who insists on the concept of a pre-cultural, universal human nature—regrets the ambiguity of the French adjective *féminine* ("female" or "feminine?"), to other critics this distinction in its very nature/culture contrast is a misleading one to begin with. In a strictly opposing attitude to this kind of "binary thinking," a number of views have emerged which perceive of human subjectivity as always already existing within culture, inseparable from human socialization. (Perhaps most prominent among these views in the American context are the ideas put forth in Judith Butler's immensely influential study *Gender Trouble*.)[25] As has become apparent with regard to the notion of language as "constitutive articulate contact," within such a theoretical framework the role of language moves from a tool to express pre-existing "facts" of human nature to a process which actively produces our experience as human beings—including our experience of sexual difference. Significantly, in developing just such a view the linguist, psychoanalyst and philosopher Julia Kristeva rejects notions of *parler femme* or *écriture féminine* which locate the feminine in the Imaginary state, before the "intrusion" of language. Insisting that Woman "does not exist with a capital 'W,' possessor of some mythical unity" ("Women's Time," 205), she elaborates: "[If] the feminine *exists*, it only exists in the order of signifiance or signifying process, and it is only in relation to meaning and signification, positioned as their excessive or transgressive other that it *exists*, *speaks*, *thinks* (itself) and *writes* (itself) for both sexes" (qtd. in Moi, "Introduction," 11).

Essential to Kristeva's view of language and its role in human existence is her notion of the "speaking subject" engaged in a "signifying process" (*sujet en procès*). In her revolutionary essay "The System and the Speaking Subject," she develops a theory of meaning which moves away from the traditional understanding of language as a representational sign-system (a monolithic, homogeneous structure, that is) to the concept of a heterogeneous (signifying) process. In this move, she criticizes such semiotic theories which work "on the basis of a conception (already rather dated) of meaning as the act of a *transcendental ego*, cut off from its body, its unconscious and also its history" ("The System," 28). With her theory, then, Kristeva — just as the theoreticians of language as "articulate contact" — rejects the notion of the Kantian-Cartesian, unified ego which utilizes language as a logical system to express pre-existing realities. Instead, she brings into play a Bakhtinian idea of language as inherently dialogic, a theory of meaning as always contextual, and a notion of the (speaking) subject as always shifting, never ready to settle into the fixed state of a closed "identity."

It is at this crucial point that Kristeva rejects any kind of theory which sees in the feminine something more basic or essential than its marginal position in patriarchal society.[26] Opposing the idea of a primally sexuate universe, she has a different vision:

> In [this] attitude, which I strongly advocate — which I imagine? — the very dichotomy man/woman as an opposition between two rival entities may be understood as belonging to *metaphysics*. What can "identity," even "sexual identity," mean in a new theoretical and scientific space where the very notion of identity is challenged? ["Women's Time," 209].

And in answer to theories which continue to stress "Woman's Difference," Kristeva expresses this "avant-garde feminist hope,"

> that having started with the idea of difference, feminism will be able to break free of its belief in Woman, Her power, Her writing, so as to channel this demand for difference into each and every element of the female whole, and, finally, to bring out the singularity of each woman, and beyond this, her multiplicities, her plural languages, beyond the horizon, beyond sight, beyond faith itself [ibid. 208].

Kristeva's vision of a universe in which sex and gender are heterogeneous traits continuously "passing through" the (speaking) subject is shared by all those who, "gendered as we are in our psychological make-up," can nevertheless "*envision* the non-necessity of gender" (Delphy 204; emphasis in the original).[27] Such visions, insisting that our world is indeed thinkable without the ever-present opposition of the sexes, take into account the intuition of anyone who feels her- or himself "to be 'really' just a person, sex unspecified" (Heilbrun 264). Virginia L. Purvis-Smith contemplates Kristeva's concept of the speaking subject as "the construal of <a network where drives, signifiers and meanings join together and split asunder in a dynamic and enigmatic process,>" a process in which our identities "<are constantly remade and reborn>." (The angle brackets, representing quotation marks, are Purvis-Smith's; see 28.) She goes on to say, "kristeva's concept of self-definiton depicts the fluid sense i have of self, the self as matrix, the self as capable of such reorientations" (56–7).[28]

Importantly, in stressing that "social construction [...] is coterminous with being human," that there is no "'human nature' [...] 'beyond' (or indeed 'before') social construction," such a view at the same time discards "the false perception that what is socially constructed is somehow shallow, or superimposed, or easily overthrown" (Delphy 204). Following a holistic epistemological understanding which recognizes that the categories of gender, "male" and "female," do not preexist their coming into relation to each other — that "the two are created one by the other and at the same time" — it entails that "human arrangements are both social — arbitrary — and material: external to the action of any given individual" (Delphy 201, 207). This, in fact, is the very same conclusion Wittgenstein draws in connection to his concept of language-games.[29] And similar to the consequences of Wittgenstein's contemplations, what follows with regard to the question of sexual difference is the understanding

> that things can change, but that it will be long and arduous, and that we do not have an infinite power over our own individual lives, nor, to start with, over our own brains. [...] [E]ven though things — including our own thoughts — present themselves to us qua individuals as external constraints, they are not imposed on us by God or Nature and [...] we, qua members of society, share in the responsibility for changing or not changing them [Delphy 207].

Once again, among the key terms of this point of view are the notions of "society," of "sharing," and of the possibility for "change" in social relations — the very concepts of communality which drive all of Susan Glaspell's works for the theater. On the basis of these theoretical concepts, then, one might argue (as I will in my subsequent readings) that any analysis which insists on retrieving the promotion of an *essentialist* female voice from these dramas does not follow Glaspell's own move away from the concept of the Kantian-Cartesian isolated self towards an understanding of human existence as irreducibly relational and intersubjective.

Artistic Expression and the Artist's Role in Society

Finally, parallel to her exploration of the subjective vantage points of "self" and "woman," Susan Glaspell frequently takes on yet another (if interrelated) position in her works: that of the "artist" in society. On the one hand, artist figures of all kinds — including an architect, a singer, several poets and novelists, a sculptor, a cartoonist and a character working with plants — abound in her plays. On the other hand, each of her dramas itself constitutes a creative act of communication. As Glaspell constantly negotiates the nature, means, and social role of artistic expression on all plains of aesthetic communication — within individual plays, from play to play, between stage and audience — a number of aesthetic theories will help to systematize these various aspects as well. Interestingly enough in the present context of language and communication in Glaspell's works, as G. L.

Hagberg points out in his study on *Art as Language: Wittgenstein, Meaning, and Aesthetic Theory*, the "belief that art is a language, or that it is in a deep sense analogous to language, is among the most pervasive of assumptions in the theory of art" (30). Indeed, this connection is inevitable if we consider that any attempt to conceptualize the nature of artistic expression ultimately deals with the question of aesthetic *meaning*. In this way, both aesthetic and linguistic theories aim at explaining the same phenomenon of "understanding" as central to human existence.

Examining various 20th-century approaches to the question of aesthetic meaning, Hagberg sets their accompanying assumptions about the nature of language against the backdrop of Ludwig Wittgenstein's language philosophy.[30] In a pervasive collection of examples, he demonstrates that virtually all examined theories can be modeled along the argumentative lines of the philosopher's so-called picture theory of meaning brought forth in his 1922 *Tractatus Logico-Philosophicus*—and in effect explain the nature of art in terms of the representational model of language. Simultaneously, Hagberg draws on Wittgenstein's later notions of his *Philosophical Investigations* in order to suggest that while the traditional view of language as a representational system of signs is unsuccessful in explaining both our experiences of language *and* of art, a fundamentally revised concept might be more appropriately applied to the ways in which we engage ourselves with both phenomena. This alternative concept, I suggest, is worked out precisely in the notion of language as constitutive articulate contact (even if Hagberg himself does not follow his observations through to this systematic conclusion). Examining how the nature and functioning of art changes against this alternative notion of language, once again my argument is that the two opposing understandings of human existence implied in this change work side by side in Susan Glaspell's creative universe.

In correlation with the representational theory of language, art has pervasively been understood as a means of transporting ideas, thoughts, or feelings from one mind (that of the artist) to another (that of the beholder). More precisely, in acknowledging the familiar notion that some experiences cannot be clothed in words, it has been perceived to pick up where language leaves off. As "one begins to feel the presence of an impenetrable barrier between aesthetic seeing and saying," artistic expression becomes the "language of the unsayable" (Hagberg 8, 17). Importantly, in this telementational model of art, what is of prominent aesthetic interest is not the outward manifestation of artistic expression itself but the "message" which it is assumed to carry.

This particular conceptual merger of language and art is brought forth by a line of thinkers whom Hagberg significantly calls "expression theorists" of art. All share the "notion that art and language are essentially alike in

serving as physical expressions of preexistent mental or imaginary objects."
Crucial to such idealist theories, thus Hagberg emphasizes, is the understanding that there is a "one-to-one correspondence between an imaginary
object of a particular mental state and its outward manifestation in language
or art," as they imply

> that for every utterance in language there is a mental experience or
> event — the imaginary object — of which the utterance is, presuming the
> work is successful, the perfect outward expression. [They] also [imply], of
> course, that the imaginary object temporally as well as logically *precedes*
> the expression. Similarly, for every physical object which we designate an
> artwork there is a determinate state of mind — the imaginary object —for
> which the physical work serves as an outward mirror [35–36; emphasis in
> the original].

Importantly, since this "analogy with language implies that the works serve
as vehicle for the communication of feelings [or mental images] whose origins are in the inner life of the artist" it also "carries with it a corresponding
conception of artistic understanding" (Hagberg 60). According to this conception, the "artwork has been understood — i.e., the content, or [...] meaning of the work has been derived from it — when the [same] feeling is excited
[or mental image called forth] in the mind of the beholder" (ibid.).

With such a view on the nature of artistic communication, the same
grounds are laid for a fundamental skepticism as are allowed in the corresponding representational theory of language. Hagberg calls the ensuing
problems in understanding the meaning of an artwork the "paradox of
expression." Noticing the "shroud of mystery covering the word 'expression'
in the philosophy of art" (119), he identifies this paradox to concern the fundamental privacy of emotions in contrast to the essential publicity of works
of art. While it seems conceptually impossible to bring the two together in
an act of successful "translation," impressive artworks nevertheless exist.
Consequently, striking parallels can be drawn "between the linguistic privacy theorist and the artistic expression theorist," as both are bound to struggle with the problem of meaning as inherently private: "we cannot really tell
if A's red is not B's blue" (Hagberg 123, 125). The implications of seeing art
as a representative system of signs, therefore, include that the only person
who can know the "true meaning" of any piece of art is the artist her- or
himself:

> The artist is believed to be in a unique position to speak for the meaning
> of the work because of some special access to the inner, nonpublic model.
> This stands as the perfect aesthetic parallel to the metaphysical problem of
> other minds; here the artist is the only one who *knows* what the content is
> behind the appearances, and for all others it is a matter of educated guess-
> work [111].[31]

With these notions in mind, Hagberg then turns from the Wittgenstein of the *Tractatus* to the philosopher's later, fundamentally different engagement with the phenomenon of language in order to demonstrate that a view corresponding to his concept of "language-games" would be of far greater help in understanding our habitual engagement with aesthetic expressions than any representational theory of art. In a process which adapts the philosopher's prominent "reminder technique" he draws out example after example which show that our aesthetic practices work in ways left unexplained by the symbol model. Discussing the concept of artistic intention, for instance, he argues that works of art often come into existence in a way which profoundly goes *against* the intentions of the artist: Writers often claim that their characters take on a life of their own in the course of a work in progress, sculptors find their forms struggling to make their way out of their raw material, and composers give their melodies space to find their own paths. As Hagberg states,

> the very idea of working things out *in art* is incompatible with the intentionalist picture. In the same way, the fact that artists often learn things about their own works after completing them deepens the suspiciousness of the view that artistic creations should be viewed as a process of making choices on every matter that could serve as the subject of deliberation [85].

Instead, "[t]hought, [feeling] and imagination [...] enter into the creation and criticism of [art] in a multitude of ways [which are] either incompatible with the correspondence theory or at least not explained by that theory" (97). As do the philosophers of language as "articulate contact," Hagberg emphasizes that "on the old way of thinking, the search for the basic in both perceptual and linguistic form was a manifestation of the desire to originate an epistemology at a point of absolute and indubitable certainty, a point immune to Cartesian doubt" (145). After a certain anti-essential movement which attempted to explain the hidden unity of the arts in terms of the Wittgensteinian concept of "family resemblances," therefore, a new search for "a necessary and sufficient condition for arthood" began as a result of the old longing for "an essence which exists, as an ontological intangible, above and beyond the physical object and its uninterpreted perception" (Hagberg 153, 146).[32] Hagberg's point in turning to the philosophy of the later Wittgenstein, of course, is to demonstrate that any such theory of essentials must inevitably lead into a dead-end.

Yet while Hagberg mentions nearly all of the most important features which would make up an alternative understanding of language and art, he falls short of combining these features into a coherent system. In a final attempt to save the art-language analogy in spite of the fact that it has proven problematic in all of the theories he has discussed, he concludes:

> Because language has been fundamental to aesthetics in the many ways we have seen, it seems fair to say that, so long as we remain mindful of the

many and various intricacies, difficulties, and dangers of art-language analogies, an investigation into language is among the best strategies at our disposal for achieving an understanding of artistic meaning and, indeed, of achieving a clear and perspicuous view of the vast range of visual, aural, and conceptual engagements that we call aesthetic experience [190].

Although Hagberg here underlines the general significance of art-language analogies, he does not attempt to clarify the basic question of exactly why such analogies are so compelling to anyone pondering over the nature of art. Criticizing many conceptions of language and art as "false" in the course of his argument, he ultimately does no more than hint at what the "true" view might consist of.[33] What is more, in this very distinction between "right" and "wrong" this scholar remains one fundamental step behind the thinkers of language as constitutive articulate contact.

Interestingly, in his concise summary of what he calls the "integra-tionist's" approach to language, Roy Harris includes some remarks on the relation between "language, art and creativity." Rejecting the traditional notion that theories of both language and art need an essential concept of rule-following the linguist states: "The integrationist view of creativity is, I think, fundamentally different from that which produces the generativist conflation with productivity" ("From an Integrational Point of View," 280). Explaining this difference in true integrationist fashion (with an example taken right out of every-day arguments on the definition of art) Harris writes further:

> An integrationist would say that throwing cans of paint randomly at a wall may or may not be a manifestation of artistic creativity, depending on the context. Furthermore, for some participants/observers it might be creative, but for others not: for different individuals will contextualize the episode in different ways. But there is in any case no question of the need for a prior rule about paint-throwing to be in place in order for the issue of cre-ativity to arise [280–81].

A little further down, he then argues for the crucial connection between lan-guage and art:

> I do think that art [...] and language involve the same creativity, and that the sense in which language is perpetual creation is no different from the sense in which art is perpetual creation. [...] [B]ecause as an integra-tionist, I hold that in artistic communication and linguistic communica-tion the source of meaning is the same; namely, the contextualized integration of human activities [281].

Here, via the concept of human creativity, Harris binds up language and art as *essentially the same kind of phenomena*. Both are uniquely human activ-ities involving the creation of meaning in reciprocal acts of communication, where communication is understood in John Stewart's sense of articulate contact. It follows that everything which I have previously demonstrated to participate in this view of the nature of *language* is also applicable to our understanding of *art*. Both *are*, in fact, communication, and in this characteristic they are constitutive of the way we make sense of our world in an ongoing, contextually delineated process. Art, then, in any of its countless manifestations, is ultimately a specific form of linguistic "worlding," or "languageing." Indeed, such an understanding is capable of incorporating the wide range of conceptual change which has occurred within various aesthetic theories during the course of the 20th century. Systematically, it extends to all works of art what has explicitly been proclaimed in the field of literary studies: that we "misconceive the nature of literature when we treat it as an object containing a message instead of an event with an experience to share" (Quigley 232).

Against this theoretical background, any notion connected to the artist as creator of her work can be approached from the two angles of a representational and an integrationist point of view. What is the meaning of an artwork? Does the artist express her inner self in her art? Does she send a "message" out into the world? Or does she enter into a dialogue with her audience in which meaning is constituted ever anew and ever differently? What is the artist's attitude towards her own work? Does it represent an instance of pure aestheticism, of art for art's sake, or is it meant to serve a (social, political, educational etc.) function?—At stake in these issues are not only the construction of the artist's identity and creative intentions, but also an understanding of her specific role in society. Who has authority over the interpretation of an aesthetic piece? Does the artist cut herself off from societal bonds or does she assume social responsibility? Last but not least, is an artist's work public or private? Whom does it belong to—the artist herself, her family and heirs, society at large?

In many of her plays Susan Glaspell engages with variations of these issues, and in most instances she comes down on the side of an intricate *connection* between the artist and society. Hence in *The People*, for instance, the dramatist argues against an avant-garde position of *l'art pour l'art* and in favor of the artist's social responsibility; in *The Verge* she defends the artist's right to create not things "more beautiful" but something "new" only to send her protagonist spinning into madness as she cuts herself off from human community; in *Alison's House* Glaspell concludes that an artist's work, although intimately private, belongs to the world in that it helps to bring about social change; and in *Springs Eternal* she thematizes the social responsibility of the writer in times of war. Yet as I will argue in each of these instances, while the connection between the artist and society is often portrayed as limiting to the artist figure's individuality (and to the female self in particular), this is not the only aspect discussed in Glaspell's works in this context. As I will show, her perception of human nature as fundamentally social contains not only the threat of restriction to the individual but incorporates positive elements as well. For in the inevitable connection between human beings Glaspell often perceives the promise of safety from loneliness and isolation, and the chance for communal creation and change. In any case, she acknowledges "togetherness" as the fundamental condition of human existence: Whether limiting or liberating, our social being is a defining feature of our humanity. And as she accepts this feature as both inescapable and full of creative possibilities, with her works Susan Glaspell frequently demonstrates the unique manner in which the artist engages with her audience in a communicative aesthetic act of "worlding reality."

Of course it must be noted in this context that the theatre, of all forms of aesthetic expression, is the very *embodiment* of art as social involvement and communicative creation. As Robert Károly Sarlós notes in his history of the Provincetown Players: "More than the other arts, theatre depends on social interaction. [...] Collective theatre, aiming to make spectators participants, is an extreme version, particularly suited to times of communal crisis. That was the potent message of Jig Cook, Dionysos in 1915" (59). Indeed, theatre needs an audience to come into existence in the common space of performance, and it is always the shared creation of various artistic minds. Debates over the social relevance of the theatre and over the prominence of one of its many participants consequently make up the history of the genre. While this study concentrates on Glaspell's plays primarily as literary texts, stressing the aesthetic stance of the dramatist over the participation of other artists in the play's theatrical productions, the character of the theatre as a uniquely communal form of art nevertheless plays a significant role in my understanding of these works—even more so since her works are part of an expressed communal philosophy as proclaimed by the group for which she wrote, the Provincetown Players.

The Provincetown Players' creative philosophy was influenced and formulated to a large extent by George Cram Cook, their undisputed *spiritus rector*. Sarlós introduces Cook's "prophetic ideas" (as quoted in Glaspell's *Road to the Temple*, 252–53) by setting them off against the opposing notions propagated by his contemporary Edward Gordon Craig, the English actor, director and theatre theoretician, in Craig's 1905 *On the Art of the Theatre*. As Sarlós explains,

> Craig carried the traditional individualistic stance to its logical extreme. He accepted Wagner's principle concerning the oneness of theatrical art, and declared it "impossible for a work of art ever to be produced where more than one brain is permitted to direct." Consequently, Craig believed the future of theatre depended on the emergence of a single Artist of Theatre, one who had mastered all relevant crafts. [...]
>
> Contrary to Craig, Cook expected the organic unity of theatre to grow

from group consciousness: "One man cannot create drama. True drama is born only of one feeling animating all members of a clan — a spirit shared by all and expressed by the few for the all. If there is nothing to take the place of the common religious purpose and passion of the primitive group, out of which the Dionysian dance was born, no new vital drama can arise in any people" [34].[34]

As Sarlós stresses in his discussion of the Provincetown Players' intentions, the members of the group understood their work (and play) as a reaction to the "social fragmentation and individual alienation from society" which they perceived as characteristic of their time. As a distinctly group-orientated enterprise, they pointedly foregrounded their artistic aim as setting in motion a social "healing process" — a process which was to be achieved with and through their creative community (36). Moreover, tracing the development of Western social thought in the 19th and early 20th centuries, Sarlós points out that Cook and the Players were "not feeling their way in a vacuum" (36):

> After worship of the individual reached its apogee [at the beginning of the 20th century], the realization came that loneliness was a liability as well as an asset; biological and social determinism revealed absolute freedom as illusory, and the need for personal interaction in a social milieu was once again recognized. The study of the individual and of society thus converged about the time of the First World War. A rising interest in philanthropy and social work, in progressive education, and in the role of creative play, all showed concern with "interpersonal relations," a term first used in 1912 [38].[35]

Sarlós thus concludes that "the emergence in 1915 of the Provincetown Players — a theatre collective, emphasizing spontaneous, amateur group creativity as an organic reaction to individual frustrations — was an autonomous manifestation of the spirit of the times" (39).

Susan Glaspell, on her part, full-heartedly agreed with the Provincetown Players' ideals as they correlated both with her personal need for community and with her desire to change society through her art. In her critical biography Barbara Ozieblo states that pursuing her professional career as a writer Glaspell "[resolved] to become 'a helper in the onward progress of society'" (*Susan Glaspell* 23).[36] In this resolve she was one with her husband George Cram Cook (as Ozieblo remarks, the "couple [...] saw themselves as creators who hoped to contribute to a better world by channeling the imagination of their audiences," ibid. 126). Nevertheless, it was not Cook (as has often been claimed) who imprinted these ideas of a social regeneration through art on Glaspell's mind. They had been present in her earliest short stories and newspaper articles and continued to drive all her art throughout her later life. As Ozieblo states in the context of the writer's 1930 play *Alison's House*, Susan Glaspell "had always grasped the didactic possibilities inherent in the theater; she understood that a skillfully developed idea could excite an audience and lead to public discussion of the evils that plague society" (*Susan Glaspell* 241).

Adequately, Ozieblo's assessment of Glaspell's didactic gesture as a writer foregrounds the element of "public discussion." With my own interpretations of her plays I confirm that the dramatist was more often concerned with fuelling a debate than with offering pre-conceived "messages" in her plays. This attitude, as I will argue, more often than not prevails in her engagement with all of the three subject positions— self, woman, and artist — that are central to her works. And although Susan Glaspell's plays frequently do seem to present rather urgent "messages" regarding the "meaning of life," the habitual vagueness of these messages might do much more than irritate her critics: It might be taken as an indication that she offers her art not as a representative system of signs which we must learn to decipher correctly, but as instances of constitutive articulate contact in which we are all free to participate.

3. Trifles (1916)

The "Female" Voice of Community?

Trifles, which premiered at the Wharf Theater in Provincetown in August 1916, is not only Susan Glaspell's first independent dramatic effort after hers and Cook's *Suppressed Desires*. Widely anthologized both as a model one-act and as an example of women's writing, it is also the single work for which she is best known today and the one drama which has most firmly set her reputation as a feminist playwright. A densely structured realist play, *Trifles* depicts two Midwestern housewives who involuntarily uncover the story behind the murder of farmer John Wright, strangled in his sleep, by deciphering the crucial significance of various details scattered across his imprisoned wife's deserted kitchen. Held by a growing sense of community which develops in the awareness of shared female experiences, Mrs. Hale and the Sheriff's wife, Mrs. Peters, decide to keep their insights into the Wrights' tragedy from their husbands and the County Attorney Mr. Henderson. The three men, who arrogantly discard the women's world of "kitchen things" as a world of "trifles," remain unsuccessful in their own officious search for clues to a motive which would win their case against Minnie Wright in court.

In her most famous drama Glaspell juxtaposes two distinct worlds, characterized by two different ways of experiencing life, which generate two opposing forms of passing judgment. This contrast is developed in the opposition between the play's male and female characters, with the women's position strongly favored as the more "truthful" and thus the more valuable one. It is this obvious division along gender lines which has led critics to read *Trifles* (and, in its wake, other plays by Glaspell) as a "statement about feminine consciousness, the feelings and perceptions associated with a female character's identity as a woman" (Friedman, "Feminism," 70). In a still ongoing discussion, both the play and its later short story offshoot "A Jury of Her

Peers" have been turned into "feminist classic[s]" — works "paradigmatic [...] for feminist criticism" (Hedges 89, 90).[1] Up to the present day, an overwhelming majority of readings has concentrated on *Trifles* either as propagating the essentialist feminist view of a female human nature in need of empowerment, or as presenting at least a kind of *écriture féminine* which will give room to the female voice (whether "essential" or not) on the American stage.

In contrast to such readings, I want to show that what Glaspell presents as the more accurate and useful approach to life in this work is not, after all, an inherently female point of view. In fact, it is for this reason that the play does not make any clear statement as to whether the approach it favors is grounded on a pre-existing *female nature* or whether it derives from women's *social position* in patriarchy. Underlying the two opposing concepts of law and justice in *Trifles* are two contrasting notions of the nature and function of communication in human existence. Glaspell suggests that Mrs. Hale's and Mrs. Peters' understanding of farmer Wright's homicide — characterized as it is by the principles of intersubjectivity, contextuality, and involvement — is more true to human experience *in general* than the male characters' approach as objective observers. Indeed, although Glaspell seems to anticipate feminist thinkers such as Irigaray and Cixous in arguing that the acceptance of the contextual nature of their lives comes intuitively, perhaps "naturally," only to the women in *Trifles*, she demonstrates that as a governing principle it holds true with regard to the men's interactions as well. Consequently, as much as it has been read to contain a preconceived "message" with regard to gender-related issues, *Trifles* simultaneously enhances the notion of meaning as created in constitutive articulate contact in a dramatic argument in which "communication" becomes equivalent to "life" itself for *all* characters.

Men Versus Women: The Opposition of the Sexes as Created in Articulate Contact

The clear division in *Trifles* between its male and female characters is introduced right from the start. When the outer door opens onto the Wrights' kitchen, it is Mr. Peters, the Sheriff, who comes in first, "*followed by the* COUNTY ATTORNEY *and* HALE" (36). While the men — all "*much bundled up*" — "*go at once to the stove*," Mrs. Peters and Mrs. Hale "*have come in slowly, and stand close together near the door*" (ibid.). Rejecting the County Attorney's jovial invitation to "[c]ome up to the fire, ladies" (ibid.), the two women, nervous and disturbed, remain in their marginal position as the two officials begin to question Mr. Hale, who found his neighbor strangled in his bed the day before.

If the separate entrance of male and female characters introduces the gender division of the play, the gesture with which Sheriff Peters turns to his witness immediately indicates the principles which govern this division. In the sheriff's movement of "*stepping away from the stove as if to mark the beginning of official business*" (36), the frame is set for the depiction of two clearly separate spheres for men and women: "The opposition between the world outside, where important events occur and murder and truths are revealed, and the kitchen, where menial and mechanical work is accomplished" (Alkalay-Gut, "'Jury,'" 2). On the grounds of this opposition, the men take for granted that nothing significant could possibly be found in the women's space:

> COUNTY ATTORNEY. (*looking around*) I guess we'll go upstairs first — and then out to the barn and around there. (*to the* SHERIFF) You're convinced that there was nothing important here — nothing that would point to any motive.
> SHERIFF: Nothing here but kitchen things [38].

In addition, the play's gender relationships are firmly set when the County Attorney finds the broken jars of Mrs. Wright's fruit preserves on an upper shelf and exclaims in disgust: "Here's a nice mess!" This accusatory remark prompts the first intervention by one of the women, which in turn triggers the threefold male commentary lending the piece its ironic title:

> MRS PETERS. (*to the other woman*) Oh, her fruit; it did freeze. (*to the* LAWYER) She worried about that when it turned so cold. She said the fire'd go out and her jars would break.
> SHERIFF. Well, can you beat the women! Held for murder and worryin' about her preserves.
> COUNTY ATTORNEY. I guess before we're through she may have something more serious than preserves to worry about.
> HALE. Well, women are used to worrying over trifles. (*The two women move a little closer together.*) [38].

This often-quoted passage is of key importance in the establishment of the play's opposition between the sexes, and it is also the first indication that an understanding of meaning not as a metaphysical entity but as created in "articulate contact" underlies the course of events in *Trifles*. The scene which lends the play its title demonstrates its gendered opposition to be *communicatively created* both in the context of the concrete situation and on the basis of conceptual patterns formed through a long "history of use" (compare Wittengenstein's term) in the characters' cultural context. On the situational level, farmer Hale's remark about "women's trifles" serves as his own admission ticket to the Sheriff's and the County Attorney's male world of significance and superiority. It is a means of strengthening his position where his role of witness in the case is only of a temporary nature. (While Mr. Peters and Mr. Henderson are referred to only as "Sheriff" and "County Attorney" in the stage directions to emphasize their official authority, their witness is simply "Hale.") Moreover, it is precisely in reaction to the men's derogatory comments that Mrs. Hale and Mrs. Peters, who are introduced as two distinctly different individuals in the opening stage directions, first "move a little closer together." If this scene offers the first sign of the women's solidarity in *Trifles*, it does so by establishing it as a defense against immediate male arrogance, not necessarily on the grounds of a supposedly innate "femaleness."

At the same time, Glaspell also shows that both her male and her female characters partake in Wittgensteinian language-games which have been established by a long history of cultural relations between the sexes. Even though Mrs. Peters and Mrs. Hale instinctively reject the men's condescending definition of their world as trivial, they have themselves internalized their society's division between a male world of official business and a female sphere of the home. In fact, Mrs. Hale's indignant objection to the men's intrusion into Minnie Wright's space reinforces the traditional system of separate spheres: "I'd hate to have men coming into my kitchen, snooping around and criticising," she vents her anger the moment the men have left the room (39). "[It] seems kind of *sneaking*. Locking her up in town and then coming out here and trying to get her own house to turn against her!" (40). And Mrs. Peters intuitively confirms the same separation when she shuts the kitchen door on the men prowling about in the Wrights' bedroom on the first floor: "[Mrs. Wright] said she wanted [...] her little shawl that always hung behind the door. (*opens stair door and looks*) Yes, here it is. (*Quickly shuts door leading upstairs*)" (40).

The Women's Voice: Closeness, Involvement, Intersubjectivity

It is in this frame of a communicatively created opposition between her male and female characters that Glaspell develops her two modes of relating to the world in *Trifles*. In contrast to the men's behavior, a distinctly "different voice" emerges in Mrs. Hale's and Mrs. Peters' interactions on stage, through the story of the absent female protagonist Minnie Wright, and through the way in which the women on stage develop this story between them.

Many scholars have pointed out the striking precision with which the verbal exchanges in *Trifles* demonstrate what Deborah Tannen, developing her sociolinguistic theory of genderlects more than seven decades after the play's premier, has described as a "female focus on closeness and rapport" and a "male preoccupation with individuality and status" (*You Just Don't Understand*). From the start, the men are intent on negotiating their individual positions at a distance not only from the women but also from each other. While all three display an acute sense of superiority over the women, there is no doubt that, as Linda Ben-Zvi has put it, their "privileged club does have a pecking order" ("Murder," 155). When Sheriff Peters tells farmer Hale to "explain to Mr. Henderson just what you saw when you came here yesterday morning" (36), he assumes the leading role in the investigation, casually ignoring the fact that "Mr." Henderson's role as County Attorney grants him the greater official authority in the case. The lawyer, in turn, promptly puts Sheriff Peters in his place by taking over the situation himself with a carefully placed insinuation that the other man might have neglected his duties:

> COUNTY ATTORNEY. By the way, has anything been moved? Are things just as you left them yesterday?
> SHERIFF. (*looking about*) It's just the same. When it dropped below zero last night I thought I'd better send Frank out this morning to make a fire for us [...].
> COUNTY ATTORNEY. Somebody should have been left here yesterday.
> SHERIFF. Oh — yesterday. [...] — I want you to know I had my hands full yesterday. I knew you could get back from Omaha by today, and as long as I went over everything here myself–
> COUNTY ATTORNEY. Well, Mr Hale, tell just what happened when you came here yesterday morning [36].

What the audience witnesses here is a struggle for position, fought out under the guise of setting straight the facts of the situation. It is won by the County Attorney as he rebukes Sheriff Peters and then addresses Mr. Hale with almost the exact same words the Sheriff had used just a moment earlier. What is more, during the following interrogation the County Attorney repeatedly cuts short farmer Hale's testimony with an air of steering him back to more relevant questions. In this way, Mr. Hale is posited at the bottom of the men's hierarchy not only because he is at the receiving end of the other two men's orders, but also through a subtle suggestion that his wordy elaborations are not to the point. (And as this underlying criticism invokes the cliché of trite — female! — gossip, it is this very frame of the men's struggle for position which makes it necessary for Mr. Hale to set himself off against the women and their trivial concerns.)

In clear opposition to the men's focus on status and distance, Mrs. Peters and Mrs. Hale (both uneasy to find themselves invading the privacy of a woman who is held for murder) are intent on establishing a connection which will give them mutual comfort and support. Although the two women are strangers to each other and do not seem to have much in common to begin with, "an immediate bond is established between [them], a kind of intimacy that has not come from long term acquaintance" (Aarons 8). As we will see, the play suggests several possible origins for this intimacy, yet in its obvious contrast to the men it leaves no doubt that this is the women's habitual way of relating to one another *as women*. Indeed, even Mrs. Hale's very presence expresses a female focus on companionship. While Mrs. Peters accompanied the men in order to collect some clothes for the imprisoned woman, Mrs. Hale joined the party for the sole purpose of keeping the other woman company. Mrs. Peters, on her part, is grateful for this favor: "I'm awful glad you came with me, Mrs Hale," she confides as they sit in Minnie's deserted kitchen: "It would be lonesome for me sitting here alone" (42). And as Mrs. Hale readily agrees ("It would, wouldn't it?"), she draws an even wider circle of female community to include the absent Minnie Wright: "But I tell you what I do wish, Mrs Peters. I wish I had come over sometimes when *she* was here. I — (*looking around the room*) — wish I had" (ibid.).

Again, this utterance stands in direct contrast to the men's focus on distance. While the women, during the further course of events, connect their feelings of desolation to the loneliness Mrs. Wright herself must have experienced in her own home, the men insist on a detached position towards the deceased *Mr.* Wright: in his status as "victim," he is objectified as nothing more than an observable fact in the case. The same contrast of female closeness and male distance which is obvious in the characters' interaction on stage, therefore, is also revealed in their differing attitudes towards the story of what might have happened between John and Minnie Wright. Marked by their functions in the official task at hand — the search for evidence on the scene of the crime — the County Attorney, the Sheriff, and witness Hale represent "the law" as a set of publicly fixed rules which need to be enforced in order to ensure just judgment. It is Mrs. Peters, the Sheriff's wife, who articulates the assumed general validity of this approach: "the law is the law" (40) she insists to the other woman, and since "the law has got to punish crime" (44) the investigators are doing "no more than their duty" (39). Significantly, such an understanding of legal judgment presupposes that in performing this duty, the men occupy a detached position as objective observers — and in complete agreement with this notion, throughout the entire play the male characters take for granted that evidence can be found by *looking around.*[2] Carefully framed as a rational, disinterested procedure, the investigation is thus supposed to bring out the "facts" to which the law will then be applied.

The women's attitude towards the unfolding case, on the other hand, is characterized not by the principles of detachment, objectivity, and the application of general rules, but by a consideration of concrete relationships, personal involvement, and the acceptance of a subjective connection between human beings. Mrs. Hale and Mrs. Peters come to an alternative understanding of the crime because they take into consideration the concrete circumstances which have led to John Wright's violent death. That they are able to do so, thus Glaspell suggests, is because a bond of similar experiences connects them to the absent woman. As the play unfolds, both Mrs. Hale and Mrs. Peters understand that the immediate situation (in which the men repeatedly barge into the kitchen on their way to more "significant" locales, making fun of the women's concerns in passing) exemplifies a structural experience of being trivialized by men which they share with the imprisoned Minnie Wright. In a process of acknowledging this connection, they gradually come to identify with the absent woman, and in this identification "break the principle of objectivity in crime detection" (Hallgren 207).

From the County Attorney's first insinuation that Mrs. Wright must have been a bad housekeeper Mrs. Hale openly rejects the men's arrogant condescension:

> COUNTY ATTORNEY. [...] (*Starts to wipe* [his hands] *on the roller-towel, turns it for a cleaner place*). Dirty towels! (*kicks his foot against the pans under the sink*) Not much of a housekeeper, would you say, ladies?
> MRS HALE. (*stiffly*) There's a great deal of work to be done on a farm. [...] Those towels get dirty awful quick. Men's hands aren't always as clean as they might be.
> COUNTY ATTORNEY. Ah, loyal to your sex, I see [38].

A farmer's wife herself, Mrs. Hale is able to sympathize with Minnie because she knows how much it takes to keep a farm household going. In her indignation at the men's disregard of women's chores she is immediately inclined to take action in protection of her neighbor. At first, her movements are simply the spontaneous empathetic gestures of a fellow housekeeper: she "*arranges the pans under* [the] *sink which the* LAWYER *had shoved out of place*" (39), picks up the bread Minnie was going to put into the bread-box, looks for a jar of fruit which has not cracked, and makes a move to wipe the messy half of the table (40). When she comes across Minnie's unfinished quilt, however, and detects the treacherously erratic needle work of the block she had last been stitching, her involvement turns into the more deliberate act of concealment:

> MRS HALE. (*examining another block*) Mrs Peters, look at this one. Here, this is the one she was working on, and look at the sewing! All the rest of it has been so nice and even. And look at this! It's all over the place! Why, it looks as if she didn't know what she was about! (*After she has said this they look at each other, then start to glance back at the door. After an instant* MRS HALE *has pulled at a knot and ripped the sewing.*)
> MRS PETERS. Oh, what are you doing, Mrs. Hale?
> MRS HALE. (*mildly*) Just pulling out a stitch or two that's not sewed very good. [...] Bad sewing always made me fidgety [41].

Whereas Mrs. Hale is the first to cross the line from uninvolved bystander to active participant in this scene, Mrs. Peters—whom the men quite bluntly take to be "married to the law" (44)—still speaks with her husband's, the Sheriff's, voice, objecting "(*nervously*) I don't think we ought to touch things" (41). When the women come across the empty, broken birdcage among Minnie's things, however, and shortly afterwards find the bird dead — its neck twisted, its tiny body wrapped in Minnie's most beautiful patch of silk — both comprehension and horror are awakened in Mrs. Peters through a personal memory which renders it impossible further to deny her connection to the other women: "(*in a whisper*) When I was a girl—my kitten— there was a boy took a hatchet, and before my eyes—and before I could get there —(*covers her face an instant*) If they hadn't held me back I would have — (*catches herself, looks upstairs where steps are heard, falters weakly*)—hurt him" (43). It is this realization of her own potential for violence against a male aggressor which finally prompts Mrs. Peters to join sides with Mrs. Hale and the alleged murderess. For the first time, she now takes an active part in the cover-up, supporting Mrs. Hale's spontaneous decision to hide the dead canary and her lie that it must have been "the cat" that got the bird: "COUNTY ATTORNEY. (*preoccupied*) Is there a cat? (MRS HALE *glances in a quick covert way at* MRS PETERS.) MRS PETERS. Well, not *now*. They're superstitious, you know. They leave" (43).

While for Mrs. Peters, then, her decision to protect the alleged murderess is framed as an act of emancipation from male dominance over her identity, for Mrs. Hale it is predominantly a way of assuming responsibility for what has happened: She defines her own guilt in the Wrights' case as her failure to link up with her distressed neighbor before it was too late. Realizing what Mrs. Wright must have suffered from her husband and remembering the lively young woman she had been before her marriage, Mrs. Hale reproaches herself for having kept away: "I could've come. I stayed away because it weren't cheerful — and that's why I ought to have come. [...] I wish I had come over to see Minnie Foster sometimes" (42).—"Oh, I wish I'd come over here once in a while! That was a crime! That was a crime! Who's going to punish that?" (44). Absolving Minnie of her desperate deed, she indicts John Wright for having choked the life out of his wife emotionally and spiritually, and herself for not having intervened. In a truly striking parallel to the women of Carol Gilligan's empirical studies, the moral dilemma Mrs. Hale and Mrs. Peters find themselves confronted with thus presents itself not as a question of abstract rules and rights (which would focus on the absolute priority of anyone's right to live) but as a matter involving the individual lives of concrete people, to be decided within the framework of a complex net of contextual factors.[3] What is more, similar to the understanding voiced by the women interviewed by Goldberger and her colleagues, "knowledge" and "truth" are not treated as abstract, objective concepts by the two women in *Trifles*: Mrs. Hale's and Mrs. Peters' understanding of the truth they have discovered acknowledges their personal connection to the absent Minnie Wright.

In an often-quoted key passage of the play, Mrs. Hale explicitly links her contextual reading of the Wrights' tragedy to her being a woman: "I might have known she needed help! I know how things can be — for women. I tell you, it's queer, Mrs Peters. We live close together and we live far apart. We all go through the same things— it's all just a different kind of the same thing" (44). Importantly, what Mrs. Hale refers to in this evocation of "the same things" all women go through is not only a common experience of male abuse. A central image in the play, the dead canary and its strangled voice at the same time symbolize a fundamental lack in Minnie's life: the lack of human interaction and communication. Indeed, the absent woman's tragedy is linked up with the same theme of a specifically female need for community which Glaspell points to in the women's relationship on stage. And thus, both Mrs. Hale and Mrs. Peters intuitively understand what the bird must have meant to Minnie in her isolation:

> MRS HALE. [...] If there'd been years and years of nothing, then a bird to sing to you, it would be awful — still, after the bird was still.
> MRS PETERS. (*something within her speaking*) I know what stillness is. When we homesteaded in Dakota, and my first baby died — after he was two years old, and me with no other then — [44].

On the grounds of their personal need for interaction, Mrs. Hale and Mrs. Peters come to realize that it was the "lack of communication, the isolation, and the social exclusion of Minnie Wright's environment [...] [that] drove her to such an extreme act of violence"— the murder of her husband (Aarons 10). Indeed, even the first pieces of information we are offered about John Wright concern his disapproval of human interaction and his indifference to the suggestion that his wife's needs in this respect might differ from his own:

> HALE. [...] I said 'I'm going to see if I can't get John Wright to go in with me on a party telephone.' I spoke to Wright about it once before and he put me off, saying folks talked too much anyway, and all he asked was peace and quiet — I guess you know about how much he talked himself; but I thought maybe if I went to the house and talked about it before his wife, though I said to Harry that I didn't know as what his wife wanted made much difference to John — [36].

Through Hale's account the audience learns that farmer Wright embraced silence and detested people who talked "too much," and the witness's wife soon adds her own doubts as to whether "a place'd be any cheerfuller for John Wright's being in it" to this emerging image of the dead man (39). Mrs. Hale knew her neighbor to be a "hard man" and shivers at the mere thought of "[passing] the time of day with him": "like a raw wind that gets to the bone" (42). To her, that John Wright strangled his wife's canary is obvious beyond even the slightest doubt ("No, Wright wouldn't like the bird — a thing that sang" 44). That he killed the creature for no other reason than that it disturbed his "peace and quiet," in Mrs. Hale's eyes constitutes the last of an endless number of factors adding up to kill off Minnie Foster's liveliness: "How — she — did — change" (43). "She used to sing. He killed that, too" (44).

For while John Wright had wanted his house to be a deadly quiet place, thus Mrs. Hale and Mrs. Peters deduct from the clues they find in Minnie's kitchen, his wife had been in desperate need of human contact for the greater part of her marriage. References to Minnie's isolated, dreary existence are scattered systematically throughout the play. Once a lively young woman active in her community, she had given up singing in the church choir and was prevented from being part even of the charitable circle of the "Ladies Aid," keeping more and more to herself (40).[4] Living in a desolate house which allowed no glimpse of the road, childless and without any comforting warmth in her partnership, she was forced to live through her solitary days without any hope for change, left to go even about her quilting on her own.[5] Depicting her as a woman whose taciturn, reticent husband "strangled her by preventing her from communicating with others" (Alkalay-Gut, "Jury," 6), the play thus seems to argue that Minnie Wright "had no control over her choice to kill" (Aarons 9).[6] Hence, thrown in with a husband's brutal exertion of patriarchal power over his wife, it seems that the salient differences between male and female attitudes toward the importance of communication and community have reached a disastrous extreme in the relationship between John and Minnie Wright.

Detachment and Objectivity as Illusory Principles: The Male Voice in Trifles

As the preceding analysis has shown, it is of course indisputable that in *Trifles* Susan Glaspell develops an alternative approach to life in her female characters' interactions on stage, in their conclusions with regard to the Wrights' murder case, and in the emerging history of the absent couple's relationship. This alternative attitude is characterized by the principles of involvement and connectedness and is directly set off against the men's approach of objectivity and detachment. A consequent reading of the play as enhancing "female ways of knowing" — as the creation, revaluation and empowerment of a distinctly "female voice" — is supported by the vast range of feminist research which has identified the principle of "intersubjectivity" as a distinctly female (or feminine) trait.

While critics readily agree on the definition of the "female voice" in *Trifles* as adhering to the notions of intersubjectivity, involvement, and connectedness, however, opinions with regard to the *origins* of the play's female attitude differ as greatly as do ideas of a female nature in feminist theory. With the help of Irigaray and Cixous, for example, *Trifles* can be read as supporting the idea of a pre-existing female nature in need of empowerment within the patriarchal Symbolic Order. In contrast, in connection to Gilligan's and Tannen's research it can also be understood as thematizing the result of women's different socialization in Western culture. Both approaches usually celebrate Mrs. Hale's and Mrs. Peters' moral judgment as the superiority of a female over a male approach — a reading which is supported by the play's harsh criticism and ironic treatment of the men's condescending attitude towards the female sphere. On the other hand, the one-act can also be read to demonstrate women's political erasure under men's law — an orientation which would focus, with thinkers such as Kristeva, on a notion of "femaleness" as nothing other than women's marginal position in patriarchal society. Such a view would shift emphasis from the "nature" of Mrs. Hale's and Mrs. Peters' alternative reading of Minnie's case to the fact that society forbids them to bring it out into the open: a theme which is clearly enhanced in the play's depiction of the women's rebellion as a necessarily secretive action.

While all of these interpretations have a firm basis within Glaspell's text, their one-sided focus on the play's gender division reads the principles enhanced in this frame only in their "femaleness," necessarily disregarding any relevance they might hold as more general, "non-gendered" notions. Yet if emphasis is shifted from the prevailing discussion of the "female voice" in *Trifles* to a reading of how the alternative it establishes relates to the play's *male* characters, what Glaspell develops here by way of presenting a "female ethics" turns out to be a universally human experience of life. For once the notions of involvement and contextuality are outlined in the play as an alternative to the men's self-assessment as detached observers, it is only a small step to the realization that as governing principles these supposedly female notions are just as valid with regard to the way the male characters communicate. Indeed, the men in *Trifles* never meet their own requirements of objectivity and distance. To the contrary, they are as involved in the Wrights' case as the women become during the course of the play, and both in Glaspell's depiction of her male characters on stage and in her presentation of Mr. Wright the dramatist shows that language and communication play the same role in the men's lives as they do for the women.

In fact, from the start the emerging relations between the play's female and male characters indicate that the Sheriff's and the County Attorney's investigation is anything *but* "objective." Even if the two officials search for signs of a break-in and still seem to consider the possibility that it was a stranger, not his wife, who killed John Wright, they soon reveal that they have already found the accused woman guilty. What the "facts" are with regard to farmer Wright's death is clear to the men even before the play begins: The woman has killed her husband and must be convicted of murder. Consequently, the County Attorney's probing glance is set on an already colored picture as he searches only for evidence which would incriminate the imprisoned woman: "No, Peters, it's all perfectly clear except a reason for doing it. But you know juries when it comes to women. If there was some definite thing. Something to show — something to make a story about — a thing that would connect up with this strange way of doing it–" (44). Indeed, the play suggests that the men *as men* have a personal interest in convicting Minnie Wright. For, as Judith Fetterley has pointed out in her influential reading of the play's short story version, "[Minnie's story] is nothing less than the story of men's systematic, institutionalized, and culturally approved violence towards women, and of women's potential for retaliatory violence against men" (153). If the male characters in the play were to confront this story, Fetterley argues, they would have to confront their own abusive position of power in a society which oppresses women. With its inherent criticism of the patriarchal social order, an honest consideration of the idea that Minnie Wright might have been justified in killing her husband would threaten the men's entire definitory universe. In this way, their premature reading of Mrs. Wright's guilt can indeed be seen as the result of utterly personal interests, and the men's pose of detached objectivity serves the very function of disguising this connection.

What is more, the men's veiled self-interest in finding Mrs. Wright guilty of murder affects the course of the entire investigation. As they cannot allow an interpretation of the crime which would threaten the very foundations of patriarchal power relationships, the men's indictment of Minnie Wright necessarily includes her derogation *as a woman*. If she killed her husband, thus they conclude, she must be a "bad," even "unnatural" woman — a definition which the County Attorney inevitably links to Minnie's supposed lack of "the homemaking instinct":

> COUNTY ATTORNEY. No — it's not cheerful. I shouldn't say she had the homemaking instinct.
> MRS HALE. Well, I don't know as Wright had, either.
> COUNTY ATTORNEY. You mean that they didn't get on very well?
> MRS HALE. No, I don't mean anything. But I don't think a place'd be any cheerfuller for John Wright's being in it [44].

That Mrs. Hale immediately reacts to the lawyer's momentous gender bias in this scene indicates that it is precisely the men's entanglement in the situation which later prompts the women to hide not only one more "sign of sudden feeling" (the quilt block) but the very clue which does "connect up with this strange way of doing it": the strangled canary, whose obvious significance the men might not have overlooked. It is the male characters' own involvement in the case, therefore, which creates the entire frame of the play's plot and predetermines its ending. In their refusal to acknowledge the context of Minnie's deed, the men make it necessary for the women to conceal what they find in the first place, and through their biased behavior towards Mrs. Peters and Mrs. Hale, they hand them a valid motivation for the cover-up.

Significantly, in misconstruing their personal approach in the investigation as objective and detached, Glaspell's male characters also fundamentally misjudge the relevance of communication and interaction in their lives. As we have seen, although they perceive of themselves as being concerned with the disinterested collection of information about the case, the men's conversation develops as an existential part of their ongoing social positioning, both among themselves and in relation to the women. Together with the various ways in which they influence the immediate course of events, this aspect of their speech indicates that the men in *Trifles*, as little as the women, employ words simply to express pre-existing "facts."

This reading is further enhanced by the key role which Susan Glaspell assigns to the character of Mr. Hale in the play. With Hale, the playwright provides a clear contrast to the other male characters, a man for whom communication as a community-enhancing activity is just as important as it is to the women. Until the farmer claims membership to the County Attorney's and the Sheriff's "privileged club" (Ben-Zvi, "Murder," 155) by volunteering his bit of wisdom about women's trifles, he speaks only when he is addressed by one of the investigators, thus accepting the male hierarchy previously negotiated. Told to relate the events of the preceding day, however, Hale does not succeed in communicating "naked facts," apparently unable to distinguish between relevant and irrelevant information. Strikingly, it is exactly in Mr. Hale's ("female") "gossiping" that he develops the notions of communication as social contact which differentiate him from the other two men and their understanding of language as a tool to transmit pre-existing truths from one mind to the other — a notion which is questionable, as we have seen, even in their own cases.

Already in his opening remark that "Harry and I had started to town with a load of potatoes" (36), Glaspell has Mr. Hale hint to her central subject of a need for community as a *generally human* phenomenon (we learn that Hale was in the company of someone with whom he was on close, first-name terms; he did not make his trip alone or with a stranger). Indeed, the mention of Hale's companion is even more relevant in this context than it seems at first sight. For, as Hale recounts, when Minnie Wright had told him that her husband "died of a rope round his neck," he immediately "went out and called Harry," thinking that "he might — need help" (37). Right from the start, then, Mr. Hale's account serves to demonstrate that it is not only the women in the play who are glad to have company at certain times.[7]

More significant than Hale's reference to his companion, however, is that the very purpose of his stop-over at the Wrights' the day before was to try and persuade John Wright to "go in with [him] on a party telephone" — a proposal which the other man had rejected once before. Here, farmer Hale explicitly joins sides with Minnie Wright, explaining that he had thought he might have an accomplice in her: "I thought if I went to the house and talked about it before his wife [...]" (36). Later, the man again links up with Wright's wife in their common need for communication as social contact (symbolized by the telephone which would have meant Minnie's open line to the outside world), as he recounts that when they were waiting for the coroner: "I got a feeling that I ought to make some conversation [!], so I said I had come in to see if John wanted to put in a telephone, and at that she started to laugh, and then she stopped and looked at me — scared" (38). Consequently, as Glaspell pointedly links the character of Mr. Hale to the women's world of community and communication, this connection indicates that the play's preference of an approach to life governed by the principles of inter-subjectivity and involvement is developed as a phenomenon which is valid for everyone, not only in women's lives.

Indeed, at the same time that the talkative Mr. Hale sets himself off against the Sheriff and the County Attorney in his ramblings, he also serves as a figure of contrast to John Wright, whose reticence Hale himself establishes in his account. In this glaring opposition, too, Glaspell frames the need of human interaction as a universally human necessity. For Hale's and Harry's intended trip "to town with a load of potatoes" evokes a frame of human contact which farmers did enjoy in their daily lives much in contrast to their wives — the social space of the community market. It is in this very evocation of his own busy farmer's life that Mr. Hale suggests that when John Wright was "out all day," leaving his wife to the prison of her dreary kitchen (Minnie has required an apron to make her "feel more natural" in jail, 40), the man had apparently had more contact with other people than he would have preferred. Set against the amiable and talkative figure of Mr. Hale, John Wright's rejection of any kind of social contact is thus presented as a profoundly "unnatural" pattern of behavior in *Trifles* — not as a typically male character trait.

In this way, Susan Glaspell sets up a second conflict in *Trifles* to supplement the play's obvious opposition of the sexes: an existential struggle for survival in which "life" itself is associated with the idea of human community and communication whereas "death" is represented by the principles of solitude and silence. Undoubtedly, the play demonstrates that Minnie's (distinctly female) existence had been a slow and creeping spiritual death for the lack of human interaction. When the play begins, however, it is her husband who is actually dead, and while it might be misdirected to see this male figure simply as a victim of his own bleak living conditions, within the play's inherent symbolic system John "Wright," just like his wife, is tragically on the "wrong," that is the losing side of the struggle. As does Minnie's emotional and psychological death, her husband's violent physical end ultimately results from his own inhumanely reticent, isolated being. Whatever the details may be with regard to her absent characters' tragic story, therefore, with John and Minnie Wright Glaspell introduces a conceptual notion of the nature and function of language which she will fully develop two years later in her one-act *The Outside*: the idea that "non-communication" (defined as a position which favors detachment and isolation) equals "death" in human existence whereas "communication" is identical to "life" itself — may it be female *or* male.

Dramatic Language and Artistic Expression: Meaning Created in Constitutive Articulate Contact

While language serves as one of Glaspell's most central themes in *Trifles*, at the same time it is also crucial in the context of the playwright's own means of artistic expression. In 1922, Ludwig Lewisohn notes about the play: "[Its] actual speech [...] is neither sufficient nor sufficiently direct. [...] [O]ne aches for a word to release the dumbness, complete the crisis, and drive the tragic situation home" (*Drama* 105). On the other hand, Glaspell's sparse use of "speech" in *Trifles* has been seen not as a weakness but as the play's unique strength by later critics. In his description of the striking way in which Mrs. Hale and Mrs. Peters "express their thoughts, fears and doubts non-verbally, with intense glances only they can interpret" (*Susan Glaspell* 118–19, my trans.), Gerhard Bach concentrates on the women's growing inarticulateness as the very way in which Glaspell creates the intensity which ultimately does "drive the tragic situation home."[8] It seems that the critical disagreement revolves around the question of whether or not Glaspell has found an adequate expression for what she meant to "say" in this play. What is significant about her way of employing a number of dramatic devices in *Trifles*, however, is precisely that Glaspell does not present her audience with an unambiguous "message." Rather, as she draws her audience into the communicative process of creating meaning the playwright initiates a concrete instance of constitutive articulate contact.

Based on varying arguments, Mrs. Hale's and Mrs. Peters' broken utterances have frequently been interpreted as the development of their specifically female voice in an act of liberation from patriarchal dominance. In Linda Ben-Zvi's words:

> [As] the awareness of their shared subjugation develops, the women begin to seek a verbal form for this knowledge. Appropriately, it is a language of stops and starts, with lacunae — dashes—covering the truths they still cannot admit or are unused to framing in words. [...] [It] is clearly their language, no longer the words of others which they have been taught to speak ["Contributions," 157].

It is true, of course, that with their growing realization of the tragedy which has taken place on the premises, Mrs. Peters and Mrs. Hale become increasingly inarticulate and communicate what they experience only in the exchange of meaningful glances. Yet their hesitant utterances do not (as has often been argued) develop an *écriture féminine* (or rather, "womanspeak") designed to break up patriarchal logic in the strict Irigarayan sense. Instead, the women's words are swept away both by their increasingly tense emotions and by their realization of the circumstantial necessity to keep their deeper knowledge of the crime from the men. Indeed, that Glaspell does not literally develop a uniquely "female language" on the figural level of the play is also evident in the fact that her female characters are not generally inarticulate when it comes to their feelings of resentment towards the men or to their expression of female solidarity. To the contrary, Mrs. Hale is very well able to formulate her objections towards the men's condescension, both in her exchanges with Mrs. Peters and directly to the men's faces. As we have seen, in its concern with aspects of connectedness and intersubjectivity the women's attitude finds its expression in Mrs. Peters' disjointed utterances (provoked by the sight of the strangled canary) *as well as* in Mrs. Hale's perfectly articulate protests against the men's arrogant behavior. Hence, no matter how the women communicate — in affluent sentences, in stammering utterances, in tellingly symbolic phrases, or in silent glances— what is important about their communication is the way in which it engages them with the present situation and with Minnie Wright's story — the way, that is, in which the women "world" the dramatic situation before the audience's very eyes.

In her influential analysis of "A Jury of Her Peers," Annette Kolodny explains Mrs. Hale's and Mrs. Peters' reading in terms explicitly taken from the field of semiotics. Her interpretation is worth quoting at length both for its immense influence on the development of feminist scholarship and for its inherent presuppositions as to the nature of communication underlying Mrs. Hale's and Mrs. Peters' utterances:[9]

> Opposing against one another male and female realms of meaning and activity [...] Glaspell's narrative not only invites a semiotic analysis but,

indeed, performs this analysis for us. If the absent Minnie Foster is the "transmitter" or "sender" in this schema, then only the women are competent "receivers" or "readers" of her "message," since they alone share not only her context (the supposed insignificance of kitchen things) but, as a result, the conceptual patterns which make up her world. To those outside the shared systems of quilting and knotting, roller towels and bad stoves, with all their symbolic significations, these may appear trivial, even irrelevant to meaning; but to those within the system, they comprise the totality of the message: in this case, a reordering of who in fact has been murdered and, with that, what has constituted the real crime in the story [56–57].

Framing the women's interpretation of Minnie's "story" in the terms of "sender," "receiver," and "message," Kolodny invokes the very concept of language as a representative system of signs which, as I argue here, Glaspell *rebukes* in her demonstration of how Mrs. Peters and Mrs. Hale come to understand what happened between John and Minnie Wright. It is interesting to note in this context that Kolodny herself only vaguely describes the "message" sent through the absent woman's "kitchen things," as a "reordering of who in fact has been murdered and, with that, what has constituted the real crime." The indeterminateness of this description is significant because Glaspell herself never makes explicit what it is the women "know" between them. Importantly, this method of leaving Minnie's message unspoken is not only an effective device of creating tension (as Gerhard Bach has argued). It involves an altogether different perception of how meaning is created than the one evoked by Kolodny's semiotic approach, and an understanding of communication which is pointedly opposed to the idea that language — including its specific form as a literary text — expresses pre-existing "messages" at all.

Throughout the entire play, Mrs. Hale's and Mrs. Peters' understanding of what happened between John and Minnie Wright comes into existence in their communicative interactions — in the very gaps of their utterances, in their connective glances, and in their body language of intense emotions. This unique way in which Glaspell's female characters stumble across ever new pieces of evidence has correctly been linked to the play's manylayered symbol of the quilt. Patch by patch the two women piece the story together in a shared act of understanding. Significantly, while the quilting image can certainly be read as a reference to the frame of female experiences, it also suggests the development of truth as a communicative activity. And while the quilting bee (as a form of social gathering exclusively reserved for women) at first sight seems to lead, once again, to an emphasis on communication as a specifically *female* activity, as we have seen the situation in which Mrs. Hale's and Mrs. Peters' reading becomes necessary in the first place is not created by the women alone. Instead, it is provoked by the men's condescending attitude towards the female sphere and developed in the women's ensuing reactions. In this way Minnie's story — even as it is presented to the audience through the eyes of the female characters— is constituted in the articulate contact between *all* characters on stage, as well as in its significant historical dimension of habitual gender relations in a patriarchal society. And thus, although the men are certainly ridiculed for underestimating the significance of "kitchen things," their main fault is not that they are unaware of female experiences. It lies in the fact that they deny their personal involvement in the situation and thus profoundly misjudge the contextual nature of their lives.

What is more, the Wrights' story is not only "worlded" between the characters on stage, but created in the very interaction taking place between the play and its audience as the plot unfolds. Interestingly, such a reading can be supported by a discussion of Glaspell's most prominent dramatic device in *Trifles*, her use of the absent protagonist. This technique lies at the heart of many feminist interpretations, since with the help of feminist language philosophies the absent woman can be understood as a symbol of the unrealized "other" in the patriarchal Symbolic Order. As Linda Ben-Zvi explains:

> Prefiguring psychoanalytic critics such as Irigaray, Glaspell actually offers on the stage the absent woman — woman as void — against whom male characters react, upon whom they impose a shape [...] — making of the absent woman a kind of palimpsest upon which to inscribe their own identities, desires, and language ["Contributions," 157].

At the same time, the female character's absence from the stage can also be seen as opening up a position of freedom from a female perspective. As Noe and others have argued, decades before Lacanian theory and contemporary feminist playwrights' reactions "Susan Glaspell created a means for woman to inhabit the subject position and at the same time elude the male gaze that objectifies and eroticizes her" (Noe, "Reconfiguring the Subject," 42). Minnie Wright's absence, this argument goes, "refracts the gaze onto the other elements of the play, elements which work in concert to establish her presence" (ibid. 37). And since these elements are all part of a distinctly female world, the implication usually is that they serve to construct Minnie's "authentic" (female) self.

As compelling as such interpretations are in light of late 20th-century feminist theories of the female subject's absence in the patriarchal Symbolic Order, both readings of the absent Minnie Wright as either the suppressed or, to the contrary, the realized female "other" incorporate a reduction which becomes apparent in the comparison. Concentrated on the theme of women's subjugation, Ben-Zvi has stressed the absent woman's co-option in male speech (in Mr. Hale's testimony and in the County Attorney's view of the murder case), but has ignored the logical parallel that the female characters, too, "speak for" Minnie Wright — that is, *in her stead*. On the other hand, Noe, who does thematize Minnie's representation through Mrs. Peters' and Mrs. Hale's reading on stage, sees this as an expression of the absent woman's "true" (female) subjectivity, and thus similarly excludes a consideration of the idea that the women, as much as the play's male characters, "impose a shape" on Minnie Wright — a shape which is closer, perhaps, to Minnie's life experience than the men's reading of her situation could ever be, but which is still not Minnie as represented by herself.

In fact, if one approaches *Trifles* from a perspective based on French feminist theories, Minnie Wright remains trapped in precisely the dilemma which such theories presuppose for all women in patriarchy: Her absence protects her from the inevitability of being made over into "more of the same" by the male Logos (in the Irigarayan sense), yet at the same time her retreat from the Symbolic Order deprives her of the possibility to realize her "other" subjectivity in language. Minnie is not there either to deny or to confirm any of the other characters' readings of what "really happened" between her and her husband, and thus her story is appropriated by the characters on stage. Significantly, as the critic Susan Kattwinkel has pointed out in her astute reading of Glaspell's absent protagonists as a dramatic technique which opens up a "site for debate," being recreated in Mrs. Peters' and Mrs. Hale's interpretation of what has happened is only the lesser of two evils: "At best [the absent woman] is appropriated by other women, who presume to speak for her, coalescing all women into a community of 'we'; at worst she is appropriated by men, who identify her in order to possess her" (51).

Consequently, any reading which pins down a concrete "message" in *Trifles* (especially if with regard to the subject of female identity) in fact appropriates Glaspell's work in the same way, as it assigns fixed meanings to an aesthetic structure which, through the very technique of the absent protagonist, ultimately denies closure. It is not surprising at all in this context that (as Kattwinkel reports), the "endings to [Glaspell's] plays [...] have often been a matter of critical debate, especially when critics assign the conclusions of her active characters to Glaspell herself" (49). Indeed, a random collection of audience responses with regard to the playwright's "message" in *Trifles* inevitably shows that when it comes to retelling the story of what "actually happened" between John and Minnie Wright, interpretations differ widely — among female critics as much as among their male colleagues. Does Glaspell imply the prototype of a "battered woman" in Minnie? Did Minnie Wright's husband systematically abuse his wife? Was John Wright a callous and brutal monster who deserved to die, or was he the pitiable product of his sparse surroundings? Furthermore, what does the playwright advocate with regard to the subject of gender relations in her play? Does she support the system of separate spheres? Does she criticize this division in exposing it so engagingly? Does she argue a superior female morality? Does Glaspell position herself at all in terms of deciding on the origins of the gender differences portrayed in her play?

Up to this day, critics have not been able to come to an agreement with regard to these issues, a fact which can be seen as a direct consequence of the dramatist's way of framing her artistic expression as an act of constitutive articulate contact in *Trifles*— as a communicative event, that is, which develops meaning in a contextual, reciprocal process. For while the play's ending, in its positive depiction of the women's cover-up, does seem to suggest that there is a definite "truth" to be found in the story of John and Minnie Wright (a truth, moreover, which only the women have been able to read correctly), this "truth" has emerged in a distinct process of worlding between all characters on stage. Moreover, in demonstrating how the situation is "languaged" between the play's characters (both male and female), Glaspell at the same time turns her audience into active participants in the ongoing process. As spectators, we are shown two language-games in action, the men's obvious power-play and the women's subversive counterpart, and we are inevitably compelled to join on the women's side. While this reader response mechanism has been interpreted as the play's active didacticism (a way of teaching the men in the audience to read as women, see Fetterley 154), the play's own technique of developing meaning interactively favors the *debate* rather than insisting on the outcome of a "correct" female reading shared by all spectators in the end.

In this very preference, as Susan Kattwinkel accurately concludes, "[Susan Glaspell's] writings reveal a belief in imagination and its power to effect change and reconcile apparently antithetical views"(39). Arguably, this belief— deeply rooted in the artist's underlying understanding of communication as an ongoing act of "worlding"— is more tangible in the theatre than in many other forms of aesthetic communication. Since dramatic art presupposes not only the interaction between the characters on stage, but between all participants involved in the theatrical experience, the theatre might prove especially suited for Glaspell's hope of changing the world through her art. How seriously, indeed, the Provincetown playwright took this understanding of the communality and social responsibility of her artistic medium is particularly evident in the theme of her next play, the 1917 one-act *The People*.

4. *The People* (1917)

Artistic Expression and Social Change

The People, first performed at the Provincetown Playhouse in New York on 9 March 1917, is Susan Glaspell's third play, another one-act after *Suppressed Desires* and *Trifles*. In her 1920 collection of plays the author simply subtitles the piece "A Play in One Act," refusing to specify any one genre or style as its leading category of expression. The text's very refusal to "[settle] on any form" (such as realism or expressionism, social idealism or satire, problem play, farce, or burlesque) has caused a considerable amount of irritation among its critics, leading some to consider this play as "one of Glaspell's more obviously flawed efforts" (France, "Susan Glaspell," 218).

The People thematizes the question of whether art can achieve social change. At first a witty satire on various revolutionary postures which Glaspell saw propagated amongst her Greenwich Village friends, midway through the action the play turns to supplement this rather playful criticism with a passionate testimony of faith in their common cause. If there is a problem of composition, however, it is not that the play makes use of a number of different dramatic styles. To the contrary, both its satirical stance and its more serious tone are employed to underline Glaspell's main point in *The People*—that lasting change can be achieved only in a communal act of creation. Instead, the play's problematic paradox lies in the fact that this idea, based as it is on the notion that meaning is created in communicative interaction, is presented in the very form of a fixed message — as a "living truth" (50) which the audience can believe or not, but in whose creation it is not invited to participate. Consequently, while on the figural level the makers of the radical magazine *The People* succeed in entering into a productive dialogue with their readers, the play itself does not draw its audience into the act of creating meaning in the same way as *Trifles* does with the device of its absent characters, Minnie and John Wright.

75

The action takes place in the New York office of *The People*, a magazine proclaiming to be "A Journal of the Social Revolution" (48).[1] The paper has serious financial problems and is about to be discontinued. On his return from an unsuccessful fundraising trip to California, the editor Ed cannot be cheered by his colleague Sara, who tries to convince him that their common cause it not yet lost. One by one, several characters enter to volunteer their ideas on what has brought about the magazine's failure — most of them drawn as stylized types to represent a number of intellectual poses. The writer/poet Oscar fights with The Artist over whether there should have been more poetry as opposed to more pictures. The Earnest Approach suggests a more sober treatment of ideas. The Light Touch proposes "frivolous lines." The Firebrand thinks the cover of every issue should have read "To hell with the bourgeoisie!" (42). And The Philosopher is convinced that the paper should have been less efficient in order to reach efficiency. While these characters still argue their positions, three actual representatives of "the people" appear on the scene: The Woman from Idaho, The Boy from Georgia, and The Man from the Cape. All three have been drawn to the paper's office from their respective corners of the country by one of Ed's editorials, which each has read in a stray copy carelessly left by visitors to their region — passionate lines calling them to "beautiful distances." Discouraged beyond any hope for new energy, Ed at first bitterly mocks his own former vision. But The Woman from Idaho refuses to accept his cynicism, and deeply moved by her passionate plea for "the people" and their need of a more truthful life, with a sudden return of his spirits Ed finally realizes that "[t]his paper can't stop." He has found "something to go on with" (58).

Reviewing *The People* for the *New York Tribune*, Heywood Broun described it as "sound" and "worth while," "built upon a gorgeous plan and developed with humor and telling eloquence, despite a trace of an intrusive literary quality" ("Looking Up"). While Broun's enthusiastic critique does not elaborate on the casually mentioned flaw of "literariness," later critics have put more emphasis on the problem of dramatic style in the play. Isaac Goldberg, for example, writes in 1922:

> *The People* is, in part, ostensibly a satire upon the cranks that infest the offices of radical publications, but the dramatist does not seem sure of her footing. Shall it be a straight satire, burlesque, or what? As a result the humor becomes too heavily freighted with the suggestion of seriousness, the characters merge into caricature, and the spectator listens to the preachment of some beautiful thoughts that live as words, as ideas, but surely not as drama [475].

Others have agreed with this negative evaluation. Arthur Waterman criticizes that the play's "high-sounding speeches are too vague" (*Susan Glaspell* 71), and Gerhard Bach describes the editorial around which its argument evolves— read out by Sara to remind Ed of his former beliefs— as a "declamatory and sentimental" piece of writing, a representation of the "stereotypical ideas" propagated by the "blurred social idealism of the twenties" (*Susan Glaspell* 103, my trans.).[2] Its change in tone from Greenwich Village satire to an expression of serious ideals, thus Bach argues, is an unsuccessful dramatic move: "The melodramatic emotionalism with which the blissful idyll of 'beautiful distances' is presented is ineffectual at this important point of the drama" (ibid. 104, my trans.).[3]

On the other hand, it is worth noting that it was this very passage— together with Glaspell's impersonation of The Woman from Idaho, the character who voices her faith in the truth of Ed's words at the end of the play— which left such a deep impression on Broun in the original Provincetown performance (a fact which Bach acknowledges, although he does not share Broun's enthusiasm). Broun had promised his readers: "If we can get hold of a copy of the play before next week we would like to print the editorial which is read, for it sounds like a capital piece of writing." And he added a remark on the actors' ability to impersonate their characters: "Susan Glaspell plays the part of the woman who heard the call with depth and spirit and George Cram Cook is good as the editor" ("Looking Up"). Indeed, if the play's speeches seem abstract and vague to many readers of the script, one might speculate that it was something about the experience of *performance* which made them so memorable to this reviewer. Interestingly enough, as one of few later critics to linger on the play's "strengths" rather than its "faults," Yvonne Shafer concludes with a similar emphasis on production experience in her interpretation of *The People* as an early experiment in expressionism: "Although *The People* is a minor work, it represents an effective theatrical challenge to realistic playwriting and *is still moving when produced*" (42; my emphasis).

This discrepancy between reactions to the play's production as opposed to its existence as text is relevant with regard to the very ideas it discusses as a piece of art, although in their focus on either criticizing or defending *The People* in its "dramatic quality" critics have not often engaged in a closer reading of the underlying principles connected to the play's central notion of social change through art. In a crucial scene, Sara reminds Ed of their common hope: "We were going to express ourselves so simply and truly that we would be expressing the people" (48). *The People*, then, thematizes the communicative potential of artistic expression, both as represented by Ed's editorial within the play and as demonstrated by the one-act's own gesture towards its audience. Significantly, throughout the play the two notions of language and art as either a representative system of signs or as constitutive articulate contact intermingle in a constant blur. On the one hand, both in Ed's editorial and in The Woman's monologue Glaspell seems to offer a

momentous *message* about "the meaning of life" — a message which remains
so vague, however, that many readers are left unconvinced. On the other
hand, in the way it develops its plot line the play promotes a simultaneous
understanding of art as a way of connecting human beings in a communal
act of "worlding" a better future — and with this gesture, perhaps, it is able
to draw more positive reactions from audiences who share in the actual performance experience.

Inherent in Ed's and Sara's explicit wish to "express the people" is an
idea of "truth" as a pre-existing essence which can be observed from a distance and communicated through language ("We were going to express ourselves so simply and truly [...]," 48). Adequately enough, accompanying this
notion throughout the play is a corresponding imagery of "sight." One might
take this paradigm to be subtly introduced when The Woman from Idaho
announces the reason for her visit early on in the play: "I came to *see* the
author of those wonderful words" (34; my emphasis). More obviously, it is
apparent in her decision to go out and "watch the people" while she is waiting for Ed's return:

> THE WOMAN. (*Thinking aloud.*) I will stand down on the street and watch
> the people go by.
> OSCAR: What?
> THE WOMAN: The people. It's so wonderful to see them — so many of
> them. Don't you often just stand and watch them? [36].

The same idea of "looking at the people" is taken up by Ed himself just
a little later, even if the editor's words do not demonstrate The Woman's (or
his own earlier) idealism but instead state his thorough disillusionment with
the notion of "expression" as a means to bring about change:

> ED. (*Wearily.*) The People. I looked at them all the way across this conti-
> nent. Oh, I got so tired looking at them — on farms, in towns, in cities.
> They're like toys that you wind up and they'll run awhile. They don't want
> to be expressed. It would topple them over. The longer I looked the more
> ridiculous it seemed to me that we should be giving our lives to—(*Picks up
> the magazine and reads.*) The People—"A Journal of the Social Revolution."
> Certainly we'd better cut the sub-title. The social revolution is dead [48].

Significantly, Sara's reaction to this loss of faith is to remind Ed of his former "vision" (48). And in fact, the editorial itself abounds with the imagery
of seeing, of darkness and of light that are so strongly indicative of the representational model of language and its related conceptions of meaning. As
this piece of writing is so central to the play's argument, it should be allowed
to "speak for itself" at this point. This is what Sara reads back to Ed when
she tries to convince him of the truth of his own words:

> "We are living now. We shall not be living long. No one can tell us we
> shall live again. This is our little while. This is our chance. And we take it

like a child who comes from a dark room to which he must return —comes for one sunny afternoon to a lovely hillside, and finding a hole, crawls in there till after the sun is set. I want that child to know the sun is shining upon flowers in the grass. I want him to know it before he has to go back to the room that is dark. I wish I had pipes to call him to the hilltop of beautiful distances. I myself could see farther if he were seeing at all. Perhaps I can tell *you*: you who have dreamed and dreaming know, and knowing care. Move! Move from the things that hold you. If you move, others will move. Come! Now. Before the sun goes down" [49].

Drawn out by these words, The Woman from Idaho, The Boy from Georgia, and The Man from the Cape have all come to ask Ed to give them what he "[has] for the people"— his visionary knowledge treated almost like an object to be passed on from one individual to the other:

> THE WOMAN. I know you will give it to us
> ED. Give *what* to you?
> THE WOMAN. What you have for the people. [...] What you made us know we need [53].

All three representatives of "the people" are convinced that Ed has seen "the living truth," and that he expressed "the right idea" with his words (55). Yet while Glaspell, with the help of The Woman, The Man, and The Boy, seems to argue the idealist stance that language can successfully transport meaning from one isolated mind to the other, the very vagueness of what it is that Ed has "given" them undermines such trust in successful communication. Indeed, Glaspell repeatedly inserts instances of a *failed* transfer of meaning into the satirical parts of her play and in this way acknowledges the skeptic's doubt as to whether people can ever "really" understand each other. Thus, the writer Oscar is left behind somewhat at a loss after The Woman from Idaho has exited to "watch the people go by," murmuring to himself: "I don't quite understand that woman" (37). And a little later the notion of a failure in communication is taken up more elaborately when The Philosopher, who claims to be "[s]peaking for the truth" (!), tries to explain to Ed:

> PHILOSOPHER. [...] You lack form in your work. By form I do not mean what you think I mean. I mean that particular significance of the insignificant which is the fundamental–
> ED. We couldn't understand it. Why tell us?
> PHILOSOPHER. No. You couldn't understand it. (*He leaves them to their fate.*) [47].

Glaspell, however, does not leave her audiences "to their fate" in the face of these failures of communication. For even if on one level of her argument she supports the notion of a metaphysical "truth" that can be "envisioned" (and, perhaps, also expressed) in her play, at the same time she demonstrates the defects of such a notion. "*Watching* the people," she seems to argue, is not the same as *engaging* with them — it keeps the observer at a distance from the lives of those he observes. As Oscar counters The Woman's assumption that he often watches the people go by: "No, madam, not often. I am too busy editing a magazine about them" (36). That the editors of "The People" are indeed remote from those they claim to be expressing is underlined by the fact that the action takes place in an "inner office." In this way, the journalists/artists are even twice removed from the world, as an "outer office" still lies between their work and the street to which The Woman has turned. ("*This is an inner office; at the rear is the door into the outer one,*" 33.) It is no coincidence, either, that all three visitors are sent to this outer room while the staff debate the journal's future. In this way, The Woman, The Boy and The Man are positioned as a *connecting link* between the editors and the people outside. What is really wrong with this paper, Glaspell argues here, is the very distance its editors have put between themselves and their fellow human beings—both physically and in their idea of "seeing the truth." Presumably, it is because of this distance precisely that not enough people have cared to buy the magazine in the first place. As Oscar is forced to resign: "it's not what we want, it's what people want, and there aren't enough of them who want us" (39).

It is as in answer to all these instances of unsuccessful communication (those in which the message is too vague or obscure to be understood, and those in which the intended receivers do not listen to it in the first place), that a simultaneous notion of language as constitutive articulate contact is discernible in the play. Indeed, central to Glaspell's main argument in *The People*—the belief in the power of writing as an agent for social change—is an idea of "connection through communication" which runs parallel (and counter) to the play's pervasive imagery of sight. Even mixed in with Ed's very "vision" is a passionate *call* to his readers—a call which evokes the same notion of involvement in empathy which has already proven central to Glaspell's understanding of "life's meaning" in *Trifles*: "I wish I had pipes to call [this boy] to the hilltop of beautiful distances. [...] Perhaps I can tell *you*: you who have dreamed and dreaming know, and knowing care" (see the quote above, 49).

If one scans the play for instances in which the idea of connection through language wins out over the contrasting images of sight and distance, already its very first scene can be taken to emphasize the notion of "voice": "Why are you writing?" the printer Tom comes in to ask Oscar, who is seated centre stage at a "*long table strewn with manuscripts and papers*":

> OSCAR. (*Jauntily*) Because I am a writer.
> TOM. But I thought you said there wasn't going to be another issue of *The People.*
> OSCAR. (*With dignity.*) I am writing [33].

While this scene could be read to suggest that Oscar follows his writing impulse in a leisurely, arrogant attitude of "art for art's sake" (regardless, that is, of whether his words will reach anyone or not), during the course of the play it becomes apparent that even to the cynical poet his writing is ultimately about affecting people. In this context, Oscar's dignified attitude in the opening scene is the result of a hope against all odds that the paper will find a way to go on. That in spite of his cynicism the poet still hopes to affect people is also evident in his (admittedly vain) insistence that it was for his poetry, not for The Artist's pictures, that "a woman in Bronxville [kept] *The People* under her bed so that her husband won't know she's reading it": "ARTIST. [...] It was my pictures got us under the bed. OSCAR. (*haughtily*) I was definitely told it was my last "Talk with God" put us under the bed" (42–43).

Importantly, when Ed decides to give up the struggle for their cause it is because he no longer believes that the effect which their paper might have on people has enough of a productive edge: "Precisely what do we do? [...] Now and then something particularly rotten is put over and we have a story that gets a rise out of a few people, but — we don't change anything" (47). In his frustration, Ed makes quite clear that to him "connection" is the prerequisite for any kind of change: "We care. I'll say that for us. Even Oscar cares, or he wouldn't work the way he has. But what does our caring come to? It doesn't connect up with anything [...]" (49). What proves most important, then, about "the people's" unexpected appearance on this rather desolate scene is not that they have *understood Ed's meaning*, but that they have *followed his call*— that with his words he did manage to reach out and establish a connection, after all. When Ed asks who she is, The Woman from Idaho replies: "I am one of the people. I have lived a long way off. I heard that call and — I had to come" (50). The Boy from Georgia "read [his editorial], and [...] didn't want to stay at school any longer" (51). Instead, he offers to go out and sell the paper on the streets, to stop people and "tell them why [he is] selling them" (55).[4] Following a similar urge, The Man from the Cape has left his chance to go in on an oyster bed: "I read what you wrote [...] and I said to myself, 'I am nothing but an oyster myself. Guess I'll come to life'" (51).

Reacting to Ed's words by setting out from their homes to the journal's office in New York The Woman, The Boy, and The Man have decided to come out of their inner isolation — to "come to life." As Oscar rightly comments: "The idealists are calling upon the intellectuals, and 'calling' them" (51). But the disillusioned poet immediately rejects his own notion of connection by insisting that Ed has "nothing to give," and that therefore the three should have stayed away: "You shouldn't have come personally. You should have sent in your needs by mail" (53). Ed, too, seems to have lost all desire to connect up with any of "the people": "It's easy enough to have a beautiful feeling about the human race when none of it is around," he states.

"The trouble about doing anything for your fellow-man is that you have to do it with a few of them" (48–49). What Ed rejects here is the negative side of the coin in the notion of language as constitutive articulate contact: the realization that if we world our reality in a communal act, the individual only has limited control over the outcome of this act of creation. Stating that "[w]hat's the matter with us is our friends," Ed wants to know: "What would we be going on for? To make a few more people like the dear ones who have just left us?" (47). Still, in the very suggestion that their endeavor has failed because it has achieved nothing more than to produce a few egocentric preachers like The Philosopher, The Light Touch, The Earnest Approach, and The Firebrand, Ed betrays his belief that their paper does have the power to affect people — even if, for the time being, he can only exclaim: "God knows [our caring] doesn't seem to be making anything very beautiful of us" (49).

In the end, Glaspell demonstrates the writer's power of connection when she has The Woman from Idaho reject Ed's bitter cynicism the very moment his "wonderful words" are read out loud:

> ED. Yes, I wrote it; and do you want to know why I wrote it? I wrote it because I was sore at Oscar and wanted to write something to make him feel ashamed of himself.
> (*While* SARA *is reading,* THE WOMAN *has appeared at the door, has moved a few steps into the room as if drawn by the words she is hearing. Behind her are seen* THE BOY *from Georgia,* THE MAN *from the Cape.*)
> THE WOMAN. (*Moving forward.*) I don't believe that's true! I don't believe that's true! Maybe you think that's why you wrote it, but it's not the reason. You wrote it because it's the living truth, and it moved in you and you had to say it [50].

One more time, the notions of an inner truth to be expressed and of a truth living only in human interaction mingle in this scene. Yet while the imagery of "seeing" is still prominent in the Woman's central speech at the end of the play, the concept of language as constitutive articulate contact does win out when she recounts how the "truth" of her own thoughts and of other's words became "real" to her only as she *spoke them out loud*:

> [It] was a wonderful ride across this country and see all the people. [*sic*] […] I had thoughts not like any thoughts I'd ever had before — your words like a spring breaking through the dry country of my mind. […] *Seeing* — that's the Social Revolution. […] Your great words carried me to other great words. I thought of Lincoln, and what he said of a few of the dead. I said it over and over. I said things and didn't know the meaning of them 'till after I had said them. I said — "The truth — the truth — the truth that opens from our lives as water opens from the rocks." Then I knew what that truth was. […] Let life become what it may become! — so beautiful that everything that is back of us is worth everything it cost [58; emphasis in the original].

With The Woman's passionate speech — spoken, if we are to believe Heywood Broun, with great effect by Glaspell herself in the original production — the playwright makes clear that Ed's "vague" words have touched three concrete human beings (who then turn into representatives both of the United States as a nation and of the entire human race). His lines have moved a woman, a man and a boy to come and meet the writer who reached out to them. What is more, at the end of the play The Woman from Idaho in turn has made a connection to Ed, changing his disillusionment into a fresh "sense of purpose" (France 218). He will now fight on to keep the paper going, and what he will keep it going for is his renewed hope for change through communicative contact: "Let life become what it may become!" (58)

In *The People*, then, Susan Glaspell stresses the act of artistic creation as a communal act and presents an ideal which claims that change is brought about in communicative interaction.[5] In this context, it is worth noting that the lighter comical tone of the play's beginning does not only serve to satirize the Greenwich Village intelligentsia of which Glaspell herself was a part. Her criticism also points to the fact that the narcissistic notions presented by The Light Touch, The Earnest Approach, The Firebrand, and The Philosopher are abstract and unconnected to people's lives. As Ed insists, the fundamental problem lies with the selfishness displayed by each intellectual position. When Oscar and The Artist fight over the significance of their respective interests ("pictures" versus "reading matter"), the editor angrily interrupts them: "I'll tell you where the fault lies. (*Points first to* THE ARTIST, *then to* OSCAR.) Here! Just this! Everybody plugging for his own thing. Nobody caring enough about the thing as a whole" (40). With the play's often-criticized contrast in tone and attitude between its first and second parts, Glaspell thus highlights her understanding that the enterprise of the journal is an entity which can only achieve its aim of reaching out to the people if all participants work together: editors, writers, artists, printer — and readers. Only in a communal effort of *caring*, she argues, can change be brought about; yet once the importance of community and communication is acknowledged in this way, social progress is indeed possible.

Importantly, this propagation of social change and the creation of life as an interactive endeavor directly corresponds to the Provincetowners' shared ideal of a communal drama.[6] In the formation of the Provincetown Players, artists from diverse social and professional backgrounds had come together to create a new, national theater which was neither inspired by a purely aesthetic understanding of "art for art's sake" nor the expression of a blunt agit-prop attitude.[7] With the same gesture with which Glaspell mocks the detached, abstract philosophical and artistic positions of her "radicals" in *The People* (if modeled closely enough on actual debates she might have witnessed in the Village),[8] she demonstrates that she takes seriously the

Provincetown's goal of social change. In fact, it should not be taken lightly that the play was written and performed in March 1917, shortly before the United States entered World War I.[9] It was in the fall of that same year that the Provincetown Players announced their decision to keep their theatre going in the face of this world crisis. As Oliver M. Sayler recounts:

> Preparations for the [Playwrights' Theatre's] third season in the city found America at its deepest engrossment in the war. The Washington Square Players had succumbed to attrition of their ranks. Seven Provincetowners were in the army at home or in France. But the rest determined to persist, [...] and issued this proclamation: "It is now often said that theatrical entertainment in general is socially justified in this dark time as a means of relaxing the strain of reality, and thus helping us to keep sane. This may be true, but if more were not true — if we felt no deeper value in dramatic art than entertainment — we would hardly have the heart for it now. One faculty, we know, is going to be of vast importance to the half-destroyed world — indispensable for its rebuilding — the faculty of creative imagination. [...] The social justification which we feel to be valid now for makers and players of plays is that they shall help keep alive in the world the light of imagination. Without it the wreck of the world that was, can not be cleared away, and the new world shaped" [97].

Could the group's conviction that they participated in a significant act of "worlding" (of "shaping a new world"!) be related more directly and more earnestly than in this proclamation — or in Glaspell's play of the same year? Reading *The People* both in this historical context and for its underlying concepts of language and art, one might argue that interpretations which criticize its passionate speeches as too "vague" fail to realize their emphasis on meaning as constituted in articulate contact. In this play, Glaspell pointedly demonstrates the artist's inseparable connection to the society s/he attempts to affect. In the creation of meaning as much as in the development of change, both are fundamentally dependent on each other.

On the other hand, the irritation with the play's "vagueness" is a frequently voiced reader response which seems to indicate that with *The People* Glaspell does not succeed in drawing her audiences into the communal act of worlding in the same way as she does in *Trifles*. As we have seen, if faced with only the *text* as opposed to being involved in a *performance*, many recipients react more immediately to the play's posure of presenting a "deeper truth" than to its simultaneous appeal to creation as a reciprocal communicative act — and come away disappointed to the degree in which they find the message they are coaxed into looking for not sufficiently specified. Without the technique of absence (which invites recipients to participate in the creation of Minnie Wright's story regardless of whether it is presented as text or as performance), and without the live experience of being addressed and included in the shared space of the theatre, successful communication between play and audience depends almost entirely on what each reader brings to the text. As a result, even though *The People* proves passionately engaging both as theatre *and* as drama if it happens to touch a chord with our personal life experiences, if it fails to appeal to its recipients' individual philosophies it seems that this play, more readily than *Trifles*, allows its audiences to lean back and refuse to participate in the "worlding" of its communal reality.

5. *The Outside* (1917)

Survival through Communication

The Outside, Glaspell's fifth play, was first staged by the Provincetown Players in New York as part of their third bill in December 1917.[1] No reviews seem to exist, and although the one-act is sometimes touched upon in comparative discussions on Glaspell's dramatic oeuvre, it has received little attention as an individual work.[2] The play centers around two women, Mrs. Patrick and her maid Allie Mayo (the latter played by Glaspell in the original Provincetown production), who have retreated from the world into a former life-saving station "*on the outside shore of Cape Cod*" (48). Two life-savers have carried a drowning victim up to the house in the face of immediate urgency, but it seems that their efforts of bringing the young man back to life come too late. The play opens with their Captain's entrance and his dogged decision to "go on [trying] awhile" against all odds (48).

When Mrs. Patrick enters the stage (introduced as "*a 'city woman,' a sophisticated person who has been caught into something as unlike the old life as the dunes are unlike a meadow*"), she is "*excited and angry*" (49). Wildly, she insists that she "must have [her] house to [herself]" (50). As the audience learns later on, Mrs. Patrick has come to hide here after the recent loss of her husband, and her hard-hearted reaction to the unexpected life-saving scene on her premises is a desperate attempt to shut out a world of feeling in which she would be forced to face her pain. However, her maid Allie, a Provincetown native who has not spoken "an unnecessary word" since she lost her own husband to the sea some twenty years ago (51), is stirred to the abrupt understanding that it is as wrong as it is illusory to retreat from life in such a way. Feeling her way back through words she did not know she still had, Allie insists on saving Mrs. Patrick from what she now recognizes as her own mistake. A verbal battle evolves between the two women which mirrors the life-savers' previous struggle for the drowned man's life, and after an increasingly elevated debate Mrs. Patrick is eventually caught by the "won-der of life," recognizing the challenge as well as the possibilities inherent in "meeting the Outside" (54).

Because of its focus on the two women and their groping language, and because of the female characters' obvious structural opposition to the three life-savers who open the play, *The Outside* has been compared to *Trifles* in thematizing "the failure of men to accomplish what women can do" (Ben-Zvi, "Susan Glaspell," 26). In her reading of the play Linda Ben-Zvi points out: "As in *Trifles*, once more Glaspell depicts the inarticulate power of women to understand the shared experiences of other women unstructured by language but nevertheless communicated through mutually shared pain" ("Contributions," 154). In addition, the opinion prevails that because "[b]oth women had originally retreated from life as a result of losing their husbands, [...] in dramatizing their re-embracing of it, the play affirms women's auton-omy" (Dymkowski 96). Indisputably, *The Outside* repeats the character con-stellation of *Trifles* in that it, too, juxtaposes two women and three men on the stage. Importantly, however, the meaning of this juxtaposition along gen-der lines is far less easily determined in *The Outside* than it is in the earlier play. In Glaspell's dramatization of the existential struggle between life and death the concepts of human community and language play a central role — in this characteristic feature, too, *The Outside* links up with *Trifles*. While in *Trifles*, however, the equation of reticence with death and of communi-cation with life provides no more than the almost casual backdrop to the play's central gender conflict, in *The Outside* the opposition between the sexes is more obviously embedded in — and complicated through — its depic-tion of life *in general* as irreducibly social.

As does *Trifles*, *The Outside* establishes its central theme in its opening stage directions. While *Trifles* is set in a kitchen — the "woman's world"— and directly points to its gendered perspective in having the men and the women enter in two distinctly separate groups, the introduction of the scene in *The Outside* identifies as its focus the existential fight for life in the face of imminent death. Not only the life-saving station itself, but even more so the fact that it has ceased to serve its original purpose and does not have "*the life-saving freshness*" any longer points to the play's thematic preoccupation with this existential conflict. It is further emphasized in the portrayal of the landscape surrounding the station. Located "*on the outside shore of Cape Cod, at the point, near the tip of the Cape, where it makes that final curve which forms the Provincetown Harbor*," the house, through its big sliding door in the back, allows an open view not only at the sea, but also at "*the line where woods and dunes meet*" (48). In this way, the play's setting introduces three symbolic sites to evoke an image of the edge where life and death engage in battle: the life-saving station which once accommodated those who risked their own lives to rescue the drowning, the open sea as contrasted by the Provincetown Harbor with its promise of safety for every ship, and the line where the woods meet the sand, where "[s]trange little things" persist to grow in spite of the dunes which ever strive to bury them in sand (53).

Obviously enough, it is this carefully built-up symbolic image of the struggle between life and death which is mirrored in the men's unsuccessful efforts to resuscitate the drowned man when the play begins—and since Glaspell makes it clear from the start that their attempts are doomed to failure, it seems just as obvious which side of the struggle the life-savers are posited on. As J. Ellen Gainor points out:

> The male drowning victim is clearly a lost cause from the start; despite the Captain's tenacious efforts, we sense no hope for his resuscitation. Rather, the ending of the play shows an alternative, symbolic resurrection. Mrs. Patrick and Allie Mayo, both of whom have given up on life, each help to "save" the other, much like Mrs. Hale and Mrs. Peters discover a bond through their examination of "trifles" [78].

On the other hand, a closer look at Glaspell's strategies of characterization in The Outside reveals that the play's assignment of "sides" in the fight for life does not take place along gender lines as clearly as such a juxtaposition of the men's failure and the women's later success suggests. After all, Glaspell introduces the three "life-savers" as characters for whom their occupation has been a long-term, serious commitment, and she does not treat their professional efforts with the same obvious irony as she does the Sheriff's and County Attorney's fruitless investigation in Trifles. If the Captain and his "boys" are too late to do anything for the drowned man in the present situation, Glaspell makes clear from the start that they have been able to save others before him:

> BRADFORD. [...] He was dead when we picked him up.
> CAPTAIN. Danny Sears was dead when we picked him up. But we brought him back. I'll go on awhile [48].

In contrast, in the open conflict between the men who are fighting to save a life and the women who want nothing to do with this fight, Allie Mayo and Mrs. Patrick are clearly associated with the notion of "death" during the opening scenes of the play. In their mute and secluded existence, both have decided to withdraw from life in order to shut out the pain it has in store for every feeling human being. As a result, the women's very presence is perceived by the men as more deadly even than the sea that has taken the sailor's life:

> BRADFORD. [...] But the sea (calling it in to the CAPTAIN) is friendly as a kitten alongside the women that live here. Allie Mayo—they're both crazy—had that door open (moving his head toward the big sliding door) sweepin' out, and when we come along she backs off and stands lookin' at us,

lookin' — Lord, I just wanted to get him somewhere else. [...] (*under his voice*) If he did have any notion of comin' back to life, he wouldn't a come if he'd seen her [48–49].

At the same time, Bradford's account of Allie's reaction to their "intrusion" — the way she "backed off" and just "looked" when the men appeared with the drowning victim — already hints at the profound change which is about to be set in motion within this female character. Indeed, the entire symbolic dynamic in *The Outside* hinges on the fact that there is a *change* in the two women's attitude, a development from "death" towards "life." Consequently, the question of what brings about this change in the first place, and what drives it to its successful completion, is of crucial significance to the play. Approaching this question from an angle that focuses on the "theme of struggle between the sexes, played out spatially as well as characterologically" in *The Outside* (Gainor, *Susan Glaspell* 75), most critics have concluded, as Gainor does, that throughout the course of events Mrs. Patrick and Allie Mayo "discover a bond" of shared female experiences on the basis of which they "each help to 'save' the other" (ibid. 78, see quote above). Read with a focus on the relevance of language and communication in this one-act, however, it becomes obvious that Allie Mayo's return to life through language is aligned far more closely with the communicative interactions of the *male* characters than linked to the denial of life which is defended so determinedly by Mrs. Patrick right up to the final curtain.

Thus, it is the Captain's dogged refusal to accept death's victory as set off against Mrs. Patrick's "wild" insistence that she will have nothing of these life-saving attempts on her premises which first reawakens Allie to a long-buried aspect of her own personality — her own will to survive. Making her entrance just as the Captain most forcibly insists that he is not yet ready to give up ("if there's any chance of bringing one more back from the dead"), Allie "*at first seems little more than a part of the sand before which she stands. But as she listens to this conflict one suspects in her that peculiar intensity of twisted things which grow in unfavoring places*" (50; my emphasis). What is more, Allie's decision to follow the Captain's example and fight for life against all odds is drawn out to full awareness precisely when one of the men confronts her straight out with the question why she would want to work for a woman who apparently "[wants] folks to die":

> BRADFORD. Well, I couldn't say, Allie Mayo, that you work for any too kind-hearted a lady. [...] (*suddenly thinking of it*) I believe [Mrs. Patrick] *likes* to see the sand slippin' down on the woods. Pleases her to see somethin' gettin' buried, I guess.
> (ALLIE MAYO [...] <u>is arrested by this last</u>— *stands a moment as if seeing through something, then slowly on, and out.*) [50; my emphasis].

Consequently, it is indeed "the appearance of the life-savers," as C.W.E.

Bigsby has pointed out in a much contended reading, which "acts as a catalyst" for Allie's move back towards life ("Susan Glaspell," 27). After twenty years of having buried herself in isolation and silence, she is prompted to "join sides" with the men as she embarks on her own fight for a life—for Mrs. Patrick's reintegration into the human community which she herself has shunned for too long.[3]

In her subsequent dramatization of both women's return from death to life, Glaspell once again gives prominence to issues of language and communication. When Mrs. Patrick arrived in Provincetown to move into the old life-saving station, she had inquired after a housekeeper who "doesn't say an unnecessary word." Allie Mayo, she had been advised, was just the right person for the job, well-known to have displayed a "prejudice against words" herself ever since her husband of two years had not returned from a whaling trip to the north (51). But now, shaken to an awareness of her mistake by the life-savers' appearance, Allie breaks her long silence. Painfully groping her own way back towards life against the unfamiliarity of language, she forces Mrs. Patrick to listen to her story. The other woman is held by the sheer intensity of Allie's efforts, and thus eventually Allie manages to coax Mrs. Patrick into an argument:

> ALLIE MAYO. I know where you're going! (MRS. PATRICK *turns, but not as if she wants to*) What you'll try to do. Over there. (*Pointing to the line of woods*) Bury it. The life in you. Bury it — watching the sand bury the woods. But I'll tell you something. *They* fight too! The woods! They fight for life the way that Captain fought for life in there! (*Pointing to the closed door.*)
> MRS PATRICK. (*with a strange exultation*) And lose the way he lost in there! [52–53].

In the verbal battle which ensues, the two women articulate the symbolic significance of the play's setting, making explicit what has found its expression only in the stage directions up until this point. Triumphantly, Mrs. Patrick argues that it is the dunes that win the battle in the ever-lasting fight between life and death, forever burying trees and vines beneath their choking sand. But Allie insists on the value of struggling on the edge. The vines— "strange little things which reach out farthest"—"hold the sand for things behind them. They save a wood that guards a town" (53). Fighting for Mrs. Patrick's life, Allie realizes that she herself must not *flee* to "the Outside," as she has done for twenty years, but *meet* it head-on. When Mrs. Patrick demands to know what "[she] ever [found] after [she] lost the thing [she] wanted," she answers: "I found — what I find now I know. The edge of life — to hold life behind me —(*A slight gesture toward* MRS PATRICK.)" In the end, Allie has succeeded in pulling Mrs. Patrick back in with her away from the far side of the edge: "MRS PATRICK. [...] *feeling her way into the wonder of life*) Meeting the Outside! (*It grows in her as* CURTAIN *lowers slowly*)" (55).

Because the two women come back to life after the men have been shown to fail in their life-saving efforts, and because they do so in a faltering language which stresses the importance of fighting on the edge, feminist interpretations have focused on the theme of women's marginality in patriarchy in *The Outside*, and on Glaspell's depiction of both the dangers and the creative potential inherent in this liminal position. Christine Dymkowski, for instance, discusses the play as part of her argument that "inherent in almost all of Glaspell's work is a consciousness that identifies women as outside the mainstream of life and thus capable of shaping it anew" (92). And Ann E. Larabee emphasizes the promise of change implied by Allie's fight on the edge: "For Allie, the struggle for a language in exile is laden with creative potential" (80). In this context the male characters (clearly "on the inside" in this play) are necessarily grouped with those frequent "spokespeople of a fixed society" in Glaspell's oeuvre whose interactions, as Linda Ben-Zvi explains, demonstrate a "glibness and verbal dexterity" which is "the mark of superficiality" ("Susan Glaspell," 25). Ben-Zvi consequently stresses that the "passive, mute Allie" is "victorious" in her "attempts to bring her mistress back to life through a recognition of the bravery inherent in a life lived at the fringe of society," whereas the men "are unsuccessful; physical activity has proven a failure." And she adds: "[as] in *Trifles*, the shared experiences of women provide a covenant that is supportive" (ibid. 25–26).

Undoubtedly, such interpretations are persuasive in that they offer a conclusive analysis with regard to the play's theme of the struggle "on the Outside," its foregrounding of women's lives on the edge, its open contrast between male and female characters, and the peculiar language employed by the women. They also make sense within the broader context of Glaspell's writing, which often deals with women's position on the margin of patriarchal society. On the other hand, interpretations which assign the sides of "life" and "death," of "creativity" and "fixity" (Ben-Zvi, "Contributions") so strictly along gender lines in this play ignore a number of elements which complicate the portrayal of gender relations in *The Outside* — aspects which include in the depiction of the women's final achievement a positive notion of what the *men* represent.[4] Thus, not only do readings concentrated on the play's "struggle of the sexes" necessarily tone down the significance of the Captain's dogged determination as the catalyst which brings out Allie Mayo's change in the first place. They also ignore the fact that all three men — quite unlike the Sheriff and the County Attorney in *Trifles*— are drawn as decidedly sympathetic figures in their struggle for life, in their interactions amongst themselves, and even in their attitude towards the women. Indeed, a concentration on the apparent contrast between "futile male activity" and "successful female communication" in *The Outside* inevitably misses the point that the three life-savers are far from being characterized only through their *actions* in this play. Significantly enough, their verbal exchanges take up the entire first half of this short one-act: For this quantitative reason alone, an analysis of the principles governing the male characters' communicative behavior seems called for in order to ascertain whether "glibness" and "superficiality" is really all that their language signifies in *The Outside*.

What is more, one aspect of Allie's argument acquires particular importance in this context. The struggle of the vines against the sand is not framed as a courageous act because it presents a life-form detached from the patriarchal Symbolic Order, where women can create their lives uninhibited by the male Logos. Instead, it is necessary and heroic precisely because the vines "*save a wood that guards a town*" (53). As Gainor notes, " the struggle has implications for the survival of civilization, emblematized by the community of Provincetown, separated from the Outside by the protecting line of woods" (*Susan Glaspell* 76). Indeed, while Allie defines "the Outside" of the play's title as the "outer shore where men can't live," the line which borders it is "an arm that bends to make a harbor — where men are safe" (53). Of course, this equation of "men" with "people" can be seen only to underline the ambivalence inherent in Allie's words: one might argue that it is really only the men who are safe in the center of society, while the women dangerously live on the edge and brave "the Outside" in a manner which men are incapable of. In spite of the appeal and usefulness of such a modern feminist reading, however, it should not be ignored that Glaspell — in Allie's very struggle to bring the other woman back to life — frames the protection of society as a pointedly positive value: "Woods. Woods to hold the moving hills from Provincetown. Provincetown — where they turn when boats can't live at sea. Did you ever see the sails come round here when the sky is dark? A line of them — swift to the harbor — where their children live" (53).

As a result, Ben-Zvi's assertion that the "direction in a Glaspell work is outward, from the confining circle of society to the freedom of 'the outside'" ("Susan Glaspell," 1982, 23) captures only one level of meaning in this play. On another level, the women's movement towards life and language is still in a direction *away* from the dangerous edge, back into the safe and comforting circle of human community.[5] What is more, it is precisely through the life-savers extensive verbal exchanges that Glaspell develops the positive understanding of human interaction which forms the very basis for the two women's return to life through language. As a close reading of the principles governing both the men's much under-discussed conversation and Allie's and Mrs. Patrick's return to language will show, therefore, in *The Outside* Glaspell presents communication *in any form* as a life-enhancing reciprocal activity — for women and men alike.

With the very first moments of the play, the male characters' interactions are shown to be defined by the same principle of status which governs the men's behavior in *Trifles*: the life-savers' hierarchical relations in the "public world" of their work are instantly established when the Captain opens the play by taking over control of the situation from his "boys" (48).[6] In contrast to the men's "pecking order" in *Trifles*, however, in this play the male characters' interrelations are not governed by an adversarial struggle for position, and the tone between the three men is genial. When Bradford refers to his captain as "the old man," it is with an air of admiration and respect as he relates the older man's twenty-seven years of service to the "Portagees" Tony, who seems comparably new at the job (49). In addition, even though especially Bradford employs strategies which signal superiority over Tony (boasting his ability and experience, employing sarcasm and irony as he demonstrates his "insider's" knowledge about the history of the place and Allie's and Mrs. Patrick's personal backgrounds), these verbal features do not serve to create distance and hostility between the men.[7] To the contrary, as nobody thinks of challenging anybody's previously assigned status, their exchanges evoke an atmosphere of closeness and camaraderie instead. The familiar way in which all three men deal with each other demonstrates that they are bound in supportive comradeship through their work and through their current — unfortunately unsuccessful — attempt to revive a victim.[8]

In this way, it is the men's conversation that establishes the notion of communication as a positive activity which generates and maintains life-sustaining relationships in the play. What is more, the life-savers *contextualize* their jobs and their current fight for life in that they evoke both the history of the old life-saving station and the town community which supports their work. Thus, the Captain relates that "Mitchell telephoned from High Head that a dory came ashore there," and former wrecks and their dead are identified by name in Bradford's boastful remembrances, implying his personal connection to the men he had once known but was unable to save:[9]

> BRADFORD. [...] There'd been dead ones carried through *that* door. [...] I carried in Bill Collins, and Lou Harvey [...]. I was here the night the Jennie Snow was out there. (*pointing to the sea*) There was a *wreck*. We got the boat that stood here (*again shaking the frame*) down that bank. (*goes to the door and looks out*) Lord, how'd we ever do it? The sand has put his place on the blink all right. And then when it gets too God-forsaken for a life-savin' station, a lady takes it for a summer residence — and then spends the winter. She's a cheerful one [49].

Importantly, too, as this last remark about Mrs. Patrick indicates, the men's way of contextualizing the current situation extends to the two women in the play as well. Indeed, it is Bradford who relates both Mrs. Patrick's and Allie Mayo's stories to Tony and the audience in the first place. His easy gossip has seldom received any closer attention in discussions of *The Outside*, yet it is noteworthy both for what it reveals about this male character's attitude towards the two "crazy" women and for the positive notions of community and communication it entails. As both the relation between the sexes and the idea of language as a life-enhancing activity play an important role in the play, Bradford's explanations are worth quoting here at length:

> BRADFORD. They're a cheerful pair of women — livin' in this cheerful place — a place that life savers had to turn over to the sand — huh! This Patrick woman used to be all right. She and her husband was summer folks over in town. They used to picnic over here on the outside. It was Joe Dyer — he's always talkin' to summer folks — told 'em the government was goin' to build the new station and sell this one by sealed bits. I heard them talking about it [...] [50].
>
> [...]
>
> BRADFORD. [...] I was in Bill Joseph's grocery store, one day last November, when in she comes — Mrs Patrick, from New York. 'I've come to take the old life-saving station,' says she. 'I'm going to sleep over there tonight!' [...] [Bill] got it out of her, not by what she said, but by the way she looked at what he said, that her husband had died, and she was runnin' off to hide herself, I guess. A person'd feel sorry for her if she weren't so stand-offish, and so doggon *mean*. [...] And then she wanted somebody to work for her. 'Somebody,' says she, 'that doesn't say an unnecessary word!' Well, then Bill come to the back of the store, I said, 'Looks to me as if Allie Mayo was the party she's lookin' for.' Allie Mayo has got a prejudice against words. Or maybe she likes 'em so well she's savin' of 'em. She's not spoke an unnecessary word for twenty years. She's got her reasons. Women whose men go to sea ain't always talkative [51].

As we can see, not only does Bradford put the women's secluded state in the context of their personal histories here, and in a surprisingly understanding way at that. His explanations to Tony also serve to connect both Allie Mayo's and Mrs. Patrick's lives to the close-knit Provincetown community, a small fishing village where communicative interactions are especially important. Indeed, it is no coincidence that Bradford assigns importance to the fact that Joe Dyer "is always talking to summer folks," and that he relates Mrs. Patrick's situation by recounting a conversation which had taken place in Bill Joseph's grocery store. In this way Bradford's narrations emphasize the inevitability of the women's association with society, even as both Mrs. Patrick and Allie Mayo vehemently strive to negate this connection in their chosen isolation.

In contrast, in direct opposition to the close note in the men's conversation and to the positive notion of social contact evoked in their talk, Mrs. Patrick insists on distancing herself from the other characters throughout the entire play. Interestingly enough, in her desperate attempts to drive the life-savers out of her house she calls on her legal right of property to the place — and in a striking reversal of the gender roles displayed in *Trifles* prompts the Captain to insist that the circumstances of the present situation are more important than abstract rules:

MRS PATRICK. You have no right here. This isn't the life-saving station any
more. Just because it used to be — I don't see why you should think — This
is my house! And — I want my house to myself!
CAPTAIN. [...] Well I must say, lady, I would think that any house could be
a life-saving station when the sea had sent a man to it" [50–51].

What is more, Mrs. Patrick does not only aim at distancing the *men* in
the play. As she uses the same defiant and aggressive tone towards Allie Mayo,
it is obvious that she wants to keep the other *woman* at bay, too. Indeed, the
two women's hierarchical relationship as that of employer/employee does not
imply anything even remotely resembling the men's notion of comradship,
and there is no admitting to any sense of "female bonding" on Mrs. Patrick's
part. To the contrary, as if to remind the other woman of the impersonal
nature of their dealings, whenever Allie addresses the concrete circumstances
which are at the heart of Mrs. Patrick's and her own situation, her employer
tells her to mind her own business: "Don't you think you've said enough?
They told me you didn't say an unnecessary word!" (52)—"[You've] bun-
gled into things you know nothing about!" (52)—"You're a cruel woman —
a hard, insolent woman! [...] What do you know about it? About me? [...]"
(54). This stubborn insistence that Allie Mayo knows nothing about her situation clearly shows that Mrs. Patrick does not accept the suggestion of a
bond of common female experiences. Instead, in an attempt to protect her
individual suffering from the intrusion of the other woman, Mrs. Patrick
makes a point of emphasizing the difference in their respective situations:
"ALLIE MAYO. [...] You're not the only woman in the world whose husband is dead! MRS PATRICK. (*with a cry of the hurt*) Dead? My husband's
not *dead*. ALLIE MAYO. He's not? (*slowly understands*) Oh" (52).

In a complete reversal of the gender roles portrayed in *Trifles*, therefore, in *The Outside* it is the male characters who represent the positive
notions of connectedness and involvement, while both women's initial symbolic position is defined by the concepts of distance, isolation, and silence.
And in this conceptual context, the fact that Allie Mayo's conversion is set
off by the men's appearance on the scene acquires additional significance yet.
For in spite of Allie's statement that it was the dead man's "face [which]
uncovered something" (52), Glaspell demonstrates that it is really the combined impact of the men's interactions among themselves, of the Captain's
argument with Mrs. Patrick, and of Bradford's direct address to Allie which
draws her out of her state of seclusion. To Mrs. Patrick Allie remarks, simply: "When you keep still for twenty years you know — things you didn't
know you knew" (52). In the play's positive emphasis on human interaction, however, and in the connection between Allie's return to life and her
return to language, Glaspell shows that the character's "knowledge" comes
into existence the moment she allows herself to engage with her surround-

ings, *not* in the twenty silent years before this day. It is for this reason that Allie cannot say what she "found" in all the years of her isolation, but that she is certain what she has found now that the men's intrusion has forced human contact upon her: "I found — what I find now I know. The edge of life — to hold life behind me–" (54).

With this emphasis on interaction in *The Outside*, it also becomes clear that once again Susan Glaspell favors an understanding of language as constitutive articulate contact over the principles connected with the model of language as a representative system of signs: Language, as Glaspell shows with this play, is not only important to the *expression* of life, communication *is* life — and it is illusory, therefore, to attempt to isolate one's self from others in order to protect one's individual authority over the creation of meaning. As is typical for the notion of language as constitutive articulate contact, Allie's situation becomes real to her only as she begins to formulate it in words. At the same time that she "[*looks*] *ahead at something remote and veiled*," the loss of her husband and the deadening pain connected to this experience materialize only in the very act of speaking: "We had been married two years. (*a start, as of sudden pain. Says it again, as if to make herself say it*) Married — two years" (52).[10]

What is more, we also learn that what caused Allie's retreat from life in the first place was not the experience of loss itself, but the way others chose to "world" this experience in their conversations with her:

> I used to talk as much as any girl in Provincetown. Jim used to tease me about my talking. But they'd come in to talk to me. They'd say —'You may hear *yet.*' They'd talk about what must have happened. And one day a woman who'd been my friend all my life said —'Suppose he was to walk *in!*' I got up and drove her from my kitchen — and from that time till this I've not said a word I didn't have to say [52].

What Allie wanted to escape from twenty years ago was the cowardly way in which people tried to create false hopes just so they would not have to admit to the tragedy that had befallen her. In contrast, Allie now wants to acknowledge Mrs. Patrick's pain and help her face it in all its intensity — and in effect leads her back to life by forcing upon the other woman the very interaction which she herself has deliberately fled for the greater part of her own life.

Significantly, indeed, while the experience that we do not "world" our reality alone drove Allie Mayo to "the Outside" twenty years ago, it is this very same experience which now draws Mrs. Patrick back inside in spite of herself. Stubbornly arguing the futility of the struggle for life at the edge, she literally attempts to re-establish her distance from Allie in a cruel gesture of rejection: "(*stepping back*) You call what you are life? (*laughs*) Bleak as those ugly things that grow in the sand!" (54). Yet in her passionate refusal to acknowledge life's persistence, Mrs. Patrick has resumed human contact and opened the door to life unwittingly. Importantly, then, in the end it is once again the very act of repeating the phrase out loud — and thus of engaging in constitutive articulate contact — which creates for her an understanding of what Allie's words really "mean":

> MRS PATRICK: (*bitter, exultant*) […] You savers of life! 'Meeting the Outside!' Meeting —(*but she cannot say it mockingly again; in saying it, something of what it means has broken through, rises. Herself lost, feeling her way into the wonder of life*) Meeting the Outside!
> (*It grows in her as* CURTAIN *lowers slowly.*) [55]

That in *The Outside* Susan Glaspell dramatizes two women's return to life through language is a reading which no recipient will have difficulties to confirm. After this common starting point, however, reactions to the play begin to diverge widely. What, precisely, is Glaspell's point in this one-act, what does she "say" about life, about the struggle for survival, about the relevance of gender or the role of language in this fight? Indeed, interpretations of *The Outside* have come to a surprisingly diverse variety of conclusions, as critics may favor the one-act's philosophical over its social dimension, its gender-relevant aspects over its "universal" appeal — and vice versa, respectively. Does Glaspell present her belief in life against all odds as the individual's struggle for a fulfilling existence in the face of an often hostile world or social environment? Does she contrast mute female understanding with blind male activity? Does she emphasize the creative potential of life on the edge (more often forced upon women than experienced by men in a patriarchal society) as set against the staleness of society's inner circle? Or does she focus on the positive aspect of safety in social interactions, both on the edge and in the center of human community? What, finally, does the play demonstrate with regard to the nature of artistic expression? Does Glaspell set a female approach to language — and, with it, a feminist reinvention of dramatic art — against the imprisoning structures of the patriarchal Logos in her gripping portrayal of the women's struggle on the edge?

As little as critics have been able to agree on the play's ultimate meaning, as little do they agree in their assessment of *The Outside* as a dramatic "success" or "failure." Once more it is the unique way in which Glaspell employs language as a dramatic medium which has caused much comment in the reception of this play — and once more it has often been perceived as a problem. In his 1922 discussion of the role of language in Glaspell's works, Lewisohn mentions *The Outside* with his remark that "at times, [Glaspell's] attempt to lend a stunted utterance to her silenced creatures makes for a hopeless obscurity" (*Drama* 103). Four decades later Arthur Waterman — if conceding that *The Outside* "is a more interesting attempt to make drama from idealism" than *The People*— similarly insists that Glaspell has once again fallen short of putting "into direct dramatic terms her concern with that vague something she calls 'the meaning of life'" (*Susan Glaspell* 71). As Waterman explains the dramatist's supposed failure: "Allie cannot show us the full life; she can only cry out against an empty one" (ibid. 72). Bach, too, identifies as the weakness of Glaspell's argument the fact that Allie herself cannot exemplify the "fulfilled life" which she struggles for so forcibly in her broken language (see *Susan Glaspell* 125).[11] And Bigsby, finally, explains Glaspell's alleged failure to argue her point convincingly in *The Outside* with the two central characters' very move from silence to loquacity:

> [In] a sense the play suffers from its own basic strategy. It works best when it is least articulate. [Allie Mayo], stunned into silence, watching the wordless efforts to bring life back to a dead body, communicates more powerfully than the over-explicit arias with which the play ends. [...] The religious fervour with which each [woman] argues her position presses language toward a poetic self-consciousness which is paradoxically bathetic ["Susan Glaspell," 28].

Of all these negative evaluations, Bigsby's is the only one to point to a crucial difference in the dramatic effect achieved by Allie's initial silence and fumbling language as opposed to the women's later verbal struggle. On the one hand, I have shown that the men's "efforts to bring life to a dead body" are by no means "wordless" in this play (as Bigsby would have it), and both their conversations and the women's move towards language serve a central function in that they stress the positive aspects of safety and understanding within human interaction. On the other hand, however, I agree with Bigsby that a striking paradox is created in *The Outside* as the debate which develops between Allie Mayo and Mrs. Patrick — meant to indicate both women's return to life-enhancing human relations— presents the audience with a philosophical argument which becomes increasingly abstract and vague. As we have seen, during two thirds of her play Glaspell sets up a contrast between an approach to communication which engenders closeness through contextualization and an opposing, distancing attitude which marks a reticent denial of life. Allie Mayo's return to language at first follows the same principles which characterize the men's conversation: when she begins to speak, it is in a personal voice, in an attempt to draw closer to the other woman by putting their present lives into a shared context. But the ensuing debate is not consistent in following the same principles. Although the women's exchanges do carry intensity when Mrs. Patrick talks about her concrete feelings in reaction to the loss of her husband, with regard to the play's central theme of the struggle for life against all odds their conversation indulges in abstractions far removed from personal life experience. In this way, Glaspell turns to employ the very strategy she has previously connected to the notion of "death" in order to demonstrate Allie Mayo's sudden understanding that life will eventually win: a language unaware of life's fundamental contextuality.

On the other hand, feminist readings have argued that Glaspell's point in *The Outside* is precisely to dramatize the creative potential of a linguistic struggle detached from imprisoning patriarchal definitions, and in this context both Allie's fumbling language and the women's later exchanges are seen to represent her very success in creating a dramatic *écriture féminine* which exists at the edge of male expectations of the theatre. In one of the earliest discussions of Glaspell's "inarticulates" Linda Ben-Zvi points out that "[the] playwright's great contribution to American dramatic language is her daring act of placing these stammerers in the center of the action, and allowing them to verbally stumble toward some understanding of themselves, often never totally framed in words" ("Susan Glaspell," 1982, 25). And in a pointed rejection of Bigsby's claim that Allie's return to language is marked by the "restoration of her fluency" (*Plays* 13), Larabee argues that, instead, her "lines are borders between silence and the social contract of language" (80)—a unique kind of verbal expression with which Glaspell revises "marginality into a position of aliveness, creativity and linguistic freedom, constrained not only by society but by dramatic representation itself" (77).

Larabee's insistence that Allie's lines in the second half of the play are "[not] simply a restoration of fluency" (as Bigsby has it) is especially significant (77). As Gainor has shown in her more elaborate discussion of style in the play, the strikingly poetic quality of Allie Mayo's and Mrs. Patrick's verbal exchanges and the very way in which this quality sets off the women's utterances against the more realistic conversation of the life-savers embody Glaspell's most important stylistic strategy in *The Outside*. In "creating a piece blending realism with symbolism and incorporating poetic language within prose dialogue," thus Gainor explains (74), "Glaspell pits the grittily real against the metaphoric, the male world of literal drowning and rescue against the female process of symbolic salvation" (79). While Allie Mayo's and Mrs. Patrick's return to life through language is depicted as an intensely symbolic process, the "male characters, intentionally, are not part of the symbolic linguistic realm of the play. They neither speak in poetic images nor envision their world through symbolism" (Gainor, *Susan Glaspell* 81).

To Gainor, this strict stylistic division of dramatic presentation along gender lines is one more proof that, as in *Trifles*, Glaspell sets the women's success against the men's failure in *The Outside*: At the end of the play it is clear that the "spiritual rescue has succeeded, and its triumph seems every bit as critical as the fate of the unnamed sailor" (81). As I have highlighted the *positive* aspects in the life-savers' representation on stage, however, the fact that their realistic conversation is strictly set off against the women's more poetic exchanges can also be seen to bear significance in quite a different way. In dramatizing the world of the men and of the Provincetown community they represent in realist terms, thus one might argue, Glaspell offers an intentionally realistic depiction of the life which the women are about to return to. It is a life in which people at times die or leave, a life in which others do not always respect one's experiences or one's personal view of the world, a life in which social relations—including the expectation to conform to traditional gender roles—set limits to one's possibility of self-creation, a life in which, ultimately, nothing can change the realization that human existence is irreducibly interconnected.[12] Inherent in Allie's symbolic argument that life will always persevere is the realization that it will do so for better or for worse: To withdraw from life is not an option, yet at the same time life is what it is, and what it is is unmistakably demonstrated in the realistic (and not entirely unsympathetic) portrayal of the play's male characters—an interactive communicative endeavor in which no single individual has authority over the creation of meaning.

Of course, from this angle, too, it is significant that *The Outside* does not end with an emphasis on the depiction of the men's social realities. That Glaspell ends her play with the poetic power of the women still poised on the edge — that she does not bring her symbolic argument to its logical conclusion by dramatizing Mrs. Patrick's and Allie Mayo's actual return to the Provincetown community and beyond—in this context signals the playwright's reluctance to admit to the downside inherent in the idea of art and language as articulate contact: that if meaning is created in interaction, it follows that the individual's freedom of creation is limited—including, of course, that of the artist herself. As we have seen, in *The Outside* Glaspell's emphasis was on the creation of meaning in interaction for the greater part of the plot. It was evident in the way in which the life-savers were shown to "world" their own and the women's realities, it governed the way in which Allie Mayo realized her mistake in her communicative engagement with the men, and it was demonstrated as both women moved from "death" towards "life" when they began to speak to each other. With the poetic style of Allie's final argument, however, Glaspell does not only move away from the men's fixed rules of social interaction, she also moves her emphasis back to an understanding of language according to the representative model, in which meaning pre-exists its expression in words. In the end, Glaspell has Allie Mayo proclaim her "message" to Mrs. Patrick and the audience: "And life grows over buried life! (*lifted into that; then,* as one who states a simple truth with feeling) It will. And Springs will come when you will want to know that it is Spring" (54; my emphasis).[13]

Consequently, then, it is the dramatist's very move from *worlding* an idea (that communication is life, or that women's position on the edge of society entails a liberating creative potential, depending on what audiences bring to this process of creating meaning) to *expressing* one (the "simple truth" that "life grows over buried life") that is responsible for many critics' impression that Glaspell fails to render her meaning convincingly in *The Outside*. Of course, as is the case in the reception of *The People*, whether or not recipients "understand" Glaspell's "message" depends both on what they take to be the play's theme in the first place and on whether their understanding of this theme links up with their personal concept of "life's meaning."[14] Nevertheless, having read three of Glaspell's early plays for their conceptualization of language, communication, and aesthetic expression, I am inclined to suggest that the more the playwright attempts to exert control over the creation of meaning by gesturing towards the expression of a momentous message, the sooner her audiences (and readers, especially) come away unconvinced and begin to question whether a certain piece is successful as dramatic art. Perhaps it should not come as a surprise, then, that in one of Susan Glaspell's next plays, her first full-length work *Bernice*, the question of control over the creation of meaning becomes one of the playwright's most central thematic concerns.

6. *Bernice* (1919)

Human Intersubjectivity — Potential and Dangers

With *Bernice*, which premiered in March 1919 at the Playwrights' Theatre as part of the Provincetown Players' fifth bill, Glaspell returned to the technique she had so effectively experimented with at the beginning of her dramatic career — that of the absent protagonist.[1] The play's three acts evolve around the life and motivations of a woman who is dead when the curtain rises. Bernice Norris lies encoffined behind the closed door of an adjacent room, yet she is still vividly present to those who, closest to her in life, have gathered in her house to mourn her sudden death. A "'mood play' of quiet yet deep emotion" (Waterman, *Susan Glaspell* 75), the drama focuses on its characters' struggle to hold on to what Bernice was to them in life. In *Bernice*, therefore, Glaspell once more approaches her theme of "life's meaning" through a debate of a woman's "innermost reality" in relation to the bonds that connect her to other human beings.

Within this frame — construed by the notions of "identity," "truth," and "understanding" — questions of gender are explored in Bernice's relationships to her aging father, her philandering husband Craig, her maid Abbie, and her best friend, Margaret Pierce. At the same time, the play touches on a number of other issues relevant to the individual's existence within the social sphere — among these the themes of social activism (Margaret is a political agitator engaged in "labor affairs"), the futility of war (Bernice's father studies Sanscrit in a withdrawal from the hopelessness engendered by World War I), and the artist's responsibility to society (Craig is a popular but superficial writer who is incapable of making a difference with his books). Adding to her cast society's personified restrictions in the character of Craig's "sensible" sister Laura, Glaspell thus continues her artistic exploration of human nature as essentially social and intersubjective. Indeed, as the circumstances of Bernice's life and dying are unraveled before the audience's

103

eyes, once more the relation between the individual and society becomes the author's central theme. For although the absent title character is described to have had an unusually *independent* personality, the audience can perceive of her only through the *influence* she still exerts over those she has left behind. Read in this context, Bernice's final act — whose meaning the audience is left to decipher together with the play's onstage characters — acknowledges the irreducible bond which connects this character to her fellow human beings.

By 1919, theatre critics had become well aware of the Provincetown Players' artistic experiments, and the plays produced in MacDougal Street were aptly commented on in the New York press. Reactions to *Bernice* were overridingly positive. In an assessment representative of many reviews, the *Nation* praised it as "a piece of such sincerity and distinction that all [the Provincetown Players'] failures and mediocrities seem worth while if they have made this one production possible" (T. H., "Drama"). Interestingly, while hailing the play for its exceptional dramatic qualities, contemporary reviewers often refused to offer their readers a comprehensive summary of its plot. As Heywood Broun stated in the *New York Times*: "It would be most unfair to Miss Glaspell to take her carefully moulded plot and reduce it into a two paragraph skeleton, with the bland remark, 'The story of the play is as follows'" ("Realism"). Still arguing along similar lines, in his 1925 study on *Playwrights of the New American Theater*, Thomas D. Dickinson announced with regard to *Bernice*: "I shall not try to outline the plot. It is profound and intense, and poised on decisions that are too delicate to follow save by the most sensitive of intuitions" (209).

Gerhard Bach has attributed such refusals to outline the play's plot to its unique structure, which he describes as "sparse with regard to outward action, but rich in inner activity" (*Susan Glaspell* 129, my trans.). Yet the difficulty of plot summary is not fully explained by the relation between "inner" and "outward" action in *Bernice*. As I argue here, many of Glaspell's plays juxtapose a notion of language as transmitter of pre-conceived messages with an idea of communication as creating reality in a reciprocal act. As her theatrical techniques often enhance the immediate experience of aesthetic "worlding," her dramaturgy often leaves essentially lacking any attempt to sum up what a particular work is "about." And while this might explain the general discomfort with plot summaries recognizable in much Glaspell criticism, in *Bernice* the conceptual tension between "message" (which could be related in a precise statement) and "event" (which would have to be experienced in an engagement with the play itself) is especially prominent. With the problem of making sense of the absent woman and her final moments in life, the question of how meaning is created in the first place becomes the very focal point of the play's plot.

As the play's on-stage characters fight over the significance of Bernice's deathbed wish, once again the creation of meaning is presented as a process which cannot be controlled by any one individual alone. In *The Outside*, Glaspell might have tried to refute the resulting sense of a loss of authorial control by reverting to an artistic gesture which highlighted the communication of a pre-conceived message. In contrast, in *Bernice* the playwright demonstrates with the help of her absent character that once an individual takes the creation of meaning to be an intersubjective act in which she is one of several "players," she can turn this understanding into an advantage by manipulating others who are also involved in the game. What is more, Glaspell herself enacts Bernice's manipulative strategy of exerting power over meaning in this play. With regard to her earlier one-acts *The People* and *The Outside*, I suggested that audiences might tend to resist Glaspell's construction of meaning especially in those instances in which she attempts to control it through the expression of an explicit message. In *Bernice*, however — as she had already done in *Trifles*— the playwright invites her audiences to participate in the act of creating meaning. As a somewhat paradoxical result, she gains control over this process in the same way that Bernice is shown to have done by the end of the play.

As quoted above, Glaspell's contemporary Heywood Broun refrained from giving his readers a summary of the play's plot by explaining that it would be "most unfair" to reduce its "carefully moulded" structure to two paragraphs with the "bland remark" that "the story of the play is as follows." However, since it is precisely the relation between the play's *story* (as the chronological order of events) and its *plot* (as the way in which these events are connected in terms of cause and effect) that provides the central dramatic interest in *Bernice*, such a summary provides the necessary basis for my following discussion of the play's "meaning."

Bernice Norris, 35 years old, married but without children, lived with her father and her servant Abbie in the seclusion of her Eastern country home. After occasional instances of not feeling well during the course of the past year and her doctor's unadhered advice to get herself checked out in hospital, she had fallen ill one bright autumn day and was dead within forty-eight hours. Sensing her near death, she had asked to telegraph her friend Margaret, but not her husband Craig, who had spent the summer months abroad and was now staying with his current lover on Long Island. Although she was dying of natural (if unspecified) causes— the doctor, who did not arrive in time to help her, could only repeat his earlier assumption that she might have been suffering from stomach ulcers— shortly before her end Bernice had implored Abbie to tell her husband that she had taken her own life.

The play is set in Bernice's living room, with the dead woman put to lie in state next door. The action begins shortly before Craig, sent for after Bernice's death, reaches the scene in the company of his sister Laura. Some time later Margaret arrives, too late to find her friend alive. At the end of the first act, Abbie fulfills her promise to Bernice and tells Craig that his wife committed suicide. Craig is shocked at this, but after a first reaction of disbelief does not further question the truthfulness of Abbie's words. In contrast, Margaret is unable to accept that Bernice could ever have done such a thing, and by the end of the second act she has pressed Abbie into telling her what really happened. At first the fact that Bernice had *wanted* Craig to believe she had killed herself is even more appalling to Margaret. Act 3, however, brings to the fore a surprising change in the shallow Craig. Convinced of Bernice's love for him as he had never been when she was alive, he vows to lead a more responsible and worthwhile existence from now on. As Margaret witnesses this unexpected transformation, she concludes that Bernice had foreseen the cathartic effect that the news of her alleged suicide would have on her husband. With this realization, the play ends on a note of awe at Bernice's final "gift to the spirit" (229).

These are the facts of the play's story. Whether Margaret's conclusion with regard to the meaning of her friend's death-bed wish — certainly framed as the valid one in the end — really presents the text's "message" to the audience, however, is left subject to debate if we take into consideration how Bernice's closest friend has arrived at this conclusion. In the way in which the play's characters reconstruct the title character's personality in their communicative interactions on stage, the influence which the dead woman still exerts over those who have surrounded her in life becomes as much the focal point of the play as do the "true nature" of Bernice's character and the meaning of the her final words.

The play's opening stage directions draw a direct link from the setting to Bernice's personality: "*The living-room of Bernice's house in the country. You feel yourself in the house of a woman you would like to know, a woman of sure and beautiful instincts, who lives simply*" (159). While this introduction sets the revering tone with which most of the play's characters will remember Bernice throughout the play, one feature is attributed to her person most consistently. As they wait for Craig and Laura to arrive, Father and Abbie have this expository conversation:

> FATHER. [...] It was nice, Abbie, the way Bernice would just laugh about things. She had no malice. [...] It was just that a good many things— well, the things that are important to most people weren't so important to Bernice. It was another set of things were important. People called her detached. [...] To you — did she seem detached?
> ABBIE. (*tenderly thinking it out.*) She was loving, and thoughtful, and gay. But always a little of what she is now —(*Faces the closed door*) off by herself [162].

This image of Bernice as "off by herself" (symbolized in this scene and others to come by the closed door behind which she lies) is confirmed by all characters in the play — even if it soon becomes clear that each contextualizes her "detached" attitude according to his or her personal relationship to Bernice. The maid Abbie, unable to reconcile the dying woman's suicide-lie with her memories of Bernice's deep and loving kindness, is eager to accept her distanced attitude as something that could (and should) not be penetrated: "You can't expect to understand a person who is 'off by herself.' Now can you?" she asks Father. "[We] should take what *we* had, shouldn't we, and not try to reach into— to where we didn't go" (163). As Father muses, Abbie lived her whole life around Bernice, and "doing things for her" had always been "the main thing" (164). Convinced that she herself is "something *more* on account of her," Abbie cannot now be unfaithful to her memories and fulfills Bernice's last request in spite of herself. In a self-protective acceptance of the notion that there were places in Bernice which no-one ever "got to," she is willing to put out of her mind this "[o]ne ugly thing in a whole beautiful life." "Let it go!" she pleads with Margaret, who is determined at first to tell Craig the truth. "Let it go! And let all the rest live!" (217)

Bernice's father, who mourns his daughter's untimely death with a grief entirely unaware of all that is going on beneath the surface, similarly admits that although he "understood Bernice," there "were things— outside what [he] understood" (163). To him, Bernice's aloofness signified that his little girl lived close to the heart of life, close to a meaning which escapes most people and which he himself was never quite able to reach. Feeling himself an utter failure, Father suspects that Bernice would have liked him to "amount to more" (222), yet he gratefully acknowledges that she always let him be himself (194). Convinced that she seemed "detached" only because "she was so—*of* [life]" (168), he had always been thankful for his daughter's "affectionate amusement," seeing in this attitude her forbearance towards those she loved but could not look up to: "I think it was gentle of Bernice to be amused by things she — perhaps couldn't admire in us she loved. [...] Affectionate amusement. Didn't you feel that in Bernice, Craig?" (222).

Like every other character in the play, Bernice's husband Craig knows the peculiar quality in his wife which his father-in-law alludes to here. Unlike her father, however, he was never able to feel anything like gratitude for his wife's elevated attitude. To the contrary, Craig is desperate at the thought of never having "had" Bernice (173): "She never seemed to need me. I never felt she —couldn't get along without me" (170). Believing that a wife's life should be "made" by her husband's (174), as long as there "was something in her that had almost nothing to do with [their] love" Craig could not be content in the love Bernice did have for him (197). That there was a part in her which was completely independent of their relationship is something he rejects as much as he attributes it to his own "failure" (174). Indeed, while no one in the play doubts that Bernice and Craig did love each other, all are aware that Craig did not dominate his wife. And thus, since in his understanding Bernice's independence marked his own ineffectiveness as a man, Craig was unable to accept it, let alone value her "aloofness" as something to be touched by.

To Craig's sister Laura, herself a stern representative of the way things "should be," Bernice's peculiar detachedness was similarly unacceptable. In an unmistakably critical tone she assures her brother: "It isn't as if Bernice were — like most women. There was something — aloof in Bernice. You saw it in her eyes; even in her smile" (177–78). That Bernice did not "have the power to hold Craig" — or, worse still, might not have wanted to "hold him" in the first place, is inexcusable in Laura's eyes: "Well, she should have wanted to. It's what a wife should want to do" (186). To her, Bernice's independent existence represented her failure to live properly *as a woman* — a concept which, as becomes clear during a clash with Margaret, includes not only a desire to "hold" one's husband and to value his work unquestioningly (both of which Bernice had been unable to grant Craig), but also the duty of taking an active part in one's community (188). Bernice, however, had kept away from any form of social involvement (Laura's charity as much as Margaret's political activism), and for Laura this facet of her sister-in law's "detachment" is one more reason to disapprove of her.

In Margaret's eyes, on the other hand, it was Bernice's very resistance to any social cause or purpose which showed that her friend was closer to "life" than she herself could ever be. At one in this feeling with both Abbie and Father, Margaret believes that "Bernice — [...] *was* life" (171). To Craig, who had cynically called her a "wreck of free speech," she admits: "I do things that to me seem important, and yet I just do *them* — I don't get to the thing I'm doing them for — to life itself. [...] Bernice did" (200). Bernice's life "off by herself," then, was an inspiration to Margaret — and like Abbie, she feels that her own life was more on account of Bernice: "Everything about her has always been — herself. That was one of the rare things about her. And herself — oh, it's something you don't want to lose! It's been the beauty in my life. In my busy practical life, Bernice — what she was — like a breath that blew over my life and — made it something" (183). Confronting Craig and his petty desire to possess his wife, Margaret cannot understand that he did not value this life-giving quality in Bernice: "[W]asn't it wonderful to you that beneath what you 'had' was a life too full, too rich to be *had?* I should think that would flow over your life and give it beauty" (173). Where Craig cannot accept the fact that he never had power over his wife's life, Margaret gratefully accepts the beauty added to her own existence through Bernice's profound way of being "herself." It is in this deep understanding and acceptance that Margaret is framed as the one character in the play who is closest to what Bernice "really was."

Indeed, this character conception of Margaret as the one character who truly "understands" Bernice is carefully developed throughout the entire play. Craig's life is "given beauty" not by his wife's inspirational autonomy but, to the contrary, by the idea of her utter dependence on his love. Yet while Craig, in his vanity, is all too easily convinced that he "was *everything* to Bernice. More than all the life we felt —" Margaret is not ready to believe that her friend would take her own life just because her husband was unfaithful: "(*After trying to take it in.*) I knew Bernice. She was life. She came from the whole of life. You are asking me to believe that because of — some little thing in her own life —" (177). Challenged by the preposterousness of Craig's changed image of her friend, she is strangely certain in her rejection:

> CRAIG. [...] You didn't know Bernice. You didn't know she loved me —*that way*. And I didn't know. But she did! [...] You say life broke through her — the whole of life. But Bernice didn't want — the whole of life. She wanted *me*. [...]
> (*He opens that door and goes in to Bernice.* MARGARET *stands motionless, searching, and as if something is coming to her from the rightness. When she speaks it is a denial from that inner affirmation.*)
> MARGARET. No! I say — No! [...] [to Abbie:] You understand — I say *no. I don't believe it.* What you told me —*I don't believe it* [203–04].

Margaret's wild certainty breaks down Abbie's resistance in this scene, but what she learns now is even worse than the idea that Bernice had killed herself in despair over Craig's infidelity. The news that Bernice had *wanted* Craig to think she took her own life dramatically calls into question everything Margaret had ever believed of her friend: "You are telling me her life was *hate*? (*Stops, half turns to the room where* CRAIG *is with Bernice.*) You are telling me she covered hate with — with the beauty that was like nothing else?" (206). Where Craig has apparently found something at Bernice's bedside, Margaret now feels she has lost her friend for good. With the unexpected change in Craig in the third act, however, the image of Bernice as her loving, kind, and insightful friend is restored to Margaret in the end. Convinced now that on her death-bed Bernice had sacrificed her own integrity for the chance of empowering her husband's life, at the fall of the last curtain her friend emphasizes this knowledge in a gesture which turns Bernice into nothing less than a saint:

> MARGARET. [...] (*Her voice electric.*) Oh, in all the world — since first life *moved*— has there been any beauty like the beauty of perceiving love? ... No. Not for words. (*She closes her hand, un-closes it in a slight gesture of freeing what she would not harm.*)
> CURTAIN [230].

In a discussion of Susan Glaspell's "absent heroines," Jackie Czerepinski states with regard to Margaret's role in *Bernice*: "Margaret Pierce is the seer in this play, the one who understands the truth and provides it for the audience" (148). With this interpretation, Czerepinski joins the majority of critical voices who have commented on this play since its Provincetown premier. As Sharon Friedman has summed up reactions to the play: "The critics essentially accept Margaret's word for Bernice" ("Bernice's Strange Deceit," 159). Indeed, whether they perceived of this work as a dramatic masterpiece or as a flawed example of theatrical expression, reviewers and critics never questioned Margaret's function as Bernice's rightful interpreter until Friedman suggested a different reading — and only few voices since then have followed this critic's claim that "multiple truths" are pointed to in *Bernice* (156).

In Glaspell's own lifetime most reviewers praised the play's "realistic staging" of a "search for truth" and its final victory. Heywood Broun wrote in reaction to the original staging:

> There is no finer adventure in the world, or in the theatre, than the search for truth, and no triumph so complete as its discovery. [...] [Bernice] is made to live because she has given something of herself to each of her friends. Not one of them knows her thoroughly, but by the gradual synthesis of the various memories *the true woman is re-created*" ["Realism"; my emphasis].

In the same issue of the *New York Times* John Corbin agrees: "At the end of the third act the whole truth transpires. And it is not until then that one knows in full measure the wisdom and beauty of [Bernice's] character" ("Seraphim and Cats"). Thirteen years later, Ludwig Lewisohn, too, still believes that with Margaret's final realization of Bernice's beautiful "gift to the spirit" new life is indeed made possible both for her and for Craig: "Nothing is done. Yet everything happens— death and life and a new birth" (*Expression* 194).

Whereas Glaspell's contemporaries were widely taken in by the play's depiction of a truth victorious, later critics reacted much less enthusiastically to its final argument. In Arthur Waterman's opinion, *Bernice* suggests that "deeply felt beliefs are best expressed in an indirect way through a gradual revelation with ever-increasing feeling," but he concludes that the play "goes too far perhaps from concrete reality. It needs something — some crisis, or motive for action — to give an outward framework to the more important inner conflicts" (*Susan Glaspell* 75, 76). Gerhard Bach has similarly argued that Glaspell's "unambiguous" presentation of Bernice as the "personification of a transcendental life which realizes itself through humanity, altruism, beauty, wisdom, and love" is not effective in dramatic terms (*Susan Glaspell* 129, 136, my trans.). And Bigsby finds the play "unconvincing in its mannered dialogue and stereotypical characters" and complains that "the absent Bernice never acquires the same reality and conviction as the desperate murderess of *Trifles* or even the solitary poet of [Glaspell's] later play, *Alison's House*" (*Plays* 16).[2]

While much of the play's commentary, both positive and negative, has paid too little attention to the relevance of the *method* with which Glaspell constructs Bernice's reality on stage (a method which, as I will argue, undermines Margaret's authority as seer), most critics' focus on Margaret as the herald of truth is neither a surprise nor a coincidence. Indeed, Glaspell uses an intricate web of dramaturgical elements to suggest that Margaret's interpretation of her friend as a kind, infinitely wise and unselfish human being is the "true" image of Bernice's character — and on this level of meaning, all the elements which make up an understanding of the world according to the notions of language and art as representative systems of signs strikingly prevail in the play.

As we have seen, even in the opening stage directions Bernice is described as "*a woman you would like to know, a woman of sure and beautiful instincts*" (159). That she "had no malice" is one of the first things we learn from Bernice's father, and Abbie tenderly muses that, if she was "detached," she was also "loving, and thoughtful, and gay." Adding piece by piece of their personal memories to the developing image of Bernice, every character confirms Margaret's vision of her friend as a woman who loved life, who could never "destroy anything" (183), and who was deeply happy in her chosen state of existence. As Father remarks: "[S]he had a happy life. [...] Oh, yes. She did. In her own way. A calm way, but very full of her own kind of happiness" (193–94). That Bernice would never have killed herself, most certainly not out of despair over Craig's infidelity, is not only established by Margaret (to Craig: "I don't think you had the power to make her very unhappy," 172). Craig's sister Laura similarly believes that her brother's affairs never hurt his wife, and Abbie had not noticed any trace of unhappiness in Bernice before she died. Even Craig himself (as much as he has suffered from his wife's indifference) was certain that in spite of her love she was somehow left unfettered by his unfaithfulness: "Bernice knew I was staying out on Long Island with [the Fredericks] while I was attending to some things about my work. I had a beautiful letter from Bernice. She was perfectly all right — about everything."

In addition to the fact that all other voices in the play clearly support Margaret's picture of Bernice as serene and beautiful, it seems that Bernice herself had trusted her friend to "see" the truth about her. Even before Father and Abbie turn to a discussion of Bernice's character, they establish the singular connection which had existed between Bernice and Margaret:

> FATHER. But Margaret Pierce will be here soon. As soon as she can get here, Margaret will come. [...]
> ABBIE. (*Apprehensive.*) You think so, sir?

> FATHER. I think so. [...] Yes, Margaret will get here the quickest way. She
> always came to Bernice when Bernice needed her.
> ABBIE. She doesn't need anyone now.
> FATHER. No. But yes—in a way, she does. She needs some one to be here
> to do what she can't go on doing. Margaret will see that — when she knows.
> Margaret sees everything.
> ABBIE. (*Frightened now.*) You think so, sir?
> FATHER. Oh, yes, she does. Bernice knew that. 'Margaret sees things,' I've
> heard Bernice say [...] [161].

Once established, Margaret's authorization as Bernice's spokeswoman
on stage is enforced through a number of additional instances. Thus, at the
very point that "the truth" seems to slip away from her at the news of Bernice's grave lie ("I've lost my seeing. It was through her I saw. It was through
Bernice I could see. And now it's dark" 215), the connection is restored when
Father movingly entrusts Margaret with his confidential account of Bernice's
dying moment. For Bernice had left this world with her friend's name on
her lips: "She breathed [your name]. It seemed to come from her whole life.
[...] Why I don't think you ever were as close to Bernice as when she said
your name and died" (220).

Certainly, at this point Margaret does not yet understand. Struck by
despair, she feels she must free Craig of the unjust burden he now carries in
thinking himself responsible for Bernice's death. But Craig himself presents
her with the missing piece in the puzzle. Now that he knows how great his
wife's love was for him (and how profound had been his influence on her),
he has found a reason to go on and become a better person:

> CRAIG. I was thinking [...] if I knew only — what I knew when I came here —
> that Bernice was dead — I wonder if I could have got past that failure.
> MARGARET. Failure, Craig?
> CRAIG. Of never having had her. That she had lived, and loved me [...] and
> died without my ever having had her. What would there have been to go
> on living for? Why should such a person go on living? Now — of course it
> is another world. This comes crashing through my make-believe — and Bernice's world get to me [*sic*]. Don't you *see*, Margaret?
> MARGARET: Perhaps— I do. (*She looks at the closed door; looks back to him.
> Waits.*] O-h. (*Waits again, and it grows in her.*) Perhaps I do. (*Turns and
> very slowly goes to the closed door, opens it, goes in.*) [226–27].

That on the grounds of Margaret's sudden understanding in this scene Bernice's "true identity" is indeed reestablished at the end of the play is emphasized not only by this character's newly-gained ability to "go in" to Bernice
(she is now certain that she has access to her friend's innermost reality). In
a further symbolic use of setting, Margaret's view is also confirmed when a
moment later she "*comes out from the room where she has been with Bernice*"
and leaves the door — symbol of Bernice's detachment throughout the entire
play —"*wide open behind her*" (228).[3] Finally, in yet another symbolic ges-

ture Bernice's image is re-established as the living-room, whose furniture Father had moved at the beginning of the first act because he could not bear the way in which "everything [was] Bernice" (160), is now "given back" to her:

> FATHER. (*Seeing what has been done to the room.*) Oh, you have given the room back to Bernice!
> MARGARET. Given everything back to Bernice. Bernice. Insight. The tenderness of insight. And the courage [229].

Significantly, in combination with the pervasive image of Bernice Norris as a divine spirit, the play's presentation of Margaret as the seer who understands the absent woman's innermost being enhances the idea of a transcendental reality which can be brought out into the open, and with it the notion of a Kantian-Cartesian self which can observe this reality from a distance. Moreover, in this conceptual context language and art are once more perceived to operate as representative systems of signs: In *Bernice*, Glaspell dramatizes her characters' attempt to hold on to the idealist belief that we can cross the gap between our isolated states of existence and express ourselves to the world.

As we have seen, Bernice's most characteristic trait was her peculiar "detachedness." Content in her isolation, she had lived with only her maid Abbie and her father for company — two people who were close to her and loved her dearly, but who admit that they never quite "understood" her. She was married, and she loved her husband, but even from this relationship a part of her — the part that was most "Bernice" — was pointedly disconnected. Closer to her inner self than anybody else had been her best friend Margaret. Margaret was the one who could reach out farthest in "getting *to*" Bernice — but even she only "got to" her "so far as she had the power" (173). And while the shut door to the room where Bernice lies in state symbolizes the distinct limits of how close one could ever get to her almost to the very end of the play, it was her "by herself-ness" which Margaret had always cherished most: "She had the gift for being herself. And she wanted each one to have the chance to be himself. [...]" (188). Indeed, as Margaret points out here, Bernice did not only insist on her own independence, she encouraged others to find their true inner selves as well.

In this context, Bernice's peculiar aloofness is seen as the expression of her unusual courage to adhere only to her own notions of life, untouched by any form of social connection or influence. In her lonesome ramblings through the woods, in her "affectionate amusement" with regard to other people's concerns, Bernice "simply and profoundly got to *life*." The play arranges this singular achievement in a sharp contrast to the other characters' manifold entangled failures to be authentic. Father once fought for his beliefs but gave up on them long ago. Margaret still keeps up the fight for what she deems important but loses herself in the struggle. Laura is made up entirely of social norms. And Craig uses his writing only to conceal his fundamental lack of purpose. In this way, each character's struggle to come to terms with Bernice's death is framed as an edging towards the truth not only with regard to the dead woman's identity, but also with regard to his or her own self—inner selves which need to be dug out from far beneath the debris of social norms and ineffective communication.

As part of this concept of a transcendental self in search for the truth about life, language is understood as the vehicle to express this truth in *Bernice*. While the idealist notion of communication is evident everywhere in the play, it is Margaret who serves as its most prominent representative. When Laura defends her brother's failure to be at Bernice's side in her last moments with the weak explanation that "there were things connected with his writing to see about," Margaret retorts: "Laura! Don't *lie* about life with death in the next room. If you want to talk at a time like this, have the decency to be honest! Try to see the *truth* about living. Craig stayed in New York with May Fredericks—and he doesn't pretend anything else" (185–86). Importantly, in her attempt to force Laura into acknowledging Craig's infidelity, Margaret overcomes her feeling that what Bernice was "about" cannot be expressed in words. Indeed, she manages to be clear enough as she approaches her point from the angle of Craig's and Bernice's relationship:

> I cannot talk to you about what Bernice "should have been." What she was came true and deep from —(*Throwing out her hands as if giving up saying it.* <u>Taking it up again.</u>) It's true there was something in her Craig did not control. Something he couldn't *mess up*. There was something in her he might have drawn from and become bigger than he was. But he's vain. He has to be bowling some one over all the time — to show that he has *power* [186; my emphasis].

While Margaret's stubborn drive at "the truth about living" is closely connected to the faculty of "sight" throughout the play, at this point she still insists that the light can be brought through *words*. In fact, in a key conversation with Craig during the second act, Margaret formulates an ardent credo of what a *writer*— as someone who uses words professionally —"might do for life" (and this, perhaps, might well be read as an expression of Glaspell's own demands on her art):

> MARGARET. [...] You write so well, Craig, but —what of it? What is it is the matter with you — with all you American writers—'most all of you. A well-put-up light — but it doesn't penetrate anything. It never makes the fog part. Just shows itself off— a well-put-up light. [...] Craig, as you write these things are there never times when you sit there *dumb* and know that you are glib and empty? [...]
> CRAIG. I should think you'd want to be good to me tonight, Margaret.
> MARGARET. Be good to you! Keep you from seeing [...] [199–200].

On the other hand, next to this belief in the power of language (and art!) to "light those never lighted places" (201), there also runs through the play a parallel notion that the heart of life cannot be expressed in words. More than of anything Margaret might actually *say* to Abbie, the maid is afraid of her piercing *look* (see 181). And as we learn, this fear is not unjustified, for Margaret is able to "see things" without "being told" (215). It is only consistent with this concept of understanding as a process of seeing rather than speaking that when Margaret wants to take Abbie in to her newly-gained knowledge of Bernice, what she knows is "not for words": "Oh — Abbie. Yes — I know now. I want you to know. Only — there are things not for words. Feeling — not for words. As a throbbing thing that flies and sings— not for the hand. (*She starts to close her hand, uncloses it*)" (229). Where language proves insufficient, a symbolic gesture is substituted as a more effective means of conveying the most profound levels of meaning here — and the same gesture is also what the audience is left with at the play's final curtain: "MARGARET. [...] No. Not for words. (*She closes her hand, uncloses it in a slight gesture of freeing what she would not harm.*)" (230).

Of course, both Margaret's belief in "honest talk" and "real writing" and her sense of knowing the truth by seeing into it directly are incidents of the idealist's notion of communication, and in the play's final scene this trust indeed seems to reign supreme. At the same time, Glaspell has added a persistent undercurrent of doubt to the play in which she tries to come to terms with the skeptic's position inevitably raised as well on the grounds of the symbol model of language. As we have seen, Margaret's certainty is severely shaken first by the news that Bernice killed herself and later by the idea that the suicide-lie was her friend's cruel revenge on her husband. And in both instances, Margaret was temporarily forced into the devastating conclusion that she had never "known" Bernice, after all.

Indeed, in the struggle between Margaret and Craig over Bernice's identity the notion of a failure to know each other gains prominence in the play. When Margaret rejects the news of her friend's suicide by insisting that it "isn't right that there should be anything in Bernice not Bernice," Craig directly attacks this character's authority to define who Bernice was: "You say it isn't right — and so you leave it out [what Bernice did because of me]? [...] "In the rightness!" Is that for you to say? Is rightness what you think? What you can see? No. You didn't know Bernice. You didn't know she loved me — *that way*" (203). Yet in the same breath he has to admit that he himself did not "know," either: "How *could* I have had that — and not *known*?" Craig asks Margaret in desperation. As he trusts Bernice's final "message"[4] to him more than his own experiential knowledge of his wife, this is the question which most seems to torment Craig. How could he have "missed" the existential quality of her love? How, indeed, can we ever "know" each other? Craig's conclusion, for the time being, is that we are ultimately incapable of bridging the gap between each other's isolated minds: "Why did I never know Bernice loved me like this? (*In anguish.*) Why wouldn't I *know* it? (*Pause.*) We don't know *anything* about each other. Do we, Margaret? Nothing. We never — get anywhere" (194).

Moreover, by the end of the play the idealist's view is reinstalled *both* for Margaret *and* for Craig — and since these two characters' interpretations of who Bernice "really was" are mutually exclusive, the play's final imagery of understanding on the basis of the symbol model serves to support the skeptic's doubts. Convinced that Bernice killed herself because she could not bear his infidelity, Craig can now "go in" to her, find "something wonderful" at her side, and come back to "return" the living-room to her presence. These, however, are precisely the same symbolic movements which later in the play indicate *Margaret's* final insight. Craig even comes to share her conviction that the most profound things in life are not for words. "I know," he misinterprets Margaret's difficulties in telling him the truth about Bernice's death. "We can't say things. When we get right *to* life — we can't say things" (225–26). Of course, the very irony of this scene lies in the suggestion that Craig has been taken further away than ever from Bernice's true self. But if Craig's and Margaret's routes to "the truth" resemble each other so closely in the symbolic language of the play as to be virtually indistinguishable, how can we be certain about who is wrong and who is right? How, indeed, do we "know?" As Craig hurls this question at his sister Laura, it remains one of the central issues explored in *Bernice*: "How do we know who's hurt? Who isn't? Who loves— who doesn't love? Don't *talk*, Laura" (178).

Three years before the premier of *Bernice*, Glaspell had formulated the same question in "A Jury of Her Peers." In her short-story version of *Trifles* Mrs. Hale asks Mrs. Peters: "[Why] do you and I *understand*? Why do we *know* what we know this minute?" (Rabkin 303). And similar to her presentation of how the two women uncover the story of Minnie and John Wright, in *Bernice*, too, Glaspell makes clear that her characters "know what they know" through their *interactional experiences of each other*. When Craig cuts off Laura's assertion that Bernice did not suffer from his infidelities, he implies that his sister's assessment is far from how things "really were." While this notion is part of the symbol model of language, in effect Craig rejects the particular part which Laura takes in "languageing" the meaning of his marriage in this scene ("Don't *talk*, Laura"). Indeed, in more ways than one this scene demonstrates that "communicative contact" (our way of experiencing life through language) is precisely how we come to "know" people in the first place. After all, Laura was never *told* that Bernice was left unfettered by Craig's affairs; she has gathered this from her personal experiences of interacting with her sister-in-law. And Craig himself, as we can conclude by the way he remembers his wife, has a similar practical knowledge of Bernice: His first intuitive reaction to Abbie's news of his wife's suicide is to accuse her of lying (see 175).

Even Margaret, for all the imagery of "seeing" connected to her character, has gathered her understanding of Bernice's identity through communicative interaction. Many times in the play she yearns to *talk* to Bernice, and even before this longing is motivated by her desire to learn the truth about Bernice's final moments, she misses their conversations as the essential experience which made their friendship. Moreover, the play's "seer" loses her grip on her image of Bernice precisely when something she learns about her does not "make sense" in relation to her life-long experiential knowledge of her friend. Hence, at the same time that Glaspell enhances the notion of a transcendental truth in *Bernice* she also dramatizes the Wittgensteinian notion that we know things to be true to the extent that we have experienced them as certain in our interactions with others.

As was already the case in *Trifles*, *The People*, and *The Outside*, *Bernice* signifies its acknowledgment of the existential connection between human beings when its imagery moves from the concept of detached observation ("seeing") to one of emotional involvement ("feeling"). This subtle change of imagery is especially effective in undermining the play's idea of abstract truth as it slips in the very moment Margaret attempts to answer Laura's question about her work as honestly as she knows how. Suddenly, the idea of "seeing" things (from a distance) is mixed with the concept of understanding achieved through empathy:

> MARGARET. [...] I am trying to get out of prison all those people who are imprisoned for ideas.
> LAURA. I see.
> MARGARET. I doubt if you see, Laura.
> LAURA. Well I don't say I sympathize. But I see.
> MARGARET. No; for if you did see, you would have to sympathize. If you did see, you would be ashamed; you would have to— hang your head for this thing of locking any man up because of what his mind sees [...] [187].

What Margaret argues here is that understanding can only be achieved through personal involvement — through a readiness to be touched both by ideas and by people's lives. Realizing how much she has antagonized Laura in her insistence on the "truth" about Craig's infidelities, she attempts to bridge the gulf between them in a telling gesture of "reaching out her hands":

> MARGARET. There's nothing insulting in trying to find the truth. (*Impulsively reaching out her hands to* LAURA, *as she is indignantly going.*) Oh Laura, we die so soon! We live so in the dark. We never become what we might be. I should think we could help each other more.
> LAURA. (*After being a moment held.*) It would have to be done more sympathetically [189–90].

Yet Margaret is unable to reach Laura precisely because she has failed to link up to her on an emotional level — something she immediately admits to: "I didn't mean to be unsympathetic. (*Watching* LAURA *go upstairs.*) I suppose that's the trouble with me" (190).

"*Thinking of this*," Margaret finds herself utterly alone with her idea of truth, and instinctively she turns to Bernice for companionship. As she realizes that her friend will never again be there to talk things over with, she calls out for Craig instead.[5] In the conversation which ensues, both acknowledge their need for human company. While Craig addresses Margaret in her function as "seer," he simultaneously calls on her faculty of sympathy: "What do you think it is is the matter with me, Margaret, that I — (*Saying it as if raw*) miss things." — "You can tell me. I'd be glad to feel some one knew. Only — don't leave me alone while you're telling me!" (196). And Margaret, in her very search for "light," acknowledges the existential principle of *connection* through a sense that our lives are strangely interrelated:

> MARGARET. (*Intensely.*) [...] It's a strange thing this has done. A light trying to find its way through a fog. (*In her mind the light tries to do this.*) Craig, why do you write the things you do?
> CRAIG. Oh, Margaret, is this any time to talk of work?
> MARGARET. It seems to be. Tonight it's all part of the same thing. Laura and I were talking of work — quarreling about it: you were talking of Bernice's father. The light — just goes there. That poor sad old man — why didn't he go on? You said he was a wreck of the Darwinian theory. Then me — a wreck of free speech [197–98].

As they go on to speak of their work, of the beliefs their lives are built on, of Bernice and all she has meant to them, Margaret and Craig thus negotiate their own identities within the web of relations which give meaning to their lives. Not what Bernice was "really like," then, is at the center of Glaspell's attention as she portrays her characters' struggle to get at the "truth" about her. What she focuses on instead is the very *process* in which Bernice is recreated through the interactions of her on-stage characters.

Eventually, it is Bernice's father who moves from the mere awareness that they are not "separate" in their grief over Bernice's loss to the attempt of creating her in a common act of remembrance. On the morning that his daughter will be "taken away" to the cemetery, he calls Craig and Margaret to sit with him in the living-room, urging them both:

> FATHER. [...] Let's not try to keep away from each other now. We're all going through the same thing — in our — our different ways. [...] She loved you so, Margaret. Didn't she, Craig? [...] She had great beauty — didn't she, Margaret? [...] I was thinking last night — malice was not in Bernice. I never knew her to do a — really unfriendly thing to any one [221].

As he draws up Bernice's presence through her relationships to her friends and family (and through the image of her "friendliness" towards other peo-

ple in general), Father suddenly stresses her "connectedness" over the detachment previously evoked as his daughter's most characteristic trait. What is
more, afraid that Bernice will "slip away" from them in death Father wants
to *speak* of her now in order to "keep [her] for us all": "You know, Margaret,
I had thought you would say things like this—and better than I can say them,
to—to keep my little girl for us all. I suppose I'm a foolish old man but I
seem to want them said" (221–22). As we know, at this point in the play
Margaret cannot participate in bringing Bernice back in such a way because
she does not "have" her anymore. Unable to place her friend's final wish into
the context of her personal experiences, she feels cut off from who Bernice
"really" was. Yet when she finally understands Bernice's "gift to the spirit"
at the very end of the play, Margaret feels a similar urge to speak of her friend
and bring her back, even if she claims she cannot express what she knows in
words. Just as Father wants the things "said" which will "keep" Bernice for
him, it is not enough for Margaret to know her friend in her heart. She has
to communicate her knowledge to others in order to make it real. As Barbara Ozieblo has pointed out in her reading of the play: "[Margaret] must
share her insight with Abbie in order to return Bernice to the living or at
least vindicate her" (*Susan Glaspell* 145).

Hence what the characters on stage have been doing in their constant
struggles over who holds the most truthful version of Bernice is to *create*
this absent character for the audience. Strikingly, of all characters in the play
it is again Margaret who points out that Bernice herself will never again be
able to set right the images circulating of her. In an attempt to protect her
friend from Laura's idea of how Bernice should have behaved in life, she
calls out: "Oh Laura, Bernice will never say one more word for herself! In
there. Alone. Still. She will not do one new thing to—to throw a light back
on other things. That's death. A *leaving* of one's life. Leaving it—with us"
(186). Indeed, the meaning of Bernice's life and dying is left with the living,
and each of Glaspell's characters pursues pointedly personal interests in the
reconstruction of the dead woman's personality. Defending Bernice's image
as detached from ordinary life because this idea is precisely what has given
her own life "beauty," Margaret scorns Craig's desire to "reshape" his wife
not only as petty, but as fundamentally impossible: "Craig! 'Reshape' Bernice!" (174). Yet a constant "reshaping" of Bernice's identity is precisely what
all characters, including Margaret, have been engaged with throughout the
play. And because Bernice is dead before the curtain rises, we have no way
of knowing whether it is the "true woman" who is recreated on stage in the
end—even if Heywood Broun's acknowledgment of Margaret's authority as
"seer" has been repeated in almost every response to the play since its first
MacDougal Street staging.

Instead, Glaspell has led her audience to witness a process in which, in

Susan Kattwinkel's words, the characters "have each constructed [Bernice's] identity in a way that fits their own needs" (43). Perhaps the most obvious of these constructions is presented in Craig's willingness to believe that Bernice "*killed* herself because she loved me so" (176). While Father, unaware of all that is going on, wants to remember her as his "little girl" who was good to everyone and who "did rejoice so in the world" (178), Craig is ready to accept the idea of Bernice's suicide because it gives him the power he had never felt over her in life. In this bizarre way, his life is given new meaning as he "reshapes" Bernice into the image of a suffering and lonesome wife desperate for her husband's love.

Where this notion gives Craig a self-confidence and direction never before experienced, it pushes Margaret into an abyss of uncertainty. Desperate to hold on to the image of her divine friend who gave beauty to her own busy life, *she* has to "leave out" Bernice's suicide, even if she is forced to accept it as "fact": "I don't say it isn't fact. I say it isn't —*in the rightness*" (203). When Margaret is finally forced to admit that she had never "known" her friend, after all, the ground under her feet gives way. The only thing left for her is to cling to the one principle which she thought had always guided her relationship to Bernice: the desire to be faithful to "the truth about living." As she insists that she must free Craig of his feelings of guilt, in her conviction that he needs to be told the true circumstances of Bernice's death Margaret struggles to protect her own sense of identity. In her confrontation with Abbie, she cries out: "I couldn't *live*—feeling I had left on him what shouldn't be there" (212). And a moment later: "I tell you there's something in me can't *stand* it to see anyone go down under a thing he shouldn't have to bear. *Why that feeling has made my life*" (215–16; my emphasis). If Margaret, already forced to view her life-long image of Bernice as a deception, were to give up her very belief in "truth" as the all-encompassing value in her life, there would be nothing left for her to live by. At the end of the play, therefore, she is ready to interpret Bernice's last act as a "gift to the spirit" because this notion restores to her the very principles her own life is built upon.

Importantly, however, Margaret's final vision of Bernice does not coincide with her original image of her friend. Although it is true that her view of Bernice as beautiful and serene is saved for her when events offer her the possibility to reconcile the suicide-lie with her personal memories of her friend, Margaret's final understanding is created in a *collaboration* between herself and Bernice's father. Indeed, in a twist which is hardly ever acknowledged in discussions of Margaret's move towards "insight," she can only interpret the change in Craig as intended by Bernice because Father has previously added to and thus changed something in Margaret's life-long perception of the other woman. Shortly before she witnesses Craig's conversion,

Father confides in Margaret that he believes Bernice did not feel right about her peculiar detachedness, after all. Pondering the way in which she had kept her innermost self from every other human being, he tells Margaret:

> I think it wasn't that she — wanted it that way. You know, Margaret, I felt something — very wistful in Bernice. [...] As if she wanted to give us more. Oh — she gave more than any one else could have given. But not *all* she was. And she would like to have given us — all she was. She wanted to give — what couldn't be given. [...] I see it now. (*After thinking.*) I think Bernice feared she was not a very good wife for Craig. (MARGARET <u>gives him a startled look</u>.) Little things she'd say. I don't know — perhaps I'm wrong [223–24; my emphasis].

Even as Father admits that he cannot be certain whether he has read Bernice correctly, his very suggestion that she might have wanted to connect to people more indicates that this, at least, is what he thinks his daughter *should* have felt. Joining sides with Laura and Craig in their belief that a man should dominate his wife, he confirms that her aloofness is something that needs to be excused or vindicated, especially in her relationship with her husband: "Craig didn't dominate Bernice. I don't know whose fault it was. I don't know that it was anyone's fault. Just the way things were. He — I say it in all kindness, he just didn't — have it in him" (224).

Margaret's final conclusion about what Bernice had done, therefore, is based on thoughts introduced by Father in order to fit his memories of his daughter to his general understanding of the world. As a result of this complex instance of "worlding," in the end Margaret has given up entirely on her original image of Bernice's independence from the world. In order to save the idea that her friend's life was "beautiful," she is forced to sacrifice one of her own most cherished abstract principles. While this sacrifice goes completely unnoticed both in the play itself and in its criticism, it nevertheless demonstrates that — as is the case with all other characters in *Bernice*— Margaret's allegedly superior "vision" of Bernice's essential identity is guided by nothing other than her own feelings towards Bernice: her love forged in a long and intimate friendship.[6]

Of all characters in the play, it is the maid Abbie who is most explicit about what is at stake in dealing with Bernice's final hour. When Margaret is about to tell Craig that the news about Bernice's suicide was a lie which his wife had wanted Abbie to tell, Abbie implores the other woman to "leave out" this "[one] ugly thing in a whole beautiful life" (217). As she tries to explain Bernice's deathbed wish to herself, her thoughts are not aimed at "finding the truth" but at creating an explanation which will enable her to keep on loving Bernice. At the same time, she introduces a new idea to the play as she pleads for the need to keep Bernice "safe" from the way in which her deathbed wish might be interpreted by others:

ABBIE. (*Her voice breaking.*) Oh, Miss Margaret, it was right at the very *end* of her life. Maybe when we're going to die things we've borne all our lives are things we can't bear any longer.

[...]

If all those years with him there was something she hid, and if she seemed to feel — what she didn't feel. She did it well, didn't she? — and almost to the last. Shan't we hide it now? For her? You and me who loved her — isn't she *safe* — with us? [216–17].

"*In a last deeply emotional appeal,*" Abbie urges Margaret to protect Bernice because she "did a great deal" for both their lives (217). "[*Going*] *nearer Margaret*" (ibid.), she thus brings to the fore the full force of the connection that links Bernice to the living. And where Margaret defends her belief in separate souls and abstract truths, Abbie does not only acknowledge the influence Bernice had exercised on the lives of those who loved her. She also recognizes that the connection goes *both ways*, as Margaret and Abbie now have the power to influence how Bernice will be remembered and interpreted in the future.

In this way, whereas Margaret, the "seer," can be understood to represent the concept of a transcendental truth (and, consequently, of language as a representative system of signs which serves to express this truth) in this play, Abbie introduces the opposing concept of a reality constituted in communicative contact. Of all the play's characters, Abbie is the one who understands that we change reality in the very way in which we use language in order to follow some experiences as "right" and decide to "leave out" others (and perhaps it is no coincidence, then, that Glaspell herself played Abbie — not Margaret — in the original Provincetown production). True enough, even Margaret as the "seer" hits on the creative (or, in her eyes, destructive) power of language as articulate contact when she is forced to face Abbie's account of Bernice's final hour: "I don't know what you're *telling* me!" she calls out in despair. "You don't know *what* you're doing. You do this *now* — after she can do nothing? (*Holding out her hands.*) Abbie! Tell me it isn't true!" (206). But Abbie is the one character who most consistently represents the idea of "doing something" with words in this play. Insisting that her fight is for Bernice and her untainted memory, she struggles for her own sanity as much as do all other characters throughout the play. She feels that she has already paid a high price in fulfilling Bernice's death-bed wish, and for this very reason she cannot now allow Margaret to change reality in a way that does not agree with Bernice's plan (even if she cannot understand what this plan might have been in the first place): "ABBIE. (*Harshly.*) Why did you *know* — what you weren't to know? But if you have some way of knowing what you aren't told — you think you have the right to do *your* thing with that? Undo what she did? What *I* did? Do you know what it took *out* of me to do this? There's nothing left of me" (213).

As Abbie here draws attention to what it would "do" both to herself and to Bernice's memory if Margaret told Craig the truth, she also raises the question of what this knowledge of Bernice's final lie would "do" to *Craig*:

> ABBIE. And you'd go to him and — what *for*?
> MARGARET. Because I can't *live*—leaving that on him — having him think — when I know he didn't. I can't leave that on him one more hour.
> ABBIE. (*Standing in the door to block her going.*) And when you take that from him —*what do you give to him*?
> (*They stare at one another*; MARGARET *falls back.*) [214].

In this way, Abbie adds an idea to the play which provides a constant under-current of meaning in *Bernice*: the notion that for those who understand the communicative mechanisms of how reality is created in interaction, the knowledge of this process entails a fair amount of manipulative power.[7]

Interestingly, this aspect of power involved in Bernice's suicide-lie is ignored both in those readings which accept Margaret's interpretation of this act as rare and beautiful, and in later interpretations that dismiss the play's construction of meaning as based on a number of unsuccessful dramatic techniques. In contrast, much more sensitive to the significance of Glaspell's technique of absence in this and other plays, feminist criticism has noted the idea of influence when it discusses Bernice's marriage as an example of the struggle for power in patriarchal gender relations. Including *Bernice* in her study of Glaspell's "women on the edge," Christine Dymkowski has underscored the creative potential in Bernice's act: "By using her death to convince Craig that he had the power over her he yearned for, Bernice, from her remote position, exercises a liberating power of her own" (97). And while it does not become entirely clear in this reading why Bernice's lie leaves her husband "free scope" in his reaction (ibid. 98), Jackie Czerepinski, too, emphasizes that "[death] — absence — gives Bernice a power she did not have in life" (149).

If it does seem, then, that Bernice is the superior player in the play's Wittgensteinian language-games, her triumph is not as positive — or even as obvious— as some interpretations suggest. Thus, Barbara Ozieblo highlights not only the empowering aspect of Bernice's final action, but also the backlash to female individuality it simultaneously entails: "Bernice, in death, shows herself to be her husband's master. Ironically, of course, she also gives him the one thing he had demanded of her all along: fuel for his sputtering ego" (*Susan Glaspell* 146). And indeed, as Sharon Friedman has pointed out, "the real Bernice remains enigmatic, silent, and inaccessible" ("Bernice's Strange Deceit," 161). As a result of her absence, the meaning of her final act can ultimately not be determined. *Bernice*, thus Friedman insists, "is a play built on a wife's deception, and the audience is left to sort out the conflicting meanings that emerge when fantasy is the instrument of revolt" (ibid.

156). The only thing the audience does know for certain by the end is that Bernice attempted to manipulate the play's on-stage characters into "playing her game" in the creation of meaning — and not even the question whether the outcome is really what Bernice had intended with her "strange deceit" (Friedman) is resolved beyond all doubt at the final curtain.[8]

It might not be possible, then, to take a final stand with regard to Bernice's deathbed lie. Regardless of how we might contextualize and evaluate the absent woman's final act, however, on the play's final note Susan Glaspell demonstrates that as human beings we do not live in a vacuum — and that communication is our very way of living. Father might be right in surmising that Bernice recognized her aloofness as a mistake (or as an unfortunate twist of her personality, or even as the detestable last resort of a woman who could not otherwise be "herself" in patriarchal society), and that she longed to "reach out" to her husband and to all those around her. Possibly, at the end of her life Bernice accepted Laura's criticism of drawing away from the social sphere, and thought of her distanced amusement with regard to other people's lives with regret. Perhaps she eventually acknowledged that she was not disconnected from others. Perhaps, as Abbie thinks, during her final hours Bernice admitted to her pain in Craig's affairs, and gave in to her feelings of revenge. In whatever way Bernice's final act is interpreted, however, if there is one "message" connected to the dying woman's final words and the play's ensuing chain of events, one more time in Glaspell's oeuvre it is that, for better or for worse, human existence is irreducibly social.[9]

Remembering his daughter as a little girl Father muses: "She was such a nice baby. She used to — reach out her hands. (*Doing this himself.*) Well, I suppose they all do" (194). Even as he immediately takes back the meaning of the gesture in its special significance for Bernice, the realization that *all* babies "reach out their hands" underscores the play's acknowledgment of all humans' fundamentally connected existence. Indeed, both the symbolism of reaching out one's hands and the theme of love in connection with the idea of "doing something" to life are repeated in Abbie's account of Bernice's final hour. And since this is the scene which calls up the most immediate image of the absent title figure in the play, the passage is crucial enough to quote it in its entirety:

> ABBIE. There were two hours when she was — quiet. Quiet — not like any quiet I ever knew. Thinking. You could see thinking in her eyes — stronger than sickness. Then, after ten, she called me to her. She took my hands. She said, "Abbie, you've lived with me all my life." "Yes," I said. "You love me." "Oh, yes," I said. "Will you do something for me?" "You know I will," I told her. "Abbie," she said, looking right at me, *all* of her looking right at me, "if I die, I want you to tell my husband I killed myself." (MARGARET *falls back.*) Yes, I did that too. Then I thought it was her mind. But I looked at her, and oh, her mind was there! It was terrible — how it was all *there.*

She said — and then she (*The sobs she has been holding back almost keep* ABBIE *from saying this*) — held out her hands to me — "Oh, Abbie, do this last thing for me! After all there has been, I have a *right* to do it. If my life is going — let me have *this* much from it!" [...] [206].

If Craig's restoration of Bernice's room as the recreation of her "true self" is based on a lie and thus highly questionable in its symbolism, the door which is opened wide between her and her fellow human beings might be read instead to admit to the ambivalent influence which the dead woman has exerted throughout the play on the act of creating meaning.

Once more in Glaspell's oeuvre, then, the very vagueness of her concept of "truth" does not point to a weakness in dramatic composition, but to a profound conceptual shift from an understanding of language as a representative system of signs towards a contradicting concept of communication as constitutive articulate contact. In *Trifles*, this shift became manifest in the way in which all characters were shown to "world" John and Minnie Wright's story in their interactions on stage. In *The People*, it was aimed at demonstrating the positive power of creating a new world through art after a devastating war. In *The Outside*, it turned to examine not only the creative power of (female) communication, but also the stifling bonds with which human community in general (and theatrical convention in particular) limits individual lives (especially women's, or those of female artists, respectively). In *Bernice*, her first full-length play, Glaspell proceeded to discuss both the limiting and the liberating effects of a philosophy which recognizes the communality of human existence in a more complex argument, including all three subject positions of "self," "woman," and "artist" in the composition. And indeed, read in this context Glaspell's decision to frame the character of Margaret as the "seer" in this play appears as a dramaturgical move which is the precise mirror image of her title character's strategy of manipulating meaning. As a result, with the particular way in which Glaspell uses her hallmark technique of the absent figure in *Bernice* she both stresses the degree of control which the concept of meaning created in constitutive articulate contact still entails for the individual, and provides, once again, a sophisticated aesthetic comment on the limits of this influence. For, once again, whether any one of the interpretations which have been offered since the first Provincetown production is really what the author "intended" when she wrote her play will of course remain as much in the dark as does its title character's own enigmatic "plan."

7. *Chains of Dew* (1919/1922)

An Artist's Social Responsibilities
and a Woman's Binding Love

Bernice, brought to the Provincetown stage in March 1919, creates the image of a woman who had always guarded her inner self against all outward demands but who acknowledges the communal nature of her existence in the hour of her death. Hidden from the spectators' view, Bernice had faced the complex consequences born out of her love for her husband, and in the competing interpretations developed through the play's onstage characters her final move is presented both as the loss of a soul's independence and as the enhancement of a woman's self-assertion. In *Chains of Dew*—first performed at the Playwrights' Theatre in 1922, but probably written during the sabbatical leave which Glaspell and Cook took from the Players after the 1918/19 New York season[1]— again a woman acknowledges the connection between her reality and that of her husband. This time, however, Glaspell leaves no room for a suggestion of freedom in the decisions open to a woman who loves. Whereas in many plays before this one Glaspell's notion of life as created in communicative interaction has suggested the possibility of a change for the better, in *Chains of Dew* this model of language and art bears only negative consequences, both for the individual and for society.

Seymore Standish is a reputable businessman and respected member of his Midwestern hometown community. Convinced of the duties attached to his prominent position, he lives out his destiny as one of the pillars of society in the roles of husband, father, bank director, and vestryman. At the same time, he is also one of the country's leading poets. The crux of this double life is that a fundamental idea of sacrifice lies at the very heart of the man's poetic inspiration. Without the illusion of being chained to the superficial world of his hometown by an unrelenting sense of responsibility, he would dissolve both as a poet whose verse lives solely in its cry for freedom, and as a human being whose very identity is forged in the terms of ever-lasting bondage. Because Bernice reaches out to her husband only at the very end of her life, she is able to gratify Craig's need for power and still reinforce her own identity. As Dotty Standish has to face the binding force of her love when she has only just awakened to a sense of her own self, she is not free to realize her desire for inward independence and outward self-assertion in the same way.

This introduction to the play's theme highlights the aspect of (female) tragedy in *Chains of Dew*. The piece, however, is subtitled "A Comedy in three Acts" and indeed presents itself as such — a social comedy — throughout its expository scenes.[2] At the rise of the first curtain, Seymore Standish is expected at the headquarters of the New York Birth Control League by his friends Nora Powers, "who works for Birth Control," and Leon Whittaker, "associate editor of the New Nation" (list of characters, 1.1). Right from the start, the poet is at the center of attention as Leon — presently seconded by James O'Brien, "a young Irishman visiting America" (ibid.) — struggles to grasp the nature of his admired friend's artistic shortcomings. Apparently, despite the promising passion of Seymore's work, even his best pieces lack an unspecifiable quality which would raise his talent to a standard of greatness comparable to that of Shelley. When Seymore eventually turns up (significantly late from a visit to his wife's aunt), he is quick to provide an explanation for what might be the matter with him. With an air of bravery he confronts his bohemian friends with the utterly conservative nature of his Midwestern existence. Befittingly appalled, Leon, Nora and O'Brien conclude that Seymore could soar to unknown poetic heights if he only broke free from his chains of respectability. At the end of the first act, Nora sets out to begin her field campaign for Birth Control in Seymore's hometown — out on a mission to free the poet by ruining the man with the help of her radical convictions and irresistible New Woman charms.

In a structural juxtaposition which prevents the male characters' existential groping for truth from taking on too many serious overtones, all throughout the first act the subject of Seymore's poetic achievements is blithely complemented by Nora's passion for Birth Control and by her flirtatious insinuations. Yet the light satire which Glaspell thus connects to the themes of bobbed hair, free love, and birth control is unexpectedly supplemented with Dotty Standish's personal tragedy when the second act moves the action to "Bluff City," the site of the poet's supposed "bondage." Indeed, a confusing mix of comic and tragic elements sets in as we learn that Dotty, far from being the dunderhead who needs to be held secure in her world of bridge and gossip, has cancelled tea and dinner parties in order to make time for new acquaintances with the local intelligentsia and for a correspondence course on poetry. When Nora whirls in to scandalize Bluff City with her freethinking attitudes, to her surprise she finds Seymore's wife more than willing to exchange her conservative hair-do for a copy of Nora's bob, and to take on the position of "first president of the first birth control league of the Mississippi Valley" (2.1.29). And Seymore's mother, too, who spends her time making dolls for church bazaars, is not at all disturbed by the illegal thrust of Nora's activities. To the contrary, conspicuously open to the project of disseminating information on how to prevent unwanted pregnancies, she offers to support the cause by "[making] some dolls for Birth Control" (2.2.9).[3] In this way, the light tone of the play's beginning runs through to the very end in the images connected to women's liberation in the social comedy of *Chains of Dew*.

At the same time, however, these images are also involved in delineating Dotty's tragic return to a life as someone to be superior to. As Greenwich Village takes Seymore's Midwestern living-room by storm, it becomes apparent that the poet is not at all pleased with this intermingling of his two heretofore neatly separated worlds. When Nora, to Dotty's great delight, announces the additional arrival of Leon Whittaker and James O'Brian on the scene, the master of the house indignantly moves to oppose "this invasion" (2.2.10). Under cover of the argument that Dotty needs protection from her own naive enthusiasm (already, she has begun to distance herself from her former friends by telling them that birth control is more important than bridge!) Seymore struggles to uphold the illusion that his regard for his family binds him to a "respectable" Midwestern life. In the end, it is his mother who comes to realize that her son would not be able to cope in a world without chains. Brought face to face with the necessity to choose between her own self-fulfillment and her love for her husband, at the fall of the final curtain Dotty cannot control her tears at the thought of her lost new life while Seymore restores his world to normalcy as he sends his friends back to New York in a heroic gesture of self-sacrifice.

When *Chains of Dew* premiered in 1922 as the last play of the Provincetown Players' final New York season, most reviewers enjoyed the witty satire of the first act but were left unconvinced by the introduction of tragedy during the further course of the action. Indeed, several first-night comments concentrate on a disturbing clash of genres in Glaspell's latest play. Writing for the *New York Evening Globe*, Alison Smith declares:

> Susan Glaspell couldn't write a commonplace play or a meaningless play however she tried, but her significant themes can meander into confusing byways—as this one does.... It is as if Miss Glaspell could not make up her mind between the hilarious satire of *Suppressed Desires* and the grim sincerity of *The Verge* and wabbled dangerously over these two attitudes, to the great injury of her craft ["The New Play," as qtd. in Bach, *Susan Glaspell* 176–77, fn. 20].[4]

And Stephen Rathbun writes in *The New York Sun*:

> Susan Glaspell's plays give one something to think about, and "Chains of Dew" is no exception to the rule. But we wonder why Miss Glaspell called the play a "comedy." To us it is tragic that a woman sacrifices her future and becomes a slave to her husband's career. It is just as tragic as though she had committed suicide. And yet, as wives are continually doing this sort of thing in real life, we might call it a grim, realistic comedy.

Of course, Glaspell had employed a mixture of conflicting styles in several plays before this one, and in these cases, too, audiences had been irritated by her way of combining comic elements with the features of a problem play or a drama of ideas. Significantly, however, in Glaspell's early one-acts the lighter touches of style and tone serve to *enhance* the respective play's serious argument.[5] By contrast, in *Chains of Dew* the ideas negotiated in the story of Dotty Standish as the play's serious thematic focus are *undermined* by the comedy that rules her husband's own story.

In fact, in the character of Seymore Standish, the poet, Glaspell sets out to ridicule a number of those "issues of expression" (Lewisohn) which she had deemed worthy of a solemn philosophical discussion in several of her earlier plays — notions such as the artist's "light of truth," the fundamental human need to be understood, the existential fear of isolation, and the difficulties inherent in living according to one's own beliefs even when this means a painful separation from one's past. The fact that Glaspell, after whole-heartedly mocking these issues in the character of Seymore Standish, turns round to approach them from a much more urgent and serious angle with the story of his wife, is bound to irritate any audience.

Seymore Standish: Artist and Society

When *Chains of Dew* was first produced by the Provincetown Players in 1922, thus Ozieblo sums up the play's original reception, "no reviewer remarked on the primary issue of Dotty's tragedy — it was lost in the staging of the play, which emphasized the situational comedy and the predicament of the businessman-poet. Even for the self-styled bohemians of Greenwich Village, *Chains of Dew* was, after all, the story of a poet, not that of his wife" (*Susan Glaspell* 166). Even if Stephen Rathbun's review in the *New York Sun* shows that at least one critic did comment on the tragedy of Dotty Standish's sacrifice, it is certainly true that under the impression of what seems to have been a very sluggish and unbalanced production, most reviewers concentrated on the character of the husband.[6] This focus, however, was not only the result of an admittedly one-sided staging. All throughout its expository act the script which Glaspell filed with the Library of

Congress confirms that Seymore Standish is set up as the protagonist in *Chains of Dew*.

At the rise of the first curtain, Nora Powers sits in front of a mimeograph, working away among stacks of "literature" and other material indicating the necessity for contraception, while Leon Whittaker *"has just put down his hat"* (1.2). Seymore's name is the first word uttered in the play:

> LEON. Seymore not here yet?
> NORA. Not yet. He's late. He's visiting his wife's aunt.
> (*After inspecting and rejecting a page*) One would suppose that would make him early.
> LEON. (*Having polished his tortoise glasses and taken some proofs from his pocket, sits down. With a sigh.*) It's a great pity he's as he is.
> NORA. Yes. Of course that can be said of most everyone.
> LEON. You hate to see a man — not there in some ways, when he's so—*there* in others
> NORA. Um, I've hated it more than once [1.2].

This opening exchange sets both the play's thematic focus (i.e. the quality of Seymore's art and its relation to his familial background) and its light comic tone. While Seymore's poetry and character provide the center of attention from the start, we simultaneously receive Nora's signal that as a guiding theme his poetic significance should not be taken too seriously. And thus, from the very beginning the "issues of expression" which Glaspell dramatizes in her central artist figure are ridiculed as nothing more than a conceited man's pitiful strategy of self-creation.

Where Nora obviously does not want to overemphasize Seymore's importance as a national poet, his editor Leon and the Irish essayist James O'Brien (who serves to underline Seymore's international renown) engage in a discussion on the shortcomings of his otherwise enlightened art. Enthusiastically, Leon introduces us to a sample of Seymore's verse, while Nora's attention is divided between poetry and birth control. This scene introduces a number of Glaspell's recurring images with regard to her interest in artistic expression and the poet's role in society:

> LEON. We're using a poem of Seymore's in this number. [...] It's to Shelley.
> [...] (*Reading*) "We need you, Shelley:
>> You whose vision had the power of light,
>> Seeing that gave sight.
>> We need the swiftness that was Shelley,
>> Swifter than harm; wider than falling darkness; more sure than—
> (*Nora, though listening, turns her machine and it squeaks; Leon pauses and looks at her in annoyance; she waits for him to begin again*)
>> "More sure than hate.
>> Who now has thoughts to life the night?
>> We need new reaches of the path of light that was your seeing,
>> Courage so pure that courage came to it as—

(*Nora is worried. She likes the poem but she must complete her operation or ruin what she has begun. Another squeak*)
NORA. (*apologetically*) Oh.
LEON. (*Folding it up*) Since you care more about birth control than you do about poetry -
NORA. I thought I could do both [1.2–3].

What is most striking about this melodramatic sample of Seymore's poetry is the way in which it exposes as hollow the very images which have served to carry Glaspell's belief in the importance of "true writing" in previous works. In *Bernice*, Margaret's understanding of the value of art is pronounced with a solemn integrity: the true artist can "see through the fog" of our lives and bring light to our human darkness. In *Chains of Dew*, Glaspell invests no strength in this idea — or, rather, she presents the easy twist with which a conceited attitude can deprive an image of its meaning even where the words ("vision," "seeing," "light," "darkness") remain the same. In fact, the very name which Glaspell has given her artist figure in this play, Sey-[i.e. "see"] "-more," mocks the idea of a superior vision which can be expressed through the voice of the artist. And thus when Seymore bewails the spiritual wasteland of the Middle West by drawing a picture conspicuously reminiscent of the moving image called forth by Ed's editorial in *The People*, Leon warns his friend: "we [should not] get lost in our own figures of speech — they are convenient spots to retire to, aren't they?" (1.27).

The obvious emptiness of Seymore's overdrawn imagery foreshadows the fundamental language skepticism presented in Glaspell's later play *The Verge*. At the same time, it serves to discredit the poet's self-imposed role as "seer" in this play. Moreover, the characterization of Seymore Standish as someone whose artistic insight must be seriously questioned undermines every other idea connected to this figure in the play, as well — including his central theme of the impossibility of freedom for the individual soul.

To Leon, Seymore's latest poem to Shelley "is the most passionate cry for freedom that has come out of this night we're stuck for" (1.4), and when Seymore himself turns up, it quickly becomes apparent that this is indeed the theme of his life. What he most envies his friends, thus Seymore declares, is their lack of dependants. Where Nora, Leon and O'Brien are free to say and do whatever they want, he is obliged to return to his Midwestern bondage — sentenced to fulfill his duties in a world he does not belong to, bound by unbreakable chains of affection as he bravely meets the responsibilities of providing for his mother, wife and children a life in safety and ease (1.19). Significantly, too, in Seymore's view of the world the freedom he longs for is not, as Nora suggests, there for the taking. His imprisonment is inevitable, as the man is nothing less than "caught by living" (1.23). For what would it do to his loved ones if Seymore decided to break out of his allotted place as leader of society and head of the family? "Say I'm weak," he challenges Nora's insistence that you "don't have to be caught by living if you don't want to be" (1.23), "[...] I just haven't got it in me the thing that would ride rough shod over all the people who love me. I can't quite believe enough in myself to overthrow their lives in order to right mine" (1.25–26). As Ozieblo accurately points out, this "confession [is] vibrant with a concern that permeates all of Glaspell's writing" (*Susan Glaspell* 161) — the playwright's constant weighing of an individual's needs against the lives of those who are closest to one's heart.

In Seymore's case, however, this worry is exposed as nothing more than a maddening pose, since the audience soon learns that his "dependants" would be more than happy to leave Bluff City and follow their provider to New York. Indeed, almost to the very end of the play the argument of Glaspell's comedy seems to be that the imprisonment of the individual through social forces is only an *idea* that can be given up at any time. Darkly predicting disaster, Seymore tries to stop his wife from giving up her Bluff City acquaintances in exchange for Nora's birth control league: "Let this madness cease! You think I am going to see our lives go to pieces before my eyes?" (3.8). As the audience has already witnessed the refreshingly liberating effects which "Birth Control" has had on his wife, however, we trust Dotty's announcement that she never will want her old life back. What is more, the shallowness of Bluff (!) City confirms her conviction that if she ever did feel a desire to return to bridge and dancing, the town would graciously receive her back: "Don't worry dear; I can get [society] back, if I want it back. I have only to say — Well, here I am — home again!" (3.8).

Already in the free-and-easy atmosphere of the play's first act, Nora, Leon and O'Brien rejected Seymore's insistence on staying in chains which, in their eyes, could be broken easily enough. After all, all three have shaken off *their* ties of social and familial obligations with headstrong determination:

> SEYMORE. [...] Have all of you gone scot free? (*To O'Brien*) Were you never caught?
> O'BRIEN. (*As if familiarizing himself with the word*) Caught? Yes, I know what you mean. Caught. Yes, I was to have been for the church. I had to tell my father I simply wouldn't think of such a thing.
> NORA. You see, Seymore? He simply told his father he wouldn't think of such a thing.
> LEON. And I shall not soon forget the day I told my father I was not going to stay in his law office. *He* didn't like it.
> O'BRIEN. It's like having a tooth pulled — violent and disagreeable, but moving in the direction of the future.
> NORA. And I used to edit "The Methodist Review." Came a time when I told them I would not edit it any longer. *They* didn't want me to stop. "They" never do [1.19].

In this early scene, too, the idea of social obligations and emotional ties is exposed as a conceited pose in the case of Seymore Standish: asserting one's own desires, supposedly, is no more painful (or harmful, for that matter) than "having a tooth pulled."

In this context, yet another central notion that is often treated seriously in Glaspell's dramatic writings is discredited in *Chains of Dew*: the conviction that communication is ultimately impossible between isolated minds. Rejecting Nora's argument that you can break your ties if you only want to, Seymore arrogantly retorts: "I'm glad you've been so gently handled. It is a bit amusing, though, to see you with this pleased sense of having emancipated yourselves. *I hardly know how to talk to you*" (1.19; my emphasis).

With his distanced reaction to his friend's personal histories Seymore here perpetuates one of Glaspell's most central themes in relation to the function of language and art — that of being "misunderstood." At first, we learn that his position as an acclaimed artist turns Seymore into an "alien" back in his hometown (a place populated by narrow-minded people with shallow concerns and petty lives). Presently, however, the poet insists that his more advanced friends in New York do not understand him, either. Once again, the idea is connected to Seymore's inability to "talk" to people who do not have the same superior knowledge of the world:

> NORA. It must be lonely to be the only grown up person in the world.
> SEYMORE. (*violently*) It *is* lonely. I see now you've never been up against life. I — I don't know how to talk to you.
> NORA. But you're getting it mixed, Seymore. We aren't the aliens. It's those ninnies out home you can't talk to [1.19].

And while Nora attempts to undermine Seymore's pose of the lonely caller in the desert with her smug remarks, his self-assessment of being doomed to a life of inner isolation stands all the more unshaken:

> SEYMORE. I'm sorry we bumped into the vestry. Life's lonely — hang it. One would like to feel one's self understood somewhere. (*Candidly, in a way to make one like him*) It really isn't any fun — what I go through. I try to get a little fun out of finding myself in such a situation, but — the joke plays out. I get awfully homesick. I get *starved*. (*As no one comments on this*) Oh, yes, I know you don't understand. I — I don't expect you to. Really, I don't see how you could [1.25].

Both the notion of Seymore's "loneliness," however, and the idea that he suffers from the impossibility to communicate his innermost thoughts to the world are ridiculed as Glaspell makes clear that the last thing this poet wants is to be "understood." Several times in the play Seymore's New York friends comment on his maddening way of shaking off all questions, and his own wife feels compelled to make an attempt at reaching him through a correspondence course on "How to Understand Poetry."[7] And even to the members of the Standishs' "unenlightened" social circles in Bluff City it is obvious that Seymore makes a point of remaining as aloof and obscure in his poetic expressions as he possibly can:

> MRS. MACINTYRE. I hear there's a new kind of poetry in New York. They say you write it about anything — bugs or hair pins or the dish cloth.
> EDITH. And they say you don't have to be a poet to write it.
> SEYMORE. That must console a lot of people.
> EDITH. I met a man the other night who said he understands your poetry. But people brag so.
> MRS. MACINTYRE. There's something I always wanted to ask you, Seymore. Do *you* understand your poetry? [2.1.17].

In this context, the artist's mother proves especially perceptive in act 2 when she reacts — if somewhat obliquely herself — to her daughter-in-law's desire to "understand" Seymore ("I wish I could understand him. Think what it would mean to him if I could understand him!") with the following soothing comment: "Don't worry, Dotty. Maybe it wouldn't mean as much as your not understanding him" (2.1.13).

In *Chains of Dew*, therefore, Susan Glaspell has her male protagonist pose as the prototype of an elitist artist who cannot — and does not want to — be "understood" by a popular audience. In Seymore's self-perception as a writer, art is a commentary on the eternal truths of life, substantially outside the social and political discourses of any specific point in time. Indeed, throughout the play, his writing features as a clear antithesis to Nora's propaganda and Leon's activism. Yet whenever he insists on a profound distance between himself and his fellow human beings, Seymore is found essentially lacking by way of comparison to the very poet whose greatness he aspires to — Percy Bysshe Shelley. When early on in the play he refuses to join a protest against the imprisonment of a fellow writer who has been locked up for writing "what he saw as the truth about life," Nora takes this behavior as an opportunity to question straight out Seymore's supposed alignment with this great classic:

> NORA. (*Throwing out her arms*) "We need you, Shelley!" (*She laughs*) I've no doubt it will be very interesting, Seymore, to read what you wrote about Shelley, but do you know, I think I'd a little rather read what Shelley would write about you.
> SEYMORE. (*Hurt now*) He might understand.
> NORA. Don't you believe it! [...] Did vestry or bank or waiting for dinner ever keep him from — You've got your nerve to *speak* to him like that! As if he'd want to hear anything you'd have to say! [1.28].

Later, when Seymore rejects his wife's idea that he should "talk for birth control" with the explanation that he is "an artist — not a propagandist," Nora again remarks: "There was once a poet who was also a simple soul. He knew what he believed — and he was even able to communicate with people who weren't poets. 'We need you, Shelley!'" (3.16).

Consequently, although Glaspell, on the one hand, stresses the role of artistic expression as a timeless and uninvolved comment on human existence (at one point Nora states: "[Seymore's] a leader of society — if you know what I mean. How can he be a poet for the whole wide world?" 1.14), at the same time she points out that artists do not exist outside of the inter-subjective web of connections which form the essence of our human experience. In the end, Seymore turns out to be wrong both in his notion of being misunderstood (in fact, especially Nora and the Mother see right through him) and in his idea that he leads his inner life in isolation (he actually needs both his home town community and his Greenwich Village friends). In a paradoxical turn of her argument, then, by exposing Seymore's stance as the misunderstood and isolated writer as utterly conceited, Glaspell once more argues here both for the notion of the artist's responsibility to society and for the more general belief that our human lives inevitably depend on each other. Importantly, however, while the playwright thus moves to prove her poet right, after all, as far as the potentially imprisoning effects of one's social ties with regard to an individual's self-fulfillment are concerned, the bitter consequences are born out in the play not by the poet himself, but by his wife. And thus, the particular stance which Glaspell takes to her various "issues of expression" is considerably confused in *Chains of Dew* by the serious twist which her social comedy receives through the character of Dotty Standish.

Dotty Standish: A Woman's Self-Fulfillment vs. A Wife's Emotional Ties

Of course, Glaspell might have chosen to prove right her male protagonist's notion of social relationships as imprisoning by presenting a Midwestern community which would indeed lose too much if it lost Seymore Standish. Such a presentation, however, would have made impossible the comic tone of the play's initial New York scene. Instead, to preserve her conceptualization of her theme as a social comedy, Glaspell upholds the image of Seymore as a conceited prig, but at the same time turns to give his ideas of human obligations unexpected weight through the character of his wife Dotty. Unfortunately, it is a direct result of this double strategy that Dotty Standish's dilemma cannot come across as a convincing one — for *why*, with the image of Seymore in mind any audience is compelled to ask, should the woman be tied by her love to a husband who is hopelessly self-centred and who will only preserve his sanity if he is never forced to acknowledge his wife as a person in her own right? Virtually out of the blue, at the end of the play's third act Glaspell expects us to believe that Seymore has his good sides, after all — as husband and father as much as in the roles of businessman and poet — and that consequently Dotty's sacrifice is both necessary and worth while. And thus, it is not only Nora Powers (as the independent New Woman of the play) who has her problems with such a view of Dotty's situation.[8] As one of many reviewers who commented on the inherent shortcomings of the play's final argument, Alexander Woollcott cites Dotty herself to make this point:

> "Do you love [Seymore] enough to be his cross?" asks the old lady [i.e. Seymore's mother, H.-B.] gravely. The young wife scowls and answers: "You don't make him out very intelligent, do you?" Which is a dangerous speech, suggesting mutiny among the creatures of Miss Glaspell's imagination. Here was one of them putting her finger right on the weak spot in the play.

What is more, with eighty years of historical distance our dissatisfaction with the play's ending only seems to have increased. As Barbara Ozieblo comments:

> The denouement [...] is [not] satisfactory. Dotty succumbs to domesticity from a sense of duty imposed on her by her mother-in-law and husband. All too briefly, we glimpse the real Dotty struggling to surface, but without Seymore's approval, she cannot stay afloat. Today, regenerated by decades of feminist thought, we can only judge her as too weak, as lacking the courage to go it alone with which Henrik Ibsen endowed his Nora in *A Doll's House* [*Susan Glaspell* 164].

In fact, while Dotty's decision to stay with her husband does not seem too consistent even within the frame of the play's own presentation of characters, to contemporary feminist taste it would arguably still be inacceptable if Seymore was less of a caricature and more of a "person."[9] Nevertheless, as Susan Glaspell forcefully perpetuates her ongoing debate around questions such as the creation of identity, the nature of social existence, and the significance of human communication both in art and in everyday life with the figure of Dotty Standish, it is certainly worthwhile to take a closer look at this female figure in *Chains of Dew*.

From the start Glaspell makes clear that Seymore's wife is geared towards catering to the needs of her husband, brought up to find her identity solely in the activities connected to the roles of wife and mother in her middle class social circles. Drawn in act 1 as a none-too-bright society goose who is entirely dependant on her husband's support, at the beginning of the second act we meet Dotty as a woman who is *"dainty, amiable-looking,* [...] *reared in what is quaintly called the polite world,"* and unobtrusively used to make herself comfortable at her husband's feet (2.1.1). In this context, even Dotty's move away from her own social circles, begun before Seymore's New York friends arrive as an outward influence, is set in motion by a wifely desire to help her husband. Despite her own feeling that it "would be nice to have some things not suited to the town" (2.1.4), her symbolic attempt of taking down the picture of the Sistine Madonna from the Standishs' living-room wall is motivated first and foremost by her belief that Seymore tolerates it only because he thinks his wife wants it there: "DOTTY. You always make fun of our having the Madonna hanging here — so I thought — I wanted to have things pleasant when you got home–" (2.1.3). Likewise, accepting her husband's ironic remarks about the conventionalism of Bluff City as expressions of his painful inner distance to their friends, Dotty has put it into her head to "free Seymore" from the obligations which stand in the way of his poetic creativity: "Seymore cares for writing as he cares for nothing else. Oh, I wish it could all be different! I wish I could —free him" (2.1.12).

Taking her husband's criticism of their hometown at face value, Dotty begins to reflect on the dull realities of their social life, and in the process she comes to see some truth in Seymore's attitude. It is into this well-prepared soil that Nora can plant her New-Woman ideas when she appears at just the right moment to achieve her own mission of "freeing the poet" in act 2. Having witnessed the admiration with which Seymore, after his return from New York, had cut one of Mother's dolls' hair (and encouraged even further by the arrival of the living, bobbed model herself) Dotty decides to change her own outward appearance as a sign of her inward transformation. On her first entrance as the new woman she has become, Glaspell's stage directions describe her change in no uncertain terms: "*Enter Dotty. Her hair is bobbed. It is extraordinarily becoming. She is young and gay and irresistible. The Dotty that never had a chance is gleaming there*" (2.2.15). At this point, the dramatist still makes clear that Dotty was only able to venture towards a new beginning for herself because she was certain of her husband's approval: "I just love it! (*Musses [her hair] affectionately*) It makes me *feel* different. I know now, Seymore, what you meant — isn't it amazing how much you cut when you cut the hair! Of course, I never would have done it if I hadn't known you liked bobbed hair" (2.2.17). And thus, as Dotty embarks on the task of introducing Bluff City to the necessity of Birth Control she is spurred on by the idea that she has found a way to make things right for her husband. Urging Seymore to give the opening speech for her campaign ("[Now] you can come straight out with your beliefs! Tell them what you think of our laws! [...] Tell them their virtues are hypocrisy and their — What a wonderful time you'll have!"), she assures him eagerly: "Why, Seymore, I'm doing all this because you are a poet!" (3.3).

On the other hand, Dotty's joy at this new experience of "breaking loose" gradually begins to overtake her initial urge to help her husband. Sensing how much she herself was walled in by the social expectations which have framed her life, she can now exchange the Sistine Madonna for the "birth control pictures" which Nora has brought along from New York and with this symbolic act energetically confirm her desire to liberate herself:

> [*O'Brien and* DOTTY] *get* [*the Madonna*] *down. Dotty takes up the mother with nine children. Over her shoulder, to Mrs. MacIntyre*) Aren't you awfully tired of Madonnas? Won't you sit down? I'm *off* Madonnas. (*She begins to pound*)
> NORA. That won't do the wall much good, Diantha.
> DOTTY. Wall? Who cares about the *wall*? (*Nailing down the words with the hammer*) If there's anything I'm sick of, it's *walls* [2.2.23].

Similarly, whereas at first Dotty had been eager to get things out of the way of Seymore's poetry, after she has assumed her post as president of the birth control league of the Mississippi Valley and has turned the Standish living-room into the league's headquarters the task of "not disturbing Seymore" becomes increasingly less important to her:

> *In flits Dotty — light, busy, happy. Halts and looks at* [*Seymore*].
> DOTTY. Oh, you here, Seymore? You're thinking aren't you?
> SEYMORE. Yes. Thinking.
> DOTTY. Will I disturb you if I do some telephoning? (*A move of his hand, as if to say, pray don't think of me*) We'll have to have another phone put in — now that there is so much going on in the house. (*Looks at a memorandum in her hand*) I'm so busy. (*Laughs happily*) I don't know what to do first. Nora is teaching me too many things! [3.1].

Interestingly, as Dotty begins to take in a completely new side of her own self, Glaspell connects the theme of her liberation to the questions of how we come to know each other in the first place, and of what constitutes our unique "identity" — two issues which have featured prominently in *Bernice*, and which in *Chains of Dew*, too, serve to juxtapose the conviction (expressed in the character of Seymore) that our transcendental souls live in isolation from each other. That Nora makes a point of addressing Dotty as "Diantha" bears a special significance in this context, implying that the name can make the woman — both in a positive and a negative sense. After Seymore, in the first act, had explained that "Dotty" is his wife's "pet name" ("Her father always called her Dotty Dimple. We've dropped the dimple" 1.18), Nora had urged him to call her by her real name as a first step of accepting his wife as a person and a partner. Importantly, it is not only Nora's perception that such a change would affect the couple's relationship — she also implies that it would allow Seymore's wife to assume more power over the construction of her own identity:

> NORA. Diantha? But that is a beautiful name.
> SEYMORE. It's not suited to her.
> NORA. How do you know?
> SEYMORE. How do I *know*? Because I know her.
> NORA. You know her as "Dotty." You call your wife "Dotty" and then claim to have respect for marriage! [1.32].

Ironically, the idea that what you "are" might have not a little to do with what people want you to be dawns on Dotty through nothing other than her husband's poetry. In a crucial scene between her and Seymore's mother, she asks the older woman:

> DOTTY. Do you think, mother, that it's hard to be any other way than the way you are? [...] Don't you think sometimes you are as you are — because you've *been* that way. [...] And you've been that way — well because you are supposed to be that way. When you do certain things— bridge and danc-ing — then you're the kind of person who plays bridge and dances. But what sort of person would you be — if you did something else? [...] You know, it's an exciting idea — that you needn't be as you are.
> MOTHER. My dear, isn't it a little too exciting? What — gave it to you?
> DOTTY. Seymore's poetry. He writes so much about being bound — things that hold us from what we might be. (*With sudden vigor*) Why do we let them do it? Why don't we get — loose? [2.1.13–14].

For a while, it seems as if Dotty were indeed allowed to turn loose — and her way of developing a sense of her own self lies through questioning the nature of her relation to other people. Once more, then, as Seymore's imagined dilemma has indicated from the start, the notion of "understanding each other" plays a crucial part in this Glaspell play. In one respect, Dotty Stan-dish foreshadows the playwright's later radical figure Claire Archer of *The Verge* when she refuses easy explanations to life's mystery and displays a yearning to get away from the simple patterns of Bluff City society: "EDITH. But what would be the fun of writing a thing you couldn't understand? DOTTY. "Didn't you ever want to get away from things you could under-stand?" (2.1.17). On the other hand, Dotty criticizes her husband in his very pose of being apart from everyone else (a criticism which, by extension, refers both back to Bernice's detached life and forward to Claire Archer's insistence on her "by-myself-ness"): "[If] no-one understands a thing," she muses with regard to her husband's obscure poetry, "perhaps that shows there's something wrong with it" (3.9). In the end, however, Glaspell's point (voiced through the character of the Mother) is that for Dotty it would sim-ply not "be 'being [her]self' to spoil things for Seymore" (3.32). And thus, with the character of Dotty Standish the dramatist once more emphasizes the essential significance of *connection* in human existence over a notion of self as a separate and independent entity.

Nora Powers and the Mother: Connectedness as Creative Potential or Suffocating Imprisonment?

As the decision of what Dotty should do is fought out in the influence exerted over her by Nora Powers on the one hand and Seymore's mother on the other, this notion of a fundamental connectedness between human beings is further supported through these two contrasting female characters. While none of the male characters (to the least Seymore himself) are able to recognize the true set-up of the poet's psychological situation, both Nora and Mother recognize Seymore's self-deception. Yet although both women sense the truth about Seymore's predicament, and even though both have a similar understanding of human community as an essential reality in our lives, they draw opposite conclusions as to what Dotty's next step should be. At the heart of their contradicting interpretations are two opposing beliefs with regard to the nature of human connectedness: While Nora has experienced it as a creative force which does not constrain her individuality but supports it through a knowledge that there are others who share her view of life, to Mother emotional ties present an unsurpassable limit to the realization of one's personal freedom — the very point which Seymore has made all along.·

From the beginning, Nora Powers is drawn as a character who has the playwright's unreserved sympathy. She is presented as a likeable and energetic woman who meets her fellow human beings in an open, straightforward way. What is more, she combines a good-natured humor with a keenly observing eye, a combination which predicates her as the center of the play's satire and its comic spirit. This function is already indicated in the very tone with which Nora is introduced in the opening stage directions:

> Nora is working a mimeograph; she is not an adept, and has a manner of trying to placate the machine. Nora has short hair. This does not mean she's eccentric — it is not that kind of short hair. It curls and is young and vital and charming short hair. Nora also is young and vital and charming — devotion to a cause really doesn't hurt her looks in the least [1.1–2].

In her frank and easy ways, Nora stands for an attitude towards life which is based on a belief in everyone's right to live according to their personal convictions, combined with an insistence on the importance of one's integrity. When O'Brien struggles to express what he finds lacking in Seymore's poetry she suggests: "Do you suppose it's sincerity you miss?" (1.7). Later on in the play Dotty quotes her new friend as having stated that "we must see ourselves if we want to have integrity," and in recruiting supporters for the cause she believes in (to Nora, informing women about effective methods of contraception is indispensable in giving them control over their lives) Nora remarks: "No, no, you don't have to do anything to your hair [to get in the birth control league]. All you have to have is a little mind and (*light and pleasant*) a little heart" (2.1.27).

Not surprisingly, then, what aggravates Nora most about her friend Seymore is the callousness with which he insists on his superior position of enlightened apartness. It is this disregard for his fellow human beings which enrages her most, even as she is attracted to the passion with which Seymore advances her:

> SEYMORE. [...] (*Suddenly* [...] *takes [Nora] in his arms and kisses her*) [...] Oh, Nora, I *need* you.
> NORA. ([...] [*H*]*olding off*) I thought it was Shelley you needed.
> SEYMORE. Oh — quit that! (*He kisses her again*) [...] Don't always *evade* so.
> NORA. That's a fine speech from you. Seymore, I think you should do your part toward getting this man free [i.e. the imprisoned writer, H.-B.].
> SEYMORE. Yes, I know you think so. Let's not talk about that now.
> [...] NORA. I'm sorry, Seymore; I like you — in spite of the things I detest about you. (*When about to be very nice to him, she thinks of something*) What is your wife's real name? [1.31–32].

In fact, while Nora impersonates the prototype of the progressive New Woman who believes in free love and does not spare a passing thought for a betrayed wife, this *femme-fatale* image of herself is clearly a pose, if an amusing one — playful within her own circles, aimed at shocking conventional society out of its complacency, but never actually followed through. True, Nora is delightedly ready to hand the Standishs' gossipy neighbors their taste of scandal when she advises them to "ask Seymore" in case they want to know something about her "personal" interest in birth control (2.1.29). It is clear, however, that she has never allowed their flirtations to go "all the way." Nora, thus Glaspell suggests, respects Seymore's social ties (i.e., his marriage) — more, in fact, than the poet himself does. And at her arrival at Bluff City she is further than ever from succumbing to Seymore's advances when she takes an immediate liking to his wife.[10]

Yet even if Nora is shown to establish an immediate bond with Dotty when she falls for the other woman's guileless openness, in the character constellation of *Chains of Dew* the Greenwich Village intellectual is drawn in correspondence not to Seymore's wife, but to the poet's mother. Like Mother, Nora intuitively objects to Seymore's pose of the lonely and misunderstood artist. Already in act 1 she senses the nature of his imprisonment when in reaction to his assurance that the "road to understanding me does not lie through my wife's aunt" she replies "(*lightly, yet darkly*) Oh I don't know" (1.9). And a little later, she is certain beyond the slightest doubt that as much as Seymore expresses his yearning for a life in New York City, he would never leave his wife and come to live with her instead (1.25). Once she has met Seymore's wife and mother, therefore, Nora can address the man's problem head-on when she advises him straight out in the second act: "You mustn't hog the sacrifice" (2.2.6).

In this way, Nora puts her finger on the spot of Seymore's central weakness just as his mother will do in the play's key scene before the last curtain. What is more, the two women also agree that the connection between human beings is the essential experience of their lives. Completely unlike Mother, however, the young Greenwich Village radical understands this basic intersubjectivity as a principle which enhances her individuality rather than inhibiting it. Indeed, when Nora comments on her relationship to her friend Leon in the first act, she preempts the gist of Glaspell's own autobiographical remembrances of the early Provincetown community in *The Road to the Temple*, as she lightly remarks to O'Brien: "Aren't [Leon's] manners awful? When people believe in the same set of things they have family manners for each other. Think of me as his sister" (1.13).[11] It is not surprising in this context that what Seymore most envies Nora and her New York friends is the intellectual companionship they share (see, for example, 2.2.14).

In the way in which she presents Nora in her New York environment during the first scenes of the play, Glaspell thus suggests that the moment the young woman separated herself from the people in her life who represented society's stifling conventions, she ventured forth to search for another community which would support her in her progressive beliefs—and found herself a new "family." Able to build upon a positive experience of emotional ties, Nora represents a creative version of life as realizing itself in the continuous constitutive articulate contact between people. Indeed, with Nora Glaspell stresses once more the notion that "truth" comes into being in communicative action. Setting Nora's joking tone against Leon's earnest attempts at "seeing the truth" with regard to Seymore's poetry in act 1 ("LEON. It's nothing to joke about, Nora. This is a time when it's important to get the truth"), Glaspell has Nora remark: "Perhaps joking is the way I sneak up on the truth" (1.19). And as this only seemingly light episode continues, Nora advocates the very possibility of constituting life *in conversation* (as opposed to Leon's concept of getting to the truth by first thinking things out and then expressing them to the world):

> LEON. Just because you can think of things to say is no reason for [...] thinking they contribute to the truth. It may be a great misfortune to have things dart into the mind — as they do into yours.
> NORA. Yes. I should think you would be sorry for me. Now I'll keep still, Leon, and you contribute to the truth. (*Silence. She looks at him.*)
> LEON. (*angrily*) I'm thinking!
> NORA. I'm glad to hear that.
> O'BRIEN. Do you always quarrel like this?
> NORA. We believe in all the same things.
> LEON. Not *all* the same things. I believe in silence.
> NORA. Then why don't you stay home by yourself?
> [...] LEON. Nora, will you let conversation be possible?
> NORA. (*cheerfully*) Sure. (*returns to the mimeograph. Decides to soak the inkpad. Nobody does anything but watch her*) Conversation?
> LEON. We are thinking preparatory to beginning a conversation. Thinking is sometimes necessary to conversation.
> NORA. Now I never would have thought of that [1.20–21].

Hence, because she believes in human community as a positive connective background for the development of the free individual, in *Chains of Dew* the character of Nora *Powers* (!) represents an understanding of life which urges on social change as both necessary and possible — much as Glaspell had already argued in her 1917 one-act *The People*.

When Nora arrives in Bluff City in the second act, she and Seymore's mother immediately hit it off with each other. In act 1, Seymore had described his mother as an old woman who has lived her "long and faithful life" and who now depends entirely on her son's support (1.16). That this picture was not exactly to the point is obvious to Nora right away: "(*Turning to [Seymore's mother] impetuously*) You *are* nice, but — I wonder if Seymore understands you?" (2.1.25). Mother, in fact, takes a keen interest in the world around her; she is as clear-sighted in her perceptions as Nora is; and she proves to be much more open to progressive ideas than her son would ever suspect. (At one point, when she is for a short moment alone on the stage with the doll whose hair Seymore has only recently bobbed, in "*passing the mirror [she] stops and turns her own hair in at the sides to get the bobbed effect.*" 2.1.12). While Seymore attempts to shoo Nora away to New York by insisting that his seventy-year-old mother must not be disturbed, Mother wants to know all about the birth control league and is even eager to get involved in the campaign herself:

> MOTHER. [...] Perhaps I can help.
> SEYMORE. It's not necessary, mother. Don't let all this disturb you.
> MOTHER. Why, it's not disturbing me, Seymore. Why should it disturb me? What's this? [...]
> NORA. I was just setting it up. It's an excess family exhibit.
> MOTHER. (*With keen interest*) How does it go together?
> NORA. (*Holding up the figure*) Here is a mother of seven children.
> MOTHER. (*Pointing to herself*) And here's another.
> NORA. Did *you* have seven children? [...] Perhaps you'd rather I didn't put this up?
> MOTHER. Put it together. I want to see it.
> NORA. Here is the kitchen stove.
> MOTHER. And here are the children. (*She takes them out and tries different arrangements of them. Seymore suddenly begins to write*)
> NORA. Here's the garbage pail — uncovered.
> MOTHER (*Brightly*) And one child falling into it. [...] How do you make the children tug at the mother's skirts. (*Inspired*) You know, I could make some dolls for birth control! [2.2.8–9].

In her son's eyes, Mother's dolls signify her sad yearning for a time long gone, when her house was full of children. Yet the woman does not in the least miss her earlier task of raising a family. Instead, it turns out that her dolls are nothing less than an artist's cutting-edge commentary on what she observes in the world around her. And again, Nora is the only one who realizes this thrust of social criticism in the dolls which Mother sells at church bazaars:

NORA. [...] Tell me — why do you make dolls? Seymore says it's because you have to be doing for others; but they haven't a do-for-others look.

MOTHER. (*With the timid eagerness of the artist*) What kind of a look have they?

NORA. They look to me — Perhaps I'd better not say it.

MOTHER. *Do*— if it's like that.

NORA. I don't know that I can — exactly. But there's something *devilish* about these dolls.

MOTHER. (*With concern*) Oh, does it show?

NORA. You were getting back at something.

MOTHER. (*Appalled, then defiant*) Well, don't you have to— one way or another? And this isn't a way that does much harm, do you think? [2.2.11].

To Mother, her dolls are her secret way of satirizing the conceited poses she watches people display in her provincial hometown. In giving their looks something of the silliness she perceives in the MacIntyres and their likes, she turns them into "*dolls which say things about people*" (2.1.1). Importantly, however, the above-quoted exchange with Nora also shows that in contrast to the free-thinking young woman from New York, Seymore's mother makes a point of giving her observations a mocking expression which is obvious *only to herself*. Intent on not doing any "harm," she is shocked to realize that Nora has been perceptive enough to unveil her secret, even if she cannot entirely conceal her artist's pride. For as Mother does not think it "safe" to upset the balance of well-established relationships, she is careful not to bring her intuitions out into the open where they would cause a lot of confusion and pain. And indeed, when Dotty, in their conversation about "understanding Seymore," states that "You don't always say things clearly, mother," she tellingly retorts: "Perhaps it's just as well" (2.1.13).

It is this understanding of imminent danger which guides the Mother in her assessment of Dotty's options when she realizes that Seymore *needs* his chains— even if they are nothing but "chains of dew." In contrast to Nora's belief in the positive potential for change in human relationships, in her eyes such change is liable to spell destruction rather than urge on new creative impulses. Just as she has previously cautioned her daughter-in-law that her new notion that "you needn't be what you are" might be rather "too exciting" (2.1.14), Mother now decides that Seymore must not be "unmade":

NORA. (*Noting the somewhat depleted head* [of the doll that looks like Seymore, H.-B.]) Are you unmaking Seymore?

MOTHER. I mustn't— unmake Seymore. It really couldn't be done. He'd become —(*pours out the rest of the sawdust, holds up the rag that was once a head*) Would you like to see him — like that?

NORA. Not permanently.

MOTHER. Then you'd better go away. [...] (*Impulsively reaching out a hand to Nora*) Oh my dear — it's hard to be a mother [3.28–29].

With the character of Seymore's mother, Glaspell thus stresses the imprisoning force of love over Nora's positive image of "family" affections as a source of an understanding which, to the contrary, can even *liberate* the self. When Dotty asks in despair at the end of the final act: "If people ought to be free — why can't *I* be free?" Mother's simple answer is "Because you love another person." And to Nora she sadly states: "When you love it isn't such a gay life. If you could only get up a love control, Nora, — then there might be some hope of controlling" (3.32, 33). Consequently, as Barbara Ozieblo concludes in her interpretation of the play: "In *Chains of Dew*, the author maintains that the bonds of love enslave a woman as surely as those of motherhood, and she offers no way out" [*Susan Glaspell* 165].

Comedy or Tragedy? Writing and Production History of Chains of Dew

When *Chains of Dew* reached the MacDougal Street stage in April 1922, reactions were overwhelmingly negative. Judging from the tenor of most opening night notices the premier of this latest Glaspell play was a truly disappointing experience for many reviewers. By 1922, Provincetown audiences might have been used to the amateur character — and charm — of the Players' stagings, yet in this case it seems the production had been not only amateur but downright sluggish: hardly a review which does not comment on fumbled lines, missed cues, or overly long waits between acts.

The exceptionally poor production of *Chains of Dew* is understandable enough with a glance at the play's singular production history. When it premiered in New York on the evening of 27 April 1922 the Provincetown Players as they had been founded in the summer of 1916 were already a thing of the past. Two months before, on 23 February, the group had decided to close its playhouse at the end of the season for a year of contemplation and reorganization, and by the time rehearsals for *Chains of Dew* were under way, Cook and Glaspell had already left for Greece. Under the circumstances the play hardly stood the chance of an appropriate staging. Originally not part of the program for that year, it had been thrown in to fill the season's final weeks after O'Neill had taken out his play *The Hairy Ape* and sold it to Broadway. As Ozieblo recounts the fate of *Chains of Dew* through the letters of Edna Kenton (one of Glaspell's and Cook's closest Provincetown friends):

> Kenton was deeply disappointed and hurt at the Provincetowners' handling of Glaspell's play. It went into rehearsal late because once Cook left, the decks were clear for what she called the "bloodless revolution," with Jimmy Light and Kenneth Macgowan fighting for control [...]. For a while it even looked as if [...] *Chains of Dew* would be struck from the program,

but Kenton stood her ground, bided her time, and loyally saw the play onto the stage, even though the best actors were either on tour with *The Emperor Jones* or uptown with *The Hairy Ape*. She lamented to Glaspell: "Your play didn't go on under the director, Sue, or with the actors I had so hoped for" [*Susan Glaspell* 201].

Inevitably, of course, the difficulties surrounding the play's production found their way into its presentation to the theatre-going public. It almost seems as if with the end of the Players' activities in sight many participants had lost their interest in the season's final engagement — and with Glaspell not there to oversee the casting of roles, the realization of sets and the cutting of lines, many of the inconsistencies remarked upon by the critics were surely overemphasized in a translation of her script onto the stage that was not authorized by the playwright herself.[12]

Nevertheless, that a majority of professional reactions to the play came down on the negative side cannot be relegated solely to its poor Provincetown production. Observers who had come to expect much from Glaspell during the past seven years of her career were openly disappointed that, even in the writing itself, the piece did not live up to her previous works (especially as compared to her two 1921 contributions *Inheritors* and *The Verge* which were still fresh in everyone's mind).[13] As unsparingly as ever, Alexander Woollcott noted in the *New York Times*: "[*Chains of Dew*], it must be admitted, does indeed seem a little stale. It has a good deal to do with bobbed hair, which it speaks of with such bated breath that one suspects the play must have been written some years ago" ("The Play"). And even reviews that faithfully strove to maintain an upbeat tone towards Glaspell's latest play agreed that in *Chains of Dew* the symbolism was too obvious, and that the characters remained unconvincing caricatures.

Indeed, one of the most unanimously negative reactions was to the depiction of Seymore Standish as hopelessly conceited and shallow, since this representation of the poet undermined the plausibility of Dotty's final sacrifice. On the one hand, this problem was clearly identified as one of incompetent performance on the part of the actor impersonating Seymore. The critic of the *New York Herald Tribune*, for instance, remarks that "Edward Reese showed little more than average talent as the poet," and Maida Castellun states even more directly: "Edward Reese, stiff and monotonous, makes Standish too obviously an ass." Certainly these reviews confirm Glaspell's own conviction that the part was not cast right, as the playwright lamented in her letters to Edna Kenton from Greece both before and after the play's premier: "Reese just hasn't got the personality to suggest what Seymore must suggest."—"I know a Seymore equal to an impression of reserve and complexity would have helped the part a lot" (qtd. in Gainor, *Susan Glaspell* 196). Yet where many reviewers criticized what they perceived as a misdi-

rected interpretation of Glaspell's male protagonist on the stage, others recognized that the problem was already integrated in the script itself. As Heywood Broun comments in the *New York World*: "In order to make [her theme]
plain [Glaspell] has adopted the unfortunate device of making Seymore Standish, her poet, a caricature. [...] [S]omewhat in the playing, but much more
in the writing he is presented as an absolute prig and idiot" (qtd. in Bach,
Susan Glaspell 175). And in a mixed assessment representative of many first
night notices Burns Mantle remarks in the *New York Mail*: "It is to be regret-
ted Susan Glaspell did not take a little more time with 'Chains of Dew.' It
promises so well in its first act, even when it is as sluggishly played as it is
at the Provincetown Playhouse, it seems a play and a theme worth working
over."[14]

    As is the case in this last review, since *Chains of Dew* had been "thrown
into the gap" to replace O'Neill's *The Hairy Ape* many reviewers were inclined
to explain the script's obvious weaknesses by assuming that in her need to
provide a fill-in Glaspell had been inappropriately rushed in the writing.
Thinking along these same lines, Alexander Woollcott called the play no
more than a "rough sketch" and mocked maliciously: "Miss Glaspell does
not think of it as a sketch. She calls it a play, turns it over to her Macdougal
Street cohorts and sails blandly away to Greece, leaving them to struggle
with it" (*New York Times* 28 Apr. 1922: 20). Interestingly enough, however,
in her literary biography Barbara Ozieblo makes a convincing argument that
Chains of Dew was not put together hastily in the spring of 1922. Instead,
with his comment on a certain "staleness" in the play's radical imagery
Alexander Woollcott might have been exceptionally perceptive in doubting
its topical timeliness. For if Ozieblo's conclusions are correct, by 1922
Glaspell's script was already more than two years old: In the chronology of
the playwright's Provincetown ventures *Chains of Dew* followed immediately after *Bernice* and was written sometime between June 1919 and Janu-
ary 1920. And what is most important with regard to this version of the play's
writing history is that Ozieblo's account does not only gratify one reviewer's
singular intuition that "the play must have been written some years ago" (see
Woollcott as qtd. above, *New York Times*): It lends an added dimension to
the frequently voiced judgment of an unsatisfactory mix of comic and tragic
elements in *Chains of Dew*.

    True to her primary critical interest, Ozieblo first places the evolution
of the play's script in the context of Glaspell's and Cooks difficult marital
relationship during the time of their sabbatical leave from the Provincetown
Players in 1919. Recounting that Cook had left Glaspell at their Provincetown home during the winter of 1919/1920 in order to meet up with Idah
Rauh in New York, the critic claims that as Glaspell spent "long, lonely
evenings tormented by visions of Jig and Rauh and flagons of wine [...] she

could not concentrate on the comedy she had planned to write. Dialogue that seemed potentially hilarious now exuded tragedy [...]" (*Susan Glaspell* 154). Ozieblo here reads the story of *Chains of Dew* as a direct follow-up to *Bernice* in that it "furthers Glaspell's exploration of her darkening predicament" in marriage (*Susan Glaspell* 158). Yet she goes on to add another explanation for the play's peculiar wavering between genres. Under the telling chapter heading "Toying with Broadway" Ozieblo argues that "[a] little miffed that O'Neill should launch himself on Broadway" with his *Beyond the Horizon* "while she was tied to the Playwrights' Theatre," Glaspell had written *Chains of Dew* "with a commercial audience in mind" (*Susan Glaspell* 155). On the grounds of Ozieblo's findings, then, one might speculate that Glaspell might have overemphasized the comedy and marital bliss in *Chains of Dew* at the expense of Dotty's self-fulfillment as she had her eye on Broadway, but that her "little theatre" roots (and personal convictions) prevented her from taking her project all the way.

Certainly, the explanation that the ultimately detrimental mix of comedy and tragedy in *Chains of Dew*—as opposed to a more successful combination of dramatic styles in many other Glaspell plays—might have been the direct result of an attempt to "toy with Broadway" bears considerable merit. Burns Mantle, in any case, commented in the *New York Mail*:

> It is a rare mind and a definite talent this playwright discloses whenever she writes anything for the stage. She suffers, or seems to, from a fear that she may be led into a dishonorable compromise of some sort with the hated commercial drama; that she might be caught writing for average intellects and ordinary playgoers; or accused by her little group of sacrificing an ideal or two in the hope of achieving a paying popularity. Some day she will conquer this foolish fear. Some day she will write simply and straightforwardly [...] and will be sharing Brother O'Neill's uptown success.

Regardless of whether we will ever be able fully to unravel the writing and production history of this play, however,[15] the impression remains that in Dotty Standish's final acceptance of her mother-in-law's "wise" view on life the playwright reinforces the idea of intersubjective ties as a bondage to the individual. In the ongoing struggle fought out in Glaspell's plays between a view of life (and art) as carrying an inherent potential to shape the world in a communal act of creation—represented by Nora in *Chains of Dew*— and the contrasting understanding—supported by Seymore's mother—that both in language and artistic expression we can only comment on realities as they stand, this time the latter view prevails. (And it seems hardly a coincidence that in the overwhelming majority of first-night reviews the Mother was perceived as the only convincingly-drawn character in the play.)[16] Alongside its predecessor *Bernice*, therefore, *Chains of Dew* might well be read as a significant transitory piece between the hopeful debates performed in Glaspell's earlier plays (such as *Trifles, The Outside,* or *The People*) and the much more pessimistic view of the relationship between the individual and society which she presents in her later play *The Verge.*

8. *The Verge* (1921)

Language and the Individual

With its combination of daringly novel form and radical subject matter, *The Verge* is not only Glaspell's most experimental work for the stage, it also remains her most controversial one. Very complex in its dramatic representation, the play takes up many of Glaspell's most prominent issues. Language, once again, is central to her discussion — and this time the question of how we can protect our sense of self within a community of others and still influence the world around us is negotiated from all three of the subject positions so relevant to Glaspell's oeuvre — the subject positions of "self," "woman" and "artist."

Claire Archer, a sophisticated New England woman of exquisite Puritan ancestry, alarms her surroundings as she devotes all her energy to a disquieting experiment of growing plants that will "[e]xplode their species" (70). Her world is her greenhouse, where she inexorably follows the vision of a living form that will make "the big leap" (70) and become something "that hasn't been" (64). Rebelling against the imprisoning conventions of society as represented by her sister Adelaide, her 17-year-old daughter Elizabeth and by the three men in her life, the proverbial Tom, Dick and Harry (friend, lover and husband), Claire strains to go beyond "the verge" herself, reaching out to a world of otherness she feels irresistibly drawn to. Full of scorn for those who fear for her mental state and implore her to get some rest and be a good sport again, she at last manages the leap into madness — "the only chance for sanity" (82) — when even her supposed soulmate Tom fails her, lapsing into the threatening mode of protective lover. Clearer than ever before Claire realizes at the end of the play that she needs to free herself before all else from this most deceptive tie to a sympathetic soul who claims to "understand." Strangling Tom in an act of unnatural strength, she burns all bridges behind her and follows her own creation — a plant called

Breath of Life that has succeeded in making the leap — over the edge to "out-ness" and "otherness."

Both the reactions to the play's original staging in November 1921 and follow-up debates over the effects of its dramatic techniques and thematic intentions bear witness to the degree to which the play divided — and still divides — its audiences.[1] As Mary E. Papke sums up first-night reactions, for most early reviewers *The Verge* was "nothing more than a 'melodrama of neuroticism'" (64), a loquacious and overwritten piece that with its "celebration of anarchic genius" (66) would appeal only to the Greenwich Village bohemian and, most of all, to "anarcho-feminist philosophers" (67). Representative of many comments, J. Ranken Towse concludes in his note for the *New York Evening Post*: "If a moral must be deduced, it must be that only the neurotic or insane have the right idea of life." And Alexander Woollcott indulges in his familiar biting mockery when he states: "'The Verge' is a play which can be intelligently reviewed only by a neurologist or by some woman who has journeyed near to the verge of which Miss Glaspell writes. And by the same token, only these would enjoy it greatly" (15 Nov. 21: 23).

On the other hand, for a select few *The Verge* was a sensational work, "extremely sophisticated in its philosophical argument" (as Papke summarizes Maida Castellun's review, 65), an artistic manifestation, in Lewisohn's words, of "that vision without which we perish" ("Drama. 'The Verge'"). Where most mainstream critics rejected the play as too confusing in dramatic form and as too appalling in its presentation of a New Woman gone mad, these voices praised *The Verge* for its experimental style and its modern creation of "a superwoman as representative of the universal rebellious spirit, the human will to create and destroy according to individual desires" (Papke 65). Indeed, to critics such as Castellun and Lewisohn, Susan Glaspell's latest work compared favorably to the writings of Shakespeare and Maeterlinck, Chekhov and Shaw, Strindberg, Goethe, and Nietzsche.

From the moment of its first staging *The Verge* has been received first and foremost as the most radical dramatic display of "the new feminist's extreme way of life" ever presented on the American stage (Waterman, "Susan Glaspell," 181). Today, like *Trifles* this play is discussed mainly for this feminist dimension — with most critics reading its central theme as the struggle of a rebellious woman against the restrictions imposed on her by patriarchal society. In addition, against the background of feminist theory since the 1970s Claire's intensely violent "linguistic 'excesses'" (Bottoms 128) about smashing things and breaking out to otherness are often read as instances of a truly Cixousian *écriture féminine* — examples of a disruptive female mode of writing which predate the theory itself by more than half a century. By analogy, from such a standpoint Glaspell's experiments with dramatic form in *The Verge* can be seen as the playwright's own attempt to break away from the traditionally male language of the theatre.

True enough, *The Verge* allows its female protagonist to reveal her story in a voice unlike anything that had been heard in American drama before. Yet where most critics have seen Claire Archer's violent attempts to "explode the species" as a fight against the male Symbolic Order, I will stress here that they are as much a struggle against the laws of human existence *in general*— a level of meaning stressed in those early responses which read Glaspell's protagonist in *The Verge* as the representation of a "female Faust." Claire's groping words and obscure language dramatize both a woman's search for her "female self" and the more universal predicament of the human soul suspicious of the possibilities of communication and distrustful of a community whose rules, in their necessity to regulate our co-existence, will ever impede the self's urge for freedom.

In addition, whether one reads the play's protagonist as representative of the "female self" or of the "modern individual," in that Claire Archer's plant experiments are presented as a form of *art* Susan Glaspell once again comments on the nature and function not only of language as such, but of artistic expression as a special case of communication. Indeed, to the extent that the play's unique dramatic structure is itself an attempt to break out of known patterns, like Claire's plant creation the play is "both a new form and a commentary on form" (Noe, "*The Verge*," 140). As C.W.E. Bigsby has pointed out, in *The Verge* Glaspell

> combined comedy and melodrama, symbolism and expressionism, feminism and a critique of feminism, social criticism and metaphysical enquiry. What begins as a play of witty social observation quickly shifts its ground. The result is a work which is challenging in the demands which it makes on producers and designers no less than on audiences ["Introduction," 19].

Where the unsettled register of earlier plays by Glaspell might or might not have served to enhance the playwright's respective argument (see my discussions of *The People* and *Chains of Dew*), in the case of *The Verge* the play's refusal to settle on any dramatic form acts out its own central theme: the hope that we "need not be held in forms moulded for us" (64). Whether either Claire Archer or Susan Glaspell are successful in their ventures of expressing and creating meaning, however, remains the focal point of the play's critical reception up to the present day. And significantly enough, the answer to this question depends to a large extent on the specific model of language and art employed in the debate.

Claire Archer: Female or Human Self?

Indeed, how we read the significance of Claire Archer's struggle against words in *The Verge* depends on whether we see her as a representative of a specifically female or, to the contrary, of a universally human self. And since, in many ways, this female character personifies the prototype of the radical New Woman rebelling against patriarchal social norms, reading her story as the struggle of "woman" against "patriarchy"—and her language as an instance of *parler femme*—certainly seems an obvious move.

With a gesture that emerges as part of the play's social comedy, from the start Claire flouts the conventional role of the angel of the house as the perfect hostess. On a fierce winter morning she has ordered all the available heat to be turned to her greenhouse, saving her plant experiments from harm but leaving her husband and guests to the bitter cold of the house. In contrast to Harry, who in turn has ordered breakfast to be served in the greenhouse, Claire is utterly oblivious to the demands of hospitality. When Dick arrives on the scene he is greeted with her outright request to "[p]lease eat as little as possible, and as quickly." This remark promptly provokes a disapproving reaction from her husband: "A hostess calculated to put one at one's ease." Claire's answer comes in no uncertain terms, if "*with no ill-nature*": "I care nothing about your ease. Or about Dick's ease" (62).

That Claire does not think it necessary to show anyone the courtesy of good manners is brought up repeatedly throughout the entire play, and always the conventional female role she thus rejects is connected to a notion of what it means to be a refined woman in the context of her noble Puritan descent. For Claire is not only expected to be "gay" and "amusing" for her guests. True to the responsibilities committed to her by her ancestors, she is supposed to represent nothing less than "the flower of New England":

> HARRY. [Claire,] be amusing. That's really you, isn't it, Dick?
> DICK. Not quite all of her—I should say.
> CLAIRE. (*gaily*) Careful, Dick. Aren't you indiscreet? Harry will be suspecting that I am your latest strumpet.
> HARRY. Claire! What language you use! A person knowing you only by certain moments could never be made to believe you are a refined woman.
> CLAIRE. True, isn't it, Dick?
> HARRY. It would be a good deal of a lark to let them listen in at times—then tell them that here is the flower of New England! [64].

Of course, it is utterly ironic that Harry should call upon his wife's Puritan ancestry in reaction to a remark with which Claire alludes to a violation of the "laws that made New England" (64) much more grave than her refusal to be a refined woman: the adultery she commits by pursuing an affair with Dick. As the image of those men who "moulded the American mind" seems to inflict real pain on her in this scene, Claire's denial of both the roles of perfect hostess and of faithful wife is linked to a shuddering abhorrence of the Puritan past that looms behind her. On the other hand, Glaspell soon makes clear that her mockery of Puritan morality, too, is nothing more than an imprisoning male pattern. For while at first Claire enjoys playing the part she has chosen for herself as Dick's secret mistress, later she perceives of the same role as a "mere escape within, — rather shameful escape within" (72). After Tom, Claire's supposed soulmate, has tragically refused her offer to "share togetherness in outness" (89), she throws herself at Dick and implores him to take her "back — to the worst we ever were." Having stood "*before what she wanted more than life, and almost had, and lost,*" at this point she wants "[o]nly a place to hide your head — what else is there to hope for?" (92).

In the same way that Claire cannot find herself in her relations with men, the idea of her role as mother is also imprisoning to her. In fact, it is the same abhorrence of her Puritan ancestors which drives her to a cruel demonstration of contempt for her daughter Elizabeth (whom she has not seen for over a year). When Elizabeth reports that Miss Lane, her teacher, had given her "a spiel one day about living up to the men I come from," Claire looks her over and coldly assures her daughter: "You'll do it, Elizabeth" (75). And when, sure enough, with her rejection of her mother's experiments the girl demonstrates that she has already taken in her ancestors' stifling morality, Claire is openly disgusted:

> ELIZABETH. You know, something tells me this is *wrong.*
> CLAIRE. The hymn-singing ancestors are tuning up.
> ELIZABETH. I don't know what you mean by that, mother but–
> CLAIRE. But we will now sing, "Nearer my God, to Thee: Nearer to–"
> ELIZABETH. (*laughingly breaking in*) Well, I don't care. Of course you can make fun at me, but something does tell me this is wrong. To do what — what–
> DICK. What God did?
> ELIZABETH. Well — yes. Unless you do it to make [the plants] better — to do it just to *do* it — that doesn't seem right to me.
> CLAIRE. (*roughly*) "Right to you!" And that's all you know of adventure — and of anguish. Do you know it is you — world of which you're so true a flower — makes me have to leave? You're there to hold the door shut! Because you're young and of a gayer world, you think I can't *see* them — those old men? [...] [77].

In answer to this scene, in which Claire rejects even the biological tie between mother and daughter ("To think that object ever moved my belly and sucked my breast!" 78), it is her sister Adelaide who voices (male) society's grave judgment: "A mother who does not love her own child! You are an unnatural woman, Claire" (84). And as Claire retorts that "at least it saves me from being a natural one," once again she insists on breaking away from the suppressive patterns of her Puritan heritage:

> ADELAIDE. A mother cannot cast off her own child simply because she does not interest her!
> CLAIRE. (*an instant raising cool eyes to* ADELAIDE) Why can't she?
> ADELAIDE. Because it would be monstrous!
> CLAIRE. And why can't she be monstrous — if she has to be?
> ADELAIDE. You don't have to be. That's where I'm out of patience with you Claire. You are really a particularly intelligent, competent person, and it's time for you to call a halt to this nonsense and be the woman you were meant to be!
> CLAIRE. What inside dope have you on what I was meant to be?
> ADELAIDE. I know what you came from.
> CLAIRE. Well, isn't it about time somebody got loose from that? [79–80].

Both in her resistance to the "natural" role of motherhood and in her desire to break loose from "what she came from," Claire's struggle with patriarchal definitions here shifts from rejecting female social roles to challenging the idea of biological essence. What this female protagonist wants to escape is determination in every sense, including the influence of her genes.

In fact, engrossed in her mysterious plant experiments and intent on making new forms of life out of old patterns, Claire Archer is presented as the daring scientist of genius, the creator figure who seizes the power both to create and to destroy. On the one hand, this representation certainly highlights this female characters' aggressive appropriation of "male spheres." Elizabeth has a feeling that Claire's experiments are wrong because she tries to do "what God did," and this is especially "unsettling" because God is traditionally perceived to be male:

> HARRY. [...] I sometimes wonder whether all this [...] is a good thing. It would be all right if she'd just do what she did in the beginning — make the flowers as good as possible of their kind. That's an awfully nice thing for a woman to do — raise flowers. But there's something about this — changing things into other things — putting things together and making queer new things — this–
> DICK. Creating?
> HARRY. Give it any name you want it to have — it's unsettling for a woman [65].

On the other hand, as Claire self-confidently appropriates a role traditionally reserved for "man" in patriarchal thinking, Glaspell claims for her female protagonist nothing other than the same right granted to any male figure in world literature: the right to represent "humankind." And thus, that the play's universally human argument can come to the forefront of reception without necessarily denying Claire her existence as a woman is evident in several first-night reactions to *The Verge*. In Stephen Rathbun's review, for instance, his readings of Claire as a "woman" and Claire as an "individual" representing "man" overlap in a way which neither denies Claire her gender nor highlights the theme of gender differences as the play's primary concern:

> Mayhap a century or two from to-day, in the year 2021 or in 2121, "The Verge" will be as much of a stage classic as "Hamlet" is today. [...] The play is an extraordinary study of the superwoman. Its heroine strives for the absolute freedom of the individual. [...] Much as man wishes happiness, we believe that he longs much more to be free. *Claire* had the vision and realized it a little. We, poor mortals, [...] are chained hand and foot by duties, inhibitions and all the other fetters of our sham civilization. Three cheers for *Claire*! If she is insane, let us have more insanity! [...] *Claire* made her own great charter [for the individual], and we should all pray for strength to follow her example. If we could, there would follow a race of supermen that Nietzsche himself would have applauded ["'The Verge'"].

On the other hand, even this emphasis on Claire as the representation of the human self in *The Verge* can be read as Glaspell's attempt to redefine "womanhood." In a contextual reading of the two plays celebrated today as the playwright's most feminist works, Liza Maeve Nelligan has demonstrated that Claire Archer's very move from "womanhood" towards "selfhood" mirrors the development of feminist political thought in the United States during the early decades of the 20th century. "[By] the late 1910s," thus Nelligan explains, "women were questioning the essentialist notion that 'woman' was a unified subject with biologically determined characteristics. Many feminists turned to the Enlightenment ideals of individualism, long considered the province of men, to shape their politics, their activities, and their concepts of self" (86). Approaching the play from this historical angle, Nelligan argues that in *The Verge* Glaspell "engages one of the central feminist paradoxes of the early twentieth century: how to achieve a healthy sense of individualism without losing some of the more valuable qualities of 'womanhood,' particularly the sense of community that had informed *Trifles*" (92).

In other words, Claire's unconditional insistence on her individual sense of self can be seen as problematic in *The Verge* because her harsh rejection of traditional feminine roles includes a specifically female notion of solidarity. Throughout the entire play, Glaspell's protagonist struggles against the "unity" of "all the girls" represented both by her daughter and her sister. At the end of the first act Claire almost strikes out at Elizabeth with the Edge Vine, her unsuccessful plant that has not made it over the edge and is now "running, back to—'all the girls'" ("It's a little afraid of Miss Lane," Claire disgustedly remarks of her failed experiment, 77). Relieved that she has liberated herself from the burden of a mother's love —"O-h. How good I feel!

Light! (*a movement as if she could fly*)"—she turns to retreat to her private quarters in a remote part of the main building, "*a tower which is thought to be round but does not complete the circle*" (78). But this space, too, is invaded at the beginning of the second act, as Harry brings up Adelaide in an attempt to help Claire get "back to normal." It is in this space that most represents Claire's unconnected individuality, that her sister urges her to "halt this nonsense and be the woman you were meant to be" (79). And in Adelaide's view of the world this phrase does not only address a woman's "natural" mother instincts, but also circumscribes a social image of women as finding their life's fulfillment in the self-effacing task of catering to other people's needs:

> ADELAIDE. [Living up to what you came from] isn't being imprisoned. Right there is where you make your mistake, Claire. Who's in a tower — in an unsuccessful tower? Not I. I go about in the world —free, busy, happy. Among people, I have no time to think of myself.
> CLAIRE. No.
> ADELAIDE. No. My family. The things that interest them; from morning till night it's–
> CLAIRE. Yes, I know you have a large family, Adelaide; five and Elizabeth makes six.
> ADELAIDE. We'll speak of Elizabeth later. But if you would just get out of yourself and enter into other people's lives—[80].

In this context, Adelaide can certainly be seen to represent the notion of a specifically female experience of life in *The Verge*, and Claire's rejection of both her sister and her daughter is a rejection of the conventional idea of female solidarity. On the other hand, as was already the case in *Trifles*, in *The Verge*, too, Glaspell engages with both the imprisoning and supporting aspects of communal relations not only in the context of *women's* lives, but as part of human existence *in general*. For even if Adelaide is "a woman who is confident in her 'womanliness'" (Nelligan 93), both in Claire's eyes and in Adelaide's own argument her belief in the necessity of living within the "main body of humanity" signifies a community of women *and* men. To Adelaide's suggestion that she should "get out of [herself] and enter into other people's lives" Claire retorts: "Then I would become just like you. And we should all be just alike in order to assure one another that we're all just right. But since you and Harry and Elizabeth and ten million other people bolster each other up, why do you especially need me?" (80). Claire's reproach that "[you] two feel very superior, don't you?" is addressed both to Adelaide and to her husband Harry: "superior to what you think is my feeling of superiority, comparing my — isolation with your 'heart of humanity.' Soon we will speak of the beauty of common experiences [...]" (80). And Adelaide also evokes a community which includes both genders when she calls upon the idea of "family" as the smallest social unit:

ADELAIDE. [...] Claire, dear, I wish I could make you feel how much I care for you. (*simply, with real feeling*) You can call me all the names you like — dull, commonplace, lazy — that *is* a new idea, I confess, but the rest of our family's gone now, and the love that used to be there between us all — the only place for it now is between you and me. You were so much loved, Claire. You oughtn't to try and get away from a world in which you are so much loved. (*to* HARRY) Mother — father — all of us, always loved Claire best. We always loved Claire's queer gaiety [...] [82].

What Claire rejects, then, is not only the conventional idea of female solidarity. She struggles against the limiting thrust of human community in general. What is more, in this struggle Glaspell once more thematizes both the negative, inhibiting aspects of human intersubjectivity and presents the notion of constitutive articulate contact as a life-sustaining inevitability. For in her way of approaching Claire, Adelaide displays "simple" and "real" feeling for her sister, and the love she offers stands as a symbol for all that Claire will lose if she continues on her path towards otherness. Likewise, just as the sympathetic portrayal of the talkative Mr. Hale serves to enhance a positive notion of human community in *Trifles*, Claire Archer's male patriarchal counterparts are drawn more positively than is often acknowledged in feminist readings of the play. As Stephen J. Bottoms recounts from a rare perspective of rehearsal dynamics, in his 1996 production the actor who played Tom "found a vulnerability, a tenderness, and a wild-eyed idealism that made Claire's fascination with him entirely believable," while Harry evolved as "a well-meaning, deeply sympathetic man who loves Claire passionately [...], but who is so much the creature of social convention that he can never comprehend the alternatives for which Claire, Tom, and even Dick live" (136).[2] To be sure, neither of Claire's men is presented exclusively as a detestable caricature of male desire for power over woman. Before her final realization that she has to go her way alone if she is to go it at all, in her longing for understanding Claire has tried three times to achieve "a satisfying relationship with a like-minded man" (Nelligan 96) — and if devotion alone could be her measuring rod, neither of the men presently surrounding her would be unworthy of her love. Their display of concern is always honest, and it is not habitually expressed in the brutal terms of taking possession with which Tom, desperately afraid for Claire's mental state, tips her over the edge in the end ("You are mine, and you will stay with me!" 99).[3]

On the one hand, then, one might argue that in rejecting the (female) community invoked by Adelaide Claire adheres to the feminist conviction of her time that the freedom of being able to "move through the social system" uninhibited by any restrictions "could only be realized if women learned to see themselves not as women but, instead, as autonomous individuals with unique attributes and desires" (Nelligan 91). On the other hand, that in the end Claire "leaps" out of the social system altogether problematizes this unconditional individualism. For while her insanity can be understood to criticize a patriarchal system which makes it impossible for "woman" to find her self within its definitory boundaries, the sympathetic portrayal of Claire's patriarchal adversaries throws more than the shadow of a doubt on Glaspell's celebration of her protagonist as a woman who has liberated herself from these ties. Whether the play's critique of Claire's self-centredness is read as the revaluation of patriarchal gender ideology in its emphasis on the notion of female community (as Nelligan has argued), or whether it is seen as the acceptance of human existence *in general* as profoundly inter-subjective — in both cases it is tragic that neither Adelaide nor Harry, Dick, or Tom can sustain Claire within the realm of contact which all of them represent. As Claire's insistence on her apartness makes human relations principally impossible, in this play Glaspell adds to her discussion of patriarchy a dark picture of the inevitable loneliness of the human soul — and thus she emphasizes the skeptic's doubt on the basis of the symbol model of language in *The Verge*.

The *"Female Voice"* in The Verge: A *Cixousian* Écriture Féminine?

Even though I will eventually stress the non-gendered aspects of Glaspell's struggle with language in *The Verge*, of course it is no coincidence that feminist theories have proven the most persistent hermeneutic lens in recent interpretations. If *Trifles* can be seen to *anticipate* the French feminists' ideal of a female language disrupting the patterns of male discourse, *The Verge* apparently *realizes* this dream. As language itself develops into one of the play's most prominent themes, Claire's utterances (opposing every other character's speech in their peculiar intensity and supposed incoherence) seem to present perfect examples of a truly Irigarayan *parler femme*. Indeed, such a reading of Claire's efforts to reach "outness" and "otherness" becomes even more enticing if one considers the play's fate in terms of its critical reception. In 1921 *The Verge* was greeted by many of its (male) critics with biting ridicule precisely on account of its being loquacious, overwritten, and hopelessly intelligible in its use of language. And even today (in a Western world in which women have achieved a considerable degree of empowerment compared to Glaspell's own time) the play is still considered obscure — an indication that the definitory frame of patriarchy still determines what is culturally successful as a work of art, and what is not.

That Claire's "linguistic excesses" (Bottoms) can be read as instances of a disruptive feminine language meant to "shoot holes" (*The Verge* 81) through the enclosing circle of the male Symbolic Order is perhaps most apparent in her outright wrath when she is confronted with the way in which both her daughter and her sister have integrated themselves into the patriarchal structure. Indeed, it is telling that Claire is most furious at Elizabeth and Adelaide — not at the men — for using words without "respect" (83). Exasperated to see that Elizabeth will have no difficulties in "[living] up to the men she came from," Claire tries to shut up her unreflected phrases:

> CLAIRE. You'll do it, Elizabeth.
> ELIZABETH. Well, I don't know. Quite a job, I'll say. Of course, I'd have to do it in my way. I'm not going to teach or preach or be a stuffy person. But now that — (*she here becomes the product of a superior school*) values have shifted and such sensitive new things have been liberated in the world–
> CLAIRE. (*low*) Don't use those words.
> ELIZABETH. Why — why not?
> CLAIRE. Because you don't know what they mean [75].

With Adelaide — a full-grown female pillar of the patriarchal order — Claire's reproach is more thorough. Read against the background of Irigarayan theory, Glaspell's protagonist can be seen to expose her sister's image of the "main body of human community" as a male concept designed to suppress a separate female sense of self as the "actual Other":

> ADELAIDE. (*beginning anew*) It's a new age, Claire. Spiritual values–
> CLAIRE. Spiritual values! (*in her brooding way*) So you have pulled that up. (*with cunning*) Don't think I don't know what it is you do. [...] [*To* HARRY:] It's rather clever, what she does. Snatching the phrase — (*a movement as if pulling something up*) standing it up between her and — the life that's there. And by saying it enough — "We have life! We have life! We have life!" Very good come-back at one who would really be — "Just so! *We* are that. Right this way, please — " That, I suppose is what we mean by needing each other. All join in the chorus. "This is it! This is it! This is it!" And anyone who won't join is to be — visited by relatives. (*regarding* ADELAIDE *with curiosity*) Do you really think that anything is going on in you? [81].

A moment later, Claire calls her sister not only a "liar and thief" but a "*whore with words*" (82; my emphasis) — an assault which underlines her belief that in "standing up" (male) phrases between herself and the life outside, for the safety of the so-called "common experiences" Adelaide has sold her female self to patriarchal definitions ("Just so! *We* are that").

On the basis of such scenes, it seems more than called for to interpret Claire's distrust of language as a rebellion of the female voice against the "language of male experience" (Ben-Zvi 157). Painfully aware of the social "limitations of her gender," thus Linda Ben-Zvi has argued, Glaspell's protagonist feels that "traditional language [is] unsuited for [women's] needs" ("Susan Glaspell's Contributions," 156), and consequently, as Ann E. Larabee has also pointed out, Glaspell portrays "woman's" urge of breaking out of the "prison of language created by patriarchy" (81). Indeed, in one of the most comprehensive analyses along these lines Marcia Noe has identified three different ways in which *The Verge* can be read to "valorize a uniquely female point of view":

> First, Claire's enterprise, the creation of revolutionary plant forms, can be viewed as analogous to the efforts of theorists such as Cixous and Irigaray to create a uniquely female form of language. Second, through setting, lighting, action, and dialogue, Glaspell sets up a number of binary oppositions that emphasize the symbolic system Claire sets out to destroy. Third, the language of the play, which almost all readers find obscure and tedious, can be seen as an attempt to create a form of *l'écriture féminine*, a uniquely female style of writing ["*The Verge*," 133].

By means of a well-chosen juxtaposition of passages in which Claire expresses her longing for "otherness," her desire to "smash things," and her yearning for the freedom of "flight," with passages from Cixous, Noe demonstrates a number of striking similarities in imagery and tone between Glaspell's character and the French feminist theorists. In this way, the critic illustrates that Claire, "like Cixous's newly born woman," "strives to transcend all limits, all bounds [...]. Claire is trying to oppose the rationality of a patriarchal system by seeking out madness, by embracing 'otherness,' by breaking through old structures to create new ones" ("*The Verge*," 134).

On the basis of an approach which reads *The Verge* through the lens of Cixousian theory, therefore, the play's "seemingly bizarre and melodramatic ending" can be understood as the realization of Claire's ultimate success. In act 3, thus Noe argues, Claire's

> enterprise comes to fruition: the Breath of Life is seen to have broken through to a new species; she has successfully undermined the masculine structures that threatened to contain her. Indeed, Claire functions in *The Verge* similarly to the way Catherine Clément describes the hysteric in the opening section of *The Newly Born Woman*: "The hysteric unties the familiar bond, introduces disorder into the well-regulated unfolding of everyday life, gives rise to magic in ostensible reason" ["*The Verge*" 136].

And certainly, this positive reading of Claire's final insanity is prepared in the character's own utterances. Throughout the entire play Claire has aspired to madness as her only chance for sanity, describing her plant experiments as a search for "the madness that — breaks through" (70):

> CLAIRE. You think I can't smash anything? You think life can't break up, and go outside what it was? Because you've gone dead in the form in which you found yourself, you think that's all there is to the whole adventure? And that is called sanity. And made a virtue — to lock one in. You never worked with things that grow! Things that take a sporting chance — go mad — that sanity mayn't lock them in — from life untouched — from life — that waits. (*she turns toward the inner room*) Breath of Life (*she goes in there*) [65].

For Dr. Emmons, too, the neurologist whom Harry has invited to the house, Claire has only one question: "It must be very interesting — helping people go insane. [...] But tell me, how do they do it? It's not so easy to— get out. How do so many manage it?" (91). And very early in act 1 she already predicts the cathartic violence which will accompany her final success: "If one ever does get out, I suppose it is— quite unexpectedly, and perhaps— a bit terribly" (63). Consequently, within her own logic Claire's final madness indeed "*is* liberating in the way she desires it," and her "ultimate linguistic collapse" (Dymkowski 92) can be seen to "[signal] the new tentative freedom of a feminist discourse that opens up a territory of limitless combinations" (Larabee 81).

Yet even from within the theory of *l'écriture féminine* and related notions, Claire's achievement at the end of the play is a highly problematic one. For one, the role of the female hysteric is not always seen as positively as it is presented in Clément's quote, introduced in Noe's interpretation above. After all, both Irigaray's concept of "womanspeak" and Cixous's idea of a feminine writing style present a conscious strategy of disruption from *within* the Symbolic Order. In contrast, the figure of the hysteric marks a retreat into the realm of the Imaginary, and thus signifies the loss of a sense of identity within language. If it should have been Claire's hope to make room for the actual (female) other within the space of the Symbolic Order (as is the proclaimed goal of *parler femme* and *écriture-au-féminine*), her retreat into insanity does not mark triumph but defeat: Instead of finding a valid identity as a female individual, Claire has lost her sense of self for good.

What is more, while Cixous's idea of a female writing style incorporates the Derridean concept of *différance* as a constant deferral of meaning (a concept, that is, which denies the possibility of a "final meaning" comprehensible in and of itself), throughout the entire play Claire's utterances suggest that she has started out on a road which will bring her "nearer God" (88) — the ultimate self-sufficient signifier. In fact, Claire's arrival in the aspired state of outness is expressed through the gropingly stammered lines of a Christian hymn, and thus what we witness at the play's final curtain is framed as her final merger with the transcendental signified:

> CLAIRE. Out. (*as if feeling her way*)
> Nearer, (*Her voice now feeling the way to it.*)
> Nearer— (*Voice almost upon it*)
> –my God, (*Falling upon it with surprise.*)
> to Thee, (*Breathing it.*)
> Nearer— to Thee,
> E'en though it be—
> (*A slight turn of the head toward the dead man she loves— a mechanical turn just as far the other way.*)

a cross
That (*Her head going down.*)
raises me; (*Her head slowly coming up — singing it.*)
Still all my song shall be,
Nearer, my–(*Slowly the curtain begins to shut her out. The last word heard
is the final* Nearer *—a faint breath from far.*)

CURTAIN [100–101].

Hence, in an interpretation of Claire's *écriture féminine* much bleaker than
that of other feminist critics, J. Ellen Gainor meets the challenge of this
female character's final religious exultation by concluding:

> Although Glaspell presents Claire as the Christ figure here, seemingly
> finally escaping all social bonds, the locus of that liberation is ironically
> problematic. Glaspell's climax permanently reinscribes her heroine in the
> ultimate patriarchal structure, as Claire embraces emblems of the Protes-
> tant Church and all it historically represented for women. Rather than a
> release, this ending marks Claire's failure to achieve an independent femi-
> nist identity — her ultimate recognition of the inescapability of the patri-
> archy ["A Stage of Her Own," 96].[4]

Such contradictory readings of *The Verge* even from within the theory
of *l'écriture féminine* itself illustrate that the various notions involved in the
creation of a female language making space for woman's "actual other" in
patriarchy have a difficult relation to the question of how to *define* this
"other" female (or feminine) subject in the first place. In this regard, both
Claire Archer's enterprise and the French feminists' theories suffer from the
same inherent paradox: that freedom from the imprisoning male patterns
of the Symbolic (defined by the very emergence of language) is supposed to
be achieved through the creation of yet more — if "other" — linguistic patterns. As Marcia Noe explains, the "feminist theorist committed to *l'écriture féminine* is caught in a vicious circle; she cannot escape structures except
through annihilation. If she tries to explain her enterprise, she must do it
with language, within the very structures she is trying to break out of. If she
doesn't explain or define it, she has no way of validating its existence" ("*The
Verge*," 140).[5] If *The Verge* is read as the outcome of a search for female otherness in the Cixousian sense, must Claire's insanity then be seen as a retreat
into the Imaginary which marks her final failure of establishing a female
sense of self in the Symbolic Order, as Gainor has it? Or is the outness she
has reached to be seen positively, as a space where all is one, where individual identities within the dichotomy of man/woman no longer exist? Has she,
to the contrary, freed herself to the possibility of realizing her "truly other"
femininity, after all? Or has Claire perhaps just bought into the notion of
"man" as the universal representative of humankind, as she appropriates the
male roles of creator and destroyer in her act of turning herself into a God-
like figure?

As it turns out, to the extent that Claire, in her hope to reach "life that waits" (62) indeed aspires to some form of (female?) essence, her attempts are doomed to failure from the outset. Inevitably, every new form (or sense of self) will turn into just another suffocating pattern within whose frame the ever-moving force of life cannot be free. In the end, Claire's plant experiments confirm this predicament. On the one hand, the Edge Vine turns out a failure because it cannot reproduce itself and thus is unable to survive as a new form of life: "CLAIRE. [...] (*looking somberly at it*) You are out, but you are not alive" (77). By contrast, Breath of Life has succeeded precisely in that it is strong enough to persist in its otherness: "The form is set," thus Anthony hails this lasting break-through when Claire is too timid to look into the flower's throbbing heart herself (96). But it is this very assurance which already addresses the fate awaiting each new form that can persist. Once it is "set," it will begin to repeat itself, and the more frequent the repetition the faster the new thing will turn into a dead pattern blocking, once again, the way to life that waits. Where Tom still pleads: "Can't this help you, Claire? Let this be release. This— breath of the uncaptured" (96), Claire already knows that her present success entails her future failure:

> CLAIRE. (*and though speaking, she remains just as still*)
> Breath of the uncaptured?
> You are a novelty.
> Out?
> You have been brought in.
> A thousand years from now, when you are but a form too long repeated,
> Perhaps the madness that gave you birth will burst again,
> And from the prison that is you will leap pent queernesses
> To make a form that hasn't been–
> To make a person new.
> And this we call creation [96].

In acquiring the strength to survive in its otherness, the new form has already been "brought in," and the only hope remaining is that "a thousand years from now" "the madness that gave [...] birth will burst again." Hence, if Glaspell's play does present us with an instance of *l'écriture féminine*, it also acknowledges that the very moment of Claire's successful self-creation tragically entails the inevitability of woman's renewed imprisonment.

The Prison-house of Language: Identity and Self-Expression

If it is questionable, then, whether Claire has managed to find a female essence "outside," and even more so whether she has found a way of inscribing a place for female otherness within the Symbolic Order, perhaps her final step "nearer God" can still be read as her discovery of a *human* essence — "sex unspecified"?[6] Certainly the predicament she so desperately struggles

against within the symbol model of language — her sense that we are incapable of expressing our innermost selves to others — is not a "female" problem alone. In fact, that Glaspell's protagonist paradoxically falls into the
stylized rhythm of poetry in the quote above as a way of escaping the stifling
patterns of familiar forms can be read as an expression of this more universal thrust in Claire's language skepticism. After all, her shift into the poetic
mode first occurs during her key confrontation with Tom, where it draws a
thematic parallel between her own desire for definitory freedom and this
male character's position as the soulmate she so desperately longs to draw
"out" with her:

> CLAIRE. [...] [Sometimes] — from my lowest moments — beauty has
>   opened as the sea.
>   From a cave I saw immensity
>   My love, you're going away–
>   Let me tell you how it is with me;
>   I want to touch you — somehow touch you once before I die–
>   Let me tell you how it is with me.
>   I do [...] not want to make a rose or make a poem–
>   Want to lie upon the earth and know. (*closes her eyes*)
>   Stop doing that! — words going into patterns;
>   They do it sometimes when I let come what's there.
>   Thoughts take pattern — then the pattern is the thing.
>   But let me tell you how it is with me. (*it flows again*) [...] (*covering her face*)
>   Stop *doing* that. Help me stop doing that!
> TOM. (*and from the place where she had carried him*)
>   Don't talk at all. Lie still and know–
>   And know that I am knowing.
> CLAIRE. Yes; but we are so weak we have to talk;
>   To talk — to touch.
>   Why can't I rest in knowing I would give my life to reach you? [87–88].

Occupying a central space within the play's dramatic structure, this
scene between Claire and Tom combines much of what the theme of language as our human (as opposed to "female") mode of existence incorporates in Glaspell's writings. On the one hand, the very fact that Claire falls
into a beautifully poetic, and thus linguistic, expression of what she longs
for demonstrates the playwright's ever-present faith in the capacity of "true"
language to reach to the heart of life (compare such earlier plays as *The People* or *Bernice*). Even Claire herself, on one level of her argument, does not
demand that we should not talk at all, but that we should "respect words."
During her confrontation with Adelaide she viciously hurls out: "I'm tired
of what you do — you and all of you. Life — experience — values — calm —
sensitive words which raise their heads as indications" (83). Here, Claire
defends the capacity of language to "reach" (ibid.) — as of course Glaspell herself does with every new piece of her writing.

On the other hand, since words inevitably turn into fixed forms even with Claire herself, who is sensitive like no other to this danger, she would rather not be forced to use this inefficient and distorting medium of communication. "Words going into patterns" — "Help me stop doing that!" she begs of Tom, and more than once she shrinks away from what she sees as utterly futile attempts to explain herself to Harry, Dick, or Elizabeth. Indeed, the fact that every time her longing to be *understood* forces her to make the effort in spite of herself merely underlines Claire's desperate predicament — a pain which only Tom can grasp:

> ELIZABETH. [...] What's the use of making [the plants] different if they aren't better?
> HARRY. A good square question, Claire. Why don't you answer it? [...]
> CLAIRE. Why do you ask me to do that? This is my own thing. Why do you make me feel I should — (*goes to* ELIZABETH) I will be good to you, Elizabeth. [...] We'll do gay things. [...] Anything else. Not — this is — Not this. [...]
> HARRY. Claire! (*which says, 'How can you?'*)
> CLAIRE. (*who is looking at* ELIZABETH) Yes, I will try.
> TOM. *I* don't think so. As Claire says — anything else. [...]
> HARRY. It'll do Claire good to take someone in. To get down to brass tacks and actually say what she's driving at.
> CLAIRE. Oh — Harry. But yes — I will try. (*does try, but no words come. Laughs*) When you come to say it it's not — One would rather not nail it to a cross of words — (*laughs again*) with brass tacks. [...]
> CLAIRE. [...] These plants — (*beginning flounderingly*) Perhaps they are less beautiful — less sound — than the plants from which they diverged. But they have found — otherness. (*laughs a little shrilly*) If you know — what I mean.
> TOM. Claire — stop this! (*To* HARRY) This is wrong [76].

Significantly, where Harry insists that putting her ideas into words will help Claire to "see more clearly," Tom understands that such struggles to "reach" when she cannot believe it possible demand too much of her. As a result, it is only with Tom that Claire can take refuge in the belief that words are "not needed," that between them there is "a way down below the way that words can go" — a connection, that is, which links two isolated souls without having to rely on the falsifying mediator of language (85).

And thus, Tom Edgeworthy's association with Claire's character in *The Verge* is the strongest indication that her distrust of words is grounded on a "universally human" fear of isolation. Although in the final scene Tom is clearly Claire's most dangerous (male!) opponent, on another level he serves as a supporting correspondence figure throughout the entire play — a parallel for which his telling last name is of course an indication. Like Claire, the man who is "worthy of the edge" has spent his adult life trying to get away from social definitions of what he should be — through Harry we learn that he refused to take up his father's publishing business, "always going to the ends of the earth to—meditate about something" (66). What is more, just like Claire, Tom cannot make the other two men understand the "business" which so intimately connects them. When he tries to explain Claire's troubled state to Harry, his words do not clarify anything for the other man: "She's left so—open. Too exposed. (*as* HARRY *moves impatiently*) Please don't be annoyed with me. I'm doing my best at saying it." (71). Likewise, when he attempts to relate his reasons for leaving Claire to his rival, Dick, Claire's current lover can only respond: "I'm afraid I'm like Harry now. I don't get you" (72). And thus, it is in her very sense of standing apart and of being unable to communicate one's most profound thoughts that Tom can understand Claire where all the other characters in the play cannot:

> CLAIRE. The idea of giving anyone a place in life.
> HARRY. Yes! The very idea!
> CLAIRE. Yes! (*as often, the mocking thing gives true expression to what lies sombrely in her*) The war. There was another gorgeous chance.
> HARRY. Chance for what? I call you, Claire. I ask you to say what you mean.
> CLAIRE. I don't know—precisely. If I did—there'd be no use saying it. (*at* HARRY's *impatient exclamation she turns to* TOM)
> TOM. (*nodding*) The only thing left worth saying is the thing we can't say.
> HARRY. Help! [70].

In this way, Glaspell draws several parallels between Claire's and Tom's marginal positions. Like Claire, Tom feels a powerful urge to "isolate self from the conventions of a society in which both feel alien" (Ben-Zvi, "Susan Glaspell and Eugene O'Neill," 26), and in sharing at least in part her feeling of "otherness," he is set apart from the other two men almost as much as Claire is herself.

On the other hand, in the end the mysterious "open way" between Tom and Claire turns out to be nothing more than an illusion. Seducing her to believe in the accessibility of what she longs for most—togetherness in otherness—Tom's understanding turns out to be more dangerous to Claire's self-realization than anything else. For at the same time that she bitterly defends her "by-herself-ness," Glaspell's female protagonist admits a deep yearning for a kindred soul. "Why can't I rest in knowing I would give my life to reach you?" she asks Tom (88), and for a brief, passionate moment she is willing to convince herself that *giving up* her "apartness" might be the very way "out" together—a way that would otherwise be so sadly lonesome:

> CLAIRE. [...] That, too, I will give you—my by-myself-ness. That's the uttermost I can give. I never thought—to try to give it. But let us do it—the great sacrilege! Yes! [...] Let us take the mad chance! Perhaps it's the only way to save—what's there. [...] Bring all into life between us—or send all down to death! [...] (*hesitates, shudders*) But yes—I will, I will risk the life that waits. Perhaps only he who gives his loneliness—shall find. You never keep by holding. (*gesture of giving*) To the uttermost. And it is gone—or it is there [...] [88–89].

It is Claire's very longing to reach out to another human being, then, to feel a true connection between herself and Tom — in body *and* soul — which makes her fall into the "trap of words." Although she is painfully aware that by putting her feelings into language she is already risking to "shut [them] up in saying" (86), she cannot rest content in Tom's assurance that he knows without words "how it is with her." Even if she herself thinks it "weak" that she has "to talk — to touch" (88), it becomes necessary because Tom, in his very acknowledgment that there is between them "an open way" beyond words, refuses to use this connection and find out where it leads. He cannot accept that Claire is not the beautiful untouched flower he takes her to be, that she is "not — all spirit" (85), nor can he hold out against his fear of that "other side" whose intensity he senses in her (87). Deterred by the unknown consequences of passing through the "door on the far side of destruction" (71), not willing to "risk everything with her," for all his understanding Tom stops short at adoring Claire in her "apartness," watching her "stand alone in a clearness that breaks [his] heart" (86). And thus, Claire finally understands that her hope for the liberating possibility of giving Tom her very "by-myself-ness" was only a desperate act of self-delusion. Suddenly seeing *"with a sight too clear"* (99) she now knows that if she ever wants to reach that outness where the stifling patterns of words cannot touch life, there is no other possibility than to go it alone. As she strangles Tom in an almost religious frenzy (*"You fill the place—should be a gate [in agony]* Oh, that it is you — fill the place — should be a gate!"*) she at last frees herself — and him — of a life which is less than truth, where the deceptive principle of language creates a tempting but cruelly mocking illusion of human community and understanding.[7]

What apparently wins in *The Verge*, then, is a bleak image of language as a system of signs ultimately incapable of signifying truth and one's innermost self, and of connecting one human soul to the other. In the end, Claire is "out," possibly close to God as the final signifier, but she is also "lonely" (100). And even within her own terms of existence this final state is not a complete success. For while Claire has followed her plant, Breath of Life, in a perfect parallel, her creation had not been finished yet; it had still awaited "reminiscence":

> CLAIRE. I want to give fragrance to Breath of Life (*faces the room beyond the wall of glass*) — the flower I have created that is outside what flowers have been. What has gone out should bring fragrance from what it has left. But no definite fragrance, no limiting enclosing thing. I call the fragrance I am trying to create Reminiscence. (*her hand on the pot of the wistful little flower she has just given pollen*) Reminiscent of the rose, the violet, arbutus— but a new thing — itself. Breath of Life may be lonely out in what hasn't been. Perhaps some day I can give it reminiscence [64].

In all her work, Claire had been convinced that even in "outness" we "need the haunting beauty from the life we've left"—yet before she was able to work on this goal she made the leap herself, leaving "Reminiscence" behind for both her plant and for herself. In vain, her faithful servant Anthony attempts to lure her back with what she had yet wanted to achieve:

> ANTHONY. Miss Claire! You can do anything—won't you try?
> CLAIRE. Reminiscence? (*speaking the word as if she has left even that, but smiles a little*)
> (ANTHONY *takes Reminiscence, the flower she was breeding for the fragrance for Breath of Life—holds it out to her. But she has taken a step forward, past them all.*) [100].

Hence, whether or not Claire has indeed found "essence" (female or human) on the "other side of destruction" (whether she has "[s]aved—[herself]," 100), what remains on the level of realistic representation is the tragic fact that she is no longer capable of communicating what is there on the outside. As Bottoms describes his experiences with staging the play's ending:

> the true agony of the situation is borne by the men left behind, who come in to cradle Tom's corpse. Claire may (or may not) have found otherness, but she has no way of communicating her discovery to these men left trapped in the gray dimension of reality/realism, who fall over themselves to cover Claire's tracks and take the blame, even while realizing the futility of these attempts [144].

Claire Archer, as the prototype of the female artist, has perhaps succeeded in her self-creation, "has broken out and is existentially free, alone in the transcendental beyond" (Ozieblo, "Suppression," 116). Yet she was able to achieve this freedom "only in the solitary icy regions of speechlessness, the silence of madness" (Bach, "Susan Glaspell—Provincetown Playwright," 254). Consequently, while with this ending Glaspell seems to prove right those skeptics who deny the possibility of "true understanding" through language, in this very suggestion she also once again stresses the need for the concept of communality in our lives—a concept which is also brought into play in the dramatist's presentation of the creative act in *The Verge*.

The Notion of (Female?) Creativity: Claire Archer and Susan Glaspell

In their discussion of female creativity in *The Verge*, feminist critics have often argued that with the character of Claire Archer Glaspell has given center stage to a woman men are rightfully afraid of. Claire is the Female Artist, the creatrix breaking out of male patterns, she is the embodiment of the naturally violent, "uniquely female capacity to give birth to new life" (Dymkowski 102), the woman "risk-taker and seer" (ibid. 101) pioneering at the outskirts of male society, set on change against the resistance of male fixity. With Claire, thus this argument goes, Glaspell dramatizes the female experience of being the Other in patriarchal society, and since in her struggle against social expectations she is "engaged in the business of self-creation" (Larabee 80), this quest can be read as the search for a uniquely female sense of self. Indeed, not only with regard to Claire's use of language, but also in the way in which Glaspell herself has translated this experience into new dramatic forms, many readers have perceived of *The Verge* as a successfully disruptive sample of *l'écriture féminine*—a dramatic writing-in-the-feminine that is indeed capable of "shooting holes through the circle" of the all-enclosing patriarchy (82).

On the other hand, one might argue that in claiming for her heroine an "unconditional freedom to choose life's patterns" (Nelligan 91), Glaspell has set Claire Archer free even from the dichotomy of man/woman itself, as the one most profound pattern still framing any discussion of the "female voice" in literature, theory, and science. With the portrayal of her protagonist as caught in an existential dilemma not exclusive to female experience, thus one might argue, in *The Verge* "Glaspell [...] wrote a play concerning the eternal difficulties of the human spirit" (Lewisohn, *Expression* 295). And although readings of Glaspell's works in this vein have become sparse, to engage with her theme of creative expression in a way which takes into consideration both a gendered *and* a more general, universally human approach may enrich today's approaches to this many-faceted play as much as it broadened the scope of critical reactions at the time of its original staging.

Once more in Glaspell's oeuvre, the playwright's central issue is one of identity in this play, debated through the two *topoi* of Claire's plant experiments and her understanding of language. As we have seen, if we read Claire Archer's aspirations as the attempt to make herself new, two opposing conclusions can be drawn. Either her madness in the end is the expression of her ultimate loss of self and, with this, her existential failure; or her final leap is seen as a successful step towards self-creation (whether as "female self" or as a "human being"). Importantly, however, what Claire aspires to is not only her own recreation as a "free, unfettered being" (Malpede 124). Yet another aspect emerges in the context of this character's work in the greenhouse: Claire wants to "explode" her entire species and create it anew for the sake of "freeing life" itself. Before we can come to know "that we *are*," thus she claims, we need to be "broken up into pieces": "I want to break it up! I tell you, I want to break it up! If it were all in pieces, we'd be (*a little laugh*) shocked to aliveness (*to* DICK)— Wouldn't we? There would be strange new comings together — mad new comings together, and we would know what it is to be born, and then we might know— that we are." It is in this context that Glaspell's protagonist sees the atrocities of World War I as a missed chance for "the madness that — breaks through": "Mankind massed to kill. We have failed. We are through. We will destroy. [...] All we had thought we were — we aren't. We were shut in with what wasn't so. [...] Break up. And then — and then — But we didn't say —'And then-' The spirit didn't take the tip" (64).

Translating her desire to destroy the fixed patterns of life so that something new and free can be created into her experiments in the greenhouse, Claire thus explains what she wants to achieve:

> Plants do it. The big leap — it's called. Explode their species— because something in them knows they've gone as far as they can go. Something in them knows they're shut in to just that. So— go mad — that life may not be prisoned. Break themselves up into crazy things— into lesser things, and from the pieces— may come one sliver of life with vitality to find the future [70].

Significantly, then, as Gerhard Bach has pointed out in his analysis of Claire's work, what underlies her scientific experiments is not an idea of evolution patterned along the lines of Darwinian thought, but a concept of species development based on the mutation theory formulated by Hugo DeVries (1848–1935) in his experimental method of analyzing the evolution of plants:

> [DeVries] discovered in his cultures of O. Mamarckiana new forms appearing among the hosts of ordinary forms, and the name of mutation was given to this method of producing new species and varieties, which he showed to arise suddenly, as distinct from Charles Darwin's variation of species through natural selection.[8]

Indeed, thus Bach explains further, Claire is fascinated with the idea of becoming the first "mutant" of her species, of turning into the "ur-mother" of a future human race (*Susan Glaspell* 167). And while even in this theoretical context the play does not decide whether Claire's final state of madness circumscribes the destruction of the *old* form (her old self) as a necessary step prior to the formation of a new species, or whether her arrival "outside" is already an expression of the *new* form (her new and other identity), one might argue that the "recognition of Claire's insanity leaves room for a peculiar optimism since she has successfully abandoned the principles of this world for those of her own devising" (Ozieblo, *Susan Glaspell* 188).

On the one hand, whether the play's ending marks Claire's success or failure, in both cases her achievement is measured by her own expressed goal of reaching the "life that waits." Throughout the play, this phrase marks a decidedly essentialist notion of human existence (referring to a form of life always already existing somewhere "outside"), and thus in this context of her plant experiments, too, Glaspell's protagonist seems to employ a notion of language and art as systems of signs which are employed to relate truths that exist both prior to and independent of their expression in these media.

On the other hand, even in *The Verge*, which seems so persistent in its philosophy of the disillusioned skeptic, a parallel notion of both language and art as forms of constitutive articulate contact is discernible on several plains.

In fact, even with regard to the very theory which serves as the basis of Claire's experiments to reach "life that waits," this character's apparent belief in essence is supplemented by a demonstration of how reality is created in *interaction*. That Claire, in Ozieblo's words, has "abandoned the principles of this world for those *of her own devising*" (see quote above; my emphasis) spells out the crucial point at which she deviates from the DeVries theory of evolution. True enough, in working with her plants Claire seems convinced that she is closer to the "heart of life"—closer to "nature"—than if she tried to bring about the leap she aspires through aesthetic expressions (in poetic language, or in abstract painting, for that matter, as Glaspell seems to add with the character of Dick). Yet where DeVries merely *described* the spontaneous "leaps" he saw his cultures take, Claire has taken on the task of *bringing them about*—and thus, her plant experiments provide a perfect parallel to the attempts of creating life in language or art which she deems so falsifying. Both her Edge Vine and her Breath of Life are nothing other than communicative media to express her own invalidated beliefs. As Claire "breathes her plants into being" through artificial cross-pollenization and other interventions, they are no more spontaneous, or immediate, or "true," than any other work of art could be. And thus, that Claire's plant experiments are indeed an artist's *construction* of reality is underlined as she, in her playing mood, explains her creation as a "trick":

> TOM. (*to take her from what even he fears for her*) But you were telling me about the flower you breathed to life. What is your Breath of Life?
> CLAIRE. (*an instant playing*) It's a secret. A secret?—*it's a trick*. Distilled from the most fragile flowers there are. [...] But here's *the trick—I bred the air*—form to strength. The strength shut up behind us *I've sent*—far out" [86; my emphasis].

What is more, if we return to Claire's unique use of language from a similar angle, it turns out that parallel to her desperate yearning to express the truth of life in her stammering utterances runs a deliberate linguistic *strategy* which frames her as the Other only *in relation to* her adversaries. Far from disrupting (as Noe has argued) the binary systems built up in the play's setting and imagery, Claire is in fact firmly set within the inside circle of the Logos as she employs these very oppositions to her own ends. Throughout the entire play, right up to the final moment of her alleged outness, Glaspell's protagonist engages with her fellow human beings in a constantly repeated pattern of drawing them close (in the expressed longing for understanding) only to push them away again (in a deliberate emphasis of her apartness). As a matter of fact, Claire *needs* the concept of the world's cold so she can "have the fire within" (59), she *needs* the darkness which surrounds the other characters in their attempts to understand her so she can be the only one who sees the light, and she essentially depends on the very concept of the detested "inside" as it enables her to position herself on the "outside," and to give this space significance in the first place. Both with her plant experiments and with her strategic use of language, therefore, Claire does nothing other than *impose* her own understanding of life on her surroundings, and her central belief in her "essential otherness" hinges on the very principle of interdependence that marks the relation between the other characters and her own — very much "communal"— self.[9] Hence, in the depiction of Claire Archer's peculiar creativity, Glaspell ultimately undermines this character's expressed adherence to the notion of language as a sign system that insufficiently mediates the essence of life.

Glaspell's Dramatic Techniques: The Possibilities of Expressing Meaning

On the other hand, if one focuses on Glaspell's more explicit meta-comments on the nature of artistic expression in *The Verge*, she seems to shift grounds once again, setting the danger of being misunderstood against the possibilities of successfully communicating meaning through art. Of course, the two most immediate (if marginal) examples of these meta-comments emerge with the play's two male artist figures: Elizabeth's father and Richard Demming (Dick). While Elizabeth's father is easily disposed of as the "stick-in-the-mud" artist who painted portraits which never interested Claire because they were "the kind people bought" (i.e. in the mimetic vein of naturalist painting, 74), the case of Dick is slightly more relevant. This artist creates abstract paintings in a mode of aesthetic expression which makes it possible to mistake a portrait for a milk-can, and thus seems to confirm Claire's doubts as to the possibility of successful communication.

Indeed, even more strongly than Tom Edgeworthy Dick agrees with Claire that "we cannot very well reach each other" (65), and in a comic sequence which takes up considerable space in the play's expository act Glaspell uses this apparent parallel between Claire and Dick as a kick-off for what can be read as a critical comment on theatrical communication. As Harry and Dick sit at the breakfast table with their backs to the locked greenhouse door (Claire has taken the key in order to prevent another opening and with it another drop in temperature), Tom tries in vain to make himself heard on the outer side of the glass. The noise he makes, which the other two men mistake for the blizzard raging outside, triggers an exchange about the power of the imagination and the communicative possibilities of abstract art:

HARRY. [...] Funny — how the wind can fool you. Now by not looking around I could imagine — why, I could imagine anything. Funny, isn't it, about imagination? And Claire says I haven't got any!

DICK. It would make an amusing drawing — what the wind makes you think is there. (*first makes forms with his hands, then levelling the soil prepared by* ANTHONY, *traces lines with his finger*) Yes, really — quite jolly.

(TOM, *after a moment of peering in at them, smiles, goes away.*)

HARRY. You're another one of the queer ducks, aren't you? Come now — give me the dirt. Have you queer ones really got anything — or do you just put it over on us that you have? (DICK *smiles, draws on*) Not saying anything, eh? Well, I guess you're wise there. If you keep mum — how are we going to prove there's nothing there?

DICK. I don't keep mum. I draw.

HARRY. Lines that don't make anything — how can they tell you anything? [...] [65].

A moment later, after their conversation has turned to Claire's strange behavior and her intimate relationship with Tom, the latter returns to the door at precisely the moment when Dick relaunches the subject of communication with the "idea that we can't very well reach each other":

(TOM *is again at the door.*)

DICK. Anyway, I think [Tom] might have some idea that we can't very well reach each other.

HARRY. Damn nonsense. What have we got intelligence for?

DICK. To let each other alone, I suppose. Only we haven't enough to do it.

(TOM *is now knocking on the door with a revolver.* HARRY *half turns, decides to be too intelligent to turn.*)

HARRY. Don't tell me I'm getting nerves. But the way some of you people talk is enough to make even an aviator jumpy. Can't reach each other! Then we're fools. If I'm here and you're there, why can't we reach each other?

DICK. Because I am I and you are you.

HARRY. No wonder your drawing's queer. A man who can't reach another man–

(TOM *here reaches them by pointing the revolver in the air and firing it.* DICK *digs his hand into the dirt.* HARRY *jumps to one side, fearfully looks around.* TOM, *with a pleased smile to see he at last has their attention, moves the handle to indicate he would be glad to come in.*) [67].

In the following slapstick scene, Harry and Tom attempt to communicate through the glass wall of the greenhouse. As no words can get through to either side, Harry — dramatically misunderstanding Tom's inquiring gestures with the revolver to indicate that he will shoot himself if he won't be let inside — begins to employ pantomime to explain that he should go and get salt for their eggs first, since Claire won't allow the door to be opened twice. Tom in turn, who has no possibility of understanding any of this, suddenly leaves after Claire, who has by now joined the scene, sneezes casually. When he returns, he brings a second thermometer and a pepper shaker.

This scene is significant for its general statement about the chances for successful communication and the lack thereof (a statement which in its deeper meaning escapes everybody but Claire), and it subtly illustrates the nuances in the particular levels of understanding which are reached between the different characters in the play. While Harry's elaborate attempts at telling Tom to get the salt resulted in a complete misunderstanding — Tom brings a second thermometer instead — Claire did not have any difficulties in getting through to her friend: "TOM. When Claire sneezed I knew — CLAIRE. Yes, I knew if I sneezed you would bring the pepper" (69).

What is more, in very obvious terms this scene satirizes the possibilities of successful expression *in the theatre*. As Ann E. Larabee has pointed out: "[Tom's and Harry's] form of communication is arduous and almost ineffectual, mocking the efficacy of performance through the illusory fourth wall" (81). And indeed, the "illusory fourth wall" of the stage is even more strongly thematized in *The Verge* with the help of another scenic device. In the second act, Glaspell uses an actual wall of glass to separate the audience from Claire's tower retreat:

> CLAIRE *is alone in the tower — a tower which is thought to be round but does not complete the circle. The back is curved, then jagged lines break from that, and the front is a queer bulging window — in a curve that leans. The whole structure is as if given a twist by some terrific force — like something wrong.* [...] CLAIRE *is seen through the huge ominous window as if shut into the tower* [78].

As does the earlier pantomime scene, this unusual arrangement emphatically underlines the idea so pervasive in Claire's distrust of words: The notion that there is a gap to be crossed from one consciousness to the other (whether in everyday speech or in the language of the stage), and that it might ultimately be impossible to achieve the connection which would have to be established if communication should nevertheless be possible.

If one relates, in a further step, Glaspell's allusion to the communicative situation of the theatre to the dramatic structure of her play itself, one might well argue that the playwright's solution to the problem she has posed is to substitute the "dead patterns" of conventional stage representation with a mix of new forms, creating a new and possibly more effective language as a vehicle to pass on her message to her audience. Featuring as the most prominent signifier within this new dramatic language would be the play's use of expressionism, with which elements both of setting (such as the "imperfect tower") and of character (in the figures of Elizabeth, Adelaide, Tom, Harry, and Dick) turn into outward manifestations of Claire's mental state.[10] Indeed, many analyses discuss Glaspell's peculiar mix of genres in *The Verge* (from realism to expressionism, from symbolism to naturalism, from farce to melodrama to social comedy) as a shift in the techniques of dramatic "language," often arguing that Glaspell has succeeded in overcoming the imprisoning male forms of the theatre in this play. Representative of several readings along these lines, Ann E. Larabee explains: "[Glaspell] has extended [her] feminist analysis of oppression to include the stage, which [she] viewed as a prison of structural language and cultural inscription" (77). And Noe extends her reading of Claire Archer's disruptive discourse to the playwright's own form of expression, as well: "Through violating the norms of dramatic discourse, the norms of logic and linear progression, Glaspell creates her own form of *l'écriture féminine*, one that is ideally suited to Claire's rebellious purpose" ("*The Verge*").

Strikingly, such readings usually discuss Glaspell's innovative use of dramatic language without questioning the effects which her new style might have on the underlying theory of expression itself. To the extent that the play's dramatic innovations are seen as a correlating comment on the ideas expressed by its heroine, in form as well as content Glaspell is usually seen to confirm the modernist notion of the isolated individual unable to articulate his innermost being in *The Verge*. As Linda Ben-Zvi has pointed out: "Like modern playwrights such as Beckett and Pinter, she recognizes that it is not enough to have subject matter discuss new ideas; a playwright must also offer a new dramatic form *appropriate to the ideas expressed*" ("Susan Glaspell's Contributions," 152; my emphasis). And she goes on to explain:

> Claire Archer is one of the first female characters in drama whose main concern is to create a new language and whose failure illustrates the difficulties in doing so. Sixty years later, in his play *Not I*, Samuel Beckett would place a gaping mouth eight feet above the stage and reenact a similar struggle for articulation of self—and a similar failure. By making language the primary focus of the struggle for selfhood, Glaspell is radically expanding the possibilities of thematic material for theater and the uses of stage language.

What is more, in a rather unfortunate parallel the play's own fate as a work of art seems to confirm Claire's dark fear that language is incapable of communicating meaning successfully. This, in any case, is what many reviewers and critics have pointed out in relation to *The Verge*. Already the play's initial staging triggered off a heated debate on what it was supposed to "mean"—a debate which never quite reached a satisfactory solution. "What 'The Verge' Is About, Who Can Tell?" the reviewer of the *New York Herald Tribune* titled, obviously frustrated with Glaspell's "message" to her audience. "Excited and Obscure" was another heading. And Alexander Woollcott judged: "[the] play, as a play, as *a medium for emptying the author's mind*, is not skillful" ("Provincetown Psychology"; my emphasis). Even critics who, unlike Woollcott, were convinced of Glaspell's singular artistic achievement with *The Verge* noted that because of its intellectual "aloofness," the play would be able to "reach and touch" only a few chosen ones (Castellun, 'The Verge').

It is tempting, then, to argue with C.W.E. Bigsby that if the play "is a call to reach beyond the comfortable confines of character, plot and language, it is also a play which finally acknowledges the price exacted for such presumption. In a sense it is the price which the avant-garde is always called upon to pay — the risk of *losing touch with one's audience*" ("Introduction," 20–21; my emphasis). As Glaspell's contemporary Kenneth MacGowan tellingly contemplates: "Perhaps the awkwardness of the word ["otherness"] with which [Glaspell] wants to make us grasp a most difficult philosophical idea is an indication of the major fault of this play. Miss Glaspell has not been successful in *translating her idea into easy terms of the theatre*."[11] And today the judgment voiced in all of these commentaries — that *The Verge*, if approached from a position based on the idea of art as a representative system of signs (as a "means of emptying the artist's mind," in Woolcott's words) fails to "come across" — has possibly become even more devastating: There seems to be a wide-spread consent among critics that the play is virtually unstageable.

Even if *The Verge* has all too seldom been tackled on the stage, however, the assumption that Glaspell's most experimental play could hardly be brought to full bloom in the theatre must appear somewhat odd if one remembers that it was written quite specifically *for* the stage. What is more, for all we know from accounts of its original staging, *The Verge* was produced successfully enough to communicate its novel expressionist note and the deep intensity which radiates from the text, especially from the figure of its female protagonist.[12] And thus, while the notion of art as a specific example of constitutive articulate contact is positioned within Glaspell's text itself (as demonstrated in my discussion of Claire's plant experiments and language strategies), it also opens up a way of engagement with this work of art which allows the incorporation of all contradicting elements surrounding both the text itself and its reception throughout history.

Indeed, what one reviewer noted in the play's original reception was not a general inability to "understand" the play — terms in which Glaspell would have to be seen as failing in the attempt to translate her thoughts into the language of the theatre — but a wide-spread unwillingness to "address [its] meaning" (see Papke 67). Gerhard Bach has approached the play's criticism "from a reader/ audience response position" along Wolfgang Iser's lines of "filling the gaps" as he describes many reviewers' refusal "to complete the text in reviewing [their] own response to it" ("Susan Glaspell: Mapping the Domains," 250). As Bach explains, what most mainstream critics balked at when *The Verge* first saw the stage in 1921 was both its disregard of the "culturally determined assumption of the purpose of the theater" (i.e. to entertain and sustain social conventions) and its inherent "[deconstruction of] its own premises of communication": "Neither language nor visual impression," thus Bach comments on the play's dramatic techniques, "function in the 'normal' patterns, facts to which the critics of the time could only respond in self-defense with such 'rationalizing' terms as *perverse, insane,* and *queer*" (ibid. 251).

To these reasons for the (predominantly male) critics' refusal to enter into a constructive debate with *The Verge* one might add their distinct displeasure with the critique of patriarchal society as it is presented in the play's realistic phase. For if mainstream critics refused to (or, for lack of precedents, could not) accept the play as a radically novel mix of dramatic genres and techniques suggesting multiple layers of "meaning," what remained of *The Verge* on its level of naturalistic representation was all the more revolting. As Alexander Woollcott complains:

> After all it is not the authenticity of the portrait at which the average passerby will strain and choke. It is the author's own reverent, heroine-worshipping attitude towards this particular manifestation of the divine discontent aforesaid which provokes combativeness in the onlooker. No one who has read a little or listened a little in this fermenting city but will recognize in part, at least, the woman now reared on the Provincetown stage through the quickening touch of Margaret Wycherly. What he will have more difficulty in recognizing is the three men who hotly pursue this distressed and distressing lady instead of running from her as if she were plague-stricken ["Provincetown Psychiatry"].

Interestingly enough in this context, recent production experience has shown that the play does not "work" if staged exclusively in the naturalist mode. As Gerhard Bach and Claudia Harris write of a 1991 performance of *The Verge* at Brigham Young University, it was its very naturalism which "created a confrontation with Claire and the issues she raises" (95).[13] And Stephen Bottoms (if from a standpoint not entirely impartial) noted on the Orange Tree production in 1996 that it "bore out" his own "conviction that the play would be unworkable if presented 'straight'":

> In order to present the play as period-set naturalism, the director of the Orange Tree version, Auriol Smith, made extensive cuts in the script, most notably reducing Claire's lengthy (and highly "unnatural") verse monologue in act 2 from 33 lines to only 12. [...] The sadly ironic result of such changes was that, though the theatre was praised for its high production standards, the play itself was almost universally dismissed by reviewers as an awkward and unconvincing piece of out-of-date naturalism "that is trying to flower into something quite different, and in spite of the care lavished upon it, doesn't quite" [129].

In fact, the play's "restlessness" in genre and technique is an integral part of the way in which Susan Glaspell deals with her central theme of human identity in *The Verge*. In approaching this play with the help of the language theory of constitutive articulate contact, therefore, its refusal to settle on a certain style does not represent a switch to another (stage) language better suited to express the author's message, but an offer to participate in the creation of meaning. This is also the approach which Stephen Bottoms seems to have taken to his own 1996 production of *The Verge*. As he reports, his version attempted to play out the various dramatic modes present in the play in a conscious effort to generate "conditions in which Glaspell's script could really breathe" (Bottoms 132). As a result of this approach, to the minds of producer and actors the rehearsal process came to underline an inherent instability of meaning in Glaspell's play. By generating a "creative dialogue between the text and performance" (ibid. 140), especially with regard to the embodiment of Claire Archer, the participants found that "Claire's search to unchain her subjectivity from the usual feminine prescriptions inspires an urge for constant 'becoming'; becoming-plant, becoming-flight, becoming-(one with)-Tom, and so on" (ibid. 141–42). Hence, since Bottoms' performance strategy — based as it was on the concepts of "dialogic performance" and the potential of a Derridean deferral of meaning for feminist literary analyses — met *The Verge* as an event of constitutive articulate contact, it came to focus (like Glaspell herself) on the mode of debate rather than on the expression of any fixed meaning potentially underlying the text. Bottoms concludes:

> I was left with the conviction that the play's greatness lies not in praising or condemning Claire, but in making all of the conflicting perspectives presented by her characters [*sic*] seem (at the very least) understandable, and so leaving the audience to negotiate their own responses to an inextricably tangled situation. If one hunts for conclusive answers from this play, they simply slip away, *en abyme* [144].[14]

On the other hand, one final point has to be made in connection to this interesting approach, which underlines a distinctly "deconstructive" streak in the set-up of *The Verge*. When Bottoms explains that if one "hunts for conclusive answers from this play, they slip away *en abyme*," he calls up the Derridean notion that meaning can never be fully present in the Logos (or in the dramatic text, in this case). Yet although I find useful both Bottoms' theoretical stance and his practitioner's experiences for my own response to this play, the notion of art as constitutive articulate contact entails that there is an experiential limit to the idea of an endless deferral of meaning. For even if Western thought during the second half of the 20th century has shifted emphasis from the notion of transcendental truth to the idea of an "ever-changing" sense of self, we still rely on certain "resting points of meaning" in our every-day human existence (see my discussion of Wittgenstein and Derrida in chapter 2). In Susan Glaspell's play, this need for Wittgensteinian "stepping stones" of meaning is acknowledged in the image of Claire's final state of madness, since with the loss of her ability to communicate Claire Archer has lost any valid sense of self in relation to other human beings. With this ending, Glaspell stresses the necessity of a communicational concept of *understanding* in our lives. Consequently, to read her play as enhancing the idea of an endless *deferral* of meaning is as problematic as pinning it down to any one particular stance.

When it comes to reading the play as a linguistic creation itself, therefore, *The Verge* confirms Glaspell's persistent belief in the potential of the theatre to create "meaning." Indeed, it is not for the first time in her career that the dramatist relies so heavily on *words* as to provoke the criticism of being "talky" and "literary," and her page-long set descriptions still arouse amused, even irritated disbelief among critics. Nevertheless, the productions of the past ten years (if sparse in number) have demonstrated "that Glaspell's infrequently performed theatre still offers fertile ground for future directors, performers, and audiences," and an engagement with this play, whether on the stage or in its written form, is still capable of seizing our imagination (Aston, "Performance Review," 231). In this way, whether the experience repels or baffles, fascinates or irritates, confuses or delights, the ongoing discussion about *The Verge* demonstrates that we can hardly be left "untouched" by the encounter — even if our experiences with this piece of art are nothing more than "temporary stepping stones" of meaning.

9. Alison's House (1930)

Speaking Across the Centuries

When *Alison's House* reached the New York stage in 1930, eight years had passed since the dispersal of the Provincetown Players. Susan Glaspell had returned to the genre of fiction as her primary medium of artistic expression, and only once before had she put her pen to drama after her return from Greece without Cook. *The Comic Artist*, the play she had co-authored with Norman Matson in 1927, does not strike one as specifically "Glaspellian" in either theme or style (see my brief discussion in chapter 11). With *Alison's House*, however, which earned Glaspell the Pulitzer Prize in 1931, the playwright revisits a number of those "issues of expression" (Lewisohn) which had been so prominent in her earlier works.

Alison's House is set in *"the old Stanhope homestead in Iowa, on the Mississippi, where Miss Agatha Stanhope still lives,"* on *"the last day of the nineteenth century, December 31, 1899"* (3). Alison Stanhope, a nationally renowned poet whose works were published posthumously by her family, has been dead for eighteen years. Now her old home is broken up at the initiative of her brother John, the patriarchal father-figure of the play, who has decided to move his aging sister Agatha to his own home up the river. As they sort out Alison's possessions, her presence is acutely felt by all members of the family — even more so when a package of unfamiliar poems turns up at the end of the second act. When they realize that here on these yellowing pages their famous relative had put down the story of her life-long love for a married man whose request to leave with her she had turned down for the sake of the family, the surviving Stanhopes find themselves faced with a serious decision: Should they burn the poems and let Alison's compromising story go down with the closing century? Or should they offer them to the world as part of her unique artistic legacy?

The play's struggle over what is to be done with Alison's poems is staged as a generational conflict fought out in the space between two centuries. Personal stakes are involved on all sides of the argument, however, and the defense of Alison's alleged interests (demanding either the protection of her privacy or the freedom to let her art speak to the future) is a matter of each character's reconstruction of the dead woman's personality. In *Alison's House*, therefore, Glaspell repeats the way she had made use of an absent title character in *Bernice*, and similar to the character constellation in that play (which seems to present Bernice's best friend Margaret Pierce as the privileged "seer" in the end), *Alison's House* apparently installs a female character's point of view as the right angle to Alison's life. Moved to a midnight gesture of reconciliation to the sound of the New Year's bells, John Stanhope entrusts the valuable package of poems to his daughter Elsa, who serves as an Alison-foil in the play. Elsa has lived the life of an outcast ever since she ran off with the love of her life, a married man like Alison's lover. The play's final scene underlines her interpretive authority on the grounds both of her generation and her gender. As Elsa is not the only representative of the younger generation who defends the public's right to Alison's art, however, it is her experience as a woman who has flouted patriarchal norms which apparently gives exclusive authority to her point of view in the end.[1] When Alison put down the agony and beauty of her love — thus another female characters asserts— she "said it —for women" (150). In handing the poems over to his daughter at the last strike of midnight, Stanhope concedes that his sister's words are "For Elsa — From Alison," a gift "from her century to yours" (154).

Glaspell had severed all ties with O'Neill's new Playwrights' Theatre in 1924, and the Theatre Guild, successor of the Washington Square Players, did not want *Alison's House* for their stage.[2] Instead, the play was put on in New York by Eva Le Gallienne's Civic Repertory Theatre, the company which had staged a revival production of *Inheritors* in 1926. It was launched on December 1—just nine days before the 100th anniversary of Emily Dickinson's birth.[3] Dickinson (1830–1886) had become a national icon with the posthumous publication of her poems. Yet more than four decades after her death very little was still known about the circumstances of her secluded life. Rumors concerning a love affair with a married man had been fostered in a first biography by the poet's niece, Martha Dickinson Bianchi, in 1924, and had been taken up in several rival studies during the centenary year. In her stage story about Alison Stanhope's illicit love and artistic legacy, Glaspell added her own aesthetic stance to the public debate about this famous poet's life and oeuvre. With *Alison's House*, thus J. Ellen Gainor points out, she "joined a group of writers participating in the creation of Dickinson [*sic*] biography, despite the fact that her play, at least on the surface, depicted the lives of fictional characters" (*Susan Glaspell* 224).[4]

Indeed, it seems that when *Alison's House* was first put on in New York it was explicitly marketed as the "Emily Dickinson story." Certainly it was perceived as such by the theatre-going public. As Mary E. Papke sums up initial reactions to the play: "Most critics [...] [noted] Alison's similarity to Dickinson and dependent on their attitudes to that poet's work [made] much or little of this" (*Susan Glaspell* 92). Nevertheless, in *Alison's House* Glaspell uses her contemporaries' interest in Emily Dickinson in order to negotiate a set of issues which have pervaded her writing from the first: questions about the nature of identity and truth, about the individual's relation to society, and about the social function of art. That something about the "Emily Dickinson story" as it was being circulated all around her at the time struck Glaspell as a theme for the stage is interesting, indeed, in the context of her other writing. It seems that for more reasons than one, the mysteries still surrounding Dickinson's life and oeuvre all but begged a revival of the playwright's technique of the absent protagonist for the stage.

As Glaspell once more puts an absent protagonist at the center of her play, similar to the events in *Bernice* the struggle that emerges between the on-stage characters in *Alison's House* focuses on the question of who the absent woman "really was." As in the earlier play the figure of absence does not only pose the question whether the "essential identity" of a character is communicable to others, but whether it exists at all. What is more, whereas in *Bernice* Glaspell added the theme of artistic expression to her interest in identity construction with an on-stage figure (Bernice's husband Craig, the writer), in *Alison's House* the absent character is also the central artist figure of the play. In this way, Glaspell uses a single cipher in this play to combine a discussion of the nature of identity with questions about the function of aesthetic communication. And as she weaves a web of thematic interests even more dense than the one presented in *Bernice*, once again the playwright's underlying conceptions of language and art mix in a contradictory tangle of ideas.

Before the scandalous poems turn up at the end of the second act, like Bernice Norris Alison Stanhope is remembered as a woman of exceptional insight and inner beauty. This image is established straight away with the play's opening scene: The first act begins with the entrance of Richard Knowles, a reporter from Chicago who came "[down] to get a little story about the house, because it is being broken up" (5). Knowles, a newspaperman with a poet's soul, begs to be allowed a last glance at "the room that was used by Miss Alison Stanhope" (4): "Won't you let me see it? It isn't just the story. It's— a feeling about it. [...] And since it's going to be broken up, and won't be any more, why not some one who has a feeling about it to— to hold it in memory, you might say" (9). An ardent admirer of Alison's art, it is this stranger to the family who first creates the revering sentiment which signals that there must have been something very special about her: "She isn't dead. Anything about her is alive" (5).

Throughout the first two acts, most of the family confirm that what lives on both in Alison's published poems and in their personal memories of her is a beautiful and divine spirit. Indeed, this image prevails even though the subject of Alison's unlawful passion for a married man is brought up early on in the play by Stanhope's daughter-in-law Louise, who fears the presence of a reporter because it might revive the town's talk (both about Alison and about Elsa's recent elopement). "I think the worst they can say about my dear sister is that she was a great soul, and a poet," Stanhope counters Louise's bickering. "It isn't going to hurt my feelings to have it said again" (13). More-over, when Stanhope's son Eben, Louise's husband, arrives on the scene, he immediately confirms this view of his beloved aunt. Introduced as a man who is *self-assured in manner, though soon one feels the inner uncertainties, hesitations, and the inner beauty* (33–34), the character of Eben Stanhope is connected to the absent Alison through this last trait, his "inner beauty"—if not through the "uncertainties" and "hesitations." On this last day of the nineteenth century, a day on which everything signals change, Eben longs for Alison's assuring insight, her capacity to "know" (36) that had always managed to calm him as a child: "Father, I'd like to hear her say once more—right now—here—Alison understands," he admits, "because—I'll be darned if I do" (37). In fact, Eben is desperate that the rest of the family (including, of course, himself) have not been able to live up to Alison's supreme exam-ple—a sentiment which is shared by his wayward sister Elsa:

> EBEN. The last day we'll ever be in her house—the last day it will be her house—how can we help but think of her—and feel her—and wonder what's the matter with us—that something from her didn't—oh Lord, *make us something!*
> (ELSA, *wearing coat, furs, hat, has stepped inside the door. She has beauty, a soft radiance.*)
> ELSA. (*in a low thrilling voice*) Yes, Eben. Yes! [39].

Significantly, in the way Alison Stanhope is conceived of both through her poetry and through her family's personal remembrances, the notion of her divine spirit once more in Glaspell's oeuvre furthers the idea of a per-sonal essence independent of any social contact, and of a metaphysical truth that can be grasped and communicated if only one has the gift of sight. In fact, that the symbol model of language and art is firmly in place where the presentation of Alison Stanhope is concerned is evident not only in the idea of her superior "knowledge." Two other leitmotifs connected to this char-acter raise both the negative and the positive implications of an understand-ing in which a Kantian-Cartesian subject faces the world at a distance: the notion that Alison was utterly "lonely" in life, and the idea that her essence can, after all, "be found" in her poetry.

In Glaspell's earlier play *Bernice*, the title character's image as a spirit who "was life" was linked to the idea of her peculiar "detachedness" from others (see my discussion in chapter 6). While this character trait was revered by most characters in that play, in *Alison's House* a similar feature translates into a distinctly negative circumstance, Alison Stanhope's profound loneliness. This theme — rarely commented on in the play's criticism — is brought up in all its crucial moments. Alison's sister Agatha, for one, is unable to destroy the poems she has kept hidden for eighteen long years because this would mean that her sister would be made to leave the world the same way she was forced to live in it — unrecognized and alone: "AGATHA. (*not speaking to any of them now*) What could I *do*? I tried — and tried. Burn them? All by themselves? (*In a whisper.*) It was— too lonely" (49). Eben and Elsa also think of how alone — and God-forsaken — Alison must have felt as they realize the full scope of their aunt's predicament: "EBEN. Afraid God left her pretty lonely at times" (103). Indeed, it is this idea of Alison's utter loneliness which makes Elsa believe that her aunt would have condoned her own decision not to deny her love: "Knowing what it is to be alone, I think she would be glad I am not alone" (147). And finally, even Stanhope changes his mind about burning the poems at the distinct realization that he does not want his sister — or himself — to be "lonely": "If she can make one more [gift], from her century to yours, then she isn't gone. Anything else is— too lonely" (154).

As the play evokes the parameters of the symbol model of art in the characters' remembrances of Alison's divine but lonely spirit, the final decision not to destroy the poems implies that the real, essential Alison will be allowed to communicate her insight to future generations and hence to remain in the world. Consequently, Glaspell once more argues the idealist stance in *Alison's House* that true understanding — and with it a bridge between isolated souls—can be achieved, after all. From the very beginning, the play's characters attempt to reach out to Alison, to find her on this last day of "her century" (36). This is the reason why Richard Knowles has come down from Chicago, and this is what Eben hopes to achieve from the moment of his first entrance. When Agatha dies at the end of the second act, her brother Stanhope calls out to her "[*softly*], *as if putting her to sleep*": "Yes. Yes. Find Alison, dear. Find Alison" (108). And united in their awe at the power of Alison's poetry, Eben and Elsa at last assure their aunt: "EBEN. (*so moved it is hard to speak*) Never mind, Alison. We have found you. ELSA. You will never be alone again" (141).

What Glaspell thus suggests in *Alison's House* (as she does ever and again in her writing), is that the medium which is truly able to express both a person's innermost being and the existential truths behind and beyond all experience is that of artistic expression. Indeed, in contrast to Glaspell's earlier absent women Alison Stanhope has left a more material mark of her personality than her family's remembrances: She has given herself to the world in her art. Through her verse, thus Glaspell makes pointedly clear when the poems are first discovered, she lives on to present her innermost self to each new generation in a handwriting that is unmistakable and unique:

> EBEN. (*reading over* [Elsa's] *shoulder*) Are they—*poems*? [...] They are Alison's. [...] Poems we never saw. (STANHOPE *examines one*.) They are her poems, aren't they?
> STANHOPE. (*slowly*) No one else—that ever lived—would say it just that way" [135].

As a result, while only Alison's family might know her through personal memories, her heart and soul can still be "found" by anyone who will look for her in her art. As we have seen, the idea of Alison's living presence is first put forth in the play by the character of Richard Knowles, a complete outsider to the family drama that is about to unfold. Knowles, of course, bears a telling name, and the legitimacy of this character's claim to "know" Alison through her poetry is underlined by the fact that he is introduced as an artist figure himself. In addition, as the third act moves into the heart of the poet's most personal space—her own room in which she used to sit and write—the notion that Alison's identity is accessible in her art is made explicit by the play's second "outsider figure," Ann Leslie: "I didn't know [Alison] but—it does seem that [she knew]. What did I say? I didn't know her? But I do know her. Her poems let me know her" (114).

On one level, then, art is a reliable channel of expression in *Alison's House*, fully capable of connecting the essential Alison to the world. On the other hand, while the elements of the representational model of language and art thus have a strong influence in Glaspell's presentation of Alison Stanhope and her poetry, at the same time matters are once again complicated by the equally persistent presence of the rival concept of meaning as created in communicative contact. For as neither Alison herself nor her poetry are ever presented directly on stage, the contextual nature of identity and meaning is once more foregrounded through Glaspell's technique of absence. In the beginning, the image called forth of Alison Stanhope is presented as a fairly consistent one by all characters in the play. When they are suddenly confronted with her secret poems, however, dissent begins to set in. As it turns out, the older and the younger generation cannot agree on what should be done with Alison's artistic legacy. And thus, as they present their contradictory arguments of what Alison herself would have wanted, Susan Glaspell makes clear that the only access which each character has to the dead poet's self (whether in personal memories or in a reading of her art) is through his or her individual convictions—and through life experiences that are governed by an endless number of social and cultural factors among which gender and age are only the two most prominent ones presented in *Alison's House*.

As the play's conflict culminates in the confrontation between Stanhope and his daughter Elsa, the final scene apparently suggests that an opposition of gender is at the heart of the play's subject matter — and as Stanhope hands over the poems to Elsa at last, Glaspell seems to give final precedence to the woman's over the man's point of view. This interpretation of the play's ending is strongly supported by the way in which the dramatist has drawn Elsa Stanhope as Alison's on-stage representative from the first moment she enters the stage. It is of course no coincidence that this character's entrance is staged just as Eben expresses his longing for Alison's spirit in his question why "something from her didn't [...] *make* us something" (39). In this way, Elsa's arrival immediately establishes her special position in relation to her aunt. On the one hand, Stanhope's daughter has clearly failed Alison's example of self-sacrifice, having lacked the older woman's strength, as one contemporary critic saw it, to "deny herself a love which she thought wrong" (Skinner, "In the Dramatic Mailbag"). On the other hand, with her air of "beauty" and "soft radiance" (39) the young woman is introduced in a positive one-to-one correspondence to the play's absent protagonist, and in this parallel Glaspell indicates that Elsa has been carrying on her aunt's struggle, walking grounds which Alison had not been free to reach in her own lifetime. As Marcia Noe describes the crucial convergence between the play's two central women in this scene: "The conversation about Alison [...] builds to an emotional peak that almost demands [her] presence; when her niece Elsa walks in at the end of the first act, it is almost as though Alison had returned" ("Reconfiguring the Subject," 41).

Hence, to the extent that the play's sympathies strengthen the similarities in Alison's and Elsa's personalities and in their experience of love over against their different choices, the "decision over whether to preserve and publish the poems [...] becomes a decision which will acknowledge the rights of feeling over convention" (Bigsby, "Introduction," 27). Throughout the entire play Elsa is presented as the unconditionally positive figure she appears right from the first: sensitive, caring, honest, and painfully aware of the suffering she has inflicted in following her love. What is more, even though Elsa herself acknowledges her moral inferiority to her aunt, through the very awe that this fallen character displays for Alison's ability "to find victory in defeat" Glaspell suggests that society's expectations can be too much for any less exceptional soul to fulfill: "What could I do— alone?" Elsa asks in defense of herself. "How could I — Elsa —find victory in defeat? For you see, I am not enough. She would know that. She would be tolerant. [...] Be happy, little Elsa, she would say" (147). At the same time that the play admits to the tragic impact of Elsa's decision to live out her feelings, therefore — both in terms of a very personal pain and in terms of an impending social instability — Glaspell insists that Alison's poems bear witness to the suffering caused by social norms which deny fulfillment to two people who have "recognized each other" as "one":

> STANHOPE. If I had known it was, as much as this—I would not have asked her to stay. [...] He was below. He had come for her. [...] She had gone East, with Father, to Cambridge, Thirtieth reunion of Father's class. She met him there. [...] At once they seemed to recognize each other. He was for her. She was for him. That was—without question. But he was married. He had children. They parted. But—they were one. I know that now [140–41].

Encountering Alison's poems thirty years after they were written, Elsa feels her aunt's presence as if she was in the same room with her now:

> STANHOPE. (to ELSA) Why did you say her name like that?
> ELSA. Because she was telling me her story. It's here—the story she never told. She has written it, as it was never written before. The love that never died—loneliness that never died—anguish and beauty of her love! I said her name because she was with me [139].

Alison's poems give voice to a story which she was unable to tell out loud, and it is precisely in the anguish caused by society's expectations (through Alison's own, internalized notion of morality) that her words reach Elsa's heart. On such a note, the character of Elsa Stanhope presents the image of the New Woman who holds up the torch of love for the absent Alison on stage—a glimmer of hope, representative of a new generation, demanding her right to emotional freedom and daring to follow her love as Alison had not been able to do.

Yet Elsa Stanhope is not the only figure whose parallel character conception serves to throw a light on Alison's personality, and if one views the play's ending in the context of its generational theme rather than its gendered oppositions, the conflict between Stanhope and his daughter enhances an entirely different view of the absent woman's identity and desires. After all, unlike Elsa Alison did not decide to follow her love, nor did she express a wish to publish any of her poems during her lifetime. On both counts she was, indeed, a woman of her own century: modest and chaste. Might the protection of her privacy, then, and of her decision to respect the social institution of marriage along with another woman's feelings, not have been what Alison Stanhope truly wanted?

This version of the absent poet's identity is strengthened in the parallel that is set up throughout the play between her and her brother John—Elsa's only remaining antagonist in the end. For John Stanhope, who on one level of meaning can be seen as the family patriarch out to stifle Alison's female voice (see my discussion further down), on another level is framed as the one character who might understand his sister better than anyone else ever could. When Eben—who himself condemns Elsa's elopement because it "made [their father] older. Nothing ever hit him as hard" (102)—tries to speak for her with the somewhat feeble remark that "[m]aybe she couldn't help it," Stanhope bitterly retorts: "'Couldn't help it'! What a weak defense. Alison helped it—and so did I" (71). Immediately afterwards, he regains control over himself and quickly brushes aside this last remark: "EBEN. What did you say, Father? STANHOPE. Never mind what I said" (ibid.). What Stanhope barely manages to conceal in this scene is finally disclosed in the play's final act when Ann breaks into the family circle and implores her employer to preserve Alison's poems "as a gift to all love." The brother who had asked Alison to "stay" had at one point been forced to make the same decision himself:

> ANN. (*going to* STANHOPE, *and sitting in a low seat beside him*) You were so good to me, always. I feel as if you were my father, though I know you're not, really. You were so good to Mother. (*Low.*) You loved her. And she loved you. Through years. And you denied your love, because of me, and Eben, and Elsa, and Ted. Well, here we all are—the children—Eben, Elsa, Ted, and Ann. Can't you let us, now when you are old, and sad, tell you what to do—for us? Won't you let Alison's words pass on—as a gift to all love—let them *be* here—when you are not here? [149].

As Stanhope was once faced with a similar situation, thus Glaspell implies, he knows the immensity of Alison's sacrifice from personal experience—better, in fact, than his daughter Elsa who—already of a different generation—has not made the same decision, after all. True enough, with her self-sacrifice Alison had succumbed to the Victorian gender image of the virtuous, chaste and obedient woman: the same notion that still marks Elsa's guilt thirty years later. With his own abstinence, however, her brother John fulfilled the equally traditional role of the responsible man who puts his family's well being (as determined by its social and financial standing) before his personal fulfillment. In this parallel between Alison and John Stanhope, the tensions alive in Alison's poems between her desire for love and the social imperatives that dictated her decision to stay with her family describe not a specifically female predicament but a generally human condition—especially as regards the 19th-century generation which both the poet and her brother represent.

From the first, Stanhope is drawn as a man who is well aware of the cruel turns which life can take, but who stands determined to keep it all together for those who depend on his protection. His character sketch introduces him as wearing "*the look of a man who has made a place for himself, who is acquainted with responsibilities. He is vigorous for a man of sixty-three, though troubled at the moment. One soon feels he has a feeling for others that makes him tolerant, though firm*" (11). What Stanhope represents more than anything else in the play is the admirable yet ultimately defeating quality of self-control — the very quality that is also held high in the image of his sister Alison.[5] When Eben furiously jumps at his younger brother Ted, who attempts to save his English grade at Harvard by providing his professor with pages of invented snippets on his famous aunt, in a typical reaction Stanhope admonishes his eldest son for being "too uncontrolled" (39). And when later Eben only half-jokingly suggests that he might "take a year off" both from his job at his father's law firm and from his wife Louise, Stanhope's criticism is even more explicit: "Come, Eben, don't talk like a weakling. What if you aren't perfectly happy with Louise? I wasn't happy with your mother, either, but I didn't run away, leaving my children to shift for themselves" (74).

Given Stanhope's unquestioning acceptance of his role as head of the family and guardian of the existing social order, Glaspell demonstrates that the man never had any other choice but to give up the love of his life as a forbidden desire, persuade his sister to do the same, and attempt to keep the poems out of the world that would make public Alison's emotional transgression. When his son Ted asks him what it is he wants out of life, Stanhope simply returns: "Hold a family together. Have some pride" (72). Against the background of the play's gendered social universe, his insistence that it is not only his right but his duty to determine the fate of the treacherous poems is in fact inevitable. What Glaspell shows us between the two male characters of John Stanhope and his son Eben is that society's gender roles can prove just as imprisoning for men as they typically are for women (a theme already hinted at with the character of Tom Edgeworthy in *The Verge*, and continued in many other male characters throughout Glaspell's oeuvre). For while it is obvious that Eben's father never wondered whether he should not simply reject his responsibilities and do as he pleased, the playwright makes clear that there are times when the steadfast patriarch secretly shares his son's longing to be freed of all obligations. After Louise has brought up the town's gossip about both Elsa and Alison, objecting to Knowles — the reporter's — presence in the house and arguing that "a family should stand together," Stanhope sinks into a chair and for a brief, unwatched moment gives way to his feelings:

> STANHOPE. (*sitting down by* ANN, *she with her pad for dictation*) Sometimes I wish I weren't the head of a family. Sometimes I wish there weren't any family. (ANN *had begun to take this, tears off the page.*) Quite so. Some things we never put down. Even Alison didn't put it all down [17].

In this scene Glaspell draws a clear parallel between Stanhope and his sister, arguing that the sacrifices forced on them by society's expectations have ultimately silenced them both. Where Alison had denied her love and hid the poems which would have given away her secret, her brother allows himself only a few "weak" seconds before he pulls himself together again and returns to his business of keeping the family's affairs in order. What is more, reading the parallel between John and Alison Stanhope in this direction one might argue that the man's social determination has been even greater than his sister's. For while Alison was at least allowed to stay "Alison"—that is, herself—in her seclusion and her poetry, her brother is identified solely by his family name, and in effect is denied any more individual or personal role than that of the "head of the family." It is telling in this context that the only time one of the other characters calls Stanhope by his first name, it is precisely to call on his patriarchal responsibilities of protecting the family: "AGATHA. I wouldn't have believed it, John. I just wouldn't have believed that you — our brother John — would break up the old place, turning me out of home" (23). In this way, in the character of John Stanhope Glaspell does not only expose the same tensions between personal happiness and social responsibility which rule the story of his sister Alison — they are given added weight since, as a man, Stanhope has obligations which make it impossible for him to live out his individuality and find release in the same way Alison was able to do in the privacy of her own home. And thus, during the play's final conflict over Alison's poems Glaspell leaves no doubt that the pressure that Stanhope feels in relation to his responsibilities is almost impossible to bear: "STANHOPE. In justification of myself—I am so tired of justifying myself that I wish — I wish I were with Agatha [his dead sister, H.-B.]—but I ask you, did [Alison] give [her poems] to the world?" (148).

Against the background of this parallel between Alison Stanhope and her brother, it is worth taking a second glance at the play's final moments, in which the family patriarch hands the poems over to his daughter Elsa. Right up to the very end, Stanhope had been determined to complete what Agatha had been unable to do: burn the poems and "shield" their sister by "giving back to her century what she felt and did not say" (154, 153). Indeed, as Stanhope ignores Elsa's objection that by pouring her feelings into her poems Alison "did say," after all, the "virtually complete convergence of Alison and her poetry" during this final scene makes "Stanhope's plan to burn the manuscripts […] tantamount to taking life" (Laughlin 227). In a last attempt to persuade him not to destroy the poems Ann pleads: "I don't want you to do it, because I have a great love for you, and I don't want you, when dying, to feel, I am guilty, I took life" (150). It is only at the very last, as he listens to the midnight clock strike out the final moments of the closing century, that Stanhope changes his mind and holds out the poems to Elsa.

Initially, as Karen Laughlin allows, "there is something very satisfying both in Stanhope's act of handing over the poems to their 'rightful owner,' Elsa, and in the reconciliation of father and daughter as the curtain falls." We are led to assume that the "powerful love poems are […] to be published, as a 'gift' from Alison's century to Elsa's […], and Elsa's sins against the old social code are forgiven" (Laughlin 228). What is more, since Alison's words are now to be passed on by a woman who understands the poet's heart with an empathy formed through similar — female — experiences, one might conclude that with this turn of events the "essential Alison" will finally be allowed to "tell her story to the world" (Noe, "Reconfiguring the Subject," 44). As Susan Kattwinkel concludes her interpretation of *Alison's House*:

> This play, Glaspell's last using the technique of the absent protagonist, offers the most positive outcome: although the absent woman must allow others to choose how she will be defined for history, through the intervention of the younger women she is essentially returned her voice and allowed to speak the words she could not speak in her lifetime [49].

Nevertheless, with its rather peculiar comment on the construction of female authorship the play's ending remains highly problematic. For despite the confirmation of Elsa's role as Alison's rightful heir it is still Stanhope who decides the poems' fate. In this context, even more significant than his highly symbolic act of "*holding the poems out to* [Elsa]" after he had himself taken them away from her in the first place (154) is his insistence that his change of heart was not brought about by anything his sister's female advocates might have said to persuade him: "It isn't — what you said," he explains to Elsa. "Or even, what Ann said. But her. [...] She loved to give her little gifts. If she can make one more, from her century to yours, then she isn't gone" (154). From a perspective concentrated on the mechanisms of women's silencing presented in *Alison's House*, the play's final scene merely underlines "the extent to which the publication of Alison's writing, and hence the expression of her desire, is mediated by her socially powerful brother, much as its subsequent interpretations may be mediated by the likes of Ted and his Harvard Professor" (Laughlin 228).[6] Indeed, it is disheartening to see that what remains for Elsa as the play's New Woman in the end is her return to the conventional role of her father's daughter:

> STANHOPE. [...] (*He holds the poems out to her.*) For Elsa — From Alison.
> ELSA. (*taking them*) Father! My father!
> STANHOPE. (*his arms around her*) Little Elsa. (*He holds her close while distant bells ring in the century.*)
>
>   CURTAIN [155].

On the other hand, since the play presents Stanhope as a sympathetic figure who can empathize with Alison's pain through personal experience, the particular stance he takes towards her poems — as representations of the very value and lasting beauty of the poet's self-denial in life — is as valid in the end as is the interpretation offered by the representatives of the younger generation. Indeed, in the way in which each character in the play experiences the intensity and presence of Alison's feelings in her words, it seems that her poems exemplify "great art" precisely in that they bear witness to the pain endured for the sake of doing right. This, at least, could be the implication as Elsa admits that she does not have Alison's strength: "I suppose it is possible [to love so much you can live without your love], if you are a very great soul, or have a very stern sense of duty" (153). Understood in this way, Alison's poems would be allowed into the world as a shining proof of her sacrificial choice to guard her own as well as another woman's home and family — not for the sake of justifying, half a century later, Elsa's betrayal of the older generation's values: "STANHOPE. (*as a cry from deep*) Oh, Elsa! Why did you go away — and besmirch the name Alison held high?" (ibid.). Certainly, in Stanhope's eyes his sister's "gift of love" to the future is one of courageously acknowledging *and accepting* the great price paid in following the call of duty. What changes his mind in favor of the poem's publication is nothing other than his desire to preserve for future generations his own image of the "essential Alison": a steadfast and responsible member of society, a woman "who loved to the uttermost, and denied, because it was right" (147).

Consequently, the play remains ambivalent with regard to Alison's message to the world and to the younger generation up to the very end. Did she say what she said "for women," urging them on to a new realization of personal freedom? Or do her poems send out a more cautious message, after all — one that carefully weighs the gains and losses at stake when one's personal happiness posits a threat to other people's feelings and to the existing social order? Significantly, the question of what Alison's poems "really mean" is not only kept open in the balance established between Stanhope and Elsa both as parallel and as contrasting figures to the absent protagonist. It is further confused through the unclear position of another character: that of Elsa's brother Eben.

Eben Stanhope is a true in-between figure in *Alison's House*. In contrast to his father, he does not have the self-command that results from the older Stanhope's acceptance of his role of patriarch. Even before Eben appears on stage Louise's characterization of her husband prefigures the image of the "weakling" Stanhope later sees in his son: "Eben isn't any too well grounded. [...] He has that same thing [Elsa has]. He could just — shake everything loose" (16–17). This introduction connects Eben's character both to Elsa and to Alison — a parallel that is reinforced as his entrance assigns to him the same "inner beauty" (34) connected to both female characters. As Glaspell suggests, Eben's "inner uncertainties" threaten the stability of the social status quo just like his sister's elopement and Alison's love (unspoken or not).

On the other hand, even if Eben himself suggests that he is like Elsa in that he does not have Alison's strength to resist "[shaking] everything loose," in the degree of his social imprisonment he is closer to the positions of his aunt and of his father than he is to his sister's situation. For although Eben wants to leave his responsibilities behind and be himself, as Elsa has chosen to do, he knows that like his steadfast aunt he "probably" never will (73). Painfully aware of the pressures exerted on him as a supposed pillar of society, he yearns to "find Alison," the aunt who always "understood," and to receive encouragement from her. And where both Elsa and Ann, the women of the younger generation, feel free to pursue their romantic love, Eben — like his father and his aunt — is held by his responsibility to protect the existing social order:

> EBEN. Are you going to marry [Knowles], Ann?
> ANN. What else can I do? (*They all laugh a little.*)
> EBEN. And go away and leave Father?
> ANN. What else can I do?
> EBEN. Poor Father. We all want to go away and leave him.
> ELSA. You won't, Eben.
> EBEN. What else can I do — but stay? [120–21].

What is more, another instance that complicates Eben's contribution to Glaspell's message in *Alison's House* is his pronounced artist's sensibility. Especially in answer to feminist interpretations that read Elsa as Alison's manifestation on stage, it is significant to note that with regard to the absent woman's self *as artist* it is not her female foil but the male figure of Eben Stanhope who is linked most directly to the absent poet. This particular correspondence is introduced with Eben's very first appearance on stage, in a scene in which he calls forth the first concrete picture of his aunt:

> EBEN. The fun we used to have down here as kids — Elsa and I. Especially when Alison was here. Remember how she was always making us presents? [...] And always her jolly little verses with them. "Alison won't tell," she'd say, when Elsa and I had run off to the river. "Alison knows," she'd say. [...] It was all so darn real today, coming down here for the last time. And the century going — her century. When I got the first glimpse of the place through the trees I had a feeling of the whole century being piled on top of her, that she couldn't get out from under [36–37].

To the practical Louise, her husband's poetic sensitivity has the dangerous twist of a sick imagination ("How *morbid.* Don't *let* your mind run on such things!" 37). The very contempt, however, that is voiced by this most prosaic character in the play moves Eben yet closer to his aunt's misjudged poet's soul. Where social expectations prevented Alison from living her passion, leaving her only the secluded expression of her pain in her poetry, Eben is allowed no room for his own poetic self in an existence ruled by patriarchal responsibilities:

> EBEN. (*with a real interest, which makes his father look at him*) [...] I would like to [write something about Alison].
> STANHOPE. Did you ever try to write, Eben?

EBEN. I used to write things—and show them to Alison.
STANHOPE. I never knew that.
EBEN. No. No one else knew—except Elsa.
STANHOPE. And did you keep it up?
EBEN. Not after I was married [76–77].

Consequently, similar to the parallel established between Alison and her brother John (as members of the same generation who have internalized the same values of responsibility and duty), the particular connection drawn between the absent poet and her nephew Eben (in his experience of imprisoning social expectations and in his presentation as an artist figure) puts into perspective those aspects which tend to grant the play's *women* exclusive insight into her personality. Indeed, since one of the play's most central arguments insists that Alison is best known through her poetry, the routes of understanding taken by the male figures of Stanhope, Knowles, and especially Eben are presented as approaches which are just as sincere, honest and direct as the empathetic understanding granted to Ann Leslie and, most of all, to the female "diviner" Elsa.

In his reading of *Alison's House* Gerhard Bach has made the point that through the play's recurrence to Emily Dickinson as a well-known historical figure whose poems were accessible to Glaspell's audiences at the time "Alison does not, like Bernice, remain an abstract idea" (*Susan Glaspell* 188–89, my trans.). True enough, in creating an image of the absent protagonist on stage Glaspell refers our imagination both to a "real" poet and to Alison's art as a concrete, material manifestation of her identity. On the other hand, both of these strategies do not help to create an image of Alison Stanhope that is any more definite than the one conjured up in the on-stage characters' conversations about her. Once again, Glaspell's absent protagonist remains an unfixed cipher in this play—not only as a woman who loved and denied her love, but also as an artist who never offered her art to the world. Indeed, the poet's own position is thrice removed from the on-stage struggle over the relevance of her art, and in this way Glaspell once again highlights the communicative constructedness of all meaning in *Alison's House.*

To begin with, what we learn of Alison Stanhope through various characters' memories implies that she never asserted herself as an artist outside the privacy of her own room while she was still alive—and in an extension of this self-imposed silence, she died without leaving any word on what should be done with her poems, which she had kept neatly folded in her desk. Her family might have been used to Alison sitting alone in her room "with her papers" (124); they might even have been aware that she was writing poetry. Eben and Elsa recall how their aunt invented little verses for them when they were children, but as far as we know Alison never read them any of her more serious poems or (even less so) attempted to bring her works out for publication. As Eben describes his aunt's secluded temperament: "She was too timid of the world. She just left [her poems], and we did the right thing, as in her heart she knew we would" (148).

Consequently, even the story of how Alison Stanhope's voice came to be heard in the world in the first place is one of *interpretation*—and critics have rightly stressed the aspect of gender as an important theme in the story of how Alison became a nationally renowned poet. In Eben's version, the modest and passive (19th-century) female trusted her male guardians to act in her interest, and Alison's brother and nephew supposedly did just that when they discovered her poems after her death and decided to edit them for publication. From the first, then, Alison's voiced was appropriated by a male perspective. For although the play states that "the family" published Alison's poems posthumously, the "we" between Eben and his father excludes Elsa and Agatha as potential female participants in the family's decision-making, and in the very process of publication Alison's words were evaluated, edited, even censored by another representative of patriarchal authority—a member of the male-dominated academic system: "EBEN. Father, we did publish all the poems, didn't we? STANHOPE. We gave them all to Professor Burroughs. He took all except a few he thought weren't so good. Those I have, as you know" (56). In this way, Glaspell makes clear that while Alison's poems were offered to the world in good faith, the decision was made on no more than a well-meaning guess on what the deceased woman herself might have wanted—and the very publication process itself already changed Alison's original aesthetic expressions.

Now, in the case of the long-hidden package of her love poems, her sister Agatha might have been able to throw some light on Alison's own take. Had she entrusted her most personal poems to her sister with instructions to destroy them, to preserve them for future generations, to watch over them? Or had Agatha simply been the first to find them after her death and had decided to take them into her possession in order to protect her sister's name? Through all the years in which she had continued to live in "Alison's House," Agatha had jealously guarded the explosive package of whose existence she alone was aware. Now that her brother decided to transplant her from the old family mansion to his home in town, she can neither bring herself to take the poems with her (away from the house to which they belong like Alison herself) nor to burn them. Unable to deal with the strain this decision entails for her at the end of "Alison's century" (which was also her own), Agatha's feeble mind and heart finally give way. After a last futile attempt to destroy the poems, she hands the package over to Elsa, and dies:

> (*With trembling fingers* AGATHA *undoes the string of her bag and takes out a small leather portfolio. Looks fearfully around, looks at the fire* [in the fireplace]. *She tries to rise.*)

ELSA. What is it, Aunt Agatha? I will do anything you want done.
AGATHA. You will — do anything — I want done?
ELSA. Why yes, Aunt Agatha. I will do anything in the world for you.
AGATHA. Elsa will do it. Elsa.
ELSA. Yes. Elsa will do it.
AGATHA. Then — (*She holds out the leather case, but withdraws it. Then suddenly gives it.*) Take it! For — Elsa. (*She falls forward.*) [107].

Significantly, this key scene is as ambivalent as are the play's final moments, in which the poems are handed to Elsa a second time. On the one hand, Agatha gives Elsa the mysterious leather case only after her niece has promised to do whatever it is she is too weak to accomplish herself — and that was to throw the poems into the burning fire of the fireplace. On the other hand, Agatha might have changed her mind in that one hesitant moment before she finally gives the package to her niece. Her final words — "For — Elsa" might indicate that Agatha finally did decide that Alison's poems should be passed on through female lineage so that they will be preserved. Yet the audience cannot be sure what Agatha's intentions really were in her dying moment (and as we know, Stanhope, for one, does not accept this last interpretation). Even less so can Alison's own intentions with regard to the explosive package be determined after Agatha has died. Shortly before the feeble woman gives the poems to Elsa, she seems to admit that while she had meant well in hiding them from the world, she had never received any explicit instructions from Alison herself: "AGATHA. But she — went away. How could I tell — what she wanted me to do?" (106). Whatever the secret behind the guarded package, Agatha dies before she can give away anything she might have known. And thus the family is left to draw their own conclusions a second time:

STANHOPE. These [poems] were not left with the others. Where were they left? What did she tell Agatha?
EBEN. We don't know their story, and now we won't know it, for Aunt Agatha can't tell us. But we know they are here, alive, and we know we will do the right thing [148].

As so many times before in the play, we are told here that there is only one "right thing" to do — and that the answer to what Alison would have wanted lies in the poems themselves, in their very presence and living power. All the more significant, then, is the poet's third removal from the stage: Although the play's action circles around Alison's art from first to last, Alison's words are never quoted. Instead, in a scene of shared remembrance between Stanhope and the reporter-poet Knowles, the two men draw closer in their "knowledge" of Alison by reading each other verses from a book she had much loved. In a gesture of "giving Alison" to the stranger who reveres her, Stanhope hands Knowles his sister's marked copy of Ralph Waldo Emerson's poems. This central scene, which points to the immortality of *Alison's art* by reading out lines from that other great American poet, gives Glaspell's play its title. And, significantly, the only direct instance of poetry in *Alison's House* is itself a comment on the nature of art:

> STANHOPE. It is called "The House."
> "There is no architect
> Can build as the muse can;
> She is skillful to select
> Materials for her plan;
> Slow and warily to choose
> Rafters of immortal pine,
> (*He glances up to the beamed ceiling above.*)
> Or cedar incorruptible,
> Worthy her design."
> Some other things, and then —(*Looking ahead.*)
> "She lays her beams in music,
> In music every one,
> To the cadence of the whirling world
> Which dances round the sun.
> That so they shall not be displaced
> By lapses or by wars,
> But for the love of happy souls
> Outlive the newest stars."
> [*He hands back the book.*
> KNOWLES. Alison's house.
> STANHOPE. Yes [98–99].

If studied for its underlying premises with regard to the nature of artistic expression, the one instance of poetry which Glaspell here connects to Alison Stanhope's own works operates along the lines of the representative model. In Emerson's presentation of the nature of art, there is a "plan" and a "design" before the fact of artistic expression, and the product of the muse's creativity, built with "incorruptible" material, then stands steadfast and unchangeable through the ages. This conceptualization corresponds to the play's notion that Alison has used her poems to communicate her innermost being to the world, and with it an eternal truth about life which will "outlive the newest stars."

On the other hand, if on one level of the play's argument Emerson's words are a legitimate stand-in for Alison's art in this scene, the absence of her own art suggests quite another view on the creation of meaning in art. As critical rumor has it, Glaspell was not granted permission to use Emily Dickinson's name or quote any of her poems (see Waterman, *Susan Glaspell* 86). Regardless of this possible historical explanation, however, the absence of the poet's own words in *Alison's House* and her simultaneous substitution through a male classic emphatically underline both the female artist's appropriation through male voices and the fundamental unavailability of Alison's personal position in the play. For while quoting Emerson certainly gives a double-edged twist to the subject of Alison's treatment as a *woman* writer (putting her on a par, that is, with the great national poet, and at the same time accepting the male tradition as a measuring rod for female art), it also adds to the fact that the audience is never given the opportunity to judge for themselves what Alison's "message" to the world might be. For all the play's emphasis on her powerful expression of life, Alison Stanhope ultimately remains silent. Hence, up until the very end of the play the poet's "meaning" remains a construction created solely through the (often contradictory) interpretations offered to us by her survivors.

If the supposed "essence" to Alison's art, then, continuously slips away from our grasp, what else might be Glaspell's argument in her representation of the artist in *Alison's House*? True enough, up to the very end the play refuses to settle on any definite meaning which might be transported in Alison's art. On the other hand, through the reactions of all characters on stage, Alison's poems are consistently (if only implicitly) characterized by their unique *presence* in the world. As Glaspell demonstrates, they create an unmediated feeling of "aliveness" for anyone who is ready to enter into a dialogue with the words on the page:

> ELSA. [...] I said [Alison's] name because she was with me. [...]
> EBEN. (*low, and in beautiful excitement*) Why that bird sang — thirty years ago, and sings now.
> ELSA. But *her—her*.
> EBEN. But the way she kept it all in life. I can see that flower bend, and smell it [139].

In this way, Glaspell argues that Alison's poems are capable of forming a connection which only "great" art can achieve: they provide a link between centuries, generations, and genders. Perhaps the path which the poems have taken — from Alison to her sister Agatha and from Agatha to Elsa — suggests that the decision over what is to be done should be left to a woman as the only rightful heir to Alison's legacy. What Glaspell demonstrates in the final dispute between Elsa and Stanhope, however, is that the secret of "greatness" in Alison's art lies precisely in its way of reaching — and eventually reuniting — *both* father and daughter. Admitting that she does not have Alison's "great soul" or Stanhope's "stern sense of duty," Elsa goes on to say: "But you know, Father, I feel Alison wrote those poems for me" (153). And while the young woman here implies that Alison would have been "on her side," Stanhope simultaneously insists that his sister's poems confirm his *own* point of view: "I feel she wrote them for me" (ibid.). In fact, Alison's art has the potential to reach out far beyond the circle of her own family to many other hearts, people who might lead very different lives and still find something in the poet's words to encourage them: "ELSA. And there will be those in the future to say, She wrote them for me" (ibid.). It is this universal quality which makes it impossible to destroy the poems in the end. They are alive not because they might reinforce traditional moral values or, on the contrary, condone a new generation's ways of self-fulfillment, but because in an empathetic way they open a place for the tensions between more than just these two opposing points of view.

Nevertheless, despite the play's inherent ambiguities, most critics have pinned down its meaning to one exclusive message, both with regard to its theme of illicit love and to what it says about the nature of art. In Glaspell's own time, few reviewers offered substantial analyses in the first place, doing little more than to note the Alison-Dickinson parallel and to complain that Glaspell's latest work for the stage (once again) was too "literary" to be effective in the theatre. Representative of many reviews, J.B. Atkinson scolded in the *New York Times*:

> No matter how earnestly the characters talk, in a strangely stereotyped prose, the image of Alison never appears for an instant. [...] And everything that might conceivably be dramatic in the narrative is consistently crowded off the stage, so that it never disturbs the rigid dullness of the spoken word ["Pulitzer Laurels"].

Yet as one of the few critics to welcome the announcement of the Pulitzer award in 1931, Richard Dana Skinner based his admiration precisely on his understanding of how successfully Glaspell's technique of the absent protagonist communicated the central message in *Alison's House*. The play was "rare, above all," he noted, "for its success in creating, by a hundred small allusions and situations, the portrait of an off-stage character which glows with life and an almost ghostly presence" ("'Alison's House'"). Importantly, what makes Alison's living image a beautiful one in Skinner's opinion — and what prepares the very ground for the public's harsh rejection of this play — is the "message of self-denial" which this critic sees the absent poet pass on to her niece Elsa: "The play says nothing more clearly," thus Skinner writes in response to the storm of protest which followed the announcement of the Pulitzer award,

> than the simple fact that Alison Stanhope became great through denying herself a love which she thought wrong. This, of course, is a challenge to nine-tenths of modern thinking. [...] Perhaps there is no space left for quiet beauty today, nor for mystic truths which poets understand, but the Pulitzer judges have had the courage to try to make space for them. That is something to their everlasting credit! ["In the Dramatic Mailbag"].

Of course, coming down strongly on Stanhope's side of the argument with regard to the "mystic truth" which Alison communicates to the next generation, Skinner is obliged to disregard all elements in the play which give legitimacy to *Elsa*'s understanding of the poet's message — elements of which the critic is well aware. Interestingly enough, he does so by arguing that he knows Susan Glaspell's characters better than the dramatist does herself. For Skinner's construction of the process of artistic communication alone (the very theme which Glaspell focuses on in her play) this passage bears quoting here at length:

> There is one period in the play when Miss Glaspell fails, I believe, to think through clearly to the full meaning of the heroic problem she has set for her characters. It is during the tense minutes of the last act when Elsa, pleading she is not as great as Alison and is unable to deny her own love for a married man, falls back on a rather sentimental feeling that Alison would have understood (which she would have!) and would have wanted only to have Elsa "happy" (which I am certain is not the truth!). Alison would wisely have looked deeper than emotional happiness to the groundwork for lasting inner peace. [...] She would not have condoned — for her acquired wisdom was too great. And Elsa, I think, knew Alison too well to say what Miss Glaspell has her say at such a time [*Our Changing Theatre*].

Firmly grounding his interpretation of *Alison's House* on the representational theory of art, Skinner suggests that the play transports a message that he, as receiver, has understood despite the fact that Glaspell, the sender, has allowed elements into her work which obscure it. In effect, Skinner is telling the playwright that her intended argument (Alison's beautiful message of self-denial) is weakened by the ambiguities she has unwittingly written into her play. On the other hand, he congratulates the Pulitzer Committee on the decision to try and make space for Alison's Stanhope's "mystic truth" in the modern world. If the jurors, then, honored the play because they understood it "correctly," and if those reviewers who protest the award-granting decision do so primarily because they reject the very message which Skinner and the jurors applaud, would this not mean that Glaspell was clear enough in making her point, after all? Indeed, it seems that what this critic himself has not "thought through" clearly enough are the conceptual premises of his own understanding of artistic communication.

Where Skinner — and the Pulitzer Committee — decided to focus on Stanhope's version of Alison's gift to the world,[7] later criticism has more often turned to the character of Elsa as the poet's — and thus Glaspell's — mouthpiece on stage. Arguing that *Alison's House* represents not much more than another of Glaspell's many literary attempts to come to terms with the adulterous beginnings of her relationship with George Cook, C.W.E. Bigsby explains somewhat disgustedly: "The playwright who presented herself as a New Woman, free of the restrictive morality and social constraints of the old world, seems intent on offering yet another justification for herself and her actions" (*Plays* 27). And Barbara Ozieblo — if with considerably less contempt — supports this point of view on the play when she writes that it "is best interpreted as a personal expression of a dilemma that Glaspell had not quite worked out of her system with the writing of *Fidelity* (1915): once again, she attempts to justify her marriage to Cook, which broke up his family unit, and argues that love is all-important in a woman's life" (*Susan Glaspell* 239).

Significantly, both the focus on Alison's self-denial as the play's message and the more recent readings which favor Elsa's decision to follow her love as the main point in *Alison's House* are based on a similar critical assumption. Highlighting either the parallel between the story of Alison Stanhope and Emily Dickinson's life or that between Elsa Stanhope's affair and Glaspell's own biography, both interpretations assume that an artist's life can help us understand what she "says" in her work. And indeed, in her suggestion that Alison Stanhope's innermost being can be "found" in her long-hidden poems, Glaspell herself seems to argue that the absent protagonist's life-story explains the poems' meaning. As the only early critic who responded more forcibly to the portrayal of the Dickinson-representative Alison Stanhope as an *artist* figure than to her presentation as a woman who denied her love, Mark Van Doren bitterly reproaches the playwright for this very take to the nature of artistic creation:

> Emily Dickinson has suffered many indignities from her biographers, but none so heavy-handed as this. The falseness of this play consists in its saying so simply that a great poet [...] is personal in this fashion. [...] Artists do not reveal themselves, or use themselves, or perhaps know themselves that well; and usually we shall find that they have had other things to bother about in their art than their strictly private affairs. So in special degree with Emily Dickinson, [...] whose recently published "love poems" are more of a mystery than biography will ever solve.

Once again, a critic argues here that Glaspell's message in *Alison's House* is simple and direct — if he considers it utterly detestable. As I have shown, however, not only with regard to the play's theme of illicit love, but also in its presentation of the nature of artistic expression, *Alison's House* allows more than one reading. Indeed, as Katherine Rodier has rightly pointed out, in "wish[ing] to exonerate the visionary Dickinson from misrepresentation as what we might now term a confessional poet," Glaspell's contemporary Mark van Doren "overlooks the play's more original elements" (199). For by introducing the character of Alison Stanhope through her technique of the absent protagonist — in representing her, that is, solely through other characters' memories — Glaspell herself problematizes precisely the kind of biographical approach to an artist's oeuvre which Van Doren so strongly objects to (and which so many critics have taken to Glaspell's own art over time). True, on the play's internal level of communication, Glaspell's characters decide on the poem's meaning on the basis of their knowledge of Alison's life and personality. Yet on the external communicative level between play and audience (where the poems themselves remain an absent force) the play's ending does not decide on one interpretation as the "right" one. And thus, while the artist's own voice remains a factor in the communicative process of creating meaning in her art, neither Alison's poems nor Glaspell's play communicate a fixed, preconceived message to their audiences on the basis of their creators' biographies.[8]

In effect, once again in her creative career Susan Glaspell presents us with a play which ultimately favors not the representational but the integrational model of language and art. Susan Kattwinkel has described the communicative relevance of Alison's poems by arguing that in *Alison's House*, Glaspell considers "whether thirty-year old poems can say something to the next generation" (50). Kattwinkel continues: "Glaspell's conclusion is clearly that they can say a great deal to the next generation, if the older generation is willing to recognize the continuity" (50). *What* they say, however, is left in the dark — and the same is true for Glaspell's play itself. As there is no absolute truth in either Alison's or Glaspell's art, the conclusions we draw from the play depend on many contextual factors, as do the characters' interpretations of Alison's art. Once Alison's poems will be accessible to the public, they will help continue the debate between "old" and "new" values portrayed in the characters' verbal struggles — just as Glaspell's play itself is still capable of doing. Rather than posit what *Alison's House* "clearly says," therefore, my contention is simply that Glaspell's seventy-year-old play can still "say a great deal" to today's audiences — if it is allowed into the language-game of creating meaning as one player in the ongoing process of aesthetic worlding.

10. *Springs Eternal* (1943)

Art and Society

With *Alison's House* Glaspell argued the power of art to unite generations, to bridge the gap between selves imprisoned by unbending gender expectations, and to initiate the creation of a better future through the very insistence on life's continuity through the ages. What is more, with her Pulitzer Prize-winning piece the playwright once again demonstrated the social role of art in a dramatic form which stressed the aspect of aesthetic expression as constitutive articulate contact. At the end of *Alison's House* all characters agree on the importance of Alison Stanhope's poems for the creation of a meaningful future, yet what precisely these works might "say" is never pinned down to a single version. Susan Kattwinkel has thus argued a linear development in Glaspell's plays towards an attitude that stresses the process of debate itself over any possible outcome: "[from] *Trifles* to *Alison's House* the debate took precedence" (52). If we include *Springs Eternal*, Glaspell's last play written thirteen years after *Alison's House*, in our view of the playwright's oeuvre, however, this development does not appear as straightforward as the comparison between *Trifles* and *Alison's House* suggests. With this play, it becomes clear that the writer never entirely abandoned the notion that art can initiate social change not by initiating a debate, but by transporting a clearly defined message from the artist's to the recipients' minds.

Susan Glaspell's final play is the only one which has never made it either onto the stage or into print, and it does not measure up to her previous works for the theatre in a number of ways.[1] Subtitled "A Comedy in Three Acts" it combines a farcical love plot with the grave theme of meeting the moral and social challenges of World War II. As Gainor rightly states, the "movement from comedy to drama worked effectively in such earlier pieces as *The Verge* and *Chains of Dew*," yet in this play the "overwhelming force

207

of the conflict abroad [...] creates both structural and tonal problems for *Springs Eternal* that Glaspell was not able to resolve" (*Susan Glaspell* 243). What is more, in a move which is certainly disappointing from a feminist standpoint, Glaspell cast a male figure in the role of the "universal artist" who is expected to initiate the creation of a better world in the end. In Ozieblo's words: "In *Springs Eternal*, Glaspell places the fate of humanity in the hands of men, relegating women to the drudgery of homemaking" (*Susan Glaspell* 271).

Yet *Springs Eternal* provides an important additional angle in the context of Glaspell's oeuvre as a whole, and thus I agree with Gainor that "[r]ather than dismiss [the play] with [such] justified observations, [...] we should read it intertextually with Glaspell's other writing to see what themes, character types, and issues still consumed her at the end of her creative life" (*Susan Glaspell* 247). Towards the end of her life, once more the writer reaffirmed her belief in the social role of art through the medium of the stage. And interestingly enough, in the context of those "issues of expression" which interested her throughout her entire career, Glaspell's final play bears witness that she never did settle on any one specific understanding of the nature and function of communication in human existence — not even on her often discernible preference for the debate itself.

Springs Eternal is set in the home of Margaret and Owen Higgenbothem, on "a day in October, 1943" (2.1). Recalling the character conception of the Father in *Bernice* (who had fled the reality of World War I in his study of Sanscrit) Owen is a disillusioned middle-aged writer who once believed in the power of the intellect to better the world, but who has now withdrawn to the study of "languages long dead" in the hope that this will "deafen [him] to [the] living language" of war (2.1). Acknowledging that the enthusiastic outpourings of his youth could do nothing to stop the world from resorting to another mass killing, Owen is further embittered when he hears that his housekeeper's son, Freddie Soames, was inspired to join the war by reading one of his books, *The World of Tomorrow*. As Freddie — off somewhere in the Pacific, risking his life in an idealistic fight for democracy and freedom — has not been heard of for several weeks, Owen is certain that the boy's mother must hate him, the man who sent her son off to war with his uselessly optimistic writings. The best he can do now, thus Owen is convinced, is to stay out of the world's affairs and avoid further harm.

Where Margaret's attempts to challenge her husband out of his self-pitying stupor have remained unsuccessful for years, and where Mrs. Soames's hope that he might have another book waiting for the boys who will return from the war only heightens his frustration, Owen is eventually drawn out of his reserve through the agency of three representatives of the younger generation — all three of them young men who have decided to go out and do something about the sorry state of the world. Dr. Bill Parks is an army doctor on sick-leave from the African front whose role is to challenge the failure of the older generation in direct verbal attacks on the embittered Owen. Mrs. Soames's son Freddie, in typical Glaspell manner, provides the play with an absent figure whose fate as a Japanese prisoner of war is capable of uniting the old and the young generations on stage. And last but not least there is Owen's own neglected and misunderstood son Jumbo, who as a painter adds another angle to Glaspell's art-as-social-action debate in this play. During the course of the final act, the alienation between father and son is resolved as Jumbo announces that he has given up his stance as a conscientious objector and will join Freddie and Bill in the fight for the world's future. Urged now by his own son to initiate the creation of a better world by writing another book, at the end of the play Owen finally accepts this weighty responsibility, his old belief in the healing powers of his writings fully restored by his son's trust.

Itself intended as a catalyst for change in a time of world crisis, it is ironic that *Springs Eternal* never reached the public space of the stage. Since no public reactions exist to this play it stands as something of an afterthought to Glaspell's eventful career as a dramatist. In its discussion of art as a social agent, however, and in its presentation of the hope for human progress through the reunion of past, present, and future generations in communicative contact, *Springs Eternal* furthers issues which have driven Glaspell's creative work ever since her earliest writings.

As Marcia Noe has pointed out, two biographical episodes from the war years emphasize Glaspell's continuing insistence on the social powers of art at this late point in her life. In "a speech delivered at the Boston Book Fair" in 1940 she "affirmed her belief in literature as a means of bringing about a better world. It is an optimistic speech entitled 'The Huntsmen Are Up in America.' The huntsmen are the huntsmen for the truth, the writers whose vision can enlighten a world menaced by the unthinking and the power mad" (Noe, *Susan Glaspell* 75).[2] Two years later, as Noe reports, Glaspell "reiterated her belief that literature offers the vision of a better world in an article in the *Chicago Sunday Tribune*," in which she "described an evening when writers gathered at her home to talk of literature and the war. Her own memories of France, heightened by Katie Dos Passos's reading of Walt Whitman's 'O Star of France,' brought her to the thought that books can hearten and guide us in a time of world crisis" (ibid.).[3]

Significantly, in both these public statements Glaspell reaffirmed her belief in the existence of a "deeper truth" behind our social and political realities—the vision of a better life which must be communicated by the world's writers. As I have shown in my previous readings, this understanding of art's social imperative often found its way into her works in the form of a clear message voiced by one of her characters (Ed in *The People*, for example, or Margaret Pierce in *Bernice*). *Springs Eternal* is a direct translation of this central belief into her art, and in this way Glaspell's last work for the stage entails an essential part of her artistic *credo*. And while the dramatist one more time mixes an understanding of art as a medium to send a message out into the world with a notion of artistic expression as capable of making this world new through communicative contact, it seems that at least with regard to Glaspell's own artistic gesture in this final play, the representative model is the one which prevails.

With the character of Owen Higgenbothem Glaspell once again thematizes one of her most central beliefs: that writing can help create a better world by awakening tolerance and understanding. Throughout the entire play Owen never rejects his housekeeper's conviction that his book "is right there in the war" ("MRS SOAMES: As much as a book can be in the war. Right after he read it Freddie joined the Marines. And when I cried he said we had to think of the world of tomorrow," 1.16). To the contrary, he seems to claim responsibility both for having led an entire generation of easily impressed youths into the hell of war and for not having prevented this terrible event of world history in the first place:

> OWEN. I feel that I owe something to the mother of Freddie. So let me tell you I have retreated to yesterday as less likely to lead anyone astray. I feel that I brought on the war. [...] I mean my generation, and particularly those people in it who were supposed to be thinking things out. [...] [The] people who were supposed to be thinking were asleep at the library table — or wherever it is that they doze. It was their business to disturb the slumbers of others [1.17–18].

Owen thus seems "to be absolutely certain of his ability to change or determine world events through the agency of his writing" (Papke, *Susan Glaspell* 97), and as the play's ending presents his determination to return to his writing table as a positive turn, Glaspell certainly suggests that Owen is right in this belief.

On the other hand, Glaspell's argument in favor of a writer's social significance is continuously challenged through the doubtful role it plays within the comedy of errors running parallel to the main events from beginning to end. Dottie, a young girl who is connected to the Higgenbothems by some entangled link of family, has apparently attempted to elope with Stewart Gleason, one of Owen's oldest friends, a Washington politician now married to Owen's first wife, Harry (christened Harriette). For some mysterious reason the plan was not carried through, and at the beginning of act 1 Dottie has locked herself into an upstairs room. As it turns out, the girl had needed Stewart's help (more precisely, his car and his war ration of gas) to elope with *Jumbo*, Owen's and Harry's son, yet the two had not been able to catch up with the conscientious objector on the run from the authorities in a chase through several states. When Jumbo finally shows up on the scene, it is only to explain that he has enlisted, after all, and does not want to marry Dottie any longer. This is not much of a disappointment to the girl, however, since in the meantime she has fallen in love with Bill Parks, the doctor. In the end, Dottie and Bill are unmistakably framed as the right match, even if Bill, too, will soon leave his girl to resume his duties at the African front-line.

Throughout the entire unfolding of this comedic love plot, Glaspell inserts references to Owen's powers as a writer in a way which both emphasizes and ridicules her argument that a book can influence people's actions. Owen's writings are held responsible for anything and everything, and the elopement is no exception. As Owen complains early on in the play: "Whenever anyone of our acquaintance gets a bumptious idea it is traced to something I have said in the past. No doubt Dottie and Stew's abortive elopement will be charged to an obsolete tract of mine" (1.13). Sure enough, the moment Stewart strides onto the stage he hurls at his old friend: "It's all your doing!" (OWEN. "I thought we'd be coming to that," 1.28). And a moment later Owen's ex-wife, too, confirms the writer's personal responsibility:

> HARRY. Owen, when you were writing the things you wrote did you think they would make people act the way they do?
> OWEN. As God is my judge I never wrote one word about elopements.
> HARRY. And yet there is something strange, and really very powerful about you. Anything anyone wants to do can be justified by something you wrote [1.31].

Importantly, Harry's last remark indicates that both with regard to the story of the elopement and in the serious main plot of the play Glaspell's presentation of a writer's social significance entails not only the chance of changing the world for the better, but also the danger of being misinterpreted and misused for various purposes. Indeed, sparing himself even the act of getting acquainted with Owen's works first, Bill reproaches the writer just a few moments later: "I never read anything you wrote but I can see you are one of those trouble-making guys who get poor helpless girls all befuddled" ("OWEN. Ah — a fresh interpretation of my work," 1.32).

As a result, in one of the play's central encounters between Owen and the housekeeper Mrs. Soames (Freddie's mother), Owen both acknowledges his writer's "influence" and expresses a determination to assume authority over the interpretation of his works:

> MRS. SOAMES *appears, carrying cloths and cleaning material; seeing* [Owen] *absorbed in work she hesitates in the archway.*
> OWEN (*not looking up from* [*his*] *book — though smiling*). Ah — my unseen audience. Pray stand right where you are and wait to be influenced. My

influence has gone out of bounds. I mean to get it back and direct it to my own advantage—for a change. [...] I am absorbed in the similarities and differences of languages long dead. My hope is it will deafen me to a living language [2.1].

Yet while Owen here betrays his desire to regain control over his own words, his son Jumbo later makes him understand that any such attempt is doomed to failure:

> JUMBO. [...] Anything can happen to a thing you've already done. I suppose the only thing we really have is the thing we're going to do.
> OWEN. Say that again.
> JUMBO. Don't you think so, Father? I mean, the only thing that is really ours is the thing that is *in* us—not yet done [3.13].

This crucial exchange between father and son demonstrates that once more Glaspell's presentation of aesthetic expression entails both an understanding of art as a vehicle for stating a pre-existing "truth" (expressing "the thing that is *in* us"), and a discussion of writing as a communicative act of constituting reality ("anything can happen to a thing you've already done"). When Owen, early on in the play, teases the young doctor that he had been "speaking like a poet," Bill answers: "At ease. I am not a poet, though if I were I'd have something to say, I think" (1.9). Likewise, Owen's friend Stewie at one point reminds him that "once you spoke the truth" (1.28)—a truth that is obviously taken to exist independent of its expression in language. On the other hand, from what we are told about Owen's book it seems that it moves his readers to action not only by what it says, but in the very way it engages people's feelings and experiences of the world. In this context, then, Glaspell once more stresses the writer's power to *do* something over what it is he might *say*:

> JUMBO. *World of Tomorrow*? I guess that's the best book I ever read. But you know, I was thinking, Father–
> OWEN. Yes?
> JUMBO. You ought to write another. I really think we need another one now. [...] Well, you—people like you—ought to fix it so there won't be any more wars.
> MRS. SOAMES. Could you do that, Mr. Higgenbothem?
> JUMBO. Father can do anything if he just puts his mind to it [2.22–23].

Once again, then, in *Springs Eternal* Glaspell discusses the nature of art as a communicative endeavor, and it is in the relation between the play's two (male) artist figures that she locates a controversial debate between the paradigms of aesthetic expression as message or event.

With the character of Jumbo, Glaspell offers a variation on her theme of the artist's role in society by introducing another medium — painting:

> *The scene* [in act 3] *is the same* [as before, i.e. the Higgenbothems' library,

H.-B.], *though* JUMBO *has made minor changes. As the curtain rises he is absorbed in his painting, working at one end of the long table, and to give proper height for his picture he has stacked up some of his father's books. To make room for this improvised easel he has pushed back other things — notebooks, papers. His paint box is on the chair in which his father usually sits* [3.1].

In the "minor changes" that Jumbo has made in Owen's library, he has in fact re-placed his father, the writer, with his painter's utensils. And sure enough, when Owen — in a rage over his son's "cowardly" decision to become a conscientious objector — storms into the room just after Jumbo has left it, the rivalry between older and younger artist over the right way to interpret the world is established as one of the play's central themes:

> OWEN. [...] Thought perhaps that son of mine was here and I could tell him what I think of him. (*Sees the heaped books on the table; paint box on chair*) He's been here, I see. So this is what my books are for! My papers—! Chaos! And for *what?* (*Snatching the picture*) Sunflowers!— is that what I see? How beautiful! Sun-flowers against the woodshed — that's how we'll win the war. We'll free Freddie with a nice picture of— It's an infernal daub! (*Tearing it*) *That* for your pictures— you little coward! Confounded impertinent — (*Tearing it again — again*) [3.7].

Importantly, Jumbo's understanding of art is related through the very painting which Owen here tears to pieces in his rage. Its motif was introduced just moments before in a conversation between Jumbo and Margaret (the only character who takes her husband's son seriously enough to call him by his real name, Harold):

> MARGARET (*looking at the picture*). It's nice, Harold. I like these sunflowers against the old gray shed.
> JUMBO. You do, Margaret? (*Standing back to look*) But something is wrong with it.
> MARGARET. The sky — do you think? Perhaps a little too dark for the shed?
> JUMBO. It is too dark for the shed. But if the sky is brighter the sunflowers lose something. That's the trouble. A thing is right for one thing and then it's wrong for something else. Kind of hard to get everything right [3.1].

Interestingly, despite the fact that the imagery of "light" and "dark" is usually connected to the notion of a pre-existing truth in Glaspell's writings, the picture of the sunflowers against the shed places an emphasis on the *interrelational* aspects of human reality. Each element of the painting stands in relation to all its other elements, and if one thing is changed in order to "correct" a certain relation, other connections are inevitably influenced. With this symbolic motif Glaspell stresses the idea of life as created in constitutive articulate contact: Meaning can only develop in the interaction of all parts, and while it might be in our power to make certain changes in life, thus she seems to argue here, we have to be mindful of the unexpected side effects these changes might have on the rest of the world.

On the other hand, the idea for Jumbo's next painting seems to stress the opposing notion that art expresses an image (and thus a message) already fully present in the artist's mind:

> JUMBO. [...] I've got another picture I want to do [...]. There are two plough horses—coming slowly. They are very tired now at close of day. The earth was russet and the sky is luminous.
> STEWIE. And this picture will register a conscientious objection to the war?
> JUMBO (*who works through most of the following talk*). Oh, not at all. Pictures really haven't much to do with the war. (*Pausing to consider*) Well— maybe. This one really does say something, I think, about — all life. [...]
> MARGARET. And what does it say, Harold?
> JUMBO. That you can be very tired and — discouraged; but beauty is all around you — though you may not know it is there [3.3].

In contrast to the sunflower-painting, Jumbo's description of the plough horses (as an image which is waiting to be translated from his mind onto the canvas) suggests that there is a reality "beyond" the world of human interrelations, a truth that can be seen by the artist and then communicated through his art. In fact, once introduced this understanding of art as a representative system of signs seems to fall back on the sunflower-painting, as well: "*Looking at* [this] *picture with dissatisfaction*" Jumbo states that he is not "doing it" right because he has not managed to visualize the scene yet: "(*putting his things down on the table*): I'll just wait a little. First you have to see it in your mind" (3.4). As a result, the conception of the sunflower painting now does not interfere any further with the notion of the artist's role in society as it is set down in Jumbo's idea for the plough-horses: In the face of an atrocious world war, the artist must envision the truth of life's eternal beauty and in this way give new hope to the world.

Importantly, too, the central conflict between Jumbo and his father (as the play's two artist figures) evolves on the grounds of the notion that our isolated selves stand at a distance from the world and are principally disconnected from each other. As Margaret states, her husband does not know who his son really is: "Owen won't *see* Harold. Because he isn't what he wanted him to be he won't see what he is" (3.4). And indeed, Owen is not ready to believe that Jumbo's decision to become a conscientious objector is an expression of his innermost being: "You can't — just overnight — become a conscientious objector. It's a philosophy — a religion. What you *are*— have been — have to be. Or else it's just running away from a gun!" (2.16). As it turns out, however, it was Jumbo's very experience of being alone with his own self which brought him to the political stance his father so detests as "cowardice":

> JUMBO (*troubled*). Now I will just have to be very honest, because this is honest business, and even more important than people's feelings— though I hope I won't hurt them — not much. [...] Well then, like I told you, I never

had the feeling anybody believed in me. [...] [T]here was me — by myself — and then there were the rest of you with each other — or that was the way it seemed to me. [...] I think it was because I felt all by myself that I never could kill anything. Not a bird — not a mouse even. Because I always thought of that bird, or whatever it was, as maybe all by itself — and having feelings [...]. And it seemed to me that you mustn't kill feelings — because, well, look! — maybe they're all you've got. So then the war came and how could I go to the war and kill men? [3.20].

As this scene explicitly addresses the need to be "oneself" even if this might hurt the people one loves, it once again emphasizes the metaphysical notion of the isolated human self disconnected from all other, equally isolated minds.

On the other hand, Jumbo's subsequent conversion from conscientious objector to soldier again marks a conceptual shift in Glaspell's representation of life in *Springs Eternal*, as it was triggered by a fundamental experience of togetherness set against his life-long sense of isolation:

JUMBO. [...] Dottie began sending me telegrams — how she believed in me and we would stand together against the world. But when she believed in me I didn't have to stand against the world — because I was in it.
(*After a pause in which each in his own way is dwelling with this*)
OWEN. So what have you done, my son?
JUMBO. Oh, didn't I tell you? Now I'm in the Army. Or I will be at nine o'clock tomorrow. [...] [That's] what I mean, Dottie — you put me on my feet. [...]
DOTTIE. But I'm sort of *staggered*. I do think it's wonderful — my putting Jumbo on his feet. But *what* feet? I mean — here I was ready to love him because he was *one* thing — and then that makes him something else! Can you explain a thing like that? [3.20].

Suddenly finding himself *in* the world of human community instead of on the outside, Jumbo feels he has no choice but to participate in the exchange which makes reality — in fact, he was "made something else" himself by Dottie's very belief in him.

It is not a coincidence, then, that in the scene which brings about the central reconciliation between Owen and Jumbo at the beginning of the third act the understanding of life as created in constitutive articulate contact takes precedence in the play's stance on the relevance and nature of art, as well. The reconciliation between the two men — father and son, both artist figures — is brought about in a collectively created idea of "coming together" with the help of Jumbo's sun-flower painting, torn to pieces by Owen in his rage:

JUMBO. ([...] *sees the scraps of his picture; just stands looking, then moves over and takes one of them*) [...] (*During the talk which follows he is fitting the pieces together*) [...] (*to his father*) You didn't like the picture?

OWEN. I lost my temper. I was—altogether wrong. I am more sorry then I can say.

JUMBO. Oh, that's all right. I can do more pictures—when I get the time. I'm always seeing things I want to do. (*Looking down at the picture*) I do sort of wish I could have finished this one. Just to see how it looked when it all came together. [...] You see this color breaking through the gray sky? [i.e. a "rift of turquoise" he had added earlier to make the picture "right," 3.2; H.-B.]

OWEN. Yes—yes—I see it.

JUMBO. Just put your fingers on the color—cover it—and I'll show you. [...] OWEN (*trying to do as Jumbo has told him*). Yes.

JUMBO. Now you can see the sky is too dark. I thought it would be good for the sunflowers—but it just about buries the shed.

OWEN (*eager to understand*). Y—es–

JUMBO. Now take your fingers off. There! Don't you see? Even though it isn't right yet you can see how it was all coming together!

OWEN. All—coming together [3.11–13].

Aesthetic expression is thus once again presented as an act of constitutive articulate contact in *Springs Eternal*. Already, Owen and Jumbo have changed their world as their interaction has created an understanding between them which has helped to "make everything come together."

Hence, the characters of Owen and Jumbo are central to Glaspell's discussion both of the role of the artist in society and of the position of the self between isolation and connectedness in this play. In addition, they act out a generational conflict also concentrated on the contrast between isolation and connection in *Springs Eternal*. Fifteen years before, the question whether the relation between the generations foregrounds the aspect of continuity or whether it, to the contrary, demonstrates a repeated break in the development of humankind had already been prominent in *Alison's House*. In *Springs Eternal*, it is once again introduced as a central theme from the start. For as Bill replaces the old family doctor in the Higgenbothem household at the very beginning of the play, his presence stands for nothing less than "the dawn of a new day" (1.7).

Initially, Glaspell suggests a deep rift between the generations, a gap which is expected to result in an inevitable failure of communication. As Margaret remarks: "Perhaps Old Doc was too old to understand modern medicine, but he did understand the Higgenbothems. You can't be expected to do that—and may not care to" (1.2). In effect, Margaret is unable to "spill" her worries to Bill because they "would spill over so many things. Things that don't belong to your generation. We were such a flop we try to hide ourselves" (1.6). This open opposition between the young and the old is further supported when Owen, too, insists that his generation has failed to create a better "world of tomorrow": "Well damn it all it needs new blood! Not men who have tried once and failed. Let them make their own world! It's *theirs*, isn't it?" (1.18). And when in one of the play's doubtful interminglings of the war-plot and the comedic love affair(s) the young doctor angrily interrupts a bickering scene of jealousy between Owen, Margaret, and Owen's first wife Harry, Bill clearly represents this "new blood" in the play:

> BILL. [...] Listen, my nutty friends. You know something? Now I know why we had a war. People are like you. *You* are the people. You don't *care*. You go in a huddle about your gains and losses—chewing it over about the past — snatching for all you can get while things go from bad to worse and straight on to hell. What's the difference who loves who among you three. You've *had* your chance. Snap out of it and give somebody else a show [1.32].

If the older generation has managed to bring the world to the point of another hideous war (thus both Owen and Bill seem convinced) this war might still be seen as a chance for the young generation to start over.[4] As a result, the idea that there is no possible route of understanding which would connect Margaret, Owen, Harry and Stewie on the one side to Bill, Jumbo, (Freddie) and Dottie on the other, is stressed once more when Margaret observes in the second act: "People who are young at the same time have some sort of key that lets them understand one another." Sadly, Stewart agrees: "That's the key we lose. Do you suppose there would be no wars if the world could stay young?" (2.33).

At the same time, Glaspell once again juxtaposes this notion of a failed communication between the generations with a contrasting idea of *connection* not only between generations, but between all human beings. In this context, too, Bill takes on a key role, as he initiates the sense that we are all "one blood" in a rather peculiar exchange with Margaret:

> MARGARET. [...] I do see how you feel. You want us to be different. But people pretty well formed in their lives don't change over-night — not even for a war.
> BILL. You're wrong. You can't imagine how wrong you are — us wanting you to change. When we're over there we think about you here. We want you to be — just the way you are. [...] Want me to tell you something? (*She nods, held by what he was saying*) [...] Well, some of the fellows are quite sentimental about the plasms. You'd be surprised. [...] They wonder whose it was [...]. How the rest of the blood is getting along. Maybe it's plowing — or it might be making love. Tending the baby —flapping the pancakes, any nice simple thing. It's quite a *bond*. I even think of it myself. Wouldn't it be funny, but perhaps we will become —*one* blood [1.9].

Just a little later, Owen resorts to the same notion of unity: "One thing we do know — now that it's too late. This home of the human race is *one*. You've got to think it as one — or be damned" (1.18). In fact, Owen's very retreat to the study of "dead old languages" as a sign of the discontinuity between the generations is unexpectedly turned into an argument for connection.

Remembering the idealism of his own youth, the writer explains: "In the beginning — as a young man — it was these dead languages I studied and loved. They aren't dead, you know. They come to life. Men spoke them once, and those men come to life" (2.9). What Owen has come to use as a way of turning his back on the future, then, was once a living exchange with the past.

And thus, in the further course of events the generations are brought closer together through the agency of the young. Towards the end of the second act it is the absent character of Freddie Soames who first reconnects the parent generation to their children. When Owen learns that Freddie was captured by the Japanese he suddenly realizes: "I feel as if — something in me — had been taken prisoner with Freddie. [...] [S]omething in me — best I've got left — for what that may be worth — is right there with Freddie" (2.3 2). As Owen and Stewart remember the beliefs they once shared about the human potential of changing the world for the better, they now come to recognize the continuity in the equally ardent idealism of the ones who are young now: "STEWIE. [...] Now you and I, Owen. Lord — the pow-wows. OWEN. Yes. [...] [The] thinkers — dreamers — making beautiful worlds out of beautiful words. (*Pause*) *And now we have Freddie*" (33–34; my emphasis). Just a moment after this scene the generations are united in the attempt of bringing the captured Freddie into their midst. As Dottie and Bill engage Mrs. Soames in a conversation about her son, these three characters come together in their thinking of Freddie:

> MRS SOAMES (*smiling at Dottie*). Freddie would like *you*.
> BILL. He can just stick to Esther [i.e. his own girl, H.-B.]. Esther is a very nice girl.
> (MRS SOAMES *laughs with* DOTTIE *and* BILL)
> MRS SOAMES. Why — we almost did it. Almost we brought Freddie into this room. Seems to me — if I was to look around now — [2.37].[5]

Importantly, if Glaspell does emphasize that the future belongs to the young at the end of the play, she also insists that the young can build their "brave new world" only on the basis of a reconnection to the generations that lie behind. When Bill takes one of the glasses of cider prepared as a refreshment for the party now gathered in the Higgenbothem library, a light remark brings him to something deeply realized:

> BILL. [...] Aren't we going to down this juice of our forebears? (*When he has said forebears he just holds the jug tilted there, repeats under his breath*) Forebears. [...]
> OWEN (*a little diffident*). Shall we drink to your brave new world?
> BILL. [...] I got — another idea. [...] When I hear all this about a brave new world — I think of another one. We really aren't starting from scratch, you know. Now take me. I had a mom and a pop [...] [3.29–30].

Bill, who was portrayed as a good-natured but cynical young man throughout the play, here acknowledges the efforts made by the parent generation to make the world a better place for their children to live in: his own "mom and pop," Margaret, Owen, Stewie — and all of them "leading up to [...] the mother of Freddie" (3.32). In the end, the generations are reconnected through the familiar Glaspellian notions of feeling and caring — and communication has made possible an exchange which is liberating instead of imprisoning for all who will belong to "the world of tomorrow": "JUMBO. [...] (*Excitedly*) You know something? Feeling doesn't go. It stays on — *in* things — in people who weren't even born when it was born" (3.34). It is in this sense that Bill completes the sentiment of the play's title when he gives out his toast at the final curtain: "But hope springs eternal as I give you — [...] Put your minds on the Brave Old World!" (3.34).

In addition to Glaspell's presentation of art as a communicative creative act in *Springs Eternal* (Owen-Jumbo) and to her specific thrust on the generational theme (Owen-Bill), there is yet another element which stresses the idea of connection between human beings in her last work for the stage: the construction of the female characters' role. Since the subject position of "woman" as a separate female identity (Irigaray's Actual Other) does not have a place in *Springs Eternal*, it does seem that Glaspell's female characters are disappointingly kept in the background in this play. Yet while it is certainly true that the women here function according to their traditional social role of silent supporters, once again they play an important part in creating the idea of human community and connection in *Springs Eternal*. In fact, quite similar to the situation in most of Glaspell's other works, the female characters are stronger, more competent, and more active than their male counterparts in this play. As was already the case in *Trifles* thirty years before, without Margaret, Mrs. Soames, or even Harry and Dottie there would *be* no world of human community which the men could fight for, and it is once again the women's role to demonstrate that the idea of the independent, isolated individual is nothing but an illusion (if a very pervasive one).

Right from the start, Margaret Higgenbothem is introduced as a typical Glaspell figure — understanding and empathetic. She is "*an attractive woman, who does not usually look her forty years — an intelligent, mobile, sensitive face, lighting with feeling — humorous, kindly*" (1.1). Throughout the entire action, it is always Margaret who connects the large Higgenbothem family (a "tree of many branches," 1.3), and in this way creates the world of the play in the first place. Where Owen, wallowing in narcissistic self-pity, has given up both himself and the world's future, his wife is determined to bring the writer back to life. As Owen himself states: "When it seems to me the world's all shot, and the things we had hoped for — (*Frowns*) We'll skip the things we had hoped for. But when it's dark, you know what comes to me like sunshine? [...] I have Margaret — that comes to me" (1.34). By the same token, Margaret is the only character who has ever believed in Owen's son Harold (Jumbo), taking him and his work as a painter seriously. As she persistently attempts to draw both father and son into the world of human interaction, Margaret's active part serves as the very expression of what Owen, Bill, Freddie and Jumbo go out to defend: the notion that "if life is all any of us have, that ought to make us feel sort of close together [...]" (3.23).

The character of Mrs. Soames, the housekeeper, also serves a key function in this context. Through the entire action it is Freddie's mother who engages the frustrated Owen in conversations which emphasize both the irresponsibility and the uselessness of his attempt to withdraw from the world. In fact, with Mrs. Soames the playwright recreates her familiar image of a simple woman who will remind the intellectuals of the reality of human community and interaction as the very basis of life (see, for instance, The Woman from Idaho in *The People*, Allie Mayo in *The Outside*, or Abbie in *Bernice*). It is the housekeeper, Freddie's mother ("*a small, trim middle-aged woman*," 1.14), who urges Owen that he should "write about another tomorrow" instead of passing his time with "languages that are dead," long before Jumbo does the same thing (1.16, 2.8). And thus, while it is true that, just like Margaret, Mrs. Soames does not succeed on her own but has to wait for Freddie and Jumbo to repeat the claim, the male figures in *Springs Eternal* further a plot whose central argument is already prepared in the interrelated understanding of life most consistently expressed through the play's female characters.

As regards the play's remaining two women, for all their triviality in connection to the comedic sub-plot they, too, are both more active and more concerned with human interaction than any of the men whom Glaspell has put into the foreground in *Springs Eternal*. In fact, if a critical discussion of gender roles is left out entirely of the *serious* argument in *Springs Eternal*, it is wittily kept just below the surface in the comedic story of the elopement. True enough, Stewie's wife is drawn as a silly, superficial woman whom Owen once married because he could feel superior to her (this last in itself a biting comment on the kind of man Owen is): "MARGARET. I honestly can't understand what you ever saw in Harry. OWEN. What do you see in a kitten? It plays. Rolls things around and amuses you — sometimes. Jumps up on your lap and cuddles quite nicely" (2.13). At the same time, Harry is presented as more "*in* things" (i.e. part of a social community) than any of the other characters. Despite the fact that Glaspell heartily enjoys ridiculing Harry's shallow personality, this female character is drawn as a rather lovable figure, who is even handed an unexpected piece of criticism now and then to throw at the male representatives of the human race.[6]

In addition, it is along the same ambivalent lines that the character of the young "elopess" Dottie is drawn. On the one hand, Dottie is a self-possessed teenage girl who falls in love with men for all the wrong reasons and causes the entire ridiculous confusion that brings the play's stock of characters into the Higgenbothem home in the first place. On the other hand, the girl functions as a way to add a good amount of authorial irony to the depiction of the men's gallant heroism, as Bill's loving yet belittling address at the end of the play signifies:

> OWEN. You're going back over there [to the African front], doctor?
> BILL. Somewhere.
> DOTTIE. You could get hurt again!
> BILL. Why I never thought of that. Ah —(smiling teasingly, tenderly) don't you think of it either, Dottie dear — Dottie darling, Dottie dove — such nice words go with Dottie. We'll omit the dimple but sometimes we might have the dumpling [...] [3.29].

While the teasing way in which Bill here talks to the woman he loves might be appropriate in its condescension because Dottie is drawn as nothing more than a childish girl throughout the play, it still throws a negative light on Bill as a patriarchal male who is not ready to take seriously his partner's perfectly legitimate fear for his life. Indeed, as Bill here repeats the diminishing attitude which Glaspell already criticized in the way in which the character of Seymore Standish treated *his* "Dotty" in her earlier play *Chains of Dew*, the demonstration of the men's belittling attitude towards their women in *Springs Eternal* complicates their presentation as the defenders of our world of interrelations. And it should not be overlooked, either, that the image of Dottie as a silly little girl who does not understand the harsh realities of life is qualified to a significant degree in that plot element which directly connects her character to the play's serious argument. It is *her* love, trust, and empathetic belief in Jumbo, after all, which first brings him into the midst of human community. As Jumbo himself insists: "Dottie, your belief in me has changed my whole life" (3.19).

From all three vantage points taken in *Springs Eternal*, then — artist, self, and woman — Glaspell once again focuses on an interrelated, connected, and integrational understanding of life and the function of communication. Moving on to the level of the playwright's own communicative act, therefore, one might ask whether Glaspell's artistic gesture itself is also designed to demonstrate how human reality is communicatively created in this play, as is the case in so many of her earlier works which foreground the same notion of intersubjectivity. Indeed, it seems that two of the play's most central scenes might be read as demonstrating the workings of art and language as constitutive articulate contact. As we have seen, Owen Higgenbothem comes to an "understanding" of his son Jumbo the very moment the two characters renew the painter's act of creating the sunflower-painting in a communicative act of interaction. And the play's old and new generations are brought together in the very way in which the play's characters create the image of the absent Freddie Soames between them.

Interestingly enough, however, both these scenes eventually result in the statement of a clear message to the play's audience. After all, in the context of the play's argument over the nature and function of artistic expression Jumbo decides not to start over with the sun-flower painting his father had torn to pieces because when he tried to explain it to Owen "Father was so nice about it that I really saw it quite clearly as I explained it to him" (3.13). Consequently, seeing the idea in his mind is more important to this artist than bringing it into being as an instance of creative worlding which would allow the participation of others in the act of creating meaning. If Jumbo "[has] any time now," thus he explains, he wants "to do [his] horses" instead — the alternative motif which favors the notion of a metaphysical truth "behind" reality over an integrational understanding of life: "(*Anxiously*) I hope I don't forget. (*As if making notes for himself*) Very tired — last strength of the day. Rough ground — *pulling. Really* pulling. Quite dark below — where *they* are — earth darkening — and wide luminous sky. Oh, yes, I've got it. I'll not forget" (3.13). And as Jumbo's explicit message in this scene lies in his conviction that "beauty is all around you — though you may not know it is there," the stance which Glaspell favors with regard to the theme of artistic production in *Springs Eternal* is this: "the only thing that is really ours is the thing that is *in* us — not yet done" (3.13). In other words, rather than considering the recipients' active participation in the bestowal of meaning to a piece of art as an integral part of the act of worlding, in this play Glaspell sees it as a falsifying influence on the artist's intended meaning — a meaning which is entirely "pure" and "true" only as long as it exists within the creator's own mind.

By the same token, even if at first sight Glaspell seems to introduce an offstage character to *Springs Eternal* in a fashion parallel to her earlier use of the absent protagonist in *Trifles, Bernice,* or *Alison's House,* there is a significant difference here. The character of Freddie Soames is not used as a "site for debate" as were Minnie Wright, Bernice Norris, and Alison Stanhope in Glaspell's earlier works. In calling forth the absent boy's image on stage Dottie, Bill, and Mrs. Soames are not engaged in a dynamic and ambivalent act of "languageing" their world together. Instead, they evoke Freddie's personality as an outward reality that is fixed and static. And thus, a clear message to the audience arises from Freddie's sympathetic image: If Mrs. Soames's son was brave enough to join the war and fight for a better future, so can all of the play's other characters, young or old — and so can the audience who watches the creation of Freddie's example on stage.

One might argue, then, that in *Springs Eternal* Glaspell did not make use of her creative medium in the same way she had often done before — in order to emphasize the point that we "world" our reality in interaction. Perhaps in this play, composed at the height of World War II, the playwright was too eagerly bent on her responsibility as one of those "huntsmen for the truth, the writers whose vision can enlighten a world menaced by the unthinking and the power mad" to encourage active audience participation in the creation of the play's meaning (Noe, *Susan Glaspell* 75) — too much concentrated, that is, on her message that humankind should be united in the fight against evil.[7] Indeed, in this context one of the scenes I have quoted before as an example of the play's comment on art as a social agent assumes added significance with regard to Susan Glaspell's own aesthetic gesture in *Springs Eternal*. At the beginning of the second act the writer Owen — his eyes on a book, not looking at Mrs. Soames who has just entered the room — addresses his "unseen" audience ("not to be spotted") with the request to "[pray] stand right where you are and wait to be influenced" (2.1). In the case of Owen Higgenbothem's socially powerful writing (the element which drives much of the play's argument), artistic expression is clearly seen as a one-way endeavor in this scene. Instead of taking part in the creation of meaning in a communicative act which is reciprocal, his audience should simply stand and "wait to be influenced." In the end, this also seems to be Glaspell's own prevalent hope as a writer in *Springs Eternal*: Addressing what was to be her last play to a world which had still not realized the hopes of her younger years, she writes to influence her audience so that humanity will eventually realize its creative potential for progress.

11. Other Works

Drama and Fiction

The preceding analyses have shown that questions of language and communication are central to many of Susan Glaspell's plays. How do we come to know something as true, and how can we communicate this truth to others? If mere words cannot be relied upon to make oneself understood, in what way might art be a more sophisticated means of communication? And what does the creation of meaning achieve in the world?

To Glaspell, understanding and empathy are the prerequisites for any kind of change, be it social, personal, or political. It is for this reason that the process of communication is a central theme in many of her plays. How is meaning created in the first place? Importantly, Glaspell does not only make this question an issue in the interaction of her characters, presenting them as locked in a struggle over the right interpretation of their lives. She also translates her interest in the nature of meaning from the internal communicative level to the external level between play and audience —first and foremost through her use of absent characters and her way of mixing various dramatic styles in a single work. As a result, her plays do not only offer a meta-comment on the function of art. They initiate an ongoing experiment in which Glaspell tests different degrees of inviting audience participation in the creation of meaning with each new work for the stage.

As I have argued, the theatre is especially suited for this kind of experiment, since the genre itself insists on the creation of meaning as a collaborative act. Yet Glaspell had developed her interest in the nature of communication well before she began writing plays, and she continued to pursue this theme right up to her final novels. On the following pages I will discuss those plays by Glaspell which have not received a detailed reading in the preceding chapters in connection to her fiction both before and after her time with the Provincetown. Seen together, Glaspell's pre-Provincetown

225

novels (*The Glory of the Conquered*, 1909, *The Visioning*, 1911, and *Fidelity*, 1915) already reveal the full range of issues related to the phenomenon of language that I have traced throughout her plays. Likewise, a look at *Norma Ashe*, her second to last long work of fiction published in 1942, the year before Glaspell wrote her final play, *Springs Eternal*, shows that she never ceased to look for meaning in *both* genres. This chapter, then, opens up the view on Glaspell's whole oeuvre as an artistic entity as it recapitulates, from this expanded angle, her life-long engagement with the most burning philosophical and aesthetic questions of her age.

Susan Glaspell's first novel, *The Glory of the Conquered*, was an immediate bestseller when it reached the market in 1909, but it has received little critical attention. Arthur Waterman, who dismissed Glaspell's fiction as generally inferior to her drama, comments that this book "does not show Miss Glaspell's maturity as a writer at all" (*Susan Glaspell* 32). Several decades later Veronica Makowski echoes this judgment when she discusses *The Glory of the Conquered* in a chapter entitled "Cultural Confusions and Apprentice Fiction," and for Martha Carpentier the book's allegedly immature craft is the reason to exclude it from her study on Glaspell's "major novels" (8). Frequently disturbed by what Waterman chided as its "sentimentality, optimism, and idealism" (*Susan Glaspell* 32), where critics *have* considered *The Glory of the Conquered* they have done so to discuss the ways in which this early novel reflects the author's interest in gender relations and the theme of woman's role in patriarchal society.

In the context of my own approach *The Glory of the Conquered* is interesting because it focuses on the same questions of truth, understanding, and communication which are so prominent in Glaspell's dramatic writings. Featuring a female artist figure whose search for meaning in life is inextricably linked to her deep experience of marital love, the novel argues the idealist stance on the basis of the symbol model of language and art. *The Glory of the Conquered* grants that words might not be capable of expressing one's inner truths. Where words must leave off in this book, however, art is fully capable of taking over.

Ernestine Stanley, a highly-accomplished painter, has just married Karl Hubers, a renowned scientist who is about to discover a cure for cancer. While Ernestine is fitting out her painter's studio in the spacious attic room of the couple's new home, Karl, through a careless handling of chemicals in his laboratory, infects his eyes and goes blind within weeks. This is a tragedy not only for his personal life, since — so close to the important breakthrough — he will not be able to continue his medical research. Karl descends into the bitterness of self-pity and cynicism, yet Ernestine is not willing to accept this verdict of fate. Ready to give up her own calling as an artist if she can help her husband continue his work, she makes a plan to "become his eyes" and begins to study the craft involved in Karl's work at the laboratory. Just when she has learned enough to be able to offer her help with the confidence needed to convince her husband of her plan, however, a final blow of fate stops her in her tracks: Karl falls ill and dies. Ernestine cannot help him accomplish his aim now, but she decides to return to her art in order to put all her knowledge of who her husband was into his death-bed portrait. At the end of the novel, this painting is the celebrated star feature of an exhibition in Paris, and Ernestine knows that she has succeeded in "revealing" Karl Hubers to the world (370).

In imagery, plot line, and argument *The Glory of the Conquered* is solidly grounded in a world view in which language and art function as representative systems of signs. The novel's characters and their innermost selves are essentially detached from each other, yet through observation and introspection they are able to gain profound insight into the fundamental truths of life. Indeed, the imagery of sight pervades this novel from first to last, dominating especially those scenes of isolation in which Karl in his laboratory, but more often Ernestine as the story's focalizer, make their most profound discoveries about the nature of life.

In this context the fact that Karl loses his eyesight is of course highly symbolic. When he realizes that he is about to turn blind, Ernestine's husband is terrified: "Blind?—*Blind?* But his eyes fitted his brain so perfectly it was through them all knowledge came to him. They were the world's great channel to his mind. It was through his eyes he knew his fellow beings" (124). To the scientist whose task it is to unravel life's secrets by looking through a microscope, it seems that with his capacity to *see* he will also lose his capacity to *know*— a paradigm which, as we know, will concern Glaspell time and again in her later writings. And indeed, given that Ernestine's work, too, is in the realm of the visual, in *The Glory of the Conquered* Glaspell insists that sight is superior to language. Thus, the chapter in which the painter sits alone in her attic studio and decides to give up her own calling in order to become her husband's eyes is entitled "Her Vision." Likewise, when on a lonely afternoon at the Oregon coast after Karl's death Ernestine makes up her mind to go back to her work as an artist in order to communicate her husband's truth to the world, the chapter bears the heading "Let There Be Light." And as Glaspell's artist figure in this first novel is a painter rather than a writer, the act of "looking" is given preference over that of "speaking." "Suppose we had to say everything in words!" Ernestine calls out early on in the novel, grateful for a long moment of silent understanding she has shared with her husband (30).

Despite its pronounced distrust of language, then, *The Glory of the Conquered* promotes an understanding of life which is profoundly idealist. Where words do not suffice to express their thoughts and feelings, the novel's characters understand each other *without* language, in their silent moments of communion — and through the medium of art. At the end of the book, Ernestine's painting succeeds in translating the truth she has seen in her dying husband's eyes onto the canvas. Indeed, it is precisely this idea of successful communication which carries the promise of the novel's final scene, in which Ernestine meets an old friend in front of her husband's portrait. "It seems so right," thus the painter exclaims, glad of her achievement: "'It seems to stand for so many things. They call it a masterpiece of light — and isn't it fine — great — right, that Karl's portrait should be a masterpiece of light?'" And with the unspoken thoughts of Karl's old friend — the doctor who was unable to save his life — Glaspell sums up her deep faith in the possibility of "perfect understanding":

> For a long time he was lost to [the portrait]. It was as she said — right. To the blind man had come the light; to the man of science the light of truth, and to the human soul, about to set out on another journey, had come the perfect understanding of what had lighted the way for him here [373].

While in *The Glory of the Conquered* Glaspell built her story on the understanding of art as a sign system capable of expressing metaphysical truths, already with her next novel she turned to the competing notion of meaning as created in social interaction. *The Visioning*, published in 1911, asks whether the individual is held hostage by his or her connection to others, or whether we can use these ties to influence the world around us — the same question that Glaspell will ask in plays such as *Bernice*, *Chains of Dew*, or *The Verge*. In the opening scene of this book Katie Jones, a young "army girl" who has always been kept safe within the well-ordered society of a U.S. Army base, saves a stranger from drowning herself in the nearby river. While Katie cannot make the girl reveal anything about herself, she succeeds in persuading her to stay at the base and take some time to reconsider her decision to end her own life. To explain her presence, Katie invents a suitable story and introduces the unknown woman as "Ann Forrest," an old friend who has stopped by for a surprise visit.

The unusual experience of making up a history and a life for "Ann" sets Katie thinking about questions of identity: "Never in her life had she been so fascinated with anything as this creation of an Ann. [...] Never before had she known any one all unencumbered, unbound, by facts" (135–36). What began as hardly more than a mere pastime for the spoilt if good-natured young woman soon has her question the casualness with which she has taken for granted her allotted place in life:

> She had come to think of Ann, not as a hard-and-fast, all-finished product, but as something fluid, certainly plastic. It was as if anything could be poured into Ann, making her. [...] That was a new fancy to Kate; she had always thought of people more as made than as constantly in the making.

> It opened up long paths of wondering. [...] Down this path strayed the fancy how much people were made by the things which surrounded them — the things expected of them. That path led to the vista that amazing responsibility might lie with the things surrounding — the things expected. It even made her wonder in what measure she would have been Katie Jones, differently surrounded, differently called upon [96–97].

Already in this early novel, then, Glaspell presents the experience of life's essential communality both as a prison for the individual and as a chance to change life for the better. Gradually Katie Jones comes to understand the degree to which she has been "made" by her history and surroundings, yet she does not conceive of her social existence as a liability that leaves her helpless. Like so many of Glaspell's later characters, this early female protagonist understands that her connection to others entails a potential for creation that presupposes a considerable amount of personal responsibility.

Moreover, where *The Glory of the Conquered* had stressed the idea that language and art serve as vehicles with which we attempt to communicate our private "vision" of life, in her second novel Glaspell focuses on the notion of communication as an intersubjective endeavor, stressing the process of the title's "Vision-*ing*" over the vision itself. As the action draws to a close, the man who has tempted Katie Jones out of her limited sphere of inquiry just as she was beginning to feel its limitations writes to her in a letter:

> You make me wonder, Katie, if perhaps it isn't less the vision than the visioning. Less the thing seen than that thing of striving to see. Make me feel the narrowness in scorning the trying to see just because not agreeing with the thing seen. Sometimes I have a new vision of the world. Vision of a world visioning. Of the vision counting less than the visioning. Those moments of glow bear me to you. Persuade me that our visions must be visioned together [413].

The context in which the idea of "visioning together" is developed here is significant in two respects. For one, as these thoughts are presented in the form of a *letter*, language gains prominence over sight in this book. Secondly, it is of course no coincidence that this idea is voiced by the man who has come to love Katie. To Glaspell love is the strongest of those emotional drives which ensure the connection between human beings and enable us to create our world together. As we have seen, this idea of understanding through empathy runs through all of Glaspell's writings. And while her novels, more frequently than her plays, foreground their female protagonist's love relationship to a man in this context, the notion that change can be achieved if we envision the world together is just as relevant to all other relationships portrayed in Glaspell's oeuvre: to same-sex friendships as well as platonic love relationships, in the relations between siblings as much as in the connection between generations.

As was already the case in *The Visioning*, in her next novel, too, Glaspell discusses human existence within a larger system of social relations. In *Fidelity* (1915) Glaspell emphasizes the individual's existential need for a life *within* the circle of social relations. The novel's protagonist Ruth Holland returns to the small-town home of her youth after eleven years of exile, hurrying to her father's death-bed. A grown woman who was never welcomed back into the circle of society after her transgression of walking away with a married man (as Elsa Stanhope will be fifteen years later at the end of *Alison's House*), Ruth must confront the fall from grace that her decision has brought on the remaining family members. At the same time, she is forced to admit to herself that as an outlaw she had never had a chance to be entirely happy. "Of this she was sure," thus Ruth reflects on the consequences of her elopement for the lives of all involved: "love should be able to be a part of the rest of life; the big relationship, but one among others; the most intense interest, but one with other interests. Unrooted, detached, it might for the time be the more intense, but it had less ways of saving itself" (233–34).

While the novel clearly criticizes the cruel impingements of society's rules on the freedom of the individual, Glaspell argues here what she will demonstrate in many of her later works, as well (both dramatic and fictional)—that we cannot survive outside the circle of social relations. Towards the end of the book she brings home this argument with an unambivalent image. Out on her farm in Colorado, one winter evening Ruth watches the sheep as they huddle together for warmth in the open pasture:

> With the first dimming of the light, the first wave of new cold that meant coming night, a few of them would get together; others would gather around them, then more and more. Now there was the struggle not to be left on the outside. The outer ones were pushing toward the centre; they knew by other nights that this night would be frigid, that they could only keep alive by that warmth they could get from one another. Yet there were always some that must make that outer rim of the big circle, must be left there to the unbroken cold. She watched them; it had become a terrible thing for her to see, but she could not keep from looking [321].

Years before Glaspell wrote such plays as the tellingly titled *The Outside* or *The Verge*, the writer thus emphasized the fatal danger of a life lived at the "edge" of society in her third novel, *Fidelity*.

Hence, when Glaspell moved from fiction to drama in the same year that saw the publication of *Fidelity*, she did not change her thematic interests with her creative medium. Questions of language and communication had been central to her art from the beginning, and the two different models (symbolic and integrational) that often work at cross purposes in her plays are as crucial to her fictional writings as they are to her plays.

Suppressed Desires, Glaspell's first work for the stage, is the result of a playful dialogue between herself and her husband George Cook, and it would be difficult to determine her concrete influence on either theme or style of this one-act comedy.[1] Nevertheless, the first play in whose writing Glaspell participated just as her third novel was out on the market relates to her overarching concern with the nature of communication in a number of interesting ways. Henrietta Brewster, a radical New Woman and burning disciple of Freud's recently developed psychoanalytical theories, with consistent nagging succeeds in urging both her unnerved husband Stephen and her sister Mabel to "get themselves analyzed" and be freed from their respective "suppressed desires." She is invariably cured of her enthusiastic worship with regard to "this new religion" (312), however, when both Steve and Mabel return from their sittings with her admired analyst Dr. Russel announcing rather unexpected diagnoses. Henrietta's sister was found to have a suppressed desire for her brother-in-law, and Stephen's desire, supposedly, is to escape from his marriage with Henrietta. Peace is restored in the Brewster household when Henrietta at last repudiates psychoanalysis, while Steve jovially advises Mabel, who by now is seriously worried about her subconscious desire for her sister's husband, that she should "keep right on suppressing it" (322).

Discarded by most critics as a trivial, if "amusing skit" (Waterman, *Susan Glaspell* 67), *Suppressed Desires* is more than a trite farce. As one of the first critics to discuss this play, Gerhard Bach has pointed to its critical concern with the abuse of Freudian psychoanalytical theory. With its prevailing satirical undertone *Suppressed Desires* presents a sharp social criticism of the popular tendency to appropriate the vocabulary of psychoanalysis in an oversimplified, pseudo-scientific manner (see *Susan Glaspell* 92 f.). Indeed, Henrietta's way of dropping isolated set-pieces of psychoanalytical terminology is attacked by Stephen's sarcastic remarks from the start, and the misuse of Freudian theories as it is exemplified by both Dr. Russell's and Henrietta's therapeutic methods are rendered as a serious threat to social peace. When Henrietta announces that "[p]sychoanalysis is simply the latest scientific method of preventing and curing insanity," Steve dryly comments: "It is also the latest scientific method of separating families" (242). In the context of Susan Glaspell's other works, *Suppressed Desires* can thus be read as an early demonstration of the destructive powers involved in the activity of communicative worlding: If therapists and "well-meaning" friends tell unsuspecting victims like Mabel that they are unhappy with their current lives, disaster will inevitably strike. At the same time, the play also seems to suggest the healing potential involved in the idea of communication as constitutive articulate contact. After all, a happy ending is secured the very moment Henrietta gives up meddling with psychoanalysis.

What is more, just like *Trifles* (Glaspell's next play) *Suppressed Desires*

invites an analysis of its characters' verbal behavior according to the understanding of "genderlects" developed by researchers such as Carol Gilligan and
Deborah Tannen. Interestingly enough, read in this way the play's "happy
ending" does not only condone Henrietta's repudiation of psychoanalysis,
but with it also seems to condemn her move into the (male) realm of public discourse and her use of language in what might be defined as the male
register of speech. Her husband, on the other hand, is confirmed in his own
use of the male genderlect: In the end, Stephen has achieved his proclaimed
aim to "be let alone about [psychoanalysis]" (312), he has regained control
over the situation, and — as he has the final word in the play — he has successfully wrestled the floor from his wife.

   Whether we read the play's ending as an enhancement or a criticism of
traditional gender roles (for one might also argue that through its well-
sustained humor *Suppressed Desires* destabilizes conservative gender expectations the moment they are installed on the stage), this first play in which
Susan Glaspell had a hand clearly supports an understanding of human reality as existentially determined by interrelations. Given that this notion is
prominent in Glaspell's writings before the Provincetown as in many of her
later works, it might be tempting to attribute the focus on social interrelations as constitutive elements of human life in *Suppressed Desires* to Glaspell's
influence rather than Cook's. Whether or not such an assumption might be
confirmed by an analysis that would consider the collaborative nature of this
play, however, this early one-act is placed squarely within Glaspell's engagement with those "issues of expression" so central to her entire oeuvre.[2]

   Glaspell's one-act comedy *Close the Book* (her fourth play after *Suppressed Desires*, *Trifles*, and *The People*) is not built around an explicit focus
on matters of language and communication, yet it offers a special take on
many familiar issues. The action of the play takes place "*in the* ROOT *home,
the library of middle-western people who are an important family in their community* [...], *and who think of themselves as people of culture*" (63). Mrs. Root
has organized a dinner for her son Peyton, an instructor of English literature at the local university, and his fiancée Jhansi, a student agitator who
prides herself in her gypsy heritage. The Root family believes that Jhansi is
a bad influence on their promising offspring, yet as Mrs. Root dryly states,
she would "rather have her sit at my table than have my son leave some
morning in a covered wagon!" (71). Indeed, in his mother's eyes Peyton's
marriage to the "gypsy girl" might turn into "a good thing" yet, since Jhansi
"won't be in a position to say so much about freedom after she is married"
(74).

   The situation swings out of control when Peyton's sister enters with the
news that Jhansi is the descendant of a respectable family, after all. Her par-
ents (who both died young of typhoid fever) had been god-fearing people

who had named their daughter "after a town in India where [her] mother's missionary circle was helping to support a missionary." Upset to "have [her] character torn down" in such a way, Jhansi vows to escape the stifling walls of respectability and dares Peyton to leave with her (84). Luckily, however, it turns out that their flight into free-love unison will not be necessary. A closer perusal of the book of "Iowa descendants of New England families" brings forth a considerable number of "crevices in [the] walls of respectability" enclosing both their families (95). While Jhansi's grandfather, to her delight, is registered in the book's fine print as having burned down a neighbor's house, one of Peyton's ancestors had earned the family fortune by "selling whiskey and firearms to the Indians" (95). As Peyton can now appease Jhansi that "whenever we feel a bit stifled we can always find air through our family trees!" his Grandmother puts an end to the debate by ordering "[w]*ith weight*": "Peyton — close that book" (96).

While the subject of language itself might not play a prominent role in *Close the Book*, many of the questions related to Glaspell's understanding of communication certainly do. As Glaspell satirizes the determination of Jhansi's identity in the space between the girl's dogged insistence on her individuality and her relation to the surrounding community, a *book* serves to thematize the communicative constructedness of human existence. Jhansi's non-conformist yearning to stand outside of society, her resistance to a feeling of being "caught" within the "walls of respectability," and her stubborn denial of any obligation to her heritage are heartily made fun of in her childish overreaction against the "charge" of coming from a reputable family. Once again, Glaspell argues that no human being can decide to live her life outside the realm of social connections. On the other hand, the legitimacy of Jhansi's struggle not to let her identity be determined by other people's readings is similarly acknowledged, and the play's ending attempts a solution of reconciliation which Glaspell will continue to look for in her later writings. As Jhansi is allowed the freedom to be "herself" *within* society, in the end she does not have to make Peyton decide between his social ties and the woman he loves. Relief can be had through a simple re-interpretation — and thus, a re-worlding — of both family's ancestral histories.

Woman's Honor, another of Glaspell's early one-act comedies, premiered in April 1918, four months after the curtain had been raised on her more serious *The Outside*. While *The Outside* had foregrounded the subject of communication in that it built its central argument around Allie Mayo's and Mrs. Patrick's initial speechlessness and subsequent return to language, *Woman's Honor* once more stages the relation between language and reality in a less explicit way. Gordon Wallace, accused of a murder he has not committed, refuses to reveal his alibi for the night in question because he is unwilling to betray the name of the woman he was with. His lawyer has leaked this story to the press in the hope that the ensuing wave of female admiration and gratitude will help to swing around the case. Revealing his male notion of the play's title concept he asserts: "Wives—including, I hope, jurors' wives—will cry, 'Don't let that chivalrous young man die!' Women just love to have their honor shielded" (125).

Neither the lawyer nor Gordon Wallace himself are prepared for the newspaper article's immediate effect. A host of women storms the sheriff's conference room, paper in hand, to stand in for the nameless woman and provide the missing alibi. While the women's individual reasons for wanting to destroy the men's concept of "woman's honor" differ widely, none is willing to allow either of the male characters to determine the story's ending. Yet as is the case in many of Glaspell's other comedies, the play's comical punch line returns the floor to the men. When the prisoner finds himself cornered by a growing number of women he has never even seen in his life, in a desperate attempt to free himself from their grasp he effectively closes the matter — and the play — when he calls out at the final curtain: "*Oh, hell. I'll plead guilty*" (156).

The theme of human reality as being communicatively constructed is once more at the very heart of Susan Glaspell's argument in this play. As in her other works that feature the character of an absent woman (*Trifles* before *Woman's Honor*, *Bernice* and *Alison's House* later on) the identity of the unseen woman — Gordon Wallace's alibi — is pieced together but never essentially pinned down through several conflicting representations on stage. The women who come in to provide the prisoner's alibi in the unknown woman's stead all bear allegorical names— the Shielded One, the Motherly One, the Scornful One, the Silly One, the Mercenary One, the Cheated One — and thus can be read to "embody the different ways that society has seen fit to categorize women" (Kattwinkel 52). When they enter a heated debate about "woman's honor" as an empty yet destructive male concept, however, these characters represent both abstract stereotypes and individual women. Their personal stories demonstrate the very real and specific effects which an ultimately meaningless social ideal has had on their lives. Indeed, for each of these women her identity as an individual is at stake in the struggle over who will be allowed to prevent the Prisoner from saving the concept of "woman's honor" all over again. And all (except for the Silly One, who completely falls for the men's "noble" and "romantic" version) are determined to take the construction of the social world out of male hands for once.

Significantly, however, in the play's final comical twist Glaspell demonstrates once more that historically developed realities cannot be changed in one day. With his decision to "plead guilty," framed as a last means of escape from the women's growing linguistic power, Gordon Wallace retains the male privilege of shaping reality, if at the expense of his own freedom. As Susan

Kattwinkel has aptly argued, the prisoner "insists on the protagonist's absence as essential for maintaining his place of privilege, if not his freedom" (43). In this context, it is hardly surprising that the play's ending has been "generally unpopular with female spectators" (ibid. 51). Arguing that the theme of women's continuing determination by male definitions is no laughable matter Ozieblo, for one, asserts that the "rudimentary comedy" in this play "is stifled as soon as the women realize that they are, in the words of the Shielded One, 'victims of men's dreadful *need* for nobility'" (*Susan Glaspell* 115).

On the other hand, if at the end of this play the floor is given back to a male character, this gesture is comic in the very way it portrays the absurdity of the Prisoner's attempt to regain control over the situation: after all, his choice is to be convicted of murder. The woman he is trying to protect might still be absent at the end of the play, but a growing number of others has decided to join the public discourse that shapes their lives. Viewed from this angle, the comedy in *Woman's Honor*— kept up right to its final line — might be read as an expression of Glaspell's optimistic determination not to let the experience of reality as communicatively constructed take authority over one's personal life. The women in this one-act might not be able to discontinue, all at once, the Wittgensteinian history of use which still makes up the concept of "woman's honor" in their world. As each has decided to counter the lawyer's story by coming out with her own, decidedly less chivalrous version, however, these women have begun to take an active part in the shaping of their reality. And thus the suggestion is that the drastic measure which Gordon Wallace is forced to take in the end to save himself from women's definitions will not be able to stop the change which the lawyer's story has set in motion. No one "worlds" reality alone — and this, once again, goes both for the women and for the men in Glaspell's play.

The nature of truth and its relation to social conventions is also the subject of *Tickless Time*, the second collaboration between Glaspell and Cook, staged at McDougal Street in December 1918. In this play Ian Joyce attempts to establish a "first-hand relation to truth" (278) by building a sun-dial in his Provincetown yard. As the curtain rises he has just completed his task. The sun-dial is "set by the North star" ("set square on the true north"), and plainly reveals that all the clocks in Provincetown are "exactly nineteen minutes and twenty seconds behind [...] [true] Provincetown local time" (277). Intoxicated by her husband's enthusiasm for cosmic truth, Ian's wife Eloise vows to have done with all clocks, and Ian immediately begins to bury every symbol of "arbitrarily imposed standards" that can be found in the house at the foot of the sun-dial (281). As Eloise watches their cuckoo clock, a wedding present, disappear in its grave, however, she begins to have second thoughts: "Eddy and Alice gave us the cuckoo. You know they're coming

[…] for dinner. They might not understand our burying their clock" (283). And even though Ian insists that their friends' "failure to understand need not limit our lives," his wife now tries to save first the old-fashioned clock her "grandmother started house-keeping with" ("IAN. [*Firmly taking the clock.*] And see what it did to her. […] She had […] a standardized mind," 284), then the watch that was her graduation present ("IAN. Symbolizing all the standardized arbitrary things you were taught!" 284), and finally the alarm clock, which tells her when to leave the house in order to catch the train for Boston ("IAN. […] In a world content with false time, we are true," 287).

With the help of various comedic plot devices the play hits home the notion that whoever insists on "cosmic truth" when all other people live by "standardized lies" will fall through the network of human relations. As Eloise warns a passing neighbor: "Oh, Mrs. Stubbs! Don't get [your husband's] supper by sun time. It wouldn't be ready. It —(*with a hesitant look at* IAN) might get cold" (289). The Joyce's own cook dashes on and off the stage in the desperate attempt to prepare dinner with the help of the sundial's passing shadow, and in the end the indignant woman can be prevented from leaving her position only by the promise that the clocks will be dug up again. In fact, the play's concern with human relations is made explicit when Eddie and Alice arrive at the scene, representing society and its arbitrary conventions:

> ELOISE. (*Pityingly.*) Don't you know that you are running by the mean solar time of Philadelphia?
> EDDIE. Well, isn't anybody else running that way?
> ELOISE. Does that make it right? […]
> EDDIE. But how are you going to *connect up with other people*? […]
> ELOISE. We will connect with other people in so far as other people are capable of connecting with the truth!
> EDDY. I'm afraid you'll be awful lonesome sometimes [295; my emphasis].

As a last straw to the waning of Eloise's trust in absolute truth she is confronted with the fact that even the sun has to be "fixed up" if it is to tell the time — and "the North star is not true north," either (302). This revelation is made when Eddie examines the curved diagram on Ian's sun-dial:

> EDDY. (*Pointing with his stick.*) What's this standardized snake?
> IAN. That's my diagram correcting the sun. […]
> ELOISE. (*In growing alarm.*) Do you mean to tell me the sun is not right with *itself*? […] Ian, you mean to say the sun only tells the right *sun*-time four days in the year?
> IAN. It always tells the 'right' sun-time, but here the said right sun-time is fifteen minutes behind its own average, and here it is sixteen minutes ahead. This scale here across the bottom shows you the number of minutes to add or subtract [300–01].

In horror, Eloise exclaims "What *is* true? What *is* true?"—to which her husband replies "(*With vision.*) The mind of man" (302). From here on out, however, the woman has had enough of the "mind of *man*" (!) and his treacherous idea of absolute truth. In the face of even the sun's and the stars' relativity she no longer sees any sense in living nineteen minutes and twenty seconds apart from her friends. She wants her ticking clocks back.

Of course, just like *Suppressed Desires Tickless Time* does not allow easy access to a determination of either Glaspell's or Cook's individual influence in the writing of this play.[3] Presenting an individual's yearning for "absolute truth" where human existence proves to be essentially social (and therefore "relative"), however, this play is once again closely related to Susan Glaspell's other works. Indeed, both in the obviously gendered contrast with which the play treats the concept of truth in the conflict between Ian and Eloise *and* in its final acknowledgment that no human being, man or woman, can exist in a state of isolation, *Tickless Time* seems especially reminiscent of the argumentative set-up in *Trifles*.

Inheritors, a full-length play staged in March 1921 (two years after *Bernice* and eight months before the premier of *The Verge*), continues Glaspell's examination of the struggle between a person's individual ("inner") existence and her or his social ("outer") relations. The play's first act is set in the "[s]*itting-room of the Mortons' farmhouse in the Middle West—on the rolling prairie just back from the Mississippi*" (104). It is the year 1879, on the afternoon of the Fourth of July. While Grandmother Morton reminisces about the old pioneer days and the early settlers' ambivalent relation to the Indians whose land they had appropriated, her son Silas, a weathered farmer nearing the age of sixty, announces that he will give away a piece of his best land to found a college for the farmers' children. Inspired by the refined spirit of his neighbor Felix Fejevary—a Hungarian count who came to America after 1848 when his country's revolution against Austria had been defeated, and who had fought next to Silas Morton in the War of Independence—the farmer defends his long-tended dream in the face of his mother's objection and his friend's doubts. "Look at the land we walked in and took! Was there ever such a chance to make life more?" (117).

After this prologue the play makes a forty-year jump in time. It is now "*October of the year 1920,*" and act 2 takes us to a "*corridor in the library of Morton College,* [...] *upon the occasion of the fortieth anniversary of its founding.*" Fejevary's son Felix II, already "*nearing the age of his father in the first act,*" has made himself a "*place in society*" as a successful banker and president of the college's board of regents (118). As the curtain rises he is in the middle of negotiations over "a state appropriation for [the college's] enlargement" with a visiting senator (119). Yet the spirit of America has changed since the college's founding days. The students work as strike-breakers in the town's steel mills, State Senator Lewis expects Fejevary to control one of the teachers, Professor Holden, who has raised his voice against the cruel treatment of conscientious objectors in American jails two years after the end of World War I, and the college is about to expel three Hindu students who have protested against British rule in their home country. It is the time of the Espionage and Sedition Acts, and in this socially and politically restrictive climate it is Madeline Morton, 21-year-old granddaughter of both Silas Morton and Felix Fejevary I, who stands in for her forefathers' ideals of democracy, freedom, and tolerance.[4]

The end of the play does not show the young woman triumphant. Madeline, who has twice attempted to prevent the arrest of the Hindu students, is taken to court from the Morton farmhouse, the setting of the play's spirited beginning. She receives no help from either Professor Holden, who has a sick wife to take care of, or from her uncle Felix, who refuses to support the destruction of his life's work, all too aware that "[if] Silas Morton's granddaughter casts in her lot with revolutionists, Morton College will get no help from the state" (140). Nevertheless, in Madeline's final reconnection to her two grandfathers Glaspell casts this ending as wistfully hopeful for the future: "MADELINE. I don't feel alone anymore. [...] Grandfather Fejevary [...]. Silas Morton. No, not alone any more" (156).

If read for its underlying concept of the nature of human existence, more strongly perhaps than any of Glaspell's other plays *Inheritors* builds on a notion of identity and truth as existing prior to and independent of our social dealings in the world. Human growth — the impulse to change life for the better — is presented as a movement towards a universal human destiny of peace and understanding in this play, and the way to reach this eternal truth is by doing it "the way of Silas Morton and Walt Whitman — each man being *his purest and intensest self*" (134; my emphasis). As clearly as she had done in her first novel, *The Glory of the Conquered*, twelve years before, Glaspell argues the idealist's stance in *Inheritors*, convinced that meaning can be communicated from one mind to another. "Ain't it queer how things blow from mind to mind — like seeds," Silas Morton reflects on his decision to found his college on a hill in act 1 — in effect expressing the aim of education on the basis of the symbol model of language (115).

Indeed, in *Inheritors* Glaspell insists that the truth of life does not change over time, even if it can be purposely misrepresented. The Hindu students are right to resort to Abraham Lincoln's "first inaugural address to Congress, March 4, 1861" in support of their protest against British rule in India, thus Glaspell argues as she has her characters go back to the original text: "'This country with its institutions belongs to the people who inhabit it.' [...] 'Whenever they shall grow weary of the existing government they can exercise their constitutional right of amending it' [...] 'or their *revolution-*

ary right to dismember or overthrow it'" (123–24; Glaspell's emphasis). That Felix Fejevary II and Senator Lewis react to the Hindu students' legitimate political aims by arguing that Lincoln's words do not apply to the present situation only highlights that these two characters do not stand on the side of truth in this play: "FEJEVARY. [Lincoln] was speaking in another age. An age of different values. SENATOR. Terms change their significance from generation to generation" (124). Hence, as is the case in *The Verge* (brought to the Provincetown stage later that same year), in *Inheritors* the medium of language is seen as a stifling pattern that distorts the truth about human existence in its repetitive use of words through the ages. "I should think you would be proud to be the granddaughter of this man of vision," Senator Lewis sternly addresses Madeline Morton in a reference to her ancestor Silas Morton, but the young woman contemptuously replies: "Wouldn't you hate to be the grand-daughter of a phrase?" (127).

In this context, it seems that the experience of life as lived in a web of social relations is understood as a purely negative phenomenon in this play. In the first act Felix Fejevary warns his friend Silas that he cannot simply decide to found a college on his own, pointing out that he would "have to have a *community in sympathy with the thing you wanted to do*" (117; my emphasis). Forty years later, his son does his best to convince Professor Holden that "No one is entirely free. That's naive. It's rather egotistical to want to be. We're held by our obligations to the (*vaguely*)—the ultimate thing" (135). And while Fejevary II is unable here to define this "ultimate thing" that makes us prisoners in life in clearer terms, in the last act a conversation between Madeline and her aunt reveals the degree to which Glaspell sees our freedom curtailed by our relation to others:

> MADELINE. It's dreadful about families!
> AUNT ISABEL. Dreadful? Professor Holden's devotion to his wife is one of the most beautiful things I've ever seen.
> MADELINE. And is that all you see it in? [*sic*]
> AUNT ISABEL. You mean the—responsibility it brings? Oh, well—that's what life is. Doing for one another. Sacrificing for one another [148].

As Holden himself remarks just a moment later: "If you sell your soul—it's to love you sell it." And Madeline sadly replies: "That's strange. It's love that—brings life along, and then it's love—holds life back" (153).

On the other hand, even if this play does not come down on the side of an understanding of language as constitutive articulate contact, in the end *Inheritors* acknowledges (just like Glaspell's previous play, *Bernice*) that life is fundamentally social—for better or for worse. This idea is developed through the character of Madeline's father Ira, Silas Morton's son. Ira, who lost his wife (Felix Fejevary's daughter) when Madeline was only two years old—she rushed out to help her neighbors' children, who had come down with diphtheria, and perished from the disease herself—and whose son had died in a war he had joined to "make the world safe for democracy," has concluded that people should mind their own business. In a complete withdrawal from human community, he has concentrated on improving his corn, developing a new kind which has already won many prizes. To Ira's dismay, however, the dust of his cornfields is blown to neighboring fields, pollinating the neighbors' plants and making them better, too:

> IRA. Nothing stays at home. Not even the corn stays at home. [...] I want it to stay in my field. It goes away. The prevailing wind takes it on to the Johnsons—them Swedes that took my Madeline! I hear it! Oh, nights when I can't help myself—and in the sunshine I can *see* it—pollen—soft golden dust to make new life—goin' on to them,—and them too ignorant to know what's makin' their corn better! [155].

Yet the very circumstance which so grieves Ira turns into an unexpected source of courage for his daughter. Life simply *is* that way, Madeline realizes: "Nothing is to itself" (156). If the play presents its argument from the base of an understanding that "reality," "truth," and "self" exist independently of our socialization, nevertheless life's fundamental connectedness is reinterpreted as a positive experience in the end. If we accept this connection, thus Glaspell argues in *Inheritors*, we can do much to bring the world closer to a life in truth and beauty—a destiny albeit understood in this play as always already awaiting us somewhere outside of our social relations.

The last play that has yet to be mentioned in my analysis of Glaspell's dramatic works is the 1927 piece *The Comic Artist*. This play was Glaspell's first return to drama after Cook's death, and it was written in collaboration with her new partner, Norman Matson. Even more so than in the case of her theatrical co-productions with Cook, the fact that *two* artists signed responsible for this play poses a problem for its interpretation (and one might speculate that Glaspell's and Matson's artistic interests were less compatible than hers and Cook's had proven to be). As Waterman has commented: "*The Comic Artist* contains an unhappy combination of serious ideas that Miss Glaspell wrote into it and frivolous comedy that, I suspect, Norman Matson was responsible for. There is an annoying inconsistency in the play, both in method and theme, as its two authors work at cross purposes" (*Susan Glaspell* 86). While I do not quite see the comedy in *The Comic Artist*, to a reader familiar with Glaspell's entire oeuvre it does seem that an aesthetic gesture other than her own won the upper hand in this case, as the play does not strike one as particularly Glaspellian in either theme or style. For while the title could suggest that *The Comic Artist* perpetuates Glaspell's interest in the nature of art as communication, the play does not discuss the artist's relation to society as do many of Glaspell's other plays (such as *The People*,

Chains of Dew or—in later years—*Alison's House* and *Springs Eternal).*
Instead, *The Comic Artist* develops the predicament of its title figure as a very
private tragedy—a tragedy, moreover, which has little to do with the artist's
work in the first place.

Karl Rolf, "*a slight boyish fellow*" (7) who is on his way to becoming a
national success with his comic strip character "Mugs," is married to Nina,
a beautiful yet utterly conceited young woman who in her loveless childhood
was neglected by a mother who preferred the status of a society woman to
the company of her daughter. The play begins as the young couple arrives
for an off-season visit on Cape Cod, where Karl's older brother Stephen, a
painter, lives with his wife Eleanor. As it turns out, Nina had been Stephen's
mistress when they both lived in Paris five years ago, a phase of his life which
he now remembers with disgust. Nevertheless, old passions flare up between
Stephen and Nina, wreaking havoc in both their marriages. Eleanor, betray-
ing her fundamental conviction that we can (and should) not "meddle" with
other people's lives, decides to tell Nina that Stephen has revived their affair
simply because he wanted to open his brother's eyes to his wife's true character. And in fact, Eleanor's revelation is half-lie, half-truth, and thus cannot be denied outright by the cornered Stephen. Running out into the stormy
night, Nina dramatically vows to die in the roaring waves of the nearby
ocean. Of course, too much in love with herself ever to think of taking her
life in earnest, she never even goes near the beach. Karl, however, having
run out after her, tragically mistakes a floating log for his wife, and drowns
in the rough autumn sea in the attempt to save her.

Although she notes the same inconsistency in the play's design which
Arthur Waterman has commented on, Barbara Ozieblo does not support
this critics' theory of two authors working at cross purposes in *The Comic
Artist.* Instead, she suspects that the play was "conceived and written mostly
by [Norman Matson]," the less experienced writer: "This play, in which passion and ambition contrive to ruin the lives of two brothers, lacks the clear
thought that characterizes Glaspell's work, and the hall mark of her writing,
the determined woman who consciously molds her own life, is absent"
(*Susan Glaspell* 234). Ozieblo's conviction that Glaspell had contributed not
much more than her name to *The Comic Artist* might be supported by the
fact that not much of the writer's heart seemed to be in this play after Matson had left her in 1932. As Ozieblo reports, "when her novel *The Morning
is Near Us* was about to come out [in 1939, H.-B.], [Glaspell] asked her publisher to strike *The Comic Artist* from a list of her plays printed in the book"
(ibid. 249).

On the other hand, *The Comic Artist* does bear a number of features
which point to Glaspell's own hand in its composition — even if, once again,
it might not be possible to prove either author's specific contribution to the

play. Most obviously, the close relationship between the artist figure Karl and his sister-in-law Eleanor is typical for Glaspell, as both characters admit to a fundamental preoccupation with the possibilities and dangers of "reaching one another." This shared concern is illustrated in their common love for Mugs, the comic strip character who continuously gets himself into awkward situations by "always trying to give people something they don't want" (28): Just like Karl himself, Eleanor likes "the comical little man" "best of all [his] pictures" (58). (Sixteen years later Margaret Higgenbothem of *Springs Eternal* will be the only character who appreciates what her stepson Jumbo has tried to do with his sunflower-painting.)

Significantly, the fact that Eleanor is so drawn to the comic-tragedy of Karl's invention indicates that even if she is convinced that it is impossible to reach another human being through deeds, words, or pictures, she believes that in our isolation we are "all in the same fix"—and thus "must have sympathy with each other" (62). While her husband Stephen rejects her "aloof, controlled" attitude (40) and her assertion that "we can't help others" as a "cold-blooded doctrine" (42), Glaspell shows that Eleanor—like so many other figures who despair of human contact in her works—does long for a feeling of connection and understanding: "ELEANOR. In the way I mean it, [that we cannot help others] is the simple truth. STEPHEN (*loudly*). It is not! You withdraw from life—calm—hoarding your strength. ELEANOR. Do I? (*Looking at him curiously.*) I'm not sure I do" (42–43). In this way, in the character of Eleanor *The Comic Artist* recalls the image that Glaspell had evoked eight years earlier of her absent protagonist in *Bernice*—and through the later play's onstage character the suspicion is strengthened that a life in isolated calm and superiority is not what these "aloof" women really want for themselves.

Hence, in Eleanor and her connection to the play's title figure, *The Comic Artist* continues Glaspell's debate around issues of human identity and the possibilities of connection through communication. The play's key exchange between Karl and Eleanor rings with familiar Glaspellian *topoi*, and for this it merits to be quoted here at length:

> KARL. I always believed [Stephen loved me].
> ELEANOR. Keep believing it. We have to have faith. If we can't draw and draw upon it—as plants from the earth–
> KARL. Not easy, sometimes.
> ELEANOR. I know that. It gets so mixed. We're not one thing, but many things.
> [...]
> ELEANOR. My grandmother was religious, in the way of her time. I don't know that the words meant a great deal to her, but when I was a little girl I heard her say them, and now they sometimes come of themselves, as if they'd sunk into life and—like Stephen's wine—been fermenting all this

time. "Now we see through a glass darkly, but one day we shall see face to
face." And when we see, what will we see, Karl? I'd give so much to know.
Sometimes it seems just too silly not to know.

KARL. We're all in the same fix there.

ELEANOR (*timidly*). And because we are — all in the same fix — we must
have sympathy one with another, don't you think? People together in a
thick fog wouldn't blame each other for stumbling.

KARL. They would, I fear. I can hear their ridiculous curses.

ELEANOR (*her voice feeling its way*). There's something in us— no one can
hurt. No one can reach. Perhaps we should know that. Perhaps we should
not refuse to know it. In words— no. We can't put it into words. But it's—
loyalty.

KARL. Loyalty — to what?

ELEANOR (*after thinking*). To what stops us with wonder in the fields. To
what we see through the glass darkly, and may see face to face.

KARL (*after dwelling with this, turns away*). No. Not for me. [...] You *want*
to be reached — even reached to be hurt! [61–62].

This passage stretches across the full space of tension available in Glaspell's
oeuvre between the concepts of isolation and connection, the hope and
betrayal of words, a representation of truth or a "being worlded" in constitutive articulate contact. As crucial as this scene is in the context of Glaspell's
dramatic oeuvre as a whole, however, in the plot development of *The Comic
Artist* it is no more than an oddly disconnected side-line. And thus, while
the play does betray Glaspell's influence in some respects, it is much less in
tune with her central artistic concerns than any of her other dramatic
works— and perhaps it is for this very reason that the author so determinedly
attempted to distance herself from this play in later years.

Significantly, in her continuous portrayal of human existence as an irreducibly social experience, the nature of communication remained an issue
even in Glaspell's latest works— both dramatic and fictional. While I have
already discussed the ways in which the author put to use the medium of
the stage with regard to these "issues of expression" (Lewisohn) in her two
final plays, *Alison's House* (1930) and *Springs Eternal* (1943), a glance at the
novel *Norma Ashe*, published in 1942, will demonstrate how once again
Glaspell carried over her thematic interests from one literary genre to the
other during the final years of her life. In fact, with regard to Glaspell's life-
long interest in issues of language and communication her second to last
novel must be seen as one of her most important works, as here the writer
takes stock of every notion she had ever negotiated in this context.

Using a retrospective point of view throughout the greater part of the
novel, in *Norma Ashe* Glaspell traces the development of her title character
from a young, idealistic university student to a disillusioned middle-aged
woman who, widowed and without support, struggles to make a living by
keeping up a run-down boarding-house. As a young woman Norma had

been part of a small discipleship of students gathered around a charismatic teacher at Pioneer College (a place of learning reminiscent of Morton College in *Inheritors*). Together they had participated in their teacher's vision that the world could be transposed if only people had the courage to believe in the possibility of "reaching" one another:

> He talked of the power of direct communication (as he to them). "We are not shut away one from another, but being one, an individual has the power to feel in another what could be his. Disease can spread, and so can the good. Be this and what you are will flow into the lives around you. This is the glorious power of life for extension. Remember, we reach one another" [156].

The nature of communication is once again among Glaspell's most central concerns in this work, and on the basis of the representative model once more the struggle is between the idealist's and the skeptic's stance. Granted a scholarship for the University of Chicago the young Norma Ashe is to become a university teacher herself and carry on the message that has transformed her own life to the next generation of students. When she attempts to explain her teacher's beliefs (and with it her own aim in life) to her suitor Max Utterbach, a young man with a mind for business who has nothing to do with her circle of university friends, language does not seem adequate for this task — which involves the difficult attempt of making him understand why she cannot marry him. Yet remembering how her teacher had reached *her* when he talked about "the power of direct communication," Norma dares to open up her deepest self to the young man:

> If you were trying to make real sunrise on a mountaintop to one who had never seen a sunrise or a mountain, you would halt in your words, feel inadequate, helpless. I am making it less, you would feel; belittling. Perhaps I should not speak of it at all. And thus Norma Ashe would halt at first, feeling inadequate. Yet no ... we could communicate; and that was a miracle great as the sunrise. It lighted, transformed, as the sunrise. Hope of a better world was in man's power to communicate. But you must speak from the truth and not about it. She almost prayed for the great vision to be there now, itself speaking. She was trying to speak for life that waited: the dream we could make come true. "Into your hands it has been committed." The time was at hand; only the awareness was lacking: awareness that we could make life what we would have it be [99].

Tragically, however, Norma Ashe fails to make herself understood in this key encounter of the novel. Max Utterbach does not understand the first thing about the young woman's beliefs. Instead, ironically her very fervor kindles a passion in him that she can only succumb to in the further course of events. From now on, her love binds her to a man whom she will not be able to "reach" in all the decisive moments of their relationship. And as she gives up her plans of becoming a university teacher for Max's dubitable business opportunities, at his side Norma Ashe's life takes a course she had not been able to foresee in her enthusiastic youth.

As Glaspell minutely demonstrates how her protagonist's life is influenced through forces other than her own will, the novel is akin to the author's most challenging plays in that it mingles aspects of a representational understanding of language and art with the contrary notion of human existence as created in constitutive articulate contact. In fact, it is as if Glaspell puts her most cherished notions to the ultimate test of experience in *Norma Ashe*— as if she wanted to determine once and for all whether her life-long belief in the power of language and art to change the world for the better could still be justified after two world wars and many personal experiences of failure, disappointment and loss.

In the end, Glaspell employs both philosophical models to reaffirm her essentially positive outlook on the possibilities of communication. On the one hand, if Norma Ashe's life has not expressed the truth she had experienced in her youth — if she has not found a medium to send her teacher's message out into the world — Glaspell's title character nevertheless returns to the conviction that the message itself had not been an illusion: "She had failed with herself: her life had deviated. But the truth that was in the dream had not deviated! Too great to be killed by her own years, or by any denying, it rose there above the lives of men, itself unsmirched, itself imperishable" (235).—"More clearly than she now saw the coffee in this cup she had seen what waited, what could be. [...] [P]erhaps we just weren't good enough, she thought. Not medium pure enough nor long enough lasting. It couldn't come through. That doesn't mean it was not there" (302). On the other hand, although she confirms the metaphysical notion of "truth" in these passages, at the same time Glaspell once again insists that it is our ideas— as part of our linguistic form of existence — that "make" our reality — and in contrast to Claire Archer in *The Verge* Norma Ashe sees this as a chance for change: "What stood in the way? Only an idea that it couldn't be. And she thought, as in the days with their teacher, if a wrong idea has that power, what couldn't the right idea do! [...] We don't know the power of our own minds. They *make* reality; a vision is as real as losing a job or having a baby" (159–60; emphasis in the original). In this context, once again Glaspell embraces the Wittgensteinian thought that language has a history of use and that historically developed language-games can influence meaning *without* denying the function of language as a "medium for your thoughts":

> The whole thing about a developed language was that we could the better understand one another. Language had a long history and many a word had the beauty of a polished stone. If you were at home in a language you had a medium for your thoughts, and by expressing them they grew.

Words were for thoughts and words could beget thoughts: all so wonderfully intertwined [316].

Importantly, too, just as many of Glaspell's plays seem to further the
idea of a metaphysical truth but highlight the process in which reality is
made in interaction at the same time, in the case of *Norma Ashe* the novel's
narrative structure demonstrates how the protagonist's reality is created in
the integrational sense. If examined for the specific mechanisms which bring
Norma Ashe back to her youthful, affirmative self, the story's plot development reveals that the old "vision" comes back to her precisely through a
(renewed) communicative engagement with others. In her youth, it had been
the community shared by the students gathered around their teacher's table
which had played a significant part in making the vision real. It is only consistent in this context that in the book's first chapter it is an uncalled-for
visit of her old friend Rosie, a member of the Pioneer College group, which
sets in motion Mrs. Max Utterbach's retrospective questioning of what has
become of her former self as Norma Ashe. Moreover, after she has thus been
set to thinking Norma happens to encounter Austin Wurthen, another member of their circle, as he cynically betrays their former vision by using it for
career purposes in a political speech. Outraged, the broken woman jumps
up from her chair to disturb her former friend's hypocritical lecture — and
in this way reaffirms her earlier self. And finally, even closer yet to the end
of the novel (and of Norma Ashe's life) it is through her stubborn will to
connect to a young student at the University of Chicago as a representative
of the young generation that her teacher's truth once again becomes real for
Norma: "She was disturbed, wondering: can't age and youth speak to one
another? Do the years of our living make a chasm not to be bridged? Does
language itself change and old words not have their old content?" (275)—
"And then, as best she could, she told him [about her teacher's vision]" (277).
Step by step, therefore, Susan Glaspell's protagonist is shown to (re-) "create" her earlier reality in communicative acts of worlding in this novel, and
the notion of communication as constitutive articulate contact is mixed in
once again with an intricate web of allusions that posit the ability of language and art to represent an individual's private meaning to other isolated
minds.

What the preceeding survey of Glaspell's works from 1909 through 1943
has shown is that both with regard to her thematic interests and with regard
to the techniques she employs in both genres to negotiate her ideas, her oeuvre stands as a consistent aesthetic entity which reflects her time's reaction
to the epistemological crisis of modernity in a complex web of ideas. Interestingly, too, while her writing was naturally influenced in many ways both
by contemporary contexts and by the advance of her personal life experience, the perspective I have taken here suggests that the oscillating angles

which Glaspell takes in each new work with regard to the nature of language and the function of art do not add up to form a neatly linear development. There is no consistent evolution from youthful idealism to mature realism or disillusionment in Glaspell's art in this context, no move from conventional form to experimentation, nor from a favoring of (female) community to a focus on (human) individuality; there is no focus zooming in at the end of her creative life on either the personal or the social significance of art, or on a final view of meaning as either created in communication or as preexisting human contact. Wherever Susan Glaspell has set her pen to paper, these notions exist side by side, and right up to her final works she continued to attempt new combinations of angles on the question which concerned her most in all of her writing — how meaning is created and sustained both in life and in art.

12. Conclusion

I said things and didn't know the meaning of them 'till after I had said them.
— The Woman from Idaho in *The People* (1917)

When you think what a writer might do for life — [...]. What is it is the matter with you — with all you American writers—'most all of you. A well-put-up light — but it doesn't penetrate anything. It never makes the fog part.

— Margaret in *Bernice* (1919)

HARRY. It'll do Claire good to take someone in. To get down to brass tacks and actually say what she's driving at.
CLAIRE. Oh — Harry. But yes — I will try. (*does try, but no words come. Laughs*) When you come to say it it's not — One would rather not nail it to a cross of words—(*laughs again*) with brass tacks.

— *The Verge* (1921)

ELSA. [...] But do you know, Father, I feel Alison wrote those poems for me.
STANHOPE. I feel she wrote them for me.
ELSA. And there will be those in the future to say, She wrote them for me.

— *Alison's House* (1930)

In Susan Glaspell's oeuvre questions of language play a crucial role. What is the relation between meaning and communication? Is language capable of expressing transcendental truths? Can it effectively relate our innermost selves to the world? Or if it cannot, if the human mind is barred from extralinguistic experience in a Nietzschean prison-house of language, does that mean that the ineffable does not exist? If language and art participate in the creation of truth, where does this knowledge leave the individual's need for a sense of identity, and how does it effect the hope for social change through artistic expression?

Questions about the nature of language and the function of art have occupied thinkers and artists of all ages. Susan Glaspell's way of negotiating these issues is firmly rooted in the experience of her own age. Her approaches to the problem of language and communication reflect a sophisticated intellectual and emotional reaction to what has come to be called the epistemological crisis of modernity. Meeting head-on the Nietzschean sense of her time that "God is dead" and that transcendental truths are no longer available, Glaspell asks for the place of meaning in human experience. Her art engages with the determinist ideas of naturalism as much as with the social criticism of more experimental European playwrights such as Henrik Ibsen, George Bernhard Shaw, and August Strindberg. Moreover, Glaspell both reacts to her modernist contemporaries' impulse to "make it new" in their search for aesthetic forms which will return a sense of order to the chaos of the modern world and responds to the complementary desire to re-enact the individual's experience of fragmentation in artistic terms—a desire evident in the works of German expressionism by playwrights such as Georg Kaiser and Ernst Toller, plays that were widely received in America.[1] In this transnational discourse on the relation between life and art Susan Glaspell develops her own, entirely unique stance. Her art is fully aware of the disturbing impact with which philosophical, aesthetic and linguistic attacks on the notion of meaning engender fundamental epistemological doubt. Nevertheless, in her persistent process of questioning, redefining, and questioning again the concepts of truth and understanding in human existence, Glaspell's belief in the power of communication is renewed time and again — insisted upon, as one might argue, out of sheer existential necessity.

For Susan Glaspell, as my readings have shown, the question of meaning resides in the tension between a sense of self as irreducibly apart from others and the contradictory experience that human existence is fundamentally communal and interrelated. Glaspell allows this tension full scope, as two concepts of language and art interact in her works: a representational understanding which presupposes the existence of the Cartesian ego at a distance from the world, and a contrasting notion which insists that meaning does not preexist the human mind's engagement with the social sphere. Significantly, the conflict between a belief that holds on to the idea of metaphysical essence and a view of life which replaces the idea of "transcendental signifieds" (Derrida) with the all-encompassing concept of human intersubjectivity is not solved anywhere in Glaspell's oeuvre. And while this is true both for her novels and her dramatic writings, I have focused on her plays because in the communal space of the theatre the social function of art inevitably gains a special, meta-aesthetic relevance thanks to the conditions of the genre itself.

In his study *Staging Depth. Eugene O'Neill and the Politics of Psycholog-*

ical Discourse Joel Pfister has argued that O'Neill's plays participated in a cultural discourse that established the concept of "depth as a timeless psychological space within the self" (5). In contrast, Pfister claims, Susan Glaspell "concentrated [her] critique on the cultural making of forms of selfhood" and thus *exposed* precisely those discursive processes that shaped the idea of "essence" for an understanding of identity at the beginning of the 20th century (188). Indeed, Glaspell did not share the pop-psychological notion of her time "that inward private subjectivity is more true to personhood than public actions and networks of collective relations" (as Alan Trachtenberg defines the notion of "depth" in his foreword to Pfister's study, xii). In many of her plays the idea of language as a vehicle to transport thoughts from one mind to another is fundamentally questioned, and the notion of communication as a process which creates truth and reality in social interaction informs her works as an unspecified idea which prefigures late 20th-century theories of human "intersubjectivity." Importantly, this idea that truth and reality are discursively constructed is presented both as a positive (i.e. creative) and as a negative (i.e. imprisoning) experience in Glaspell's plays. Assuming that human beings participate in an ongoing process of "worlding," Glaspell insists that there is a chance to change life for the better, as we are free to embark on this communal project at all moments. This is the hopeful argument with which plays such as *Trifles, The People, The Outside, Bernice, Alison's House* or *Springs Eternal* end. On the other hand, because the individual does not "world" alone or from scratch, no single self has ultimate control over the mechanisms that create the defining frame of his or her life. Hence, the same plays which suggest a hopeful outlook on the future often also admit (directly or indirectly) to the idea of a loss of control in the creation of meaning — an argument which I have foregrounded in my readings of *Trifles, The Outside,* and *Bernice.*

Consequently, I agree with Joel Pfister that Susan Glaspell's plays are "about dismantling cultural constructions of personal life" (198). On the other hand, my analyses have also shown that Glaspell often grounds her works in the representational model of language and art at the same time. One of her most burning questions is whether or not human beings are capable of communicating the truth about their "innermost beings" from one isolated mind to the other. Indeed, although Glaspell is concerned with communicative constructions of selfhood in everything she writes, she does not entirely abandon the image of the human self as defined by such principles as "isolation," "essence," and "interiority"—concepts which belong to the (pop-) psychological notion of "depth" developing in the early 20th century as much as to an older idea of the individual as an autonomous entity.

Significantly, Glaspell's idea of the individual — whether in essentialist terms or as a product of discursive processes—includes both the sense of a universal human nature and an understanding of the self as a distinctly gendered entity. This tension in Glaspell's awareness of the self as simultaneously marked and unmarked by gender was acknowledged early on in her dramatic career. In his book *The Drama of Transition* (1922) her contemporary Isaac Goldberg included her in his discussion of new developments on the international dramatic scene (next to chapters on innovative playwrights from Spain, Italy, South America, France, Germany, Yiddish Drama, and Russia). Goldberg was possibly the first critic to claim that "Glaspell [...], as a serious dramatist—one of the few Americans whose progress is worth watching with the same eyes that follow notable European effort—is largely the playwright of woman's selfhood":

> That acute consciousness of self which begins with a mere sense of sexual differentiation (exemplified in varied fashion in *Trifles, Woman's Honor, The Outside*) ranges through a heightening social sense (*The People, Close the Book, Inheritors*) to the highest aspirations of the complete personality, the individual (*Bernice, The Verge*) [474].

The notion of "woman's selfhood" does not develop into the idea of a specifically female self in Goldberg's reading of Glaspell's plays, however, as he goes on to point out: "And there is *more than rebellious womanhood* in these dramas; there is consciousness of valid self, or of a passion for freedom, of dynamic personality; there is craving for life in its innermost meaning" (ibid. 475; my emphasis). With this qualifier Goldberg firmly re-establishes the idea at the end of his argument that Glaspell's plays are not about female subjectivity but about "life's innermost meaning" in a sense that has nothing to do with gender differences.

Of course, it is Glaspell's dramatization of the *female* self that has re-established her in the American literary canon at the end of the 20th century. A substantial number of studies has demonstrated the ways in which Glaspell's plays anticipate late 20th-century notions of Woman as the unrealized Other in the patriarchal Symbolic Order. In her female characters' stammering utterances and pervading silences, and in her characteristic use of absent female protagonists (thus Linda Ben-Zvi, Elaine Aston, Barbara Ozieblo and many others have argued) Glaspell formulates "her rejection of the 'symbolic' and desire for the 'semiotic'" in the Kristevan sense (Aston, 1995, 119). As Aston sums up the gist of such readings: "Glaspell's women on the margins, locked in/ out of language, represent the inability of the 'female' self to take a place" (ibid.).

While feminist thought has rightfully taken issue with a critical stance in which the experience of *man* is still taken to denote "humankind," the focus on a specifically female position in Glaspell's oeuvre has necessarily rejected the idea of "universally human" experiences altogether—both with regard to the works in question and as a viable concept as such. The tension between a vantage point of the individual as unmarked by gender and the experience of a decisively female self is nowhere to be resolved in Susan Glaspell's works, however. Glaspell does resort to notions of "essence" within the frame of the representative model of communication, yet her plays oscillate continually between the two understandings of the self as either "irreducibly female/male" *or* as essentially "human" (compare, for instance, *Trifles, The Outside,* or *The Verge*). What is more, arguing within the contrary frame of an integrationist approach to language, Glaspell at the same time strives to work against *all* discursive patterns that might imprison the self in notions of fixed essences—including those which assume a preexisting female self in need of empowerment. As Pfister notes with regard to one of Glaspell's early comedies:

> The point of *Woman's Honor* is not to delve into "womanly depth," but rather to demystify the ideological invention of it. Glaspell's play acknowledges sexuality as an important part of a woman's humanity (as does her later drama, *The Verge*) without inflating it into the very essence of her humanity. Female sexuality is not blown up into a hermeneutic — the key to a woman's mysterious self [198].

Pfister's point is taken here against Freudian readings of a female essence as they were becoming popular in the dramatist's own time. The same criticism, however, can be extended to late 20th-century readings of Glaspell's works along the lines of French feminist theories (which, after all, have their roots in Lacan's reinterpretation of Freudian psychoanalysis). These theories postulate female *jouissance* as a key factor in woman's essential "otherness." While such readings have provided potent insights into the gendered workings of Glaspell's plays, their underlying understanding of the "female self" carries the danger of claiming an essence for the subject position of woman which turns out to be just as imprisoning to the individual as the patriarchal constructions of womanhood which it was meant to contend — an idea of female essence which Glaspell, in fact, never quite follows through in her plays. In her dramas Glaspell frequently thematizes the experience that we are essentially "made" by different forms of communication. At the same time, she tests the degree to which we, as individuals and as members of a diachronic as well as synchronic human community, have the power to create our own realities (and identities) in continuous acts of linguistic "worlding." Importantly, this experience of the workings of language and art as constitutive forms of communication is ultimately valid for both genders in Glaspell's oeuvre. The dangers and potentials inherent in our human existence as irreducibly social and fundamentally linguistic affect us all — regardless of whether we are men or women.

Finally, Susan Glaspell's persistent interest in the function of language and communication includes a discussion of the nature of art as a communicational medium, and with it a questioning of the artist's role in society. On the one hand, we have seen that in this context, too, Glaspell often supports the idea of metaphysical essences by postulating that an artist's social obligation is to communicate a truth which is first formed as a "vision" within her (or his) mind and then expressed in works of art in order to "make the fog part" for others. This is obvious in Ed's editorial in *The People*, Margaret's plea in *Bernice* that Craig use his creative gifts in a more responsible way, Stanhope's reception of his sister's poems in *Alison's House*, and Owen's decision to write another book for the boys about to return from the war in *Springs Eternal*. In fact, even in *The Verge*, the play which most directly deals with the epistemological crisis of the modern age, Claire Archer's desperate desire to "shoot holes" through the surface of reality implies that there is something behind and beyond the discursive patterns of language which separate us from extralinguistic experience (*The Verge* 82).[2] On the other hand, Claire longs to get through to an "outside" which, as she is forced to admit time and again, "she doesn't know is there" (83). The same plays, therefore, which suggest the existence of a transcendental beyond often demonstrate how Glaspell's characters create their reality in the process of communicative interaction. And for her artist figures, too, this idea implies both the loss of authorial control over the process of interpretation and a personal obligation to take a conscious part in the communal process of worlding. Indeed, even more than of her ordinary characters, Susan Glaspell expects of her *artists* to develop new language-games out of old ones.

Of course, these discussions of the relation between life and art are also relevant to Glaspell's own position as a playwright. As I have shown, time and again Glaspell's works seem to make an attempt at regaining control over the "message" they send out to the theatregoer or reader — to the extent that Ed and The Woman From Idaho in *The People*, Allie Mayo in *The Outside*, or Margaret in *Bernice* gesture towards the existence of a transcendental truth, each play's ending seems to insist that there is only one authoritative interpretation of its meaning. On the other hand, many of Glaspell's innovative dramatic techniques emphasize that the creation of meaning takes place in a reciprocal process between dramatist, play, theatre, and audience. These techniques—first and foremost Glaspell's use of off-stage characters and her mixing of various modes of theatrical expression and styles in a single play — encourage an understanding of art as constitutive articulate contact. This understanding works hand in hand with the notion of the theatre as an inherently communal endeavor as it was favored by the Provincetown Players' explicitly formulated aesthetic philosophy. And read in this context, Susan Glaspell's works for the stage demonstrate the ways in which meaning is created in the realm of human intersubjectivity, not within (or even prior to) the "visions" of our isolated minds.

Noting the ever-present importance of language in Susan Glaspell's dramatic art, her contemporary Ludwig Lewisohn described her as "a dramatist a little afraid of speech"— as an artist whose attempts to "speak out" circumscribed a painful and often fruitless effort: "She brooded and tortured herself and weighed the issues of expression" (*Expression in America* 93–94). Glaspell's evident distrust of language may have been an expression of the modern individual's epistemological insecurity, and it may prefigure the postmodernist notion of meaning as endlessly deferred in the free play of signifiers. In any case, Glaspell's plays fully embrace the idea that meaning is a discursive construction. And while she recognizes the potential for existential despair in this notion and allows such feelings ample space in her works, she always insists that it bears a positive, creative potential as well. Susan Glaspell's characters develop their lives in an ongoing dialogue with each other, aware of those influences that lie outside the sphere of their own selves but testing ever new ways of cooperation rather than resistance. Indeed, in Glaspell's art the oppressed and discontented have a greater chance of influencing their world if they enter into a constructive exchange with established discourses than if they embark on a deadly combat in the conviction that life needs to be created from scratch.[3]

Importantly, too, even if Glaspell meets the challenge of the so-called linguistic turn in 20th-century philosophy and art on all possible plains, her art ultimately insists on the importance of the concept of meaning as such. Our interpretations, whether of life or of art, may be no more than temporary resting places— stepping stones of meaning in the Wittgensteinian sense. Nevertheless, Glaspell's characters never cease to look for "relief in words," acknowledging that it is the act of communication itself which makes them part of a human community.[4] And it is in this same sense that Susan Glaspell herself, too, is temporarily relieved of her inclination to "brood and torture herself" (Lewisohn) through her words on the page — and manages to communicate, after all. Glaspell's art allows that meaning might be neither transcendental nor controllable. And yet, like Alison Stanhope's poems in *Alison's House*, her plays challenge her audiences across time, space, and all differences of gender, nationality or cultural context to participate in the creation of meaning as a fundamental necessity in human existence — and the only route towards any kind of change.

Notes

Introduction

1. Ozieblo, *Susan Glaspell* 178. For a brief overview of Glaspell criticism along similar lines, see Gainor, *Susan Glaspell* 1–9. For a thorough presentation of both primary and secondary sources up to 1992, consult Mary E. Papke's *Sourcebook*.

2. Linda Ben-Zvi's long awaited biography of Susan Glaspell appeared when my own study was already well into the publication process. I regret that I was thus unable to refer to it.

3. See Gainor, *Susan Glaspell* 5. In her afterword Gainor rightly points to the crucial significance of defining one's own understanding of the term "feminism" when applying it to Glaspell's works (or to any other writer, for that matter): "As scholarly debates of the past two decades demonstrate, there is no longer a sense of a monolithic 'feminism' but, rather, multiple 'feminisms' that emanate from a range of subject positions in their social and historical contexts. They may indeed conflict with one another" (*Susan Glaspell* 264–65).

1. Social Rebel or Conventional Woman?

1. The following account is based on Noe's and Ozieblo's full-length biographies, as well as on Papke's short presentation of Susan Glaspell's life in her *Sourcebook*. For a discussion of the rationale to refer to the artist's biography as one of many possible intertexts for her works, see also Gainor, *Susan Glaspell* 4.

2. Glaspell herself listed the year of her birth as 1882. This is the year which many biographical sources stated in her lifetime, and it is also cited on her gravestone in Cape Cod. Reliable research, however, has established Glaspell's birth date as 1 July 1876 (see Noe, *Susan Glaspell* 13, and Ben-Zvi, "Susan Glaspell's Contributions," 163).

3. See Papke, *Susan Glaspell* 5–6. The degree and nature of Cook's—and other men's—influence on Glaspell are a frequent source of contention among critics.

4. In *The Road to the Temple* Glaspell writes about her husband's vision: "Quite possibly there would have been no Provincetown Players had there not been Irish Players. What he saw done for Irish life he wanted for American life—no stage conventions in the way of projecting with the humility of true feeling" (218).

5. "I had meant to do it as a short story, but the stage took it for its own, so I hurried in from the wharf to write down what I had seen. Whenever I got stuck, I would run across the street to the old wharf, sit in that leaning little theater under which the sea sounded, until the play was ready to continue" (Glaspell, *Road* 256). See chapter 3 on *Trifles*, as well as Gainor's astute remarks on this stylized version of Glaspell's entry into the world of the theatre, *Susan Glaspell* 37 f.

6. See Ben-Zvi, "O'Neill's Cape(d) Compatriot," 130: "For Isaac Goldberg, Heywood Broun, Ludwig Lewisohn and other eminent theatre critics of the early 1920s, O'Neill was the undisputed father of American drama, Glaspell the mother [...]."

7. In Glaspell's drama *Chains of Dew* this "family" function of the Greenwich Village community is expressed through the character Nora Powers; see my interpretation of this play in chapter 7.

8. For detailed background information on the foundation, development, and "fall" of the Provincetown Players see contemporary and critical histories such as those by Edna Kenton, Helen Deutsch and Stella Hanau, Mary Heaton

Vorse, Lawrence Langner, Robert Károly Sarlós, Leona R. Egan, and Cheryl Black.

9. For an account of Cook's and Glaspell's stay in Greece, as well as for a closer analysis of the couple's intimate relationship, see Ozieblo's biography.

10. See Sarlós 144: "The practical reason for incorporation and interim stemmed from a desire to protect the Provincetown Players' name (and perhaps the theatre and its personnel as well) from being used by artists with clearly professional aspirations who were only too eager to fill the vacuum left by Cook's departure. The wording of the Certificate of Incorporation along with a number of Kenton's letters to Greece indicate that the legal maneuver had a specific tactical goal: the prevention of non-amateur, noncollective, in a word non-Provincetown Player-like pursuits under the Players' name." See also Edna Kenton's newly edited remembrances of the Provincetown Players and their end, *The Provincetown Players and the Playwrights' Theatre, 1915–1922*.

11. Glaspell to "Fitzie, though not to Fitzie alone, but to all those new members of the Provincetown Players," 23 May 1924, Harvard Theatre Collection; as qtd. in Sarlós, *Jig Cook* 150–51.

12. In addition, the Berg Collection at the New York Public Library contains the first act of one further drama, an undated and incomplete draft.

13. See Cheryl Black's study on *The Women of Provincetown*.

14. In a curious parallel, Glaspell's early one-act *The Outside* celebrates two women's return to life who had withdrawn from human community in reaction to having lost their husbands: one to death, the other to infidelity (see my discussion of this play in chapter 5). The connection between Glaspell's personal problems and her prolonged "writer's block" is, of course, only an assumption. On occasion of the publication of her next novel eight years later a journalist reports: "[Miss Glaspell] did say she was glad to have got her book written, since for several years previously she had simply been unable to write, for no reason.... She wished to avoid any phrase that could be made to sound like 'waiting for inspiration,' but certainly there are dry spells for a writer, when neither specific ideas, good intentions nor the most earnest and laborious toll will produce the least result.... And though a writer may not be exactly happy while writing, she added resignedly, he or she is even less happy when not writing...." ("Turns With a Bookworm," spaces in the original).

15. The Federal Theatre Project was closed down only one year later, as Rachel France reports in the introduction to her *A Century of Plays by American Women*: "A hostile Congress ended the Federal Theatre Project in 1939.

Largely an amalgam of the remnants of the Little Theatre movement and, in New York, elements of the left-wing workers' theatres, the project had been in operation for little more than four years" (21).

16. *The Morning is Near Us* (1939), *Norma Ashe* (1942), *Judd Rankin's Daughter* (1945); *Cherished and Shared of Old* (1940).

17. The theme of illicit love and the tensions between an individual's obligations to herself and to society would occupy Glaspell for the rest of her life, surfacing again and again in her works. That she had no particular desire to shock Davenport society is also apparent in the fact that although she never legally married Norman Matson, she pronounced him her husband both to her mother and relatives at home and to the general public. (Biographical entries written in Glaspell's own lifetime in fact all state her to have been married twice.)

18. See Waterman, *Susan Glaspell* 28: "[Glaspell] tried throughout her career many different ways of expressing the idealist's unusual but meaningful approach to life."

19. See, for instance, Arthur Hobson Quinn: "[Eugene O'Neill] has pictured with rare skill the striving of the individual soul against the crushing adverse forces of fate, or the insistent clutch of circumstances, or the progress of disease and death, or the overmastering impulse of the forces of nature [...]" (*Contemporary American Plays* xii). Compare also Pfister on *Eugene O'Neill and the Politics of Psychological Discourse*.

2. Language and Communication

1. While Wittgenstein starts his *Philosophical Investigations* with a narration of the fourth-century scholar St. Augustine about how he learned to speak as a child, both Harris and Stewart trace this model of language back to ancient Greece. See Harris, "From an Integrational Point of View," 249: "[W]e are dealing with a language myth that is so deeply entrenched in the Western tradition that for more than two thousand years theorists and lay commentators alike have simply taken its validity for granted."

2. In the following summary of these features I mainly follow Stewart's explanations, see especially his chapters 1–3.

3. Roy Harris points out in this context that the discipline of linguistics has traditionally insisted on its self-definition as a "science," taking for granted the idea that language can be studied from the viewpoint of an objective and

detached observer. See "From an Integrational Point of View," 272 f.

4. Modern-day linguists, for instance, have invented the so-called fixed-code theory of language. As another example, the philosopher Gottlieb Frege posited thoughts to be independent entities which exist outside of the thinking subject and are therefore generally accessible.

5. Roy Harris, for example, claims that any theory which would make "communicational sense" should illuminate our "day-to-day communicational practices" and act "as a guide to understand [our] experience of language" ("From an Integrational Point of View," 254). Stewart, too, misses the attributes of "coherence, plausibility and applicability" in the symbol model (xii, see also 16).

6. Since Stewart develops his concept of language as constitutive articulate contact out of a line of thought which explicitly includes the ideas of both Wittgenstein and Harris, I roughly follow his argumentation to explain the notions shared by these and other 20th-century thinkers.

7. Stewart 116, emphasis in the original. Stewart here paraphrases Gadamer's thoughts as put forth in his *Truth and Method*.

8. From this point of view, it is a fundamental error of traditional linguistics to perceive of language as an object open to scientific scrutiny: "Language does not present itself for study as a neatly disengaged range of homogeneous phenomena, patiently awaiting description by the impartial observer, as is suggested by the misleading expression *linguistic data*. [...] On the contrary, language [...] offers a paradigm case of interference by investigation. The interference arises from the fact that in linguistics language becomes both the object and the instrument of investigation, as well as the medium in which the linguist's conclusions are ultimately formulated" (Harris, "From an Integrational Point of View," 272–73, emphasis in the original).

9. It is a result of the very nature of these contemplations that Wittgenstein presents his own thinking on language as a process instead of a statement on objective reality. His work displays a "peculiar aggregate of loosely related paragraphs which offers no detailed statement of intended goals, no sustained elaboration of a narrative thread, and no triumphant summary of achieved conclusions" (Quigley 209; compare also Wittgenstein, *Investigations*, "Preface," ix.). Hence, in contrast to thinkers such as Harris and Stewart, Wittgenstein does not create an alternative model to the understanding of language as a representational system of signs. Instead, *he demonstrates an alternative way of going about the question*.

10. As Roy Harris explains: "No linguistic act is contextless, and every linguistic act is uniquely contextualized." — "Contextualization, for the integrationist, not only varies according to the past experience of the individuals in question (and is thus irreducibly different for different individuals) but is itself a dynamic process. In short, contexts do not precede communication but are constructed in the course of communication" ("From an Integrational Point of View," 282, 285).

11. This term is borrowed from Julia Kristeva; see part 2 of this chapter, p. 43f.

12. See Altieri 1404: "Derrida, of course, would agree with [Wittgenstein's] denial of a constitutive self definable through self-consciousness, but he goes on to make too easy a leap to denying any criteria of identity or possibility of self-knowledge. It seems likely, however, that if we cannot know the self as an independent entity, we can come to understand the various procedures it has for acting in the world and even for establishing emotional and conceptual attitudes toward its actions."

13. See, once again, Altieri 1404 (my italics): "As Sidney Shoemaker has shown, the most important source of our sense of identity is the way we use the spatio-temporal location of our body to make basic physical distinctions between here and there, in front and behind, etc. *Those who cannot make these distinctions and use personal identity in this way need therapy not self-reflexive philosophy.* And this physical sense is supplemented on a public level, as J. F. M. Hunter has shown, by a wide variety of legal and behavioral constructs which define modes of seeing oneself as possessing an identity." Compare the publications by Shoemaker and Hunter.

14. In *The Verge*, for instance — one of Glaspell's most controversial works — the protagonist Claire Archer reaches a state of madness after having cut all ties to her fellow human beings; see chapter 8.

15. While these ideas originated in France and are consistently linked to the names of Luce Irigaray, Hélène Cixous, Jaques Lacan, Jaques Derrida and Julia Kristeva, an argument can be made that Anglo-American literary criticism has appropriated the thoughts of these writers in an invention of "French Feminism" which has lost nearly all affinity to the debates led in that country (see Delphy 190–221). However, in my discussion of various circulating approaches to the notion of a "female voice" I will not, in the first place, try to disentangle what these writers have "actually said" from what might have been their "misinterpretations" or "inventions" on the Anglo-American scene. Crucial to my interpretation of Glaspell's plays are the various theories of a women's language as they exist in criticism today, regardless of their origins or history.

16. See Irigaray, "The Question of the

Other," 10: "In *Speculum*, I interpret and critique how the philosophical subject, historically masculine, has reduced all otherness to a relationship with himself—as complement, projection, flip side, instrument, nature—inside his world, his horizons. As much through Freudian texts as through the major philosophical methods of our tradition, I show how the other is always the other of the same and not an actual other."

17. For a definition of this term, see Jones, n. 2: "*Jouissance* is a word rich in connotations. 'Pleasure' is the simplest translation. The noun comes from the verb *jouir*, meaning to enjoy, to revel in without fear of the cost; also, to have an orgasm. [...] A note to Introduction 3 in *New French Feminisms: An Anthology*, ed. Elaine Marks and Isabelle de Courtivron (Amherst: University of Massachusetts Press, 1980) explains feminist connotations of *jouissance* as follows: 'This pleasure, when attributed to a woman, is considered to be of a different order from the pleasure that is represented within the male libidinal economy often described in terms of the capitalist gain and profit motive. Women's jouissance carries with it the notion of fluidity, diffusion, duration. It is a kind of potlatch in the world of orgasms, a giving, expending, dispensing of pleasure without concern about ends or closure.' [P. 36, n. 8]."

18. See Moi, *Sexual/Textual Politics* 143: "Irigaray's theory of 'woman' takes as its starting point a basic assumption of analogy between woman's psychology and her 'morphology' (Gr. *morphé*, 'form'), which she rather obscurely takes to be different from her anatomy. Woman's form is repressed by patriarchal phallocentrism, which systematically denies woman access to her own pleasure: female *jouissance* cannot even be thought by specular logic. Male pleasure, she claims, is seen as monolithically unified, represented as analogous with the phallus, and it is this mode that is forcibly imposed upon women. But as she argues in the article 'This sex which is not one,' woman's sex is not *one*: her sexual organs are composed of many different elements (lips, vagina, clitoris, cervix, uterus, breasts) and her *jouissance* is therefore multiple, non-unified, endless."

19. Compare the numerous discussions on the nature of Irigaray's "essentialism" in Schor and Weed. See also Christine Delphy: "Most French Feminists do not hold up essentialism as a 'Good Thing.' But they often promote it by saying that it is not essentialism" (212).

20. See Cixous' writings as collected in Susan Seller's *The Hélène Cixous Reader*.

21. On the relationship between the author/artist and the meaning of her work see also part 3 of this chapter, p. 45f, esp. 47.

22. "Phallogocentrism" is another Derridean term which combines his coinage of "logocentrism" (privileging the *Logos*, the Word as a metaphysical presence) and "phallocentrism" (privileging the phallus as the symbol or source of power). See *Moi, Sexual/Textual Politics* 179, n. 6.4 and 6.5.

23. See Irigaray, "The Question of the Other," 16: "This difference between the statements of female and male subjects is expressed in one way or another throughout the majority of responses to a series of questions which seek to define the sexualized characteristics of language. (The research was conducted in a variety of languages and cultures, mostly Romance and Anglo-Saxon.)"

24. See, for example, Deborah Tannen and her inclination "to regard socialization (that is, cultural experience) as the main influence shaping patterns of behavior." *Gender and Discourse* 13.

25. Judith Butler entered the discussion of women as the subjects of feminist studies by fundamentally questioning the distinction between the concepts of "sex" and "gender:" "[What] is 'sex' anyway? Is it natural, anatomical, chromosomal, or hormonal, and how is a feminist critic to assess the scientific discourses which purport to establish such 'facts' for us? [...] Are the ostensibly natural facts of sex discursively produced by various scientific discourses in the service of other political and social interests? If the immutable character of sex is contested, perhaps this construct called 'sex' is as culturally constructed as gender; indeed, perhaps it was always already gender, with the consequence that the distinction between sex and gender turns out to be no distinction at all" (*Gender Trouble* 10–11). See also Purvis-Smith, 46: "while the distinction [between 'sex' and 'gender'] has provided a corrective to biological determinism, to make such a distinction is to imply that an identification of <naturally> determined traits as opposed to <culturally> determined ones can be made, a distinction that sets up yet another dichotomy of nature/ nurture." (On the reasons for this critics' unusual diction, see n. 28 below.)

26. See Moi, *Sexual/Textual Politics* 166: "If 'femininity' has a definition at all in Kristevan terms, it is simply, as we have seen, as 'that which is marginalized by the patriarchal symbolic order.' This relational 'definition' is as shifting as the various forms of patriarchy itself, and allows her to argue that men can also be constructed as marginal by the symbolic order, as her analyses of male avant-garde artists [...] have shown."

27. See also Derrida as qtd. by Moi, *Sexual/Textual Politics* 172–73: "'What if we were to approach ... the area of a relationship to the other where the code of sexual marks would no longer be discriminating?' [...] 'The relationship would not be a-sexual, far from it,

but would be sexual otherwise: beyond the binary difference that governs the decorum of all codes, beyond the opposition feminine/ masculine, beyond homosexuality and heterosexuality which come to the same thing. As I dream of saving the chance that this question offers, I would like to believe in the multiplicity of sexually marked voices. [...]'"

28. The quote continues: "this concept has reinforced my resolve to incorporate the textual device of not capitalizing in the dialogue that is this essay, especially not the personal pronoun <i,> except in quoted material. capitalization would imply a solid, objective entity that could be identified and permanently tagged. i only capitalize within quoted material, which is identified by the modified parentheses, and then only to display more graphically bakhtin's heteroglossia."

29. Indeed, Delphy sees in this holistic approach "the matrix of all twentieth-century schools of thought" (201).

30. Hagberg's discussions include theories developed and addressed in works by Susanne Langer, R. G. Collingwood, C. J. Ducasse, Leo Tolstoy, Arthur Danto, George Dickie, Joseph Margolis, and others.

31. Compare Derrida's comments on the concept of a "transcendental signified" as referred to earlier in this chapter.

32. The idea of "family resemblances" is what Wittgenstein sets against any essentialist definition of language: "[S]omeone might object against me: 'You take the easy way out! You talk about all sorts of language-games, but have nowhere said what the essence of a language-game, and hence of language, is: what is common to all these activities, and what makes them into language or part of language. [...]' And this is true.— Instead of producing something common to all that we call language, I am saying that these phenomena have no one thing in common which makes us use the same word for all, — but that they are *related* to one another in many different ways. And it is because of this relationship, or these relationships, that we call them all 'language.' [...]"— "I can think of no better expression to characterize these similarities than 'family resemblances' [...]" (*Investigations* §§ 65, 67).

33. Here, Hagberg's understanding of art as "conceptual engagements in aesthetic experience" is especially striking. At other points of his discussion, he stresses the importance of "context" for the emergence of meaning, or the aspect of art as communicative action.

34. For a more detailed account of Cook's ideas, see Sarlós 34 f. and Bach, *Susan Glaspell* 56 f.

35. In a footnote, Sarlós explains that "Paul Emanuel Johnson, *Psychology of Religion* (New York, 1959), p. 43, mentions Robert McDougal

as the first user of the term 'interpersonal relations,' in discussing the kinship of Moreno's *Einladung zu einer Begegnung* (1914) and Buber's *Ich und Du* (first draft, 1916; published, 1923)" (213).

36. The quote is from Charles Blanchard's *Building for the Centuries: A Memorial of the Founders and Builders*, and formulates the idealistic ethics of Drake University, Glaspell's alma mater, with which she identified.

3. Trifles *(1916)*

1. In his generic comparison between the play and the short story Leonard Mustazza has drawn attention to the fact that "thematic criticisms of the respective pieces are virtually indistinguishable, most of these commentaries focusing on the question of assumed 'roles' in the works" (489). For interpretations which focus on the play or story's division of gender, see, for example, the readings by Fetterley and Kolodny, Nelligan, Stein, Aarons, Alkalay-Gut, Smith, Mael, and others. See also J. Ellen Gainor's summary of feminist criticism on these two works through 2001 (*Susan Glaspell* 271–72, n. 8).

2. The County Attorney asks Mr. Hale how Mrs. Wright "looked" when she told him that her husband was dead, and he wants the witness to "point it all out" upstairs where he found the dead man (37). The Sheriff wants to "take a look" at the windows (45), and both officials are careful to ensure that nothing has been "touched" (36).

3. See Mael's interpretation along these lines, as well as Alkalay-Gut, "'Jury,'" 8–9.

4. As Elaine Hedges explains, the "Ladies Aid would have been a female society associated with the local church, where women would have spent their time sewing, braiding carpets, and quilting, in order to raise money for foreign missionaries, for new flooring or carpets, chairs or curtains for the parish home, or add to the minister's salary" (102).

5. The image of quilting serves as possibly the most significant symbol for the female community from which Minnie Wright is so painfully excluded: "Through quilting [...] and through the institutions, such as the 'bee,' that grew up around it, women who were otherwise without expressive outlet were able to communicate their thoughts and feelings" (Hedges 102). See also Stein's explanations on the process of quilting and the techniques involved: "The patchwork squares are pieced together in solitude, often in between and after the completion of the round of chores which was women's lot. The quilting itself, however, [...] was done in a communal setting, the quilting bee. Groups of women, friends and skilled seamstresses,

would gather around the quilting frame to cooperate in the tedious task of quilting. The quilting bee was one of the main social events for women whose daily lives kept them isolated from each other" (255).

6. In her historical reconstruction of the living conditions on Midwestern farms at the turn of the 19th century, Elaine Hedges points out: "That the loss of her music, in the shape of a bird, should have triggered murderous behavior in Minnie Wright is [...] neither gratuitous nor melodramatic. [...] In the monotonous expanses of the prairie and the plains, the presence of one small spot of color, or a bit of music, might spell the difference between sanity and madness" (100).

7. In the short story, Harry is farmer Hales' son, but in the play this relation is never implied and thus acquires no additional relevance.

8. See Bach, *Susan Glaspell* 118–19: "Glaspell hat hier zu einer eigenen Darstellungsform gefunden: die Frauen, von Anfang an weniger wortgewandt als die Männer, drücken ihre Gedanken, Ängste und Zweifel nicht-verbal aus, mit eindringlichen Blicken, die nur sie selbst interpretieren können. Es fällt ihnen schwer, Worte für das zu finden, was sie empfinden. [...] [D]er nachhaltige Eindruck des inneren Ringens um ein jedes Wort, das Abwägen um ein Für und Wider, überwiegt in diesem Drama und vermittelt jene nach einer Lösung strebende Intensität des dramatischen Geschehens."

9. While it bears a certain significance with regard to Glaspell's act of aesthetic communication in each respective case that both Kolodny and Fetterley deal with the short story as opposed to the play, the female characters' method of reading Minnie's "clues" is the same in both texts.

4. The People *(1917)*

1. Entirely unconcealed, the journal of *The People* is modeled on Max Eastman's *The Masses*, ambitious and belligerent organ of New York's intelligentsia at the time. See Gainor for a discussion both of the many parallels between the real-life model and its dramatic counterpart and for an assessment of the creative changes made by Glaspell (*Susan Glaspell* 61–67).

2. Bach, *Susan Glaspell* 103: "[D]eklamatorisch und sentimental zugleich präsentiert Glaspell jene stereotype Vorstellungswelt eines verschwommenen *social idealism* der zwanziger Jahre [...]."

3. Bach, *Susan Glaspell* 104: "Das melodramatische Pathos, mit dem die paradiesische Idylle von 'beautiful distances' vorgetragen wird, hinterläßt, zumindest an dieser Rede

zugedachten wichtigen Punkt des Dramas, keine Wirkung."

4. As Gainor reports, the real-life context to The Boy's announcement that he will sell the paper on the street (as well as to Oscar's "Talk With God") lies in the "ban on the sale of the *Masses* in New York's subway newsstands" in 1916 after the publication of a poem "with a distinct spin on the tale of Mary and Joseph" (*Susan Glaspell* 64–65).

5. It is for this emphasis on intersubjectivity in *The People* that I disagree with Yvonne Shafer, who reads the play as a theatrical experiment in expressionism. According to Shafer's interpretation, the editor Ed is the protagonist of the play, since all other characters appear "[a]s if called up by his mind, [...] the pleas of his own enlightened consciousness" ("Susan Glaspell," 41). A reading which places Ed in the center of the one-act in such a way concentrates on the idea of the detached, isolated individual intent on expressing a message. The debate which goes on between different philosophies and values would be a debate going on within Ed's mind, not a truly interpersonal dialogue. As I have shown, however, the emphasis in *The People* is not on Ed alone, but on the interaction between him and the other characters, especially the three people he has "called"—The Boy from Georgia, The Man from the Cape, and The Woman from Idaho.

6. See also Gainor's discussion of the institutional parallels between the Provincetown Players and *The Masses*, the magazine that served as a model for the journal of *The People* (*Susan Glaspell* 61 f).

7. Compare my accounts in chapters 2 and 3; see also Sarlós on the Provincetown philosophy.

8. See Gainor, *Susan Glaspell*, 61 f.

9. I am grateful to Professor Fritz Gysin of the University of Berne for his useful comments in this context.

5. The Outside *(1917)*

1. Between *The People* and *The Outside*, the Players staged Glaspell's satire *Close the Book* in November 1917 (see chapter 11 for a brief discussion of this one-act).

2. Exceptions are Bach's interpretation (*Susan Glaspell* 120–26), the analyses offered by Bigsby (*Drama* 27–28, *Plays* 12–15), and Gainor's detailed reading of the play (*Susan Glaspell* 73–81). Waterman deals with *The Outside* in his chapter on Glaspell's one-act plays (*Susan Glaspell* 71–72), and it is also touched upon in discussions of the author's dramatic works by France ("Susan Glaspell," 219),

Dymkowski, Larabee, and Ben-Zvi, ("Susan Glaspell;" "Contributions," 154–55). See also Schwank's article on *The Outside* and *The Verge*.

3. Glaspell underlines Allie's change of sides from death to life (and from Mrs. Patrick to the men) with a small symbol of human warmth and social normalcy. Immediately after her exit in this scene Bradford remarks: "Some coffee'd taste good. But coffee, in this house? Oh no. It might make somebody feel better" (50). When Allie reenters—just moments before she makes her first move to "save" Mrs. Patrick—she is "carrying a pot of coffee," which she sets down when she sees that the men are already on their way out (51). Of course, from an angle focused on the gender struggle in *The Outside* this detail serves only to signify the men's arrogance and insensitivity, as Gainor's interpretation confirms: "Bradford simply assumes it is Allie's job to meet the needs of the men who have invaded the station. [...] Soon Allie returns with a fresh pot of coffee, just in time to see the men leave, having realized their work is futile and having of course forgotten the woman's work they in effect demanded" (*Susan Glaspell* 80). Yet while Glaspell is sensitive to "the way that men construct female identity and make assumptions about women's roles" (ibid.) in this play as she is in all her other works, she favors social relations (gender-determined as they might be) over her female characters' denial of life in *The Outside*—and the detail of the coffee pot might well be seen in this context.

4. Arguing that "in dramatizing [the women's] re-embracing of [life], the play affirms women's autonomy," Dymkowski at the same time concedes: "The relationship between women and men in the play is, however, more complex than this statement suggests [...]" (96). Unfortunately, however, without further identifying the complexities she mentions Dymkowski goes on to assert that "Glaspell's focus is unquestionably on the women [...]" (96).

5. The human need for society is often thematized alongside a contrasting desire to get away from stifling social norms in Glaspell's works. See, for example, my discussion of *The Verge* in chapter 8.

6. The hierarchy Captain—Bradford—Tony is also emphasized in this very way of identifying the male characters in the stage directions: official title—last name—first name (see also the designation of the men as "Sheriff" and "County Attorney" versus "Hale" in *Trifles*).

7. See Bradford's turns addressed to Tony on pages 49–51, for example: "Last night wasn't the best night for a dory. (*to* TONY; *boastfully*) Not that I couldn't 'a' stayed in one. Some men can stay in a dory and some can't [...]" (49).

8. See, for example, the following exchanges: "TONY. Lucky I was not sooner or later as I walk by from my watch. BRADFORD. You have accommodating ways, Tony. No sooner or later. I wouldn't say it of many Portagees. [...]" (48).—"(*The* CAPTAIN *comes out. He closes door behind him and stands there beside it. He looks tired and disappointed. Both look at him. Pause.*) CAPTAIN. Wonder who he was. BRADFORD. Young. Guess he's not been much at sea" (51).

9. By the same token, the life of one they did save is also made concrete in Bradford's remark right before they leave: "Danny Sears is tendin' bar in Boston now" (51). And the identity of the drowned man the life-savers are faced with now is also important to the Captain: "You know who he is, Joe? BRADFORD. I never saw him before" (49).

10. The experience that something becomes "real" or "true" only in the very act of saying connects Allie—and also Mrs. Patrick at the end of the play—with the character of The Woman from Idaho in *The People*, and the playwright will use this idea repeatedly in later works as well.

11. Bach, *Susan Glaspell* 125: "[Allie Mayo] selbst steht nicht exemplarisch für das, was sie mit Worten nur schwer und unvollkommen ausdrücken kann. Der fehlende Gegenpol als Paradigma des erfüllten Lebens steht in ursächlichem Zusammenhang mit der unbefriedigenden Lösung, die Glaspell anbietet. Nur am Beispiel der naturhaften Elemente im Kampf um den Lebensraum kann Glaspell andeuten, was für sie 'life's meaning' heißt."—[Allie Mayo] herself does not exemplify what she can only express imperfectly with words. The missing opposite as a paradigm of the fulfilled life stands in a causal relation to the unsatisfactory solution which Glaspell offers. Only through the exemplary struggle for survival fought out by the natural elements can Glaspell hint at what 'life's meaning' is for her" (my trans.).

12. Read in this context, in a parallel to the image of the coffee pot (see n. 3 above) another image connected to the men's traditional understanding of women's role could be seen to symbolize this notion of life's inevitable "connectedness." Surveying the bleak surroundings in which Allie Mayo and Mrs. Patrick have opted to live, at one point Tony remarks in surprise: "A woman—she makes things pretty. This not like a place where a woman live. On the floor there is nothing—on the wall there is nothing. Things—(*trying to express it with his hands*) do not hang on other things" (49). While this complaint of course might be read along the lines of the County Attorney's complaint in *Trifles* that Minnie Wright did not have "the home-making instinct" (see also Gainor's interpretation,

Susan Glaspell 78), the image that in Mrs. Patrick's house "things do not hang on other things" could also be read to emphasize the women's illusory attempt to withdraw from all social contact.

13. It is striking with which regularity critics, whether they read the presentation of Allie's argument as a success or a failure, frame the meaning of the play in terms of the woman's "vision"—a conceptualization along the lines of the representative model of language and opposed to the notion of "voice" which accompanies the concept of language as articulate contact. See, for example, Dymkowski 96 ("the triumph of Allie's vision"), Papke 31 ("Allie's powerful vision"), Bigsby, *Plays* 14 ("a confident vision of meaning"). See also Waterman's assessment that the "broken speech of Allie [...] states the meaning of the play [...], the abstract message" (*Susan Glaspell* 72).

14. In another parallel to *The People* it also seems to be the case that the female characters' poetic language in *The Outside* is more engaging when experienced in the theatre instead of as dramatic text. As I have not yet witnessed a performance of *The Outside* myself, I am grateful to Linda Ben-Zvi and Elaine Aston for bringing this possibility to my attention in their reactions to my paper on *Trifles* and *The Outside* at the Glaspell Conference in Tel Aviv, May 2000.

6. Bernice *(1919)*

1. After *The Outside*, Glaspell had contributed two more one-acts to the Provincetown stage: the comedies *Woman's Honor* (1918), and (in the same year) *Tickless Time*, her second collaboration with Cook. For a short discussion of these plays see my chapter 11.

2. With Alison Stanhope of *Alison's House*, Glaspell completed her series of "absent protagonists" for the American stage in 1930; see my discussion in chapter 9. (The absent character Freddy Soames of Glaspell's last play, *Springs Eternal*, is only a minor character.)

3. See, for example, Ozieblo's interpretation of this scene: "Margaret finally reaches the truth: in opening the door to the room where Bernice lies, she transcends the alienation inherent in death as well as in life and comprehends the motives of another human being [...]. Coming from the room of death, she now leaves the door—which until then symbolized the inability to reach out to others and, in its intractability, dominated the set—'wide open behind her' [...]" (*Susan Glaspell* 145).

4. At various times in the play Glaspell suggests that what Abbie has to tell Craig is a "message" from Bernice. See, for example: "ABBIE. Mr. Norris! (*Her tone halts him.*) There's something I must tell you. CRAIG. A—message she left? ABBIE: Message? No. Yes—perhaps. Before you go in there I must tell you—" (170; see also 166 and 175). This idea directly opens up the play's conceptual contrast between language as expressing facts or as creating reality interactively. See my discussion of this aspect further down.

5. "MARGARET. [...] I'm down here alone—lonely. [...] I wanted so to talk to Bernice, and when I couldn't I—called to you. CRAIG. I was glad to hear my name. It's too much alone" (190–91).

6. Even Craig's sister Laura, a minor character when it comes to her relation to Bernice, in her assessment of the absent protagonist's character is led by her own feelings. Laura remembers Bernice's "aloofness" not only as a hostile attitude towards society, but also as her sister-in-law's failure to fulfill her proper role as wife—a role she herself has whole-heartedly accepted for her own life. In this way, she vindicates her own identity as guided by the strict rules of Victorian gender-relations and the image of the "True Woman." In disapproving of Bernice, Laura can hold up her own chosen position in life as stable and unthreatened.

7. In fact, the idea of the potential (or impossibility) of influencing reality has accompanied the play from the very beginning, in bylines such as Father's resigned observation that "now the war is over, [...] some of the people who fussed around about it influenced it as little as I" (169), or as Laura's insightful self-assessment that "[r]eally I do like control" (209).

8. The conflicting meanings which stand unresolved in the play, thus Friedman agrees with Kattwinkel, arise from the fact that the absent woman remains poised between the three "perspectives that [...] informed [all of] Glaspell's work: the Romantic, the Feminist, the Modernist" ("Bernice's Strange Deceit," 160). On the one hand, as Margaret and all other characters seem to suggest, Bernice might indeed have possessed "a nineteenth-century Romantic sensibility, perceiving truths that transcend mundane conflict, even gender-based conflict" (ibid.). On the other hand, thus Friedman points out in her astute and detailed reading, this suggestion "ignores the power that Bernice, in creating this deception, sought for herself: the power to create an autonomous existence, which her husband's needs denied her, and the power to undermine the sanctity of her husband's vision now predicated on complete falsehood" (ibid.). Consequently, one might speculate indeed that, "[in] order to insure Margaret's compliance, [...] [Bernice has] duped her as well into seeing the nobility

of her sacrifice against her initial and perhaps better judgment" (ibid.). Yet "[v]iewed through still a different lens," thus Friedman subsequently suggests, "Bernice's reticence to act directly might imply the Modernist's preoccupation with struggle rather than victory" (ibid. 161–62).— See also Susan Kattwinkel, who argues that in *Bernice*, "the characters of Craig, Laura, and Margaret embody the social forces through which the absent woman will eventually be defined. Through their individual constructions of Bernice we see the ideals of nineteenth-century conventionalism struggling against the concepts of modern feminism. [...] [W]oman as nurturer is placed in debate with woman as individual" (44).

9. That Bernice's "detachment" was not such a desirable quality, after all, is hinted at in the idea that she might have been saved had she not lived too far out of medical reach. As Laura states: "It's a great pity you couldn't get a doctor. That's the worst of living way up here by one's self" (180).

7. Chains of Dew *(1919/1922)*

1. In her recent biography Barbara Ozieblo has presented a convincing argument for this assumption. See my discussion of the play's writing and production history at the end of this chapter.

2. Apart from her last dramatic effort, *Springs Eternal*, *Chains of Dew* is the only one of Glaspell's plays which was never published. Glaspell's carbon copy typescript is hosted at the Library of Congress.

3. While Ozieblo states in passing that "[the] campaigns promoted by Margaret Sanger and Emma Goldman to inform women about birth control add to the topicality of [Dotty Standish's] personal drama" (*Susan Glaspell* 158), Gainor has concentrated on *Chains of Dew* as a "drama of birth control" in the context of several agitprop plays written during the late 1910s. Yet the question of birth control is indeed not Glaspell's focus in this play. As Gainor herself concludes: "From the complex network of characters and plot in act 1 alone, it is obvious that Glaspell's *Chains of Dew* is different from the other dramas of birth control. Although the movement is certainly important to the play, it is not exclusively a politically or socially motivated work [...]" ("*Chains of Dew*," 186).

4. By the time *Chains of Dew* reached the Provincetown stage, New York audiences had encountered two more Glaspell plays after *Bernice*: *Inheritors* (1921) and *The Verge* (1921).

5. See my discussion of *The People* in chapter 4. The same complementary effect of com-

edy and tragedy can also be found in the one-acts *Close the Book* and *Woman's Honor*, which I will briefly comment on in chapter 11. *The Verge*, staged before *Chains of Dew* but probably written around the same time, is the most complex example of how Susan Glaspell combines various dramatic styles in her drama (see the following chapter).

6. Only one critic comments on the gender implications inherent in the play's plot. Maida Castellun (one of the few female reviewers of the lot) writes: "So subtle is the satire here and so heavy the characterization that one fears the spectator may see only the obvious theme of the martyr rejoicing in his sacrifice because he has no other claims to distinction. But there is much more implied — among other things the showing up of the male as your only true conservative in matters social and spiritual. [...] As a social iconoclast the female of the species again proves more daring than the male" ("The Plays That Pass"). More on the play's writing and production history at the end of this chapter.

7. See, for example, the following exchanges: "SEYMORE. Oh, you don't get it at all. LEON. Why isn't it your business to see that we do? Since we're friends? SEYMORE. But apparently it's impossible [...]" (1.29).— "NORA. Your way of telling me what you are seeing is to tell me that I don't see it. SEYMORE. Very well, no use going into it" (2.2.5).— "SEYMORE. [...] But you can't [?don't? H.-B.] know what I mean. NORA. I might if you'd tell me. SEYMORE. Never mind" (2.2.7).— "SEYMORE. [...] As if I couldn't tell you how to understand poetry. DOTTY. Maybe you could — but you don't. [...] I want to understand you, Seymore. I want to *reach* you. SEYMORE. Fat chance you have of reaching me through a correspondence course in poetry." (2.2.7).

8. NORA. [*to the* MOTHER] [...] [What] you're saying about Seymore makes me think Diantha had better pack a trunk and come with me. Let Seymore stay here and get up some new way of feeling himself. DOTTY. I don't think you should talk that way about Seymore. You — a nice impression you've given Nora, mother. You haven't said anything about the nice things — the delightful things. And the *great* things. Everyone knows that Seymore is a poet. Well, certain peculiarities — go with gifts" (3.34).

9. In 1931, Susan Glaspell turned the idea of *Chains of Dew* into the plot of a novel, *Ambrose Holt and Family*. As I argue elsewhere, in this work the wife's decision to stay with her husband is ultimately more convincing because change and a growing understanding are deemed possible within the couple's marriage. And indeed, Glaspell already hints at this pos-

sibility at the end of *Chains of Dew*, as she has Seymore promise that from now on, he will take Dotty with him to New York every once in a while. (Compare my article on "Male Rebels in Susan Glaspell's Writings" in the upcoming collection of essays edited by Barbara Ozieblo and Martha Carpentier, *Disclosing Intertextualities*, Rodopi 2006.)

10. "NORA: [...] [Mrs. MacIntyre] asked me if birth control meant anything to me personally, and I said — ask Seymore. And now I ask you, Seymore, wasn't that a good reply? (*Turning to Dotty*) You see — (*But it isn't so easy to make her see*) Oh, well, never mind. (*She keeps looking at Dotty, and as if she likes Dotty. Of a sudden, and with the exhilaration of one who has an inspiration, and is taking a big chance for putting it over*) Seymore, let me introduce you to Diantha Standish, first president of the first birth control league of the Mississippi Valley. (*To Dotty*) Am I right?" (2.1.29). Ironically, it turns out that while the relationship between Seymore and Nora never was a "complete affair," the poet did have such an affair with Dotty's friend Edith, Mrs. MacIntyre's daughter (3.4–5).

11. See *Road* 235–36 ("We were supposed to be a sort of 'special' group — radical, wild ..."); as already qtd. in chapter 1, p. 74.

12. In fact, as we know from letters going back and forth between Edna Kenton and Glaspell during her time in Greece, Glaspell was "chagrined" and "appalled" both at the watercolors she saw of Leon Throckmorton's set to her play and of the cut script that Kenton had sent her (Ozieblo, *Susan Glaspell* 201). The playwright was also explicit enough in her letters to Kenton about what she thought of her colleagues' casting decisions: "I saw there was nothing for me to do but get drunk, and so deaden the first pangs in the thought of [Edward] Reese as Standish, Blanche [Hays] as Dotty and little Marion Berry as the on-to-herself Nora" (qtd. in Gainor, *Susan Glaspell* 196).

13. See, for instance, Ludwig Lewisohn: "This play is plainly inferior to both 'Inheritors' and 'The Verge'" ("Drama"). For a discussion of *The Verge* see chapter 8; *Inheritors* will be commented on in chapter 11.

14. See also Stephen Rathbun: "While the idea is carried through to its logical conclusion, the play might have been written much better in the second and third acts, and the ensemble acting left much to be desired. But it is a bright, wise little comedy, and the players caught the spirit of the play, even if they fumbled a line now and then and were leisurely in taking their cues" (*New York Sun*).

15. According to Ozieblo's research, Glaspell — far from "taking little time" with *Chains of Dew* — revised it several times before its eventual production (see *Susan Glaspell* 156, 157, 197). Yet the Library of Congress file seems to be the only known version of the play's text. See also Gainor on the "textual problems" we are confronted with in the case of *Chains of Dew* (*Susan Glaspell* 198).

16. See, for example, Alexander Woollcott's statement that "That play might be dismissed with a wave of the hand, if it were not for the interesting figure of the mother, a role written with so much insight and so much tenderness that it fairly forbids a slighting review of the entire work" (*New York Times*). See also Stephen Rathbun's review in the *New York Mail*, and Maida Castellun's *New York Call* piece, in which she notes with regard to character conceptions in *Chains of Dew*: "Only the mother is sketched with the little touches that spell life" ("The Plays that Pass").

8. The Verge *(1921)*

1. For an overview of the play's critical reception until 1992 see Papke 64–69. *The Verge* was restaged four times since its original production: in 1925 at the Regent Theatre in London; in 1991 as part of a conference entitled "Susan Glaspell — Rediscovering an American Playwright" at the Brigham Young University in Provo, Utah; and twice in 1996, at the Orange Tree Theatre in Richmond, Surrey, UK, and at a University of Glasgow conference entitled "Suppressed Desires: The Struggle for Expression in the Theatre of Susan Glaspell and her Contemporaries." For a discussion of these different stagings and related criticism see the end of this chapter.

2. "Tom, Dick, and Harry's development," thus Bottoms adds, "was matched by [a similar discovery] made by Ashley Ross — who played Claire's sister Adelaide as far more than the embodiment of smug bourgeois religiosity she is often taken to be" (137).—Two instances I find especially noteworthy with regard to character conception in *The Verge*. For one, in this play Glaspell was more successful than she was with Seymore Standish in *Chains of Dew* in combining both caricature and realistic representation in the characters of Harry, Tom, and Adelaide. On the other hand, the characters of Elizabeth and Dick remain types to a greater degree than do the other figures in the play. In this context, Claire's rejection of her daughter turns into a much less scandalous scene if this character is seen not as a "real[istic]" child, but as an "oppressive presence [of conformity] that Claire urgently [needs] to get rid of"—a fact which Bottoms underlined in his production as the part of Elizabeth was played "on live, closed-

circuit feed from the dressing room," projecting "an enormous close-up of the actor playing Claire's daughter" onto video screens looming over three sides of the stage (134). In the case of Dick, I would argue that Glaspell uses a "type" conception for the same ends as with such characters as "The Philosopher" or "The Light Touch" in *The People*: as a way of criticizing the art-for-art-sakers' refusal to take up social responsibility with their art.

3. From his practitioner's point of view, Bottoms argues that the staging process can bring out elements in the play which must go unnoticed in any "mere" reading of the text. But of course, a close *reading* of Glaspell's play can arrive at the same experience of Adelaide, Harry and Tom as sympathetically drawn characters as the staging process might. Both, after all, are instances of interpretation which start out from the same base — the dramatic text itself.

4. Although Gainor's Freudian interpretation goes very far in drawing direct parallels between Claire's fate and the significance of concrete male influences on Susan Glaspell herself (especially Cook's alleged "co-optation" and "manipulation" of her dramatic works), her reading of *The Verge* as "a study of female hysteria" (85) deserves a hearing especially with regard to its analysis of the play's ending, and with the discussion of the role played by Claire's son David, who died in infancy.

5. In *The Newly Born Woman* Clément remarks: "I see no way to conceive of a cultural system in which there would be no transmission of knowledge in the form of a coherent statement." And Cixous herself concedes: "At the present time defining a feminine practice of writing is impossible with an impossibility that will continue; for this practice will never be able to be *theorized*, enclosed, coded, which does not mean it does not exist" (both qtd. in Noe, "The Verge," 140).

6. See my discussion in chapter 2 (the quote is Carol G. Heilbrun's, see p. 44).

7. As Stephen Bottoms has astutely noted, overwhelmed by the forceful pain of her isolation Claire lapses into the first person plural in realizing that it is "because we are tired — and lonely — and afraid, [that] we stop with you. Don't get through — to what you're in the way of" (*The Verge* 98). Within Claire's logic, the murder of Tom is a necessary act of self-defense, yet at the same time she also sees it as a gift to him. As Bottoms puts it, by "giving him the 'gift' of oblivion embraced by her [infant son, David], she seeks to free him from the all-too-adult temptation to assume that he has understood; free him, that is, from becoming Elizabeth" (Bottoms 143–44).

8. *Encyclopedia Brittanica*, VII (London 1962), 294, as qtd. in Bach, *Susan Glaspell* 166 (n. 58).

9. I am grateful to my colleagues Torsten Graff and Ralph Poole at the Amerika-Institut in Munich for drawing my attention to this element in Glaspell's use of language. As Graff pointed out in reaction to my reading, it is no coincidence in this context that Claire *chokes* Tom at the end of the play. Preventing him from further taking part in the mutual constitution of their reality, she silences the most creative alternative version of life other than her own.

10. For interpretations of *The Verge* as one of the first example of expressionism on the American stage see Rachel France, Yvonne Shafer, Arthur Waterman, and Klaus Schwank.

11. Kenneth MacGowan, *Theatre Arts Magazine* VI (2 Apr. 1922): 94; as qtd. in Bach, *Susan Glaspell* 170 (n. 68); my emphasis.

12. The performance of the professional actress Margaret Wycherly was applauded in almost every review. See, for example, Maida Castellun in the *New York Call*: "Miss Margaret Wycherly, an actress who has always scorned the patterns of the stage, lends her intelligence, her sensitive intuition, her poetic beauty, and her artistic sincerity to make Claire live, and transcends anything she has done before. She does not soften the arrogance of the artist-creator in Claire, nor shrink from expressing the passion of the woman. The signs of genius on the verge of madness are delicately indicated and the final scene of madness is relentless in its truth" ("'The Verge'").

13. Mary E. Papke writes of this performance: "My own critique of this production would commend the effort but question the clarity of directorial intention. The play was staged naturalistically and so could not do justice to Glaspell's elaborate symbolist intervention into realism or her expressionist effects meant to foreground the philosophical issues essential to the play's meaning" (69).

14. The allusion is to Elam's *Feminism and Deconstruction: Ms. en Abyme*: "Many of Elam's arguments hinge around a discussion of the term *mise en abyme* [...], a phrase which derives from heraldry, referring to the quadrant of a coat of arms that restates in miniature the coat of arms as a whole, and so has another quadrant within itself restating the same scheme again, and so on, ad infinitum (*en abyme*). In deconstructive analysis, *mise en abyme* becomes a conceptual metaphor for the endless deferral of conclusive meaning, for the inevitable slippage of all attempts at fixing identity" (Bottoms 131).

9. Alison's House *(1930)*

1. Elsa's argument that the poems have to be published is supported on various grounds

by her brothers Ted and Eben, as well as by two additional characters who represent the outside world in what would otherwise be solely a family affair: Ann Leslie, Stanhope's secretary (another daughter-figure in the play), and Richard Knowles, a young Chicago journalist and poet who has come to gather a story about Alison before "her house" will cease to exist.

2. See Ozieblo, *Susan Glaspell* 238.

3. Apparently, there had been a first staging in England shortly before, as Katherine Rodier reports: "A newspaper clipping in the Susan Glaspell file of the Berg Collection of the New York Public Library documents a preliminary run for the play in Liverpool, November 1930" ("Glaspell and Dickinson: Surveying the Premises of *Alison's House*," 214, n. 1).

4. See Katherine Rodier and J. Ellen Gainor, *Susan Glaspell*, for a detailed discussion of the Alison-Dickinson connection and its historical context.

5. One might even argue that Stanhope's self-control in staying away from his love had to be greater yet than Alison's, for he saw Ann's mother daily "through years" (149), while Alison's Harvard professor left the house never to return after the day she had sent him away.

6. Stanhope's patriarchal stance is symbolically paralleled in the position of his youngest son. Although he misjudges his own influence, Ted seems determined to continue the protective responsibilities of the "head of the family" into the next century: "TED. Now here I object. Here *I* step in. *I'll* protect Alison. I'm younger than you are. I can do it better. [...] I won't leave it to anybody! I am Alison Stanhope's nephew and I will not have her poems burned. Understand? [...] I'll be alive when the rest of you are dead. Then *I'm* the one to look after them. (*With a swift movement he puts some of the papers in his pocket, reaches for others*)" (143). In addition, a moment later he also prefigures Stanhope's condescending way of "entrusting" the poems to Elsa: "TED (*looking hard at her*): All right, Elsa. I trust them to you. Not Eben. Not Father. I leave them with Elsa" (146).

7. Indeed, it seems that the play's supposed defense of conventional American values was one aspect to influence the Pulitzer decision. See Karen Laughlin's, Barbara Ozieblo's and J. Ellen Gainor's discussion of this point in their analyses of *Alison's House*.

8. In fact, even on the basis of a biographical approach to the play, many other readings are possible in addition to a simple confirmation of either Stanhope's or Elsa's view on Alison's poems. Compare Rodier and Gainor for a detailed discussion of *Alison's House* as a comment on biographical accounting.

10. Springs Eternal *(1943)*

1. Glaspell's last play exists only in its manuscript form, which is hosted at the New York Public library. All quotes refer to this carbon copy.

2. Glaspell's "The Huntsmen Are Up in America" can be found in the Susan Glaspell Papers, Berg Collection, New York Public Library.

3. "Susan Glaspell Says We Need Books Today as Never Before," *Chicago Sunday Tribune* 6 Dec. 1942, typescript, Susan Glaspell Papers, Berg Collection, New York Public Library.

4. In *The Verge*, too, Glaspell suggested that World War I might have been a chance to create a new world. In that play, however, the idea has a much more violent character than it does in *Springs Eternal*, and it is not primarily framed in the context of a generational conflict. See my interpretation in chapter 8.

5. That Jumbo first appears at this very moment stresses the fact that he, too, plays his part in reconnecting the generations in this play: "MRS SOAMES. Why—we almost did it. Almost we brought Freddie into this room. Seems to me—if I was to look around now—(JUMBO *can be seen in the hall; about to come into the room, but steps back uncertainly. No one has seen him.*) OWEN. Don't look around, Mrs. Soames. MRS SOAMES. No; I know better than that. (*And yet she does look around—then she rises.*) Why—(*peering*) No. That's not Freddie" (2.37). By the same token, after Jumbo's passionate account of how he turned from conscientious objector to soldier, Owen's friend Stewie exclaims: "It's my youth. [Jumbo] dumped my youth right back on my lap" (3.25).

6. "HARRY. [...] Of course the reason why Stewie has to be connected with so many important things [in Washington] is that he has this inferiority complex. And that gives me an idea. OWEN. There is always that danger. HARRY. Quite possibly all men in public life have inferiority complexes. Don't you see my line of reasoning?" (1.21).

7. Indeed, besides *Springs Eternal* there are three other plays in Glaspell's dramatic oeuvre which might be read as stressing the gesture of presenting a message rather than as demonstrating the workings of art as constitutive articulate contact: *The People* (1917), *The Outside* (1917), and *Inheritors* (1921). All of them might be read as "war plays" in one way or another.

11. Other Works

1. In *Road to the Temple* Glaspell remembers that she and Cook "had a good time writ-

ing 'Suppressed Desires.' Before the grate in Milligan Place we tossed the lines back and forth at one another, and wondered if anyone else would ever have as much fun with it as we were having" (250). In Ozieblo's opinion (one of few critics who has dealt with this one-act at some length), the play's "fun" must be attributed mostly to Cook, since she observes that "[in] later plays and in her novels Glaspell's ambivalence toward the ideas she examines mars any incipient humor" ("Suppression and Society," 112). To the extent that I find Glaspell's humor in plays such as *Woman's Honor, Chains of Dew*, or *Springs Eternal* to be more successful than Ozieblo does, I disagree with this assessment of who is responsible for the wit in *Suppressed Desires*. Such an assertion, however, of course only underlines the degree to which such claims must remain purely subjective without a well-reflected method to assess either artist's influence on their collaborative works.

2. Next to the subject positions of the "individual" (the popular abuse of a scientific discourse by both men and women) and "woman" (Henrietta's advance into and retreat from the male realm of public discourse), the position of the "artist" is also already hinted at in *Suppressed Desires* with the figure of Stephen Brewster, whose creativity as an architect is seriously impaired by Henrietta's unnerving worship of psychoanalysis.

3. For discussions of how (and why) the play was written, and on the question of each author's possible influence on its theme and humor, see the conflicting versions of Arthur Waterman (*Susan Glaspell* 72) and Barbara Ozieblo (*Susan Glaspell* 136).

4. This, of course, was also Glaspell's own present. As Linda Ben-Zvi explains, "[i]n order to appreciate the risks taken in this work, it is necessary to have some idea of the climate in which the play was written in 1920. [...] The [1917] Espionage Act, on pain of a ten-thousand-dollar fine and twenty years in jail, made it illegal to refuse duty or impede recruitment in the military. The appended Sedition Act went further and prohibited uttering, printing, or writing any disloyal, profane, or scurrilous language about the form of government in the United States. Various alien laws made it a crime, punishable by deportation, to speak out against America or any of its allies. [...] Glaspell's *Inheritors* was the exception to [the theatre's] escapist fare" ("Susan Glaspell's Contributions," 160).

12. Conclusion

1. See, for instance, Kenneth McGowan's and Robert Edmond Jones' *Continental Stage-*

craft (1922) and Isaac Goldberg's *The Drama of Transition* of the same year.

2. With this idea, as with the imagery Glaspell employs in relation to Claire Archer in this play, her protagonist is directly linked to the project of the international avant-garde of the 1910s and 1920s. As Richard Murphy describes these artists' frame of mind in his study *Theorizing the Avant-Garde*: "[The] awareness of being enclosed within an ideological system of fictions placing limitations on experience brings with it the pervasive sense of alienation from a more 'genuine' realm of being, an alternative dimension of experience which the expressionists can only gesture towards, and which they hope to attain through the pursuit of what they term 'spirit,' 'essence' or 'power'" (54). Murphy quotes the painter Franz Marc as an "example of this widespread tendency" from his 1914 "Der Blaue Reiter:" "Wherever we saw a crack in the crust of convention, that's what we pointed to: only there, for we hoped for a power beneath which would one day come to light" (ibid. n. 14, trans. Murphy from *Manifeste Manifeste. 1905–1933*, 56). It is in this context that what critics usually refer to as Claire Archer's senseless gibberish in *The Verge* gains both precision and significance: "CLAIRE. [...] Here is the circle we are in. (*describes a big circle*) Being gay. [The preposterous thing said] shoots little darts through the circle, and a minute later — gaiety all gone, and you looking through that little hole the gaiety left. ADELAIDE. (*going to her, as she is still looking through that little hole*) [...] We always loved Claire's queer gaiety. Now you've got to hand it to us for that, as the children say. CLAIRE. (*moved, but eyes shining with a queer bright loneliness*) But never one of you — once — looked with me through the little pricks the gaiety made — never one of you — once, looked with me at the queer light that came in through the pricks" (*The Verge* 82).

3. Glaspell's willingness to include established discourses in the recreation of the world is evident (with regard to women's situation in patriarchy) in plays such as *Trifles, The Outside, Bernice* or *Alison's House*, or (with regard to the revolutionary impulses of the younger generation) in *Alison's House* or *Springs Eternal*. It is worth noting that in this stance especially, Glaspell develops a personal take on the communicational creation of reality which is distinctly different from the need for revolution as it is expressed in the generational and class conflicts displayed both in the plays of German expressionism such as Walter Hasenclever's *Der Sohn*, Ernst Toller's *Die Wandlung* and Georg Kaiser's *Masse Mensch*, and in Eugene O'Neill's family dramas.

4. In Glaspell's 1915 novel *Fidelity*, as so often in her writings a wordless glance first

makes real the power of Ruth Holland's love for Stuart to her friend Deane, who up to this moment was unable to understand her passion for a married man: "He could not rage against that look; he had no scorn for it. It lighted a country between them which words could not have undarkened" (82). Yet "after that," as Glaspell goes on to say, Ruth "found relief in words, the words she had had to deny herself so long. It was as if she found it wonderfully good to talk, in some little measure linking her love, as love wants to link itself, with the other people of the world, coming with the human unit" (ibid.).

Bibliography

Primary Sources — Plays

Glaspell, Susan. *Alison's House. A Play in Three Acts.* London and New York: Samuel French, 1930.
_____. "Bernice." *Plays by Susan Glaspell.* Boston: Small, Maynard and Co., 1920. 157–230.
_____. *Chains of Dew.* Ts. Library of Congress.
_____. "Close the Book." *Plays by Susan Glaspell.* Boston: Small, Maynard and Co., 1920. 61–96.
_____, and Norman Matson. *The Comic Artist.* London: Ernest Benn Ltd., 1927.
Glaspell, Susan. "Inheritors." *Plays by Susan Glaspell.* Ed. C.W.E. Bigsby. Cambridge: Cambridge University Press, 1987. 102–57.
_____. "The Outside." *Plays by Susan Glaspell.* Ed. C.W.E. Bigsby. Cambridge: Cambridge University Press, 1987. 97–117.
_____. "The People." *Plays by Susan Glaspell.* Boston: Small, Maynard and Co., 1920. 31–59.
_____. *Plays by Susan Glaspell.* Boston: Small, Maynard and Co., 1920.
_____. *Plays by Susan Glaspell.* Ed. C.W.E. Bigsby. Cambridge: Cambridge University Press, 1987.
_____. *Springs Eternal.* Ts. Berg Collection. New York Public Library.
_____, and George Cram Cook. "Suppressed Desires." *Plays by Susan Glaspell.* Boston: Small, Maynard and Co., 1920. 231–72.
_____. "Tickless Time." *Plays by Susan Glaspell.* Boston: Small, Maynard and Co., 1920. 273–315.
Glaspell, Susan. "Trifles." *Plays by Susan Glaspell.* Ed. C.W.E. Bigsby. Cambridge: Cambridge University Press, 1987. 35–45.
_____. "The Verge." *Plays by Susan Glaspell.* Ed. C.W.E. Bigsby. Cambridge: Cambridge University Press, 1987. 57–101.
_____. "Woman's Honor." *Plays by Susan Glaspell.* Boston: Small, Maynard and Co., 1920. 119–56.

Primary Sources — Novels

Glaspell, Susan. *Ambrose Holt and Family.* New York: Stokes, 1931.
_____. *Brook Evans.* New York: Stokes, 1928. London: Persephone Books, 2001.
_____. *Fidelity.* Boston: Small, Maynard and Co., 1915. Pref. Laura Godwin. London: Persephone Books, 1999.

_____. *Fugitive's Return.* New York: Stokes, 1929.
_____. *The Glory of the Conquered.* New York: Stokes, 1909.
_____. *Judd Rankin's Daughter.* Philadelphia: J.B. Lippincott, 1945.
_____. *The Morning Is Near Us.* New York: Literary Guild of America, 1940.
_____. *Norma Ashe.* Philadelphia: J.B. Lippincott, 1942.
_____. *The Visioning.* New York: Stokes, 1911.

Primary Sources — Other Works

Glaspell, Susan. "The Huntsmen Are Up in America." Typescript. Susan Glaspell Papers, Berg Collection, New York Public Library.
_____. "A Jury of Her Peers." *Lifted Masks and Other Works.* Ed. Eric S. Rabkin. Ann Arbor: University of Michigan Press, 1993. 279–306.
_____. "Pollen." *Harper's Magazine* 826, Mar. 1919: 446–51.
_____. *The Road to the Temple.* New York: Stokes, 1927.
_____. *Lifted Masks and Other Works.* Ed. Eric S. Rabkin. Ann Arbor: University of Michigan Press, 1993.
_____. *Cherished and Shared of Old.* New York: Julian Messner, 1940.

Secondary Sources

Aarons, Victoria. "A Community of Women: Surviving Marriage in the Wilderness." *Rendezvous: Journal of Arts & Letters* 22.2 (1986): 3–11.
Alkalay-Gut, Karen. "'Jury of Her Peers:' The Importance of Trifles." *Studies in Short Fiction* 21.1 (1984): 1–9.
_____. "Murder and Marriage: Another Look at *Trifles.*" *Susan Glaspell: Essays on Her Theater and Fiction.* Ed. Linda Ben-Zvi. Ann Arbor: University of Michigan Press, 1995. 71–81.
Altieri, Charles. "Wittgenstein on Consciousness and Language: A Challenge to Derridean Literary Theory." *MLN* 91 (1976): 1397–1423.
Aneja, Anu. "The Medusa's Slip: Hélène Cixous and the Underpinnings of *Écriture féminine.*" *Literature Interpretation Theory* 4.1 (1993): 17–27.
Aries, Elizabeth. "Gender and Communication." *Sex and Gender.* Eds. Philip Shaver and Clyde Hendrick. Newbury Park et al: Sage, 1987. 149–76.
Aston, Elaine. "Meeting the Outside: The Theatre of Susan Glaspell." *Difference in View: Women and Modernism.* Ed. G. Griffin. London: Falner, 1994. 155–67.
_____. "Performance Review. *The Verge.*" *Theatre Journal* 49.2 (1997): 230.
_____. "The 'Prisonhouse of Criticism': Susan Glaspell." *An Introduction to Feminism and Theatre.* London and New York: Routledge, 1995. 109–19.
Atkinson, J.B. "Pulitzer Laurels. 'Alison's House' as the Most Unsatisfactory Dramatic Award Made During the Past Few Years." *New York Times* 10 May 1931, sec. 8: 1.
Bach, Gerhard and Claudia Harris. "Susan Glaspell — Rediscovering an American Playwright: Conference and Theatre Performance, Brigham Young University Provo, Utah, 16 March 1991." *Theatre Journal* 44.1 (March 1992): 95.
Bach, Gerhard. "Susan Glaspell — Provincetown Playwright." *The Great Lakes Review: A Journal of Midwest Culture* 4.2. (1978): 31–43.
_____. "Susan Glaspell und die Provincetown Players. Eine Studie zur Frühphase des modernen amerikanischen Dramas und Theaters." Diss. Marburg, Ger., 1971.
_____. "Susan Glaspell: Mapping the Domains of Critical Revision." *Susan Glaspell: Essays on Her Theater and Fiction.* Ed. Linda Ben-Zvi. Ann Arbor: University of Michigan Press, 1995. 239–58.

_____. Rev. of *Susan Glaspell: Voice from the Heartland*. By Marcia Noe. *Western Illinois Regional Studies* 7.2 (Fall 1984): 97.

_____. *Susan Glaspell und die Provincetown Players: Die Anfänge des Amerikanischen Dramas und Theaters*. Frankfurt am Main: Lang, 1979.

Ben-Zvi, Linda. "Introduction." *Susan Glaspell: Essays on Her Theater and Fiction*. Ed. Linda Ben-Zvi. Ann Arbor: University of Michigan Press, 1995. 1–14.

_____. "'Murder, She Wrote': The Genesis of Susan Glaspell's *Trifles*." *Theatre Journal* 44.2 (1992): 141–62.

_____. "O'Neill's Cape(d) Compatriot." *The Eugene O'Neill Newsletter* 19.1–2 (Spring/Fall 1995): 129–38.

_____. "Susan Glaspell and Eugene O'Neill." *The Eugene O'Neill Newsletter* 6.2 (1982): 21–29.

_____. "Susan Glaspell and Eugene O'Neill: The Imagery of Gender." *The Eugene O'Neill Newsletter* 10.1 (1986): 22–27.

_____. "Susan Glaspell's Contributions to Contemporary Women Playwrights." *Feminine Focus: The New Women Playwrights*. Ed. Enoch Brater. New York and Oxford: Oxford University Press, 1987. 147–66.

_____, ed. *Susan Glaspell: Essays on Her Theater and Fiction*. Ann Arbor: University of Michigan Press, 1995.

_____. *Susan Glaspell: Her Life and Times*. New York and Oxford: Oxford University Press, 2005.

Bigsby, C.W.E. "Susan Glaspell." *A Critical Introduction to Twentieth-Century American Drama, vol. 1, 1900–1940*. Cambridge: Cambridge University Press, 1982. 24–35.

_____. "Introduction." *Plays by Susan Glaspell*. Ed. C.W.E. Bigsby. Cambridge: Cambridge University Press, 1987. 1–31.

Black, Cheryl. "Technique and Tact: Nina Moise Directs the Provincetown Players." *Theatre Survey* 36.1 (May 1995): 55–64.

_____. *The Women of Provincetown, 1915–1922*. Tuscaloosa and London: The University of Alabama Press, 2002.

Bottoms, Stephen J. "Building on the Abyss: Susan Glaspell's *The Verge* in Production." *Theatre Topics* 8.2 (1998): 127–47.

Broun, Heywood. "Looking Up, Down and Around with the Provincetown Players— Susan Glaspell and 'The People.'" *New York Tribune* 18 Mar. 1917, sec. 4: 3.

_____. "Realism Has Special Thrills of Its Own." *New York Times* 30 Mar. 1919, sec. 4: 2.

Brown, John Mason. "Prize Play. 'Alison's House' as the Winner of the Pulitzer Award and the Reasons Which make It an Unhappy Choice." *New York Evening Post* 9 May 1931, sec. 4: 1.

Burke, Carolyn, Naomi Schor, and Margaret Whitford, eds. *Engaging with Irigaray. Feminist Philosophy and Modern European Thought*. New York: Columbia University Press, 1994.

Butler, Judith. *Gender Trouble. Feminism and the Subversion of Identity*. 1990. Pref. Judith Butler. New York and London: Routledge, 1999.

Canfield, John V. "The Community View." *The Philosophical Review* 105.4 (Oct. 1996): 469–88.

Carpentier, Martha C. and Barbara Ozieblo, eds. *Disclosing Intertextualities*. Amsterdam: Rodopi, 2006.

_____. "Susan Glaspell's Fiction: *Fidelity* as American Romance." *Twentieth Century Literature: A Scholarly and Critical Journal* 40.1 (1994): 92–113.

_____. *The Major Novels of Susan Glaspell*. Gainesville: University Press of Florida, 2001.

Castellun, Maida. "The Plays That Pass—'Chains of Dew,' by Susan Glaspell." *New York Call* 30 Apr. 1922: 4.

_____. "'The Verge,' Daring Venture in Drama by Susan Glaspell." *New York Call* 16 Nov. 1921: 4.

Chipp, Herschel B., ed. and trans. *Theories of Modern Art*. Berkeley: University of California Press, 1968.

Cixous, Hélène and Catherine Clément. "The Newly Born Woman." *The Hélène Cixous Reader*. Ed. Susan Sellers. London: Routledge, 1994. 35–46.

_____. "First Names of No One." *The Hélène Cixous Reader*. Ed. Susan Sellers. London: Routledge, 1994. 25–33

_____. "Preface." *The Hélène Cixous Reader*. Ed. Susan Sellers. London: Routledge, 1994. xv–xxii.

_____. *The Hélène Cixous Reader*. Ed. Susan Sellers. London: Routledge, 1994.

Collingwood, R.G. *The Principles of Art*. Oxford: Oxford University Press, 1938.

Corbin, John. "Seraphim and Cats." *New York Times* 30 Mar. 1919, sec. 4: 2.

Craig, Gordon. *On The Art of the Theatre*. London, 1905.

Czerepinski, Jackie. "Beyond *The Verge*: Absent Heroines in the Plays of Susan Glaspell. *Susan Glaspell: Essays on Her Theater and Fiction*. Ed. Linda Ben-Zvi. Ann Arbor: University of Michigan Press, 1995. 145–54.

Danto, Arthur. "Description and the Phenomenology of Perception." *Visual Theory*. Ed. Norman Bryson, Michael Ann Holly, and Keith Moxey. New York: HarperCollins, 1990. 201–15.

_____. *The Philosophical Disenfranchisement of Art*. New York: Columbia University Press, 1986.

_____. *The Transfiguration of the Commonplace*. Cambridge: Harvard University Press, 1981.

Delphy, Christine. "The Invention of French Feminism: An Essential Move." *Another Look, Another Woman*. Ed. Lynne Huffer. Yale French Studies 87. New Haven: Yale University Press, 1995. 190–221.

Deutsch, Helen, and Stella Hanau. *The Provincetown: A Story of the Theatre*. Introd. Kenneth MacGowan. New York: Farrar & Rinehart, 1931.

Dickie, George. *Art and the Aesthetic*. Ithaca: Cornell University Press, 1974.

_____. *The Art Circle*. New York: Haven Press, 1985.

Dickinson, Thomas D. *Playwrights of the New American Theater*. 1925. St. Claire Shores, MI: Scholarly Press, 1972.

Ducasse, C.J. *Philosophy of Art*. 1929. New York: Dover, 1966.

Dummett, Michael. "Language and Communication." *Reflections on Chomsky*. Ed. Alexander George. Oxford: Basil Blackwell, 1989. 192–212.

Dymkowski, Christine. "On the Edge: The Plays of Susan Glaspell." *Modern Drama* 3.1 (1988): 91–105.

Egan, Leona R. *Provincetown as a Stage*. Orleans, MA: Parnassus Imprints, 1994.

Elam, Diane. *Feminism and Deconstruction: Ms. En Abyme*. London: Routledge, 1994.

"Excited and Obscure. Susan Glaspell's New Play, 'The Verge,' as Produced by the Provincetown Players in New York — A Puzzling, an Occasionally Absurd Piece in Which She Does herself Scant Justice." *Boston Evening Transcript* 16 Nov. 1921: 1.11.

Fetterley, Judith. "Reading about Reading: 'A Jury of Her Peers,' 'The Murders of the Rue Morgue,' and 'The Yellow Wallpaper.'" *Gender and Reading: Essays on Readers, Texts and Contexts*. Ed. Elizabeth A. Flynn. Baltimore: John Hopkins University Press, 1982. 147–64.

France, Rachel, ed. *A Century of Plays by American Women*. New York: Richard Rosen Press, 1979.

France, Rachel. "Susan Glaspell." *Twentieth-Century American Dramatists*. Dictionary of Literary Biography 7. Ed. John MacNicholas. Detroit: Gale Research, 1981. 215–23.

Friedman, Sharon. "Bernice's Strange Deceit: The Avenging Angel in the House." *Susan Glaspell: Essays on Her Theater and Fiction*. Ed. Linda Ben-Zvi. Ann Arbor: University of Michigan Press, 1995. 155–63.

_____. "Feminism as Theme in Twentieth-Century American Women's Drama." *American Studies* 25.1 (1984): 69–89.

Frye, Marilyn. "The Necessity of Differences: Constructing a Positive Category of Women." *Signs: Journal of Women in Culture and Society* 21.4. (1996): 991–1010.

Gadamer, Hans-Georg. *Truth and Method*. 2nd ed. Trans. J. Weinsheimer and D.G. Marshall. New York: Crossroad, 1989.

Gainor, J. Ellen. "A Stage of Her Own: Susan Glaspell's *The Verge* and Women's Dramaturgy." *Journal of American Drama and Theatre* 1.1 (Spring 1989): 79–99.

_____. "*Chains of Dew* and the Drama of Birth Control." *Susan Glaspell: Essays on Her Theater and Fiction*. Ed. Linda Ben-Zvi. Ann Arbor: University of Michigan Press, 1995. 165–93.

_____. "The Provincetown Players' Experiments with Realism." *Realism and the American Dramatic Tradition*. Ed. William W. Demastes. Tuscaloosa: University of Alabama Press, 1996. 53–70.

_____. *Susan Glaspell in Context. American Theater, Culture, Politics 1915–48*. Ann Arbor: University of Michigan Press, 2001.

Gasbarrone, Lisa. "'The Locus for the Other': Cixous, Bakhtin, and Women's Writing." *A Dialogue of Voices. Feminist Literary Theory and Bakhtin*. Eds. Karen Hohne and Helen Wussow. Minneapolis and London: University of Minnesota Press, 1994. 1–19.

Gilligan, Carol. *In a Different Voice: Psychological Theory and Women's Development*. Cambridge: Harvard University Press, 1982.

Goldberg, Isaac. *The Drama of Transition. Native and Exotic Play Craft*. Cincinnati: Stewart Kidd Co., 1922.

Goldberger, Nancy Rule, Blythe McVicker Clinchy, Mary Field Belonky and Jill Mattuck Tarule. "Women's Ways of Knowing: On Gaining a Voice." *Sex and Gender*. Eds. Phillip Shaver and Clyde Hendrick. Newbury Park et al.: Sage, 1987. 201–28.

Guignon, Charles. "Philosophy after Wittgenstein and Heidegger." *Philosophy and Phenomenonological Research* Vol. L, No. 4 (June 1990): 649–72.

Hagberg, G.L. *Art as Language. Wittgenstein, Meaning, and Aesthetic Theory*. Ithaca: Cornell University Press, 1995.

Hallgren, Sherri. "'The Law Is the Law — and a Bad Stove Is a Bad Stove': Subversive Justice and Layers of Collusion in 'A Jury of Her Peers." *Violence, Silence, and Anger. Women's Writing As Transgression*. Ed. Deirdre Lashgari. Charlottsville: University Press of Virginia, 1995. 203–18.

Hapgood, Hutchins. *A Victorian in the Modern World*. 1939. Seattle: University of Washington Press, 1972.

Harris, Roy and Talbot J. Taylor. *Landmarks in Linguistic Thought: The Western Tradition From Socrates to Saussure*. London: Routledge, 1989.

Harris, Roy. "From an Integrational Point of View." *Linguistics Inside Out. Roy Harris and His Critics*. Eds. George Wolf and Nigel Love. Amsterdam and Philadelphia: John Benjamins, 1997. 229–310.

_____. *Language, Saussure and Wittgenstein. How to Play Games With Words*. London: Routledge, 1988.

_____. *The Language Myth*. London: Duckworth, 1981.

_____. *The Language-Makers*. London: Duckworth, 1980.

Hebel, Udo J. "'Superior in Unity and Economy'? Produktivität, Komplexität und Konventionalität einer gattungsübergreifenden Wirkungsstruktur amerikanischer Einakter seit Eugene O'Neill und Susan Glaspell." *Kurzformen des Dramas. Gattungspoetische, epochenspezifische und funktionale Horizonte*. Tübingen, Ger.: Francke, 1996. 285–314.

Hedges, Elaine. "Small Things Reconsidered: Susan Glaspell's 'A Jury of Her Peers.'" *Women's Studies: An Interdisciplinary Journal* 12.1 (1986): 89–110.

Heidegger, Martin. *Being and Time*. Trans. J. Macquarrie and E. Robinson. New York: Harper and Row, 1962.

_____. *History of the Concept of Time*. Trans. T. Kisiel. Bloomington: Indiana University Press, 1985.

Heilbrun, Carolyn G. "Androgyny and the Psychology of Sex Differences." *The Future of Difference*. Eds. Hester Eisenstein and Alice Jardine. New Brunswick: Rutgers University Press, 1985. 258–66.

Heller, Adele and Lois Rudnick. *1915. The Cultural Moment. The New Politics, the New Woman, the New Psychology, the New Art, and the New Theatre in America*. New Brunswick, NJ: Rutgers University Press, 1991.

Hohne, Karen and Helen Wussow, eds. *A Dialogue of Voices. Feminist Literary Theory and Bakhtin.* Minneapolis, London: University of Minnesota Press, 1994.

Hunter, J.F.M. *Essays After Wittgenstein.* Toronto: University of Toronto Press, 1973.

Irigaray, Luce. "The Power of Discourse and the Subordination of the Feminine." *The Irigaray Reader.* Ed. Margaret Whitford. Oxford: Blackwell, 1992. 118–32.

_____. "The Question of the Other." *Another Look, Another Woman.* Ed. Lynne Huffer. Yale French Studies 87. New Haven: Yale University Press, 1995. 7–19.

_____. "The Three *Genres.*" *The Irigaray Reader.* Ed. Margaret Whitford. Oxford: Blackwell, 1992. 140–53.

_____. *The Irigaray Reader.* Ed. Margaret Whitford. Oxford: Blackwell, 1992.

_____. "Questions." *The Irigaray Reader.* Ed. Margaret Whitford. Oxford: Blackwell, 1992. 133–39.

_____. *Speculum. De l'autre femme.* Paris: Minuit, 1974. Trans. Gillian C. Gill. *Speculum of the other Woman.* Ithaca: Cornell University Press, 1985.

Johnson, Paul Emanuel. *Psychology of Religion.* New York, 1959.

Jones, Ann Rosalind. "Writing the Body: Toward an Understanding of *L'écriture féminine.*" *Feminist Studies* 7.2 (Summer 1981): 247–63.

Kattwinkel, Susan. "Absence as a Site for Debate: Modern Feminism and Victorianism in the Plays of Susan Glaspell." *New England Theatre Journal* 7 (1996): 37–55.

Kenton, Edna. *The Provincetown Players and the Playwrights' Theatre, 1915–1922.* Ed. Travis Bogard and Jackson R. Bryer. Jefferson, North Carolina, and London: McFarland & Company, 2004.

Kolin, Philip C. "Therapists in Susan Glaspell's *Suppressed Desires* and David Rabe's *In the Boom Boom Room.*" *Notes on Contemporary Literature* 18.5 (1988): 2–3.

Kolodny, Annette. "A Map for Rereading: Gender and the Interpretation of Literary Texts." *The New Feminist Criticism: Essays on Women, Literature and Theory.* Ed. Elaine Showalter. London: Virago Press, 1986. 46–62.

Kristeva, Julia. "The System and the Speaking Subject." *The Kristeva Reader.* Ed. Toril Moi. Oxford: Blackwell, 1986. 24–33.

_____. "Women's Time." *The Kristeva Reader.* Ed. Toril Moi. Oxford: Blackwell, 1986. 187–213.

_____. *The Kristeva Reader.* Ed. Toril Moi. Oxford: Blackwell, 1986.

Lakoff, Robin. "Philosophy of Language Meets the Real World; or, When is 'Enough' Enough?" Kim Hall et al., eds. *Proceedings of the Sixteenth Annual Meeting of the Berkeley Linguistics Society. February 16–19, 1990. General Session and Parasession on the Legacy of Grice.* Berkeley: BLS, 1990.

Langer, Susanne. *Feeling and Form.* London: Routledge & Kegan Paul, 1953.

_____. *Philosophy in a New Key.* New York: Mentor, 1951.

_____. *Problems of Art.* New York: Scribner's, 1957.

Langner, Lawrence. *The Magic Curtain: The Story of a Life in Two Fields, Theatre and Invention by the Founder of the Theatre Guild.* New York: E.P. Dutton and Co., 1951.

Larabee, Ann E. "'Meeting the Outside Face to Face': Susan Glaspell, Djuna Barnes, and O'Neill's *The Emperor Jones.*" *Modern American Drama: The Female Canon.* Ed. June Schlueter. Rutherford: Fairleigh Dickinson University Press, 1990. 77–85.

Laughlin, Karen. "Conflict of Interest: The Ideology of Authorship in *Alison's House.*" *Susan Glaspell: Essays on Her Theater and Fiction.* Ed. Linda Ben-Zvi. Ann Arbor: University of Michigan Press, 1995. 219–35.

Lewisohn, Ludwig. "Drama. 'The Verge.'" *The Nation* 113, 14 Dec. 1921: 708.

_____. "Drama." *The Nation* 114, 24 May 1922: 627.

_____. *Expression in America.* New York and London: Harper, 1932.

_____. *The Drama and the Stage.* New York: Harcourt, Brace and Co., 1922. New York: Johnson Repr. Co., 1986.

Lindroth, Colette. "Lifting the Masks of Male-Female Discourse: The Rhetorical Strategies of Susan Glaspell." *Susan Glaspell: Essays on Her Theater and Fiction.* Ed. Linda Ben-Zvi. Ann Arbor: University of Michigan Press, 1995. 303–16.

McGowan, Kenneth and Robert Edmond Jones. *Continental Stagecraft*. Harcourt, Brace and Co., 1922.

MacGowan, Kenneth. "The Portrait of a Season." *Theatre Arts Magazine* 6, 2 Apr. 1922: 94.

Mael, Phyllis. "*Trifles*: The Path to Sisterhood." *Literature-Film Quarterly* 17.4 (1989): 181–84.

Makowsky, Veronica. "Forging a Woman's Identity in Susan Glaspell's Fiction." *Susan Glaspell: Essays on Her Theater and Fiction*. Ed. Linda Ben-Zvi. Ann Arbor: University of Michigan Press, 1995. 317–30.

_____. "Susan Glaspell and Modernism." *The Cambridge Companion to American Women Playwrights*. Ed. Brenda Murphy. Cambridge: Cambridge University Press, 1999. 49–65.

_____. *Susan Glaspell's Century of American Women. A Critical Interpretation of Her Work.* New York and Oxford: Oxford University Press, 1993.

Makward, Christiane. "To Be or Not to Be ... A Feminist Speaker." Trans. Marlène Barsoum, Alice Jardine, and Hester Eisenstein. *The Future of Difference*. Eds. Hester Eisenstein and Alice Jardine. New Brunswick: Rutgers University Press, 1985. 95–105.

Malone, Andrew E. "Susan Glaspell." *Dublin Magazine* 2 (Sept. 1924): 107–11.

Malpede, Karen. "Reflections on *The Verge*." *Susan Glaspell: Essays on Her Theater and Fiction*. Ed. Linda Ben-Zvi. Ann Arbor: University of Michigan Press, 1995. 123–27.

Mantle, Burns. "Plays of the Week. 'Chains of Dew' at the Provincetown Playhouse." *New York Mail* 29 April 1922: 7.

_____. *Contemporary American Playwrights*. New York: Dodd, Mead and Co., 1938.

_____, ed. *The Best Plays of 1930–31 and the Year Book of the Drama in America*. New York: Dodd, Mead and Co., 1931.

Margolis, Joseph. *Art and Philosophy*. Atlantic Highlands: Humanities Press, 1980.

Marks, Elaine and Isabelle de Courtivron. Eds. *New French Feminisms: An Anthology*. Amherst: University of Massachusetts Press, 1980.

Maufort, Marc, ed. *Eugene O'Neill and the Emergence of American Drama*. Amsterdam: Rodopi, 1989.

Miller, Terry. *Greenwich Village and How it Got That Way*. New York: Crown, 1990.

Moi, Toril. "Men Against Patriarchy." *Gender and Theory. Dialogues on Feminist Criticism*. Ed. Linda Kauffman. Oxford: Blackwell, 1989. 181–88.

_____. "Patriarchal Thought and the Drive for Knowledge." *Between Feminism and Psychoanalysis*. Ed. Teresa Brennan. London: Routledge, 1989. 189–205.

_____. "Introduction." *The Kristeva Reader*. Ed. Toril Moi. Oxford: Blackwell, 1986.

_____. *Sexual/Textual Politics. Feminist Literary Theory*. London: Methuen, 1985.

Murphy, Richard. *Theorizing the Avantgarde. Modernism, Expressionism, and the Problem of Postmodernity*. Cambridge: Cambridge University Press, 1998.

Mustazza, Leonard. "Generic Translation and Thematic Shift in Susan Glaspell's *Trifles* and 'A Jury of Her Peers.'" *Studies in Short Fiction* 26.4 (1989): 489–96.

Nelligan, Liza Maeve. "'The Haunting Beauty from the Life We've Left': A Contextual Reading of *Trifles* and *The Verge*." *Susan Glaspell: Essays on Her Theater and Fiction*. Ed. Linda Ben-Zvi. Ann Arbor: University of Michigan Press, 1995. 85–104.

Noe, Marcia. "Reconfiguring the Subject/ Recuperating Realism: Susan Glaspell's Unseen Woman." *American Drama* 4.2 (Spring 1995): 36–54.

_____. *Susan Glaspell: Voice from the Heartland*. Western Illinois Monograph Series 1. Macomb, IL: Western Illinois University, 1983.

_____. "*The Verge*: L'Écriture Féminine at the Provincetown." *Susan Glaspell: Essays on Her Theater and Fiction*. Ed. Linda Ben-Zvi. Ann Arbor: University of Michigan Press, 1995. 129–42.

Ozieblo, Barbara. *Susan Glaspell. A Critical Biography*. Chapel Hill and London: University of North Carolina Press, 2000.

_____. "Rebellion and Rejection: The Plays of Susan Glaspell." *Modern American Drama: The Female Canon*. Ed. June Schlueter. Rutherford: Fairleigh Dickinson University Press, 1990. 66–76.

_____. "Suppression and Society in Susan Glaspell's Theatre." *Susan Glaspell: Essays on Her Theater and Fiction*. Ed. Linda Ben-Zvi. Ann Arbor: University of Michigan Press, 1995. 105–22.

Papke, Mary E. *Susan Glaspell. A Research and Production Sourcebook*. Modern Dramatists Research and Production Sourcebooks 4. Westport, CT: Greenwood Press, 1993.

Pfister, Joel. *Staging Depth. Eugene O'Neill and the Politics of Psychological Discourse*. Chapel Hill and London: University of North Carolina Press, 1995.

Purvis-Smith, Virginia L. "Ideological Becoming: Mikhail Bakhtin, feminine *écriture*, and Julia Kristeva." *A Dialogue of Voices. Feminist Literary Theory and Bakhtin*. Ed. Karen Hohne and Helen Wussow. Minneapolis and London: University of Minnesota Press, 1994. 42–58.

Quigley, Austin E. "Wittgenstein's Philosophizing and Literary Theorizing." *New Literary History* 19 (1987/88): 209–37.

Quinn, Arthur Hobson, ed. *Contemporary American Plays*. New York: Scribner's, 1923.

Rabkin, Eric S. "Introduction." Susan Glaspell. *Lifted Masks and Other Works*. Ed. and introd. Eric S. Rabkin. Ann Arbor: University of Michigan Press, 1993.

Radel, Nicholas F. "Provincetown Plays: Women Writers and O'Neill's American Intertext." *Essays in Theatre* 9.1 (1990): 31–43.

Rathbun, Stephen. "Susan Glaspell's 'Chains of Dew' is a Bright, Realistic Little Comedy." *The New York Sun* 29 Apr. 1922: 4.

_____. "'The Verge,' the Provincetown Players' First Bill, Is an Extraordinary Study of the Superwoman." *The Sun* 19 Nov. 1921: 4.

Rodier, Katharine. "Glaspell and Dickinson: Surveying the Premises of *Alison's House*." *Susan Glaspell: Essays on Her Theater and Fiction*. Ed. Linda Ben-Zvi. Ann Arbor: University of Michigan Press, 1995. 195–218.

Ruhl, Arthur. "'Alison's House,'" *New York Herald Tribune* 2 Dec. 1930: 18.

Sarlós, Robert Károly. *Jig Cook and the Provincetown Players: Theatre in Ferment*. Amherst: University of Massachusetts Press, 1982.

Sayler, Oliver M. *Our American Theatre*. New York: Benjamin Blom, 1923. Repr. 1971.

Schor, Naomi and Elizabeth Weed, eds. *The Essential Difference*. Bloomington and Indianapolis: Indiana University Press, 1994.

Schwank, Klaus. "Die dramatischen Experimente Susan Glaspells: *The Outside* und *The Verge*." *Amerikastudien* 34.4 (1989): 413–21.

Seabright, Paul. "Explaining Cultural Divergence: A Wittgensteinian Paradox." *Journal of Philosophy* 84 (1987): 11–27.

Sellers, Susan. "Introduction." *The Hélène Cixous Reader*. Ed. Susan Sellers. London: Routledge, 1994.

Shafer, Yvonne. "Susan Glaspell." *American Women Playwrights, 1900–1950*. New York: Lang, 1995. 36–57.

_____. "Susan Glaspell: German Influence, American Playwright." *Zeitschrift für Anglistik und Amerikanistik* 36 (1988): 333–38.

Shaver, Phillip and Clyde Hendrick, eds. *Sex and Gender*. Newbury Park et al.: Sage, 1987.

Shay, Frank. "Drama." *The Greenwich Villager* 1, 23 Nov. 1921: 7.

Shoemaker, Sidney. *Self-Knowledge and Self-Identity*. Ithaca: Cornell University Press, 1963.

Sievers, David W. *Freud on Broadway: A History of Psychoanalysis and the American Drama*. New York: Hermitage House, 1955.

Skinner, Richard Dana. "'Alison's House.'" *The Commonweal* 13, 17 Dec. 1930: 187–88.

_____. "In the Dramatic Mailbag. In Defense of 'Alison's House' — Critics As the Theatre's Middlemen." *New York Times* 17 May 1931, sec. 8: 2.

_____. *Our Changing Theatre*. New York: Dial Press, 1931.

Smith, Alison. "The New Play." *New York Evening Globe* 28 Apr. 1922.

Smith, Beverly A. "Women's Work — *Trifles*? The Skill and Insights of Playwright Susan Glaspell." *International Journal of Women's Studies* 5.2 (1982): 172–84.

Sochen, June. *The New Woman: Feminism in Greenwich Village, 1910–1920*. New York: Quadrangle, 1972.

Stein, Karen F. "The Women's World of Glaspell's *Trifles*." *Women in American Theatre*. Eds. Helen Krich Chinoy and Linda Walsh Jenkins. New York: Crown, 1981. 253–56.

Stewart, John. *Language as Articulate Contact. Toward a Post-Semiotic Philosophy of Communication*. New York: State University of New York Press, 1995.

"Susan Glaspell Says We Need Books Today as Never Before." *Chicago Sunday Tribune* 6 Dec. 1942, typescript, Susan Glaspell Papers, Berg Collection, New York Public Library.

"Susan Glaspell's 'Chains of Dew' Is Sharp Satire. Provincetown Players' Production Attacks Bobbed Hair and Birth Control." *The New York Herald Tribune* 28 Apr. 1922: 10.

T.H. "Drama. Little Theatres." *The Nation* 108, 3 May 1919: 703.

Tannen, Deborah. *Gender and Discourse*. New York and Oxford: Oxford University Press, 1994.

_____. *You Just Don't Understand: Women and Men in Conversation*. New York: Ballantine Books, 1990.

Taylor, Talbot J. "Communicational Scepticism and the Discourse of Order." *New Departures in Linguistics*. Ed. George Wolf. New York and London: Garland Pub., 1992. 163–79.

Tolstoy, Leo. *What Is Art?* Trans. Aylmer Maude. Oxford: Oxford University Press, 1930.

Toohey, John. *A History of the Pulitzer Prize Plays*. New York: Citadel, 1967.

Towse, J. Ranken. "The Play." *New York Evening Post* 15 Nov. 1921: 9.

Trachtenberg, Alan. "Foreword." *Staging Depth. Eugene O'Neill and the Politics of Psychological Discourse*. Joel Pfister. Chapel Hill and London: University of North Carolina Press, 1995. 11–13.

"Turns with a Bookworm." *New York Herald Tribune Books* 31 Mar. 1940. Sec. 9: 2.

Van Doren, Mark. "The Pulitzer Prize Play." *The Nation* 27 May 1931: 591–92.

Vanden Heuvel, Michael. *Performing Drama/ Dramatizing Performance*. Ann Arbor: University of Michigan Press, 1991.

Vorse, Mary Heaton. *Time and the Town: A Provincetown Chronicle*. New York: Dial Press, 1942. Ed. Adele Heller. New Brunswick: Rutgers University Press, 1991.

Waterman, Arthur E. "A Critical Study of Susan Glaspell's Works and Her Contributions to Modern American Drama." Diss. U of Wisconsin, 1956. *DA* 16 (1956): 2170.

_____. "Susan Glaspell and the Provincetown." *Modern Drama* 7.2 (1964): 174–84.

_____. "Susan Glaspell's *The Verge*: An Experiment in Feminism." *The Great Lakes Review: A Journal of Midwest Culture* 6.1 (Summer 1979): 17–23.

_____. *Susan Glaspell*. New York: Twayne, 1966.

"What 'The Verge' Is About, Who Can Tell?" *New York Herald Tribune* 15 Nov. 1921: 15.

Wheeler III, Samuel C. "Wittgenstein as Conservative Deconstructor." *New Literary History* 19.2 (Winter 1988): 239–58.

Whitford, Margaret. "Introduction." *The Irigaray Reader*. Ed. Margaret Whitford. Oxford: Blackwell, 1993.

Wittgenstein, Ludwig. *On Certainty*. Trans. Denis Paul and G.E.M. Anscombe. New York, 1969.

_____. *Philosophische Untersuchungen*. Trans. G.E.M. Anscombe. *Philosophical Investigations*. Oxford: Blackwell, 1953.

_____. *Tractatus Logico-Philosophicus*. 1922. Trans. D.F. Pears and B.F. McGuinness. Atlantic Highlands, NJ: Humanities Press, 1974.

Woollcott, Alexander. "The Play. Provincetown Psychiatry." *New York Times* 15 Nov. 1921: 23.

_____. "The Play." *New York Times* 28 Apr. 1922: 20.

Young, Stark. "After the Play." *The New Republic* 29 Dec. 1921: 47.

Index

Numbers in **boldface** represent main entries.

as expressing the truth about life ("light of truth," "true writing") 130, 132; the artist's responsibility to society 136; character conception in (Seymore Standish as caricature/type vs. his wife Dotty, Nora Powers and especially the Mother as individuals) 137, 147–148, 149; character constellation: Nora Powers and the Mother as contrasting and corresponding female characters 141, 142; connectedness as creative potential or suffocating imprisonment 140–146, 149; creation of identity (artist, woman, individual) 128, 131, 137, 139–140; the creation of meaning in 132, 143; creation of truth in 143; dramatic quality of (clash of genres, Seymore an unconvincing caricature) 129–130, 147, 148; dramatic subgenre: tragedy vs. comedy 128–130, 131, 136, 146, 148, 149, 153, 207; ending of 129, 136–137, 149; the fundamental human need to be understood 130; human community as positive: parallel between Nora Powers and Susan Glaspell 143–144; the human condition as irreducibly social and intersubjective 136, 140–143, 149; the human need of community (fear of isolation) 130, 136, 143; the individual's control over the creation of meaning 139; isolation vs. connection in 134, 140; language and art as constitutive articulate contact 127, 139–140, 142–43, 149–150; language skepticism ridiculed in 132, 134; modernist art as elitist and obscure vs. art as social action 135; the Mother as artist figure 144–145; Nora Powers as New Woman 128–129, 137, 138, 142; plot development 127–129; possibility of (social) change in 139, 144, 145; reception of 129–130, 146–147; setting: Greenwich Village vs. the Midwest 127–128, 129, 132, 134, 137; Seymore Standish's dilemma of "being caught" (theme of social imprisonment) 127–128, 132–133; sluggish Provincetown staging of 130, 146–147, 147–148; social conventions as imprisoning 127, 128, 132, 133, 138–140, 149–150; theme of the human condition as irreducibly social played out in the story of a woman's binding love for her husband 127–128, 136–140, 141, 145–46, 149; theme of the human condition as irreducibly social played out in the story of an artist's imprisonment in social obligations 127, 132–34; writing and production history of 146–150

change, possibility of 6, 45, 225, 229, 234–235, 245, 251, 255; *see also* social change; for individual works *see* separate entries
character conception *see* separate entries for individual plays
character constellation *see* separate entries for individual plays
characters, male and female 1, 4, 6; *see also* female characters; male characters; *and* separate entries for individual works
Chekhov, Anton 4, 152
Chicago 12, 13, 18, 185
Chicago Evening Post 12
Chicago Sunday Tribune 209
Christianity 36, 250; as theme in Glaspell's works 155, 156, 163–164, 169; *see also* Puritanism
Civic Repertory Theatre *see* Le Gallienne, Eva
Cixous, Hélène 1, 5, **35–38**, 38, 56, 65, 152, 160–165; *see also écriture féminine*
Close the Book 7, **232–233**, 252; communicative constructedness of human existence (imprisonment and creative potential of) 233; identity between individuality and communality 233; plot development 232–233; reconciliatory ending 233
collaboration, artistic (question of influence) 6, 7, 13, 17, 225, 230–231, 232, 235, 240, 241–242; *see also* separate entries for *The Comic Artist, Suppressed Desires, Tickless Time*
comedy (social) in Glaspell's works 75, 79, 83, 128–130, 131, 133, 136, 141, 146, 148, 149, 153, 174, 176, 207, 210–211, 220, 231, 234, 235, 236, 240; *see also* humor; *and* separate entries for individual works
The Comic Artist 7, 17, 183, **240–243**; art as communication in 240; the artist and society not a prominent theme in 240–241; collaboration between Glaspell and Norman Matson: question of influence 240–241, 241–242; as comedy 240; language and art as representative systems of signs or as constitutive articulate contact 243; place in Glaspell's oeuvre 243; plot development 241; theme of isolation vs. connection through communication 242–243; typical Glaspellian character constellation: the artist figure Karl and Eleanor 242–243
communality 5; as essential human mode of being in Glaspell's works 31, 45; as a source of power in Glaspell's works 31, 74; *see also* community